Putin's Russia

Past Imperfect, Future Uncertain

Seventh Edition

Edited by
Stephen K. Wegren

ROWMAN & LITTLEFIELD
Lanham • Boulder • New York • London

Executive Editor: Susan McEachern
Editorial Assistant: Katelyn Turner
Senior Marketing Manager: Amy Whitaker

Credits and acknowledgments for material borrowed from other sources, and reproduced with permission, appear on the appropriate page within the text.

Published by Rowman & Littlefield
An imprint of The Rowman & Littlefield Publishing Group, Inc.
4501 Forbes Boulevard, Suite 200, Lanham, Maryland 20706
https://rowman.com

6 Tinworth Street, London SE11 5AL, United Kingdom

British Library Cataloguing in Publication Information Available

Library of Congress Cataloging-in-Publication Data
Names: Wegren, Stephen K., 1956– editor
Title: Putin's Russia : past imperfect, future uncertain / edited by Stephen K. Wegren.
Description: Seventh edition. | Lanham, Maryland : Rowman & Littlefield Publishing Group, Inc., 2019. | "First edition published 2002." | Includes bibliographical references and index.
Identifiers: LCCN 2018029091 (print) | LCCN 2018030614 (ebook) | ISBN 9781538114278 (ebook) | ISBN 9781538114254 (hardcover : alk. paper) | ISBN 9781538114261 (pbk. : alk. paper)
Subjects: LCSH: Russia (Federation)—Politics and government—1991– | Russia (Federation)—Foreign relations. | Putin, Vladimir Vladimirovich, 1952– —Political and social views.
Classification: LCC DK510.763 (ebook) | LCC DK510.763 .P88 2019 (print) | DDC 947.086/3—dc23
LC record available at https://lccn.loc.gov/2018029091

Printed in the United States of America

Contents

Preface to the Seventh Edition

Since the publication of the sixth edition, Vladimir Putin was elected to a fourth (nonconsecutive) term in March 2018. Putin will serve as president until 2024, meaning that his rule spans nearly a quarter of a century. The purpose of the seventh edition is to analyze the final years of Putin's third term (2015–2018) and to look forward to the challenges that exist for his fourth term. Russia remains at a crossroads, and critical questions are more salient than ever. In the domestic sphere, the question is what kind of society is Russia evolving into? Is Russia stable and is managed democracy an enduring system? In economics, will oil revenues be sufficient to fund economic development and modernization, or will they hinder democratization, the so-called resource curse? Can Russia diversify its economy to become less dependent on natural resources? Regarding Russia's relations with the world, the major questions concern Putin's adversarial relations with the West, so-called Russian adventurism, and the expanded definition of its national security interests. The decades-old schism between Westernization and Russian exceptionalism continues to resonate today. Will the agricultural sector continue to be a source of economic strength that gives the Kremlin options in foreign policy?

Analyzing wide-ranging policy issues requires the combined efforts of an excellent group of scholars. Because trends in Russia are often difficult for nonspecialists to discern, the book offers clearly written analysis by respected scholars whose expertise is Russia. Most of the authors who wrote chapters for the sixth edition are included in the seventh edition. Building on the success of previous editions, the seventh edition adds four new contributors: Laura Solanko, who revised the chapter on economic policy; Stefan Hedlund, who writes on energy; Jeanne Wilson, who writes on Russia-China relations; and Bettina Renz, who writes on the Russian military. In addition,

Thomas Remington contributes a chapter on inequality, a change from his previous contributions on executive-legislative relations. I note the retirement of Dale Herspring, who served as editor for the first three editions of this book, starting in 2003. Even after I assumed the editorship starting with the fourth edition, Dale continued to contribute chapters on military reform. The field of Russian studies is indebted to Dale for starting this project. I am deeply grateful to all authors who contributed to this seventh edition.

I would like to thank several people at Rowman & Littlefield: Susan McEachern for her continued enthusiasm for this project; Katelyn Turner for discovering the book cover and for general production support; and Janice Braunstein for her excellent editorial skills in producing this book.

Finally, this book is dedicated to our collective students so that they may better understand the riddle, wrapped in a mystery, inside an enigma that we call Russia.

Introduction

Prospects during Putin's Fourth Term

Stephen K. Wegren

The seventh edition of *Putin's Russia* covers the last years of Vladimir Putin's third term and takes the analysis into the first months of his fourth term that will run 2018–2024. The purpose of this introductory chapter is to outline broad trends and issues, leaving detailed analysis for the individual chapters. This introduction examines prospects in domestic politics, in the economy, and in foreign policy.

POLITICAL PROSPECTS

Leading up to the 2012 presidential election, there was speculation in the West and Russia whether then president Dmitry Medvedev would run for reelection. Medvedev repeatedly stated that he wanted to run for reelection and had grown to like the job, but he nuanced his statements by saying that he and Putin would decide together what was best for the country. In September 2011, Dmitry Medvedev conceded to Vladimir Putin, who announced that he would return to the presidency (thus anticipating an electoral victory). Putin in turn indicated that he would nominate Medvedev to be his prime minister. The main drama surrounding the March 2018 election was the late date that Putin announced his candidacy. There was no question that Putin would win if he decided to run; the question was whether he wanted another six years. Putin finally announced his candidacy in December 2017. In March 2018, Putin was elected with 76.6 percent of the vote, his highest level ever, with 67 percent turnout, thereby exceeding the 65 percent that election officials had established as a target. Reports of voting fraud were curious because it was completely unnecessary. In any event, Putin was inaugurated in May 2018 for his fourth term. Unless there are unforeseen developments, for example Putin becoming prime minister again in 2024 (at age seventy-two) and serving "in tandem" with a new president, this will be Putin's last term in the executive branch. Another scenario for 2024 and beyond is for Putin to assume a British monarch-type role in which he retains political power but does not hold a formal office. After Putin serves his fourth term, he would have led Russia for twenty-four years, a period almost as long as Stalin ruled over Soviet society (1928–1953).

Prospects for Political Stability

Starting with the protest movement in 2011–2012, one of the crucial questions that Western analysts have wrestled with since 2012 is the extent to which the method of rule and the type of regime Putin has created makes Russia politically stable. Many analysts are repulsed by Putin's criminal state.[1] They cite the use of violence against journalists and political opponents and the strengthening of authoritarian rule to argue that Russia is unstable and that the Putin regime could collapse.

Lilia Shevtsova, for example, argued that "either the society succeeds in transforming the system of personalized rule that suffocates it, or Russia will lose its energy and end in rot or implosion. There is only one way out of this civilizational trap, and that is through pressure from below."[2] Can a regime that drives honest opposition to flee the country, that tolerates assassinations of political opposition, and that interns those who dare to expose corruption be considered stable?[3] Analysts argue that authoritarian, corrupt regimes are doomed to fail, citing the color revolutions in the post-Soviet space and the Arab Spring of 2011. Gel'man notes, however, that the collapse of Putin's authoritarianism could be replaced by another authoritarian regime. In other words, there is nothing deterministic about Russia ending up with democracy, and it is possible that a new regime could be worse, for instance, even more nationalist or more anti-West.[4]

A second question is whether Russia has changed—has a genuine civil society emerged that is frustrated by the fact that the "supply" of democracy is inadequate to the demand? Advocates of this point of view cite the aftermath of the March 2012 presidential election when there were demonstrations in nearly every region of Russia and more than one hundred cities. The most notable protest occurred in Bolotnaya Square in Moscow in May 2012 when Putin was inaugurated, at which an estimated 100,000 people turned out and four hundred people were arrested. For the first time, the Russian people protested against Putin as leader. Some protestors carried signs that read "Russia without Putin." In June 2012, a demonstration estimated by supporters at 120,000 took to the streets in Moscow, the largest protest in

Moscow since the August 1991 coup attempt against then-president Mikhail Gorbachev (official estimates were closer to twenty thousand). Based on these events, it appeared that a genuine civil society had emerged in Russia. A passive population that had tolerated political games, manipulation, and dishonesty for twenty years suddenly awoke in 2011–2012. As one Russian academic argued, "the decade of economic growth and socio-political stability led to the appearance of a layer within society that wants to have the right to its own voice and is ready to put pressure on the authorities."[5] Russian society differed significantly from the Russia of 2000 when Putin first took power, marked by a willingness by at least some of the population to be politically active, to protest, and to demonstrate. Alfred Evans discusses trends in civil society and nuances of popular protest in his chapter.

The large popular protests over fraudulent elections in 2011–2012 had by 2014 run their course, with very little to show for their efforts, and the opposition was left with an uncertain future. Idealists wanted to see the 2011–2012 protests as the first signs of "creeping democracy" from below that could lead to the collapse of the Putin regime. Aside from the fact that the number of active oppositionists in 2011–2012 was extremely small, less than 0.1 percent of Moscow's population, the sudden collapse of the Putin regime seems unlikely. There were smaller protests in 2014 over the war in Ukraine and again in 2016 over leadership corruption. Even the 2016 protests were not regime threatening, despite the seriousness of the allegations that reached all the way to Prime Minister Dmitry Medvedev. As a top organizer of anticorruption protests, Aleksei Naval'ny emerged as the leading oppositionist to Putin and his regime. He also has political ambitions. In December 2016, Naval'ny attempted to register as a candidate for the 2018 presidential election, but he was rejected based on a previous criminal conviction that his supporters argue was politically motivated. In the aftermath, he called for a boycott of the March 2018 election, but that was ineffective. For Putin's inauguration in May 2018, Naval'ny organized protests that again led to his arrest as well as the arrest of over one thousand other protestors nationwide, but overall the demonstrations had little impact on what was otherwise an ornate ordeal.[6]

A third question is whether any system that depends upon one person to hold itself together and to operate can possibly be stable. Myers argues that Putin returned to the presidency in 2012 "with no clear purpose other than the exercise of power for its own sake."[7] Putin had made himself indispensable. No Putin, no Russia. Myers writes that "he had unified the country behind the only leader anyone could now imagine because he was . . . unwilling to allow any alternative to emerge."[8] If the leader were to become chronically ill, suddenly die, or be assassinated, the system would have a difficult time operating. When Putin disappeared for ten days in March 2015, panic and paralysis gripped the political elite.

The questions above are valid and need to be taken seriously in any analysis of political stability in Russia. That said, the visceral antipathy toward Putin, his regime, and his policies by the Western media overlooks factors which suggest that the Putin regime is unlikely to collapse. In this regard, it is useful to think broadly about sources of stability in authoritarian regimes. While it may be true that authoritarian regimes eventually end, the "eventually" can span very long periods of time. The Soviet system existed for more than seven decades and would have existed even longer if Gorbachev had not tried to reform an unreformable system. The Chinese system has existed since 1949 and shows little sign of impending collapse.

Dix posits several factors that contribute to the breakdown of authoritarian regimes based on experiences in Latin America: failure of performance, particularly in the economic sphere; regime delegitimation; regime narrowing and the emergence of negative coalitions; the defection of regime elites; and exit guarantees among them.[9] It is true that authoritarian regimes may collapse suddenly, without warning, with the signs of collapse becoming apparent only after the fact. At this point, however, there is very little evidence to suggest the presence of delegitimation of Putinism among the majority of Russians.

The discussion below explores alternative views to the Russia-will-collapse thesis. First, long before Donald Trump became president based on his "Make American Great Again" slogan, Putin was making Russia great again. During the 1990s, Russians wanted three things from their government: an end to economic instability, the restoration of greatness, and an end to the war in Chechnya. One can argue that Putin has delivered on all three points. Despite some dips in the economy, there is no doubt that Russians have lived better in the Putin period than in the 1990s, witnessed by a growth in real income, an increase in real GDP per capita, and the emergence of an urban middle class. The political importance of economic revival is that in the minds of Russians, Putin is associated with the rebirth of Russia as a great power and with improvement in their daily lives as consumers. Based on this cognitive association, Putin remains enormously popular among Russians. To be sure, his popularity is fueled by an impressive propaganda machine and state-controlled media.[10] The cult of personality is partly manufactured and partly reflects genuine support for his leadership.

Even without the omnipresence of pro-Putin media, however, it is likely that he would be a popular leader. Maybe his approval numbers would not be in the eightieth percentile, but they also would not be as low as for Donald Trump. Western media are quick to focus on any indicator of waning popularity or discontent. Western sources, for example, pounced on the fact that Putin's popularity at the end of 2013 was lower than at any time since 2000, but they deemphasized the fact that his approval rating remained above 60 percent, a level of support that many Western leaders could only dream of achieving.[11] The reality is that Putin remains popular across gender, occupation, region, and income level. Further, during the political "crisis" period of 2011–2013, two-thirds of Russians believed that conditions had gotten generally better during Putin's rule, while less than 19 percent felt that things had gotten worse.[12] After Russia annexed Crimea in 2014, Putin's approval rating soared above 80 percent as his nationalism resonated with the population.[13] By early fall 2014, Putin's approval rating had reached an all-time high above 85 percent and has remained steady at more than 80 percent since then.

Second, the literature on instability and revolution asserts that an alternative ideology and alternative leader must exist and have support among the population.[14] In Russia today there is no viable alternative ideology—political liberalism died in the 1990s and liberal parties are shut off from power—and no alternative leader who could displace Putin. Much attention has been given to Aleksei Naval'ny as an oppositionist candidate and as a populist.[15] Supporters of Naval'ny point to the 27 percent of the vote that Naval'ny received when he ran for mayor of Moscow in 2013 as evidence of his popularity. Moscow, however, is not representative of Russia, and Putin remains much more popular in the regions. In the run-up to the March 2018 presidential election, voters perceived him to be experienced, decisive, and energetic, a person who was able to formulate long-term strategies for the nation.[16] It was difficult to find anyone who believed that Naval'ny could actually win the presidential election, except Naval'ny himself.[17] Naval'ny, in short, did not represent a viable alternative to Putin for a number of reasons. Another liberal candidate in the presidential election of March 2018, Ksenia Sobchak, received less than 2 percent of the vote.

A third factor that augurs for stability is that Putin is firmly in control of the political machine that helps him rule.[18] One aspect of the political machine is to oversee electoral outcomes: from registering the candidates, to manning the polling stations, to counting the votes. Masha Gessen describes how the 2011 Duma election was controlled.

> The Kremlin did not allow any strangers on the ballot, so the election did not need to be fixed. And still it was fixed. Ballot boxes were stuffed, numbers were doctored, phantom precincts reported, and conscripts were bused in to vote early and often. Not that it even mattered who got into parliament, which existed only to rubber-stamp the Kremlin's policies. But the bad theater of it all, in which you were invited up onstage for a millisecond and not allowed to open your mouth, was insulting.[19]

Control over electoral processes is further evidenced by wins for the pro-Kremlin party United Russia in regional elections in 2012, 2013, 2014, 2015, and 2017 despite reports of unpopularity of the party.[20] At the national level, United Russia again won the September 2016 election for the State Duma, as it had in every national election since 2004, receiving 54 percent of the vote (although with only 48 percent voter turnout) and emerging with 343 seats, thereby ensuring passage of bills drafted by the executive branch. There were no protests surrounding the 2016 Duma election. United Russia, which originally was created to support the Kremlin and ensure passage of presidential bills, remains loyal to Putin and controls at least a majority in all regional legislatures.[21] As of January 2018, United Russia also controlled eighty-one of eighty-five governorships, but three of the four are "token" opposition leaders.[22]

Further, Putin retains influence over the political elite and control over who occupies positions of power. The struggle with oligarchs was decided long ago in favor of Putin. People who want power, riches, or both must be loyal to Putin. Putin replaced several governors during 2015–2016 under the pretext of rooting out corruption. In late 2016, the minister of economic development, Aleksei Ulyukaev, was removed from Putin's cabinet over corruption charges. Whether it was corruption or something else we will probably never know. The important point about changes in governors and the cabinet is that turnover supports the idea that Putin is in control of personnel and that loyalty is necessary to remain in office. Although there may be differences of opinion or nuances of emphasis among elite members, Putin is unlikely to face contenders or challengers to his position from within the existing political elite, probably until the 2024 presidential election grows nearer and political jockeying can be expected.

Although Putin is far from infallible,[23] his counterstrategy against political opposition has been effective.[24] The strategy combined a crackdown on NGOs, the internet, and political activity. It is a valid question whether a strategy based on coercion will work over the long term. That said, if believers in "the Putin regime will collapse" scenario are expecting the middle class to support the political opposition, they are likely to be disappointed. Unlike the 2011–2012 protests when the middle class joined demonstrations against unfair elections, separate studies show that middle-class values have changed since then and now tend to be conservative and status quo.[25] Moreover, Levada Center polls show a low willingness to participate in protests, implying that it is easier for Russians to become apolitical than risk arrest or fines.[26] The bad news for opponents to Putin is that economic motivations for protest rank low among Russians, suggesting that the hope that economic sanctions may spur regime change are unlikely to succeed.[27]

A fourth factor is the institutionalization of Putinism, which enhances presidential power. The 1990s failed to create stable institutions. According to Kotkin, it was not until after 2000 that Russia began to create stable governing institutions and to address issues surrounding governability.[28] What is the institutional order that took hold that we call Putinism? Steven Fish identifies the Putin regime as conservative, populist, and personalistic.[29]

It is conservative in that it prioritizes the status quo and opposes anything suggesting instability, which Putin often defines as liberal values found in the West. Putin's populism overlaps with conservatism in its opposition to gay rights and women's equality but extends to ethnonationalism that glorifies Russia and Russian culture but also presents itself as inclusive of other cultures and religions—a model of "intercommunal harmony" to be emulated by other societies. Finally, Putinism is a personalistic autocracy, in which the leader is answerable only to himself. Putin did not inherit this type of regime; he created it, and he has been very successful. We may add the following characteristics:

- A centralized and authoritarian state
- An unfree media
- The redefinition of center-periphery relations, with a shift of power to the center at the cost of regional autonomy
- The bringing of political parties under control, and the rule of a "party of power"
- Less competitive elections
- A less independent court and legal system
- The use of coercion and violence against oppositionists
- The centrality of the state in all realms of political life
- Structural limitations on political opposition
- Russian nationalism and xenophobia

These elements of Putinism are important because they are not just a set of policies; they define the system of rule. Putinism has become a political system with an identifiable political culture, behavior, and characteristics. That said, Putinism is not a static system but has evolved over time. Robertson sees changes in the regime as a factor of longevity, arguing that "the Putin regime has invented and reinvented itself without greatly transforming the key formal institutions of the Russian political system."[30] Conversely, Shevtsova asserts that "Russia's system is growing ever more dependent on strategies that already proved useless in sustaining the USSR. . . . While there are grounds for cautious optimism regarding Russian society's future outside the doomed system, the same repressive tactics that have rendered the regime ever more brittle are also narrowing the window for a negotiated exit from a situation of rising tension."[31]

A different way of looking at the stability of Putinism considers the relationship between the values of those who govern and those who are governed. In a provocative thesis, Masha Gessen argues that Putinism as a system of governance resonates with the values and characteristics of *Homo Sovieticus*—the Soviet regime's attempt to remake a Soviet man. Decades before Gessen, Sheila Fitzpatrick had argued that Stalinism as a system was successful because it resonated with the value system of the population. The system bred obedience, conformity, and subservience. For a brief period— during Gorbachev's perestroika and into the "liberal" 1990s—it appeared that *Homo Sovieticus* was dying off, to be replaced by a value system closer to that found in the West. Values began to change and become more tolerant. The values of Stalinism as a system were discordant with the new values held by the population. Stalin's historical standing began to decline. That decline of *Homo Sovieticus* stopped in the late 1990s. According to Gessen, a series of events, such as the financial crisis of 1998, the West's bombing of Serbia and support for an independent Kosovo in 1999, and the rise of Putin in 1999–2000, revealed that *Homo Sovieticus* had not died off. *Homo Sovieticus* was the foundation that Putin needed to create a new, post-Soviet totalitarianism, evidenced by growing intolerance and a willingness to use violence against people with different sexual orientations, liberals, and those who were suspected of being "foreign agents" of the West, which came to mean anyone who did not buy into Russian nationalism.[32] Gessen's argument is supported by Vladislav Inozemtsev, who argues that "Putinism has deep roots in Russia's political traditions and imperial history; in its economic foundations; and in widespread norms and expectations in Russian society."[33] In short, Putinism is not a foreign ideology or system; it was born from the womb of Russian society and history. The implications of Putinism as a system are further discussed by Petrov and Slider in their chapter on regional politics, by Hendley in her chapter on the judicial system, and by Lipman in her chapter on the media.

The fact that Putinism is being institutionalized and finds fertile soil in Russian society suggests that its lasting power may be underappreciated by Western analysts. Fish argues that "Putinism's greatest liability may be its thoroughgoing personalism and lack of foundations that transcend the individual leader."[34] This may be true, but for today and the foreseeable future, it is important to understand that Putinism is probably stronger than ten years ago. We need to recognize that Putin has been remarkably successful in avoiding the fate of other post-Soviet states that fell to color revolutions. In 2003–2004 there was a perceived threat of contagion from color revolutions in Georgia and Ukraine. Russia avoided contagion by restricting political rights. In 2003–2004, conditions inside Russia were different from those in Georgia and Ukraine, so the threat was probably exaggerated by the Kremlin. In Russia, the regime abolished elections for governors and changed the way the State Duma was selected, moving decisively to "managed democracy." To be sure, Russia's middle class prospered after 2003 and today arguably has a stake in regime stability (although suffering through two recessions). Put another way, there is little evidence today that the middle class has an appetite for instability brought about by regime change. Similarly, the oligarchs have made their billions and have no desire to risk it all on societal upheaval.

A final factor is that Putin's Russia is not the USSR. The Soviet Union collapsed because of intra-elite conflict from above, which as noted earlier either does not exist or is controlled in Putin's Russia. Nationality problems and independence movements added pressure on the Soviet system, which have been effectively muted under Putin. It collapsed because the ideology on which society was organized became delegitimated. Putin has been accused of having no ideology other than wanting power; that may or may not be true, but he has deftly identified his regime with the Russian nation, with the church, and with Russian history, pillars that are more durable than Marxism-Leninism. Marxism-Leninism was an ideology that became discredited over time. The Russian state and the Orthodox Church are unlikely to become delegitimated. Economic weakness did not cause the collapse of the USSR, but it undermined support for the regime.

Further, Russian consumers today are more prosperous than in Soviet times. Travel to foreign countries is possible for anyone with the money for an air ticket. There is access to foreign films, news, and movies on TV and the internet. In mid-2016, home computer usage was above 76 percent, and cell phone ownership in 2017 was above 103 million (in a population of about 143 million), which means that just about every adult owned a cell phone in Russia. The point is that Russians today have more freedoms and conveniences than their Soviet counterparts did.

ECONOMIC PROSPECTS

Former president Medvedev emphasized that if Russia wanted long-term economic growth, it needed to diversify and modernize its economy. Medvedev envisioned a process of development that was predicated on good relations with the West, from whom credit and technology would be obtained. Medvedev wanted to create an innovation economy and hoped to build a high-tech Russian equivalent of Silicon Valley—the Skolkovo Innovation Center located in Skolkovo, a distant suburb of Moscow. Putin has never denied the need for modernization but does not embrace it as much as Medvedev did, perhaps because he is wary of spillover effects into the political system and how this might affect his ability to retain political control. Since 2012, and especially after 2014, it has been clear that Putin's modernization means Russia will go it alone and cannot depend on Western assistance. In July 2014, after hostilities in Ukraine broke out, Putin called for more protection of the economy against a hostile West. Igor Yurgens, a former adviser to the Kremlin, summarized Putin's choices at the time as "either autocracy and isolation or modernization."[35] Perhaps that formulation was too stark, but it does raise vexing questions whether Russia can modernize without financial and technological assistance from the West, with whom the relationship has deteriorated and rapprochement is unlikely.

In order to diversify and modernize the economy Russia needs capital in the form of investment and loans. Although Russia has signed investment agreements with Japan and China, the West historically has been the most important source of capital. Few people believe that Russia's tilt to the East will be able to compensate for the loss of Western financing. In 2017, neither China nor Japan were in the top ten nations for foreign direct investment (FDI) into Russia. It is not clear that the pivot to China and other Asian countries can bring Russia modernization. Jeanne Wilson in her chapter, for instance, notes the low level of Chinese foreign direct investment into Russia. Further, FDI to Russia has been vulnerable to political events, and generally levels have not been high. FDI into Russia equaled $53.4 billion in 2013, $29.1 billion in 2014, a bit less than $12 billion in 2015, and $37.6 billion in 2016.[36] For comparison, in 2013 China received $117.6 billion in FDI, $128.5 billion in 2014, $135.6 billion in 2015, and $133.7 billion in 2016, making it the third most popular destination for FDI after the United States and the United Kingdom.

Economic Challenges

Aside from the need for modernization, Russia faces a variety of economic challenges. The first challenge concerns the need to improve economic growth and general macro-performance such as GDP.[37] In 2014, the economy contracted as GDP fell to $2.0 trillion, down from $2.2 trillion in 2013. In 2015 the economy went into recession as real GDP contracted 3.7 percent and another 2 percent in 2016. The economy recovered to 1.7 percent growth in 2017, but GDP remained far below the 2013 level. Growth in GDP is forecast to remain below 2 percent for the next few years. Laura Solanko and Pekka Sutela examine economic policy in their chapter.

A second challenge is to diversify sources of revenue and growth. An economy that is based on the export of natural resources and is integrated into global markets is vulnerable to price fluctuations in commodity markets. This is true whether a country exports coffee, bananas, or oil and gas. Russia's government has depended on oil and gas revenue for a long time. About 40 percent of Russia's GDP comes from the energy sector; energy accounted for 52 percent of government revenues and 70 percent of export earnings in 2013.[38] When the price of oil fell from over $100 in 2013 to the $30s in 2016, the consequences were reduced domestic investment, reductions in federal and regional budgets, deficit spending, and a drawdown on the sovereign reserve fund.[39] The price of oil rebounded into the $50s in the second half of 2017, into the low $60s in early 2018, and then into the high $60s and low $70s by mid-2018, which will give a boost to the economy and govern-ment revenue. But the prospect of returning to $100 per barrel of oil is unlikely anytime soon. Stefan Hedlund discusses energy policy in his chap-ter.

Significant consequences resulted from reduced state revenue as the price of oil fell. One consequence was that Putin's 2013 decree "On the State's Long-Run Economic Policy," which laid out long-term goals for the econo-my, was unlikely to be fulfilled.[40] In October 2014, Putin indicated the need to cut state spending by up to R1 trillion.[41] Another consequence was a contraction in state investment and available credit for investment. In the past, Russian banks and companies could turn to global financial markets for capital. In 2013, for example, Russian banks borrowed €15.8 billion ($21.3 billion) from the EU, equal to almost one-half of their capital loans.[42] West-ern sanctions, however, prohibit any Russian bank that is 50 percent or more owned by the state from restructuring or acquiring new debt in US or Euro-pean capital markets for a term longer than thirty days. Debt that would have been automatically renewed in the past no longer will be.

Another challenge concerns the effort to improve Russia's ranking in the World Bank's ease of doing business index. Putin's 2013 goal was to rise to 20th place by 2018.[43] In 2013, it ranked 62nd.[44] In 2016, Russia rose to 40th, and in 2017 to 35th place.[45] Thus, the trajectory is positive, but the original goal was not reached by 2018. Russia's attraction for investors and for start-ing a business is affected by continual high corruption. In 2016, Russia ranked 131st out of 176 nations with a score of 29/100, with 100 being defined as "very clean."[46] In 2017, Russia fell a bit to 133rd place. It is unlikely that Russia will improve significantly on the corruption scale for reasons that Louise Shelley examines in her chapter.

A fourth economic challenge concerns improving the personal welfare of Russians. In particular, incomes, poverty, and jobs are discussed. For many years (2000–2013), the real incomes (adjusted for inflation) of Russians in-creased every year except 2009. During 2000–2007, the real increase was in double digits when the price of oil was climbing. In nominal rubles, the disposable monetary monthly income for urban residents rose from R1,894 during the fourth quarter of 2000 to R18,056 in the first quarter of 2013.[47] During this period, pensions, the minimum wage, and the subsistence mini-mum that defined the poverty line were repeatedly raised. A large portion of the increase in income for the working and nonworking population was at-tributed to revenues generated from energy exports, allowing the government to fund development programs and support domestic investment to create new jobs in advanced sectors of the economy.

- *Personal incomes.* The slowdown in the economy starting in 2014 af-fected personal income. Real incomes fell by 9.5 percent in 2015, but even in the "good" years of 2014 and 2016, real incomes rose just 1.2 percent and 0.7 percent, respectively. Per capita GDP fell from R24,880 in 2014 to R24,026 in 2016, reflecting the erosion in real income (inflation adjusted). Further, compared to 2000–2007, the rise in disposable incomes slowed considerably. In nominal rubles for an urban dweller, disposable monetary monthly income rose from 22,783 rubles per month in the fourth quarter of 2013 to R26,043 in the fourth quarter of 2016.[48] But real (inflation-adjusted) disposable income decreased by 3.2 percent in 2015 and by 5.9 percent in 2016.[49] Disposable income is important because consumer spending serves as a main driver of economic growth. The slowdown in the growth of disposable income reverberates throughout the entire economy. As consumption slows, so too does the economy.

During 2014–2015 the depreciation of the ruble meant that the dollar equivalent of individuals' monthly income plummeted from $935 in 2013 to $427 in 2016.[50] The fall in dollar-denominated incomes made foreign consumer goods too expensive, and the same was true for foreign travel. Russians began to vacation domestically, which was good for Russian tourism companies but represented a reversal of the increase in foreign travel that had been ongoing for many years. For companies, the devaluation of the ruble meant that the price of foreign products increased, making purchases of foreign equipment and technology prohibitive for many businesses. Economists estimate that Russia's economic performance could improve with Western managerial techniques and modern equipment, but an unfavorable exchange rate hinders the acquisition of foreign technology and equipment.[51]

- *Poverty.* The number of people officially living in poverty rose from 15.5 million in 2013 to 19.8 million in 2016. Needless to say, millions of others live on the edge of poverty and move in and out of official classification of poverty but never escape the conditions. People on the borderline of poverty have standards of living that differ little from those who are classified as below the subsistence minimum.[52] The problem of the working poor— employed but living in poverty—remains chronic and acute. At the same time, high inequality persists in Russia, characterized by enormous disparity between rich and poor. Thomas Remington analyzes inequality and its social consequences in his chapter.

- *Jobs.* The number of employed persons in the formal economy was 71.3 million in 2013.[53] The 2015–2016 recession slowed job creation, as the number of employed rose to just 72.3 million in November 2017, far off the pace to meet Putin's goal of 25 million new jobs during 2013–2020. Although unemployment did not rise significantly, there are regions where unemployment is much higher than the national rate of 5.1 percent in 2017; for example, the North Caucasus federal district had an unemployment rate of almost 11 percent in November 2017.[54] Further, the economy faces a deficit in skilled labor for key sectors and occupations, which constrains the creation of an innovation economy. Although the federal government has been active in the labor market, the Moscow office of the International Labor Organization believes that there remains a mismatch between market demand by businesses and the supply of labor that is produced by the educational system.[55]

The upshot of this discussion is that while the Russian economy is not in a crisis, it certainly faces several serious challenges. It will not be easy because the conditions that fueled economic growth during 2000–2007 are no longer present: the rising price of oil and access to Western credit. That said, despite the deep financial crisis in 2008–2009 and a recession in 2015–2016, the Russian people are resilient. They endured much worse in the 1990s. Economic conditions are less likely to motivate protest than political issues. The government has the patience of the Russian people and time to introduce corrective policies without fear of being thrown out of office, one way or another.

The Positive

One of the main economic positives during Putin's third term and especially since 2014 has been the agricultural sector. When Putin announced Russia's food embargo against Western nations in August 2014, it is unlikely that anyone in the political leadership expected the degree of success agriculture has had. The decision to ban food imports from selected Western nations— borne out of anger and a desire to punish the West for its sanctions against Russia—produced protectionism that has benefited actors in the entire food chain, from producers to processors and from distributors to retail chains.[56] To be sure, the agricultural sector continues to be plagued with serious problems. Some of those problems include continuing village depopulation; a shortage of skilled workers and people with managerial experience; access to credit, particularly for households, private farmers, and small farm enterprises; and slow remechanization of production processes, which still has far to go to recapture the levels of 1990. The year 2017 revealed shortages in train cars to transport grain to ports for export, and there was inadequate storage, which made export necessary. There was also a deficit of storage for about three million tons of vegetables.

That said, the agricultural sector has grown faster than national GDP since 2013, as well as for nine of the past eleven years dating back to 2008 (covering the period 2008–2017). Since 2008, the nominal ruble value of agricultural production more than doubled from R2.46 trillion in 2008 to over R5 trillion in 2016 and 2017. Farm profitability is up. Russia has emerged as a major grain producer and global exporter, capturing the top spot for wheat exports in two of the past four years, finishing second behind the United States the other two years. More and more unused and unclaimed land is being brought into production so that grain production levels will increase in the future. Thus, the agricultural sector not only is not a disaster, but it emerged as a bright spot in an otherwise dismal economy during the recession of 2015–2016.[57]

Although production in the agricultural sector only accounts for 4–5 percent of national GDP, its importance is felt in other ways. First, increased food production is creating jobs up and down the value chain. Higher grain production creates the need for more farm machinery, so machine-building jobs are increasing. Grain exports create the need for more grain storage facilities, for train cars to transport grain, for dockworkers to load the grain, and for shipbuilding to transport grain across the ocean, for example to South America and Mexico. Higher food production means that processors are increasing capacity, and their income is growing annually. Increased food production means not only higher farm profitability, some of which is reinvested in production processes that create jobs, but ordinary workers have benefited. For example, the Ministry of Agriculture reported that workers in agricultural production had the highest rate of income growth since 2014 of any sector in the economy.[58]

Moreover, agricultural production is branching out in new directions. The construction of industrial-type greenhouses is increasing to replace imported tomatoes and cucumbers, which in turn creates demand for metal frames, glass, wiring, and robotics. Land reclamation creates jobs for the construction of dams and levees. Efforts to develop domestic high-yield seed and pedigree livestock create demand for research and scientific personnel. Retail chains are experiencing higher profits and opening new stores across the country, which creates jobs in the construction of stores but also employees who work in the stores. Overall, while the number of agricultural workers involved in food production on farms continues to decline, one hundred thousand new jobs were created in the agroindustrial complex in 2016, jobs that were not in food production.[59] Higher levels of production, more grain exports and revenue from it, improved farm profitability, and job creation are the reasons that former minister of agriculture Alexander Tkachev referred to the agricultural sector as a "driver of the nation's economy."[60] In 2014, Russia's political leadership did not know what their self-induced protectionism would bring, but the results have undoubtedly exceeded their expectations. In their chapter, Wegren and Nikulin consider how the rebound in agriculture allows food to be used as an instrument of foreign policy.

FOREIGN POLICY

Russia's estrangement from the West is now in its fifth year as this book goes to press. This section sets the context for more detailed discussions by Andrei Tsygankov, Jeff Mankoff, Jeanne Wilson, Bettina Renz, and Stephen Wegren and Alexander Nikulin. The reset in US-Russia relations that occurred in 2010 between former president Obama and former president Medvedev seems ancient history. US-Russia relations began to sour late in Medvedev's term and came fully undone after Putin returned to the presidency in May 2012. In December 2012, the United States passed the Magnitsky Act, and Russia retaliated when President Putin signed the Dima Yakovlev Law shortly thereafter that imposed a ban on the adoption of Russian children by US parents. In February 2014, Michael McFaul, former US ambassador to Russia, announced his resignation following the 2014 Olympic Games in Sochi, Russia. The atmosphere in Moscow turned so vehemently anti-American that McFaul felt that he was essentially driven from office. [61] In July 2018, during the summit between Presidents Trump and Putin, the Russian side requested permission to interview McFaul on US soil for his "crimes" while serving in Russia; McFaul was considered an enemy of Russia. The Trump administration initially was receptive to the idea but then reversed course one day later after an uproar from political leaders and the media.

US-Russia relations since 2014 have been especially acerbic. In March 18, 2014, following the annexation of Crimea, Putin delivered a speech to the Federation Council and State Duma in which he defended Russia's actions in Crimea and lambasted the West and in particular the United States for its lies, hypocrisy, and hegemonic behavior that threatened Russia's interests. [62] As the relationship became increasingly bitter, President Obama indicated that Russia was a greater threat to global stability and order than Islamic State or the Ebola outbreak in Liberia, something that enraged Putin. [63] Putin again lashed out at the West in an October 2014 speech in Sochi in which he excoriated the United States for its unilateral actions that threaten world peace, its continuation of a Cold War mentality, and its attempt to impose its will on other countries in a way that Putin considered to be unlawful international behavior. [64] Dmitry Trenin, head of the Carnegie Center in Moscow, concluded that Putin "clearly does not trust America and sees no point in talking to it." [65] Continuing his theme in November 2014, Putin accused the United States of trying to subjugate Russia. [66] In his annual address to the Federal Assembly in December 2014, Putin criticized the West's "hypocritical statements on the protection of international law and human rights" as nothing more than blatant cynicism. He also argued that the United States is controlling its European partners in their relations with Russia, so that "we will have to protect our legitimate interests unilaterally and will not pay for what we view as erroneous policy." [67]

Since that watershed year in 2014, Russia's relations with the West have been characterized by increasing disagreement, antipathy, and distrust. After 2014, positive interaction between Russia and the United States virtually stopped in the period prior to the July 2018 summit between Trump and Putin. The European Union renewed its sanctions against Russia several times. Russia extended its food embargo ("countersanctions") against the West through 2019. The United States accused Russia of meddling in its 2016 presidential election, a charge that Putin has repeatedly rejected. The United States was behind the banning of Russian athletes from the 2018 Winter Olympics. The United States and Russia disagree on all of the key international hot spots around the world—Ukraine, Syria, North Korea, and Iran.

Relations between Russia and the West were set back even more in March 2018 when an attack occurred using a military-grade nerve gas on ex–double agent Sergei Skripal and his daughter in Salisbury, England. Almost immediately, the British government alleged that Putin had ordered the attack, based on the fact that the nerve agent Novichok had been produced in the Soviet Union during the Cold War. Building on the poisoning of Alexander Litvinenko in 2006, also a former Russian spy, the Skripal case reinforced impressions that Russia under Putin is a thug state. Putin denied Russian involvement, and in fact many questions remained about putative motivations for the attack.[68] In fundamental ways the official story coming out of London made no sense, leading to conspiracy theories that the British government had initiated the attack to bolster the political ratings of Prime Minister Theresa May, or that Sergei Skripal had accidentally poisoned himself.[69] In any event, the damage to Western-Russian relations quickly intensified. About two dozen Western countries displayed solidarity with UK prime minister Theresa May by expelling 150 Russian diplomats, led by the United States, which expelled sixty Russians. Russia, of course, retaliated and expelled the same number of Western diplomats, including sixty Americans, and closed the US consulate in St. Petersburg. The United States placed more sanctions on Russia, but President Donald Trump backed away from a second round of economic sanctions that was even tougher, a move that rekindled speculation that Putin did in fact have compromising information on Trump as alleged in the controversial Steele dossier.

Another blow to US-Russia relations came in April 2018 when Syrian president Bashar al-Assad was alleged to have used chemical weapons against his own people again. He had used chemical weapons in 2017, and then again in a smaller attack in March 2018, for which the Trump administration did not have any response options prepared. After the April attack, the United States threatened a military response, to which Putin said that Russia would shoot down any incoming missiles. Posturing on both sides ensued, and the prospect for war between the United States and Russia loomed. In the end, Trump essentially gave notice of an impending attack through one of his tweets, thereby allowing Syria to remove any stored chemical agents to different locations. The Trump administration also alerted Russia to the attack and likely indicated areas to be targeted, thus avoiding political pressures to retaliate if Russian soldiers were killed. In the end, the US missile attack on Syria was an act of symbolism. The episode was aptly described by a columnist in the aftermath:

> It was the perfect limited strike. It did not spark a wider conflict. Casualties were minimal. The strike's modest goals provided Moscow and Tehran an opportunity to back down gracefully from their rhetoric. Trump has an opportunity to brag. And Americans who were justifiably horrified by images of children gasping for breath can comfort themselves with the consolation that at least we did something. But, really, nothing has changed. [70]

The remainder of this section adopts a big-picture perspective to examine Russia's relations with the West and prospects for improvement, leaving more detailed analyses of foreign policy to separate authors in their respective chapters. Foreign policy entails policy choices. The political climate and the personalities that are involved make a change in course difficult. US policy makers and the media for the most part are distrustful of Putin. For his part, Putin has been wary of the West and its intentions since at least 2007, and his orientation is not going to disappear magically. There are several schools of thought about relations between the West and Russia that are presented as hypotheses below.

Hypothesis 1. There is a new Cold War between the West and Russia that flows from the authoritarian nature of the Russian political system and its values. This school of thought sees disagreement and conflict between the West and Russia as structural in nature. The new Cold War flows from Russian behavior, which has turned assertive, aggressive, and even adventurist since 2008. Russia intends harm to the West. Shevtsova goes so far as to argue that the Ukraine crisis of 2014 "is in truth the product of the Russian system of personalized power, which, having reached a certain point in its decay, can no longer exist in a state of peace."[71] The conflict over Ukraine represents "civilizational confrontation with liberal democracy."[72] In this view, Russia is not just expansionist; it represents an "existential" threat to the West, an idea that resonates with the Trump administration as it identified Russia (and China) as the main threats in its National Defense Strategy, released by the Pentagon in January 2018. Remediation can only come from internal change within Russia. Until that point, military containment is an appropriate response. [73]

Hypothesis 2. There is a new Cold War between the West and Russia that redefines the relationship that had vacillated between friendly and unfriendly cycles since the mid-1990s. The 2014 Ukrainian crisis and subsequent annexation of Crimea represents a break from the previous cycle. Following the crises in Ukraine/Crimea, relations deteriorated so badly that they represent a new Cold War, reflecting the depth and all-encompassing scope of the relationship. [74] The damage done to the relationship is so deep and the prospects for improvement are so poor that "rivalry" or even "enduring rivalry" do not do justice. [75] This new Cold War shares many characteristics with the first, although ideological competition is not one of them. [76] Both the United States and Russia engage in demonizing the other side and assume the worst motivations, unable and unwilling to find common ground or understand the perspective of the other. In this view, the only way to prevent the new Cold War from lasting as long as the first is for both sides to travel the path toward rapprochement together. Legvold calls on the United States to take the first step because of its overwhelming economic, military, and strategic advantages. If the Putin regime is unresponsive—"unredeemable"—the United States "has the time and wherewithal to shift course." [77]

Hypothesis 3. There is no new Cold War. This argument has been postulated two ways, but both argue that the Cold War framework is misleading. First, Trenin argues that US-Russia relations resemble great power rivalry from the nineteenth century and British-Russian competition, the Great Game. [78] The second view is that US-Russia relations reflect asymmetrical rivalry. In this view, Russia is motivated to gain recognition and more influence in the Western-controlled global order. Russia is in no position to challenge the Western global order and cannot defeat the other side. Instead, Russia uses asymmetrical methods such as social media, cyber power, hybrid military intervention, and targeted economic sanctions. [79]

Hypothesis 4. Russia's foreign policy behavior reflects an effort to reclaim the great power status that it lost when the Soviet Union collapsed. Russia's imperialist drive reflects rejection of integration with the West. Some analysts date the imperial drive as a reaction to the 1990s when Russia was politically and economically prostrate. [80] Others date the imperial impulse to the Soviet period, arguing that Russia's "imperial syndrome" was a fatal flaw in Soviet foreign policy. Rejecting the view that Gorbachev's perestroika doomed the USSR, Kovalev argues that, "in fact, the Soviet Union's defeat in the Cold War had occurred long before the start of Gorbachev's perestroika." [81] Soviet leaders before Gorbachev failed to realize that the Cold War had *already* been lost through the effort at an empire and competition with the West, a competition that the USSR could not possibly win. He argues that Putin's Russia is making the same mistake: isolation from the West and engaging in competition in which it cannot prevail.

Hypothesis 5. Russia has national interests, and its foreign policy reflects constructivist theory in that relations are conditioned by the international system and interactions within it. In the Russian version, its behavior is merely an attempt to recapture its "rightful place" that was temporarily lost during the 1990s.[82] Putin signaled as early as 2005 that Russia would not play a diminished role in the world forever.

Russia's foreign policy conundrum is policy based but has elements of a structural problem, namely, that Russia is a lonely power.[83] Russia has no close friends, and alliances are instrumental rather than based on shared interests and outlooks. In the late 1980s, Seweryn Bialer described the USSR as a country surrounded by hostile communist nations. Russia today is surrounded by noncommunist nations, which if not hostile are not exactly friendly. Russia and Ukraine are at war. The Baltic states have drawn closer to NATO. The president of Russia's supposed ally, Alexander Lukashenko in Belarus, has yet to support the annexation of Crimea, and Russia is engaged in chronic trade disputes with Belarus involving the reexport of banned food into Russia. Relations with Georgia have improved but are hardly warm. Russia has attempted to draw closer to Armenia through trade, but the Armenians remain cautious. Relations with Kazakhstan are normal despite petty trade disputes that arise from time to time, but President Nursultan Nazarbayev, who has been in office since 1991 and is seventy-eight years old, won't be around forever. Nazarbayev has shown signs of wanting closer relations with the United States, indicated by his meeting with President Trump twice in Trump's first year in office. Putin may have reason to worry. Russia's "ally," China, is a client for Russian weapons and natural gas, but Russia is terrified of it. In reality, China is as much a competitor as an ally, but the Kremlin does not want to acknowledge this reality. Russia's friendliest relations are with nations that lie outside the Western orbit—Iran, North Korea, Venezuela, Cuba, and Syria—a reality that pokes the West and demonstrates Russian "independence," but also limits economic relations and the potential for credit and technology. Russia has chosen to align with the weak and isolated. The conundrum is that, having withdrawn from integration with the West, there are few routes to global leadership.

DISCUSSION QUESTIONS

1. What are the prospects for political stability in Putin's fourth term as president?
2. What are the economic challenges that Putin faces in his fourth term as president?
3. What are the challenges in foreign policy that Putin faces in his fourth term as president?

SUGGESTED READINGS

Dawisha, Karen. *Putin's Kleptocracy: Who Owns Russia?* New York: Simon & Schuster, 2014.

Gessen, Masha. *The Future Is History: How Totalitarianism Reclaimed Russia*. New York: Riverhead Books, 2017.

Kovalev, Andrei A. *Russia's Dead End: An Insider's Testimony from Gorbachev to Putin*. Translated by Steven I. Levine. Omaha, NE: Potomac Books, 2017.

Legvold, Robert. *Return to Cold War*. Cambridge: Polity, 2016.

Myers, Steven Lee. *The New Tsar: The Rise and Reign of Vladimir Putin*. New York: Vintage, 2015.

Sakwa, Richard. *Russia versus the Rest: The Post–Cold War Crisis of World Order*. Cambridge: Cambridge University Press, 2017.

Trenin, Dmitri. *Should We Fear Russia?* Cambridge: Polity, 2016.

Tsygankov, Andrei P. *Russia's Foreign Policy: Change and Continuity in National Identity*. 4th ed. Lanham, MD: Rowman & Littlefield, 2016.

NOTES

1. See Karen Dawisha, *Putin's Kleptocracy: Who Owns Russia?* (New York: Simon & Schuster, 2014).

2. Lilia Shevtsova, "The Next Russian Revolution," *Current History* 111, no. 747 (2012): 251.

3. Steven Lee Myers, *The New Tsar: The Rise and Reign of Vladimir Putin* (New York: Vintage, 2015), 475–78.

4. Creeping democratization envisions an "incremental and sometimes quite lengthy process of transition from authoritarianism to democracy through a series of strategic interactions between the ruling group and the opposition, who adjust their strategies in response to each other's moves." See Vladimir Gel'man, "Political Opposition in Russia: A Troubled Transformation," *Europe-Asia Studies* 67, no. 2 (2015): 177–91.

5. Andrei Yakovlev, "Russia's Protest Movement and the Lessons of History," *Russian Analytical Digest*, no. 108 (2012): 9.

6. Andrew E. Kramer, "For Putin's 4th Term, More a Coronation than an Inauguration," *New York Times*, May 7, 2018.

7. Myers, *The New Tsar*, 480.

8. Myers, *The New Tsar*, 480.

9. Robert H. Dix, "The Breakdown of Authoritarian Regimes," *Western Political Quarterly* 35, no. 4 (1982): 54–73.

10. Arkady Ostrovsky, *The Invention of Russia: The Rise of Putin and the Age of Fake News* (New York: Penguin Books, 2015).

11. Steve Gutterman, "Approval for Russia's Putin Lowest since 2000," Reuters, December 3, 2013, http://www.reuters.com/article/us-russia-putin-approval/approval-for-russias-putin-lowest-since-2000-opinion-poll-idUSBRE9B212G20131203 (accessed July 19, 2014). The Levada Center placed the level of trust in Putin at just under 60 percent starting in July 2012 and continuing into mid-2013. Levada Tsentr, *Obshchestvennoe mnenie—2013* (Moscow: Levada Center), 90.

12. Levada Tsentr, *Obshchestvennoe mnenie—2013*, 88.

13. Abby Abrams, "Putin's Approval Rating Reaches Record High in Russia," *Time*, July 18, 2014, http://www.time.com/3005439/putin-approval-ratings (accessed July 19, 2014).

14. Jack A. Goldstone, *Revolution: A Very Short Introduction* (Oxford: Oxford University Press, 2014), 26–40.

15. Jussi Lassile, "Aleksei Naval'nyi and Populist Re-ordering of Putin's Stability," *Europe-Asia Studies* 68, no. 1 (2016): 118–37.

16. Levada Tsentr, *Obshchestvennoe mnenie—2016* (Moscow: Levada Center, 2017), 87.

17. AP, "Opposition Leader Says He Could Beat Putin in Fair Election," December 18, 2017, in *Johnson's Russia List*, no. 236, December 19, 2017.

18. Konstantin Gaaze argues differently, asserting that whereas before Putin ran a "well-oiled machine," now "his personal power is diminishing" and his role is "being quietly challenged." Gaaze divides governance between "daylight rulers" over which Putin still has power,

and "nighttime rulers," who operate semi-independently of him. He bases his argument on the trial of former minister of economic development Aleksei Ulyukaev and "other instances of intimidation and force exercised by men in the shadows." See Konstantin Gaaze, "Between Night and Day: Who Will Control Putin's Fourth Term?," Carnegie Moscow Center, December 21, 2017, http://carnegie.ru/commentary/75087 (accessed December 21, 2017).

19. Masha Gessen, *The Future Is History: How Totalitarianism Reclaimed Russia* (New York: Riverhead Books, 2017), 335.

20. In October 2012, United Russia (UR) won all five gubernatorial elections, putting loyalist governors to the Kremlin in office. In 2013, UR won all sixteen regional elections due to vote-splitting manipulation and restrictive nomination procedures. In the September 2014 regional elections, Kremlin-backed governors and legislators swept to power, showing the continued strength of the regime and its ability to influence electoral outcomes to its benefit. In 2015, UR won all eleven regional legislative elections. In 2017, UR won all six regional legislative elections. For analysis, see Aleksandr Kynev, "Russia's September 14 Regional Elections: Strengthening the Rules and Reducing Competition against the Background of the Ukrainian Crisis," *Russian Analytical Digest*, no. 156 (2014): 2–10; Grigorii V. Golosov, "The September 2013 Regional Elections in Russia: The Worse of Both Worlds," *Regional and Federal Studies* 24, no. 2 (2014): 229–41; Grigorii V. Golosov, "The September 2015 Regional Elections in Russia: A Rehearsal for Next Year's National Legislative Races," *Regional and Federal Studies* 26, no. 2 (2014): 255–68.

21. Interestingly, over time we see evidence of a split in popular opinion toward the political leadership. On the one hand, Putin remains very popular. On the other hand, there is discontent toward legislative deputies and regional leaders. In 2015, the Levada Center found that 71 percent of respondents either knew "practically nothing" about the activity of their representatives or had no interest. Only 19 percent were satisfied with the performance of their representatives. It is for these reasons that Putin ran as an independent in 2018 and not as a member of United Russia as in 2012. Levada Tsentr, *Obshchestvennoe mnenie—2015* (Moscow: Levada Center, 2016), 140–41.

22. I thank Darrell Slider for this information.

23. According to the Levada Center, respondents did not like that he was connected to big capital, he was associated with corrupt politicians, and he had other interests than those of the common Russia. Levada Tsentr, *Obshchestvennoe mnenie—2016*, 87.

24. For a review of the 2011–2012 protests and the Kremlin's reactions, see Graeme Robertson, "Protesting Putinism: The Election Protests of 2011–2012 in Broader Perspective," *Problems of Post-Communism* 60, no. 2 (2013): 11–23.

25. Evgeny Gontmakher and Cameron Ross, "The Middle Class and Democratisation in Russia," *Europe-Asia Studies* 67, no. 2 (2015): 269–84; Mikhail Dmitriev, "Lost in Transition? The Geography of Protests and Attitude Change in Russia," *Europe-Asia Studies* 67, no. 2 (2015): 224–43.

26. Levada Tsentr, *Obshchestvennoe mnenie—2015*, 150; Levada Tsentr, *Obshchestvennoe mnenie—2016*, 135.

27. Tomila Lankina and Alisa Voznaya, "New Data on Protest Trends in Russia's Regions," *Europe-Asia Studies* 67, no. 2 (2015): 336.

28. Stephen Kotkin, *Armageddon Averted: The Soviet Collapse, 1970–2000*, updated ed. (Oxford: Oxford University Press, 2008).

29. M. Steven Fish, "What Is Putinism?," *Journal of Democracy* 28, no. 4 (2017): 61–75.

30. Grame Robertson and Samuel Greene, "How Putin Wins Support," *Journal of Democracy* 28, no. 4 (2017): 86–100, quote on 89.

31. Lilia Shevtsova, "Paradoxes of Decline," *Journal of Democracy* 28, no. 4 (2017): 101–9, quote on 101.

32. Masha Gessen, *The Future Is History*, 59–66, 395–418.

33. Vladislav Inozemtsev, "Why Putinism Arose," *Journal of Democracy* 28, no. 4 (2017): 80–85, quote on 80.

34. Fish, "What Is Putinism?," 73.

35. Kathrin Hille, "Vladimir Putin Starts to Show the Strain as Outrage Mounts over MH17," *Financial Times*, July 22, 2014, http://www.ft.com/content/058a2a9e-11b5-11e4-a17a-00144feabdc0 (accessed July 22, 2014).

36. One cannot talk about FDI without mentioning capital flight. Capital flight from Russia was negative in every year during 2008 through 2016 and in many years exceeded the level of FDI. The flight reversed itself temporarily in early 2017 before resuming. For data on capital flight from Russia, see BNE Intellinews, March 2, 2017, http://www.intellinews.com/russian-capital-flight-reverses-for-the-first-time-since-2015-116834 (accessed December 23, 2017).

37. See Peter Rutland, "Back to the Future: Economic Retrenchment in Russia," *Russian Analytical Digest*, no. 180 (2016): 2–7, and "Russia's Current Economic Indicators in International Comparison," *Russian Analytical Digest*, no. 180 (2016): 14–21.

38. Steve Hargreaves, "Russian Energy Should Keep Flowing," Money.CNN, March 3, 2014, http://www.money.cnn.com/2014/03/03/news/economy/russia-oil-prices/index.html (accessed July 20, 2014).

39. For trends in the reserve and national welfare funds, see BNE Intellinews, March 2, 2017, http://www.intellinews.com/russian-capital-flight-reverses-for-the-first-time-since-2015-116834 (accessed December 23, 2017).

40. Some of the goals included the creation of twenty-five million new jobs by 2020, investment was to reach 25 percent of GDP by 2018, production of high-tech products was to increase by 30 percent, and labor productivity was to increase by 50 percent over 2012.

41. Alexander Panin, "Putin Promises Rosy Future for Russia's Economy despite Sanctions," *Moscow Times*, October 2, 2014, http://www.themoscowtimes.com/articles/putin-promises-rosy-future-for-russias-economy-despite-sanctions-40046 (accessed October 3, 2014).

42. Reuters, "EU Sanctions on Russian Banks Would Stifle Investment, Lending" *Moscow Times*, July 25, 2014, http://www.themoscowtimes.com/articles/eu-sanctions-on-russian-banks-would-stifle-investment-lending-37672 (accessed July 27, 2014).

43. Peter Rutland, "The Political Economy of Putin 3.0," *Russian Analytical Digest*, no. 133 (2013): 3.

44. World Bank, *Doing Business 2015: Going Beyond Efficiency* (Washington, DC: World Bank, 2014), 213.

45. World Bank, *Doing Business 2018: Reforming to Create Jobs* (Washington, DC: World Bank, 2018), 113. Russia ranked 35th out of 190 countries for ease of doing business. High rankings included measurements for starting a business (28th), registering property (12th), getting electricity (10th), enforcing contracts (18th), and getting credit (29th). Low rankings included dealing with construction permits (115th), trading across borders (100th), resolving insolvency (54th), paying taxes (52nd), and protecting minority owners (51st). In recent years, the World Bank noted reforms in registering property, enforcing contracts, and starting a business. See World Bank, "Russia Accelerates Reforms Pace to Improve Business Climate: Doing Business Report" (press release no. 2018/102/ECA, October 31, 2017), http://www.worldbank.org/en/news/press-release/2017/10/31/russia-accelerates-reforms-pace-to-improve-business-climate-doing-business-report (accessed December 23, 2017).

46. Transparency International, "Corruption Perceptions Index 2016," January 25, 2017, https://www.transparency.org/news/feature/corruption_perceptions_index_2016 (accessed December 23, 2017).

47. Goskomstat, *Dokhody, raskhody i potreblenie domashnikh khoziaistv v III–IV kvartale 2000 goda* (Moscow: Goskomstat 2001), 77; Rosstat, *Dokhody, raskhody i potreblenie domashnikh khoziaistv v I kvartale 2013 goda* (Moscow: Rosstat, 2014), 14.

48. Rosstat, *Dokhody, raskhody i potreblenie domashnikh khoziaistv v IV kvartale 2013 goda* (Moscow: Rosstat, 2014), 14; and *Dokhody, raskhody i potreblenie domashnikh khoziaistv v IV kvartale 2016 goda* (Moscow: Rosstat, 2017), 15.

49. Rosstat, *Sotsial'no-ekonomicheskoe polozhenie Rossii 2016 god*, no. 12 (2016): 250.

50. "Russia's Current Economic Indicators in International Comparison," 18.

51. Samuel Ramani, "World-Renowned Economist Sergei Guriev on the Russian Economy: Takeaways from His Speech at the Oxford Guild," *Huffington Post*, February 19, 2016, https://

www.huffingtonpost.com/samuel-ramani/worldrenowned-economist-s_b_9272876.html (accessed December 24, 2017).

52. Rosstat, *Sotsial'no-ekonomicheskie indikatory bednosti v 2013–2016 gg.* (Moscow: Rosstat, 2017), 12.

53. Rosstat, *Rabochaia sila, zaniatost' i bezrabotitsa v Rossii* (Moscow: Rosstat, 2016), 14.

54. Rosstat, "Zaniatost' i bezrabotitsa v Rossiiskoi Federatsii v Noiabre 2017 goda," http://www.gks.ru/bgd/free/b04_03/IssWWW.exe/Stg/d03/261.htm (accessed December 23, 2017).

55. Olga Koulaeva, "What Are the Challenges behind Russia's Plan to Boost Job Creation?," May 21, 2012, http://www.ilo.org/global/about-the-ilo/newsroom/comment-analysis/WCMS_181133/lan--en/index.htm (accessed December 23, 2017).

56. See Stephen K. Wegren, Frode Nilssen, and Christel Elvestad, "The Impact of Russian Food Security Policy on the Performance of the Food System," *Eurasian Geography and Economics* 57, no. 6 (2016): 671–99.

57. Aleksandr Rybakov, "Komentarii. A. Tkachev: sokhranit' zadannuiu traektoriiu razvitiia," December 18, 2017, http://kvedomosti.ru/news/kommentarij-a-tkachev-soxranit-zadannuyu-traektoriyu-razvitiya.html (accessed December 18, 2017).

58. "V APK Sodano 100 tys. novykh rabochikh mest," April 12, 2017, http://www.agromedia.ru (accessed April 12, 2017).

59. "V APK Sodano 100 tys. novykh rabochikh mest."

60. "Aleksandr Tkachev: proizvodstvo sel'khozproduktsii v etom godu prevysit uroven' 2000 goda pochti v dva raza," December 26, 2017, http://kvedomosti.ru/news/aleksandr-tkachev-proizvodstvo-selxozprodukcii-v-etom-godu-prevysit-uroven-2000-goda-pochti-v-dva-raza.html (accessed December 26, 2017).

61. See David Remnick, "Watching the Eclipse," *New Yorker*, August 11 and 18, 2014, 52–65.

62. "Address by President of the Russian Federation," March 18, 2014, http://eng.kremlin.ru (accessed March 19, 2014).

63. Neil Buckley, "Putin Makes West an Offer Wrapped up in a Warning," *Financial Times*, October 26, 2014, http://www.ft.com (accessed October 27, 2014).

64. Vladimir Putin, "Meeting of the Valdai International Discussion Club," October 24, 2014, http://eng.news.kremlin.ru (accessed November 4, 2014).

65. Quoted in "Hard Talk," *The Economist*, November 1, 2014, 51.

66. Darya Korsunskaya, "Putin Says Russia Must Prevent 'Color Revolution,'" November 20, 2014, http://www.reuters.com/article/us-russia-putin-security/putin-says-russia-must-prevent-color-revolution-idUSKCN0J41J620141120 (accessed November 22, 2014).

67. "Presidential Address to the Federal Assembly," December 4, 2014, http://eng.news.kremlin.ru/events/president/news/53379 (accessed December 5, 2014).

68. See the very insightful essay by Richard Sakwa, "The Skripal Affair," *Johnson's Russia List*, no. 54 (March 23, 2018).

69. See for example, Rob Slane, "The Three Most Important Aspects of the Skripal Case so Far . . . and Where They Might Be Pointing," *Johnson's Russia List*, no. 62 (April 5, 2018), http://www.theblogmire.com/the-three-most-important-aspects-of-the-skripal-case-so-far.

70. John M. Crisp, "Airstrikes Changed Nothing," *Dallas Morning News*, April 17, 2018, 9A.

71. Lilia Shevtsova, "Russia's Political System: Imperialism and Decay," *Journal of Democracy* 26, no. 1 (2015): 174.

72. Shevtsova, "Russia's Political System," 173.

73. Edward Lucas, *The New Cold War: How the Kremlin Menaces Both Russia and the West* (London: Bloomsbury, 2007).

74. Robert Legvold, *Return to Cold War* (Cambridge: Polity, 2016), 11–13.

75. Legvold, *Return to Cold War*, 21–24.

76. Legvold, *Return to Cold War*, 33–40.

77. Legvold, *Return to Cold War*, 138–39.

78. Cited in Legvold, *Return to Cold War*, 15.

79. Andrei P. Tsygankov, "Russia and the West: A New Cold War?," December 22, 2017, https://sustainablesecurity.org/2017/12/22/russia-and-the-west-a-new-cold-war (accessed December 27, 2017).

80. Jeffrey Mankoff, *Russian Foreign Policy: The Return of Great Power Politics*, 2nd ed. (Lanham, MD: Rowman & Littlefield, 2012), 1–52.

81. Andrei A. Kovalev, *Russia's Dead End: An Insider's Testimony from Gorbachev to Putin*, trans. Steven I. Levine (Omaha, NE: Potomac Books, 2017), 238.

82. Fyodor Lukyanov, "Putin's Foreign Policy," *Foreign Affairs* 95, no. 3 (2016): 30–37.

83. Kotkin, *Armageddon Averted*, 209.

Part I

Domestic Politics

Chapter One

Political Leadership

Richard Sakwa

> It is clearly too early to assert that, this time, Russia will complete her real convergence with the West. But it is not too early to assert that, in the normal course, she hardly has anywhere else to go. . . . As has ever been the case since Peter, if Russia wants to be strong, she will have to Westernize. With her Communist identity gone, and with no other ideological identity possible, she has little choice but to become, as before 1917, just another "normal" European power, with an equally normal internal order.
>
> —Martin Malia[1]

The Putin phenomenon remains an enigma. Putin studied law but then spent a large part of his formative adult years in the security apparatus, and then, following the fall of the communist system in 1991, he threw in his lot with the democratic leader of St. Petersburg, Anatoly Sobchak. Elected president for the first time in March 2000, Vladimir Putin presided over the development of a market economy and constantly reiterated his commitment to democracy, yet following reelection for his second term in 2004, the system veered toward a type of state capitalism. Dirigisme in the economy was accompanied by suffocating restrictions on the free play of political pluralism and democratic competition in society. Putin came to power committed to the "normalization" of Russia, in the sense of aligning its internal order with the norms practiced elsewhere and establishing Russia's foreign policy presence as just another "normal great power," yet there remained something "extraordinary" about the country. In May 2008 Putin left the presidency, as prescribed by the constitution adopted in December 1993. Power was transferred to his nominee, Dmitry Medvedev, while Putin himself became prime minister and was thus able to ensure that "Putinism after Putin" would continue.

The "tandem" form of rule during 2008–2012 ensured that neither the liberalizing aspirations of Medvedev nor Putin's more conservative inclinations could be given free rein. This was a prescription for stalemate and stagnation, as well as frustration for those who hoped that Medvedev's liberalizing rhetoric would be translated into more concrete action. His presidency was unable to reconcile the contradiction between the regime's avowed commitment to the development of a modern capitalist democracy, accompanied by declarations in favor of "modernization," with the consolidation of a power-hungry power system that absorbed all independent political life and stifled the autonomy of civil society. The contradictions continued into Putin's renewed presidency.

In May 2012 Putin returned to the Kremlin, while Medvedev swapped positions with him to become prime minister. The move was formally legitimized by elections, yet it was clear that Putin's decision was decisive. The regime had become increasingly personalistic, focused on Putin himself, and in his third term his personality towered over every substantive decision. However, Medvedev's continued membership on the reconfigured Putin team indicated that modernization and reform remained on the agenda. This was reflected in the relatively liberal composition of Medvedev's cabinet, with a strong bloc of reformers leading the economic ministries.

On September 12, 2017, Putin passed Leonid Brezhnev to become the longest-serving leader since Stalin's death in 1953, a total of eighteen years. In March 2018 he was reelected for a fourth term in a landslide victory, winning 77 percent of the vote with 67 percent turnout. While there was some vote stuffing, it was clear that Putin enjoyed the support of the overwhelming majority of the Russian people, although the depth of that support may be questioned. Few expected major changes in Putin's renewed presidency, although some of the old challenges remained. The task of this chapter is to indicate some of the dimensions of Russia's continuing engagement with the problem of "becoming modern" and to present an analysis of the leadership dynamics accompanying this challenge.

THE DUAL STATE AND POLITICS

Under the leadership of Boris Yeltsin in the 1990s, Russia emerged as a dual state. The divergence between, on the one hand, the formal constitutional order, the rule of law, and autonomous expression of political and media freedoms and, on the other hand, the instrumental use of law and attempts to manage political processes was already evident as early as the 1996 presidential election, which was effectively stolen by Yeltsin. Under Putin the gulf widened and defined his system of rule. Putin's administration was careful not to overstep the bounds of the letter of the constitution, but the system of "managed democracy" conducted itself with relative impunity and lack of effective accountability. It was located in the gray area of para-constitution-alism, a style of governance that remains true to the formal institutional rules but devises various strategies based on technocratic (rather than democratic) rationality to achieve desired political goals. Putin's para-constitutionalism did not repudiate the legitimacy of the constitution but in practice under-mined the spirit of constitutionalism. For example, from 2012 regional governors were once again elected, but a "municipal filter" was introduced (requiring a candidate to be endorsed by a set proportion of local councilors) that allowed undesirables to be filtered out. This prevented a return to the situation of the 1990s, when all sorts of criminals and gangsters had become governors, but it also filtered out those who were politically undesirable, as seen from the perspective of the Kremlin. Equally, in most normal cases the legal system operates with a high degree of impartiality, but in a small number of political cases the judicial system is suborned.

The interaction of real constitutionalism and nominal para-constitutional-ism in Russia can be compared to the development of the dual state in Germany in the 1930s. Ernst Fraenkel described how the prerogative state acted as a separate law system of its own, although the formal constitutional state was not dismantled. Two parallel systems of law operated, where the "normative state" operated according to sanctioned principles of rationality and impartial legal norms while the "prerogative state" exercised power arbi-trarily and without constraints, unrestrained by law.[2] The contrast between the *constitutional state* and the *administrative regime* defines contemporary Russia. To reflect the distinctive features of Russian development, I use these terms in place of Fraenkel's "normative" and "prerogative" states. The fun-damental legitimacy of the regime is derived from its location in a constitu-tional order that it is sworn to defend, yet on occasion it applies the law in ways that subvert the independence of the judiciary. The most egregious case of such abuse was the attack on Mikhail Khodorkovsky, the head of the Yukos oil company. In October 2003 he was arrested, and in the following year Yukos was dismembered, with most of the spoils going to the state-owned oil company, Rosneft. Although the rule of law in Russia remains fragile and, as the Yukos affair amply demonstrated, is susceptible to manip-ulation by the political authorities, no full-fledged prerogative state has emerged. Instead, the administrative regime grants itself considerable lati-tude but formally remains within the letter of the constitution. Russia remains trapped in the gray area between a prerogative and a genuine constitutional state. The regime is able to rule *by* law when it suits its purposes, but the struggle for the rule *of* law is far from over.

Two political systems operate in parallel. On the one hand, there is the system of open public politics, with all of the relevant institutions described in the constitution and conducted with detailed regulation. At this level parties are formed, elections are fought, and parliamentary politics are conducted. However, at another level, a second para-political world exists based on informal groups and factions operating within the framework of the inner court of the presidency. This Byzantine level never openly challenges the leader but seeks to influence the decisions of the supreme ruler. This second level is more than simply "virtual" politics, the attempt to manipulate public opinion and shape electoral outcomes through the exercise of manipulative techniques.[3] However, by seeking to reduce the inevitable contradictions that accompany public politics into a matter of technocratic management, tensions between groups within the regime are exacerbated. Putin places a high value on civil peace and thus opposes a return to the antagonistic politics typical of the 1990s, but this reinforces the pseudo-politics typical of court systems. The restraints on public politics intensify factional conflicts within the regime. Putin's political genius lies in ensuring that no single faction predominates over the others, while also ensuring that he remains the arbiter above them all.

The divisions of the dual state were exacerbated by the modernization program pursued by Putin. His rule is committed to the development of Russia as a modern state and society comfortable with itself and the world. However, at the same time, it seeks to overcome the failings of what it considered to be the excesses of the 1990s under Yeltsin, notably the pell-mell privatization, the liberalism that gave rise to inequality epitomized by the enormous wealth of a handful of "oligarchs," and the "anarcho-democracy" characterized by the hijacking of the electoral process by business-dominated media concerns and regional elites. However, instead of strengthening the state, it was the administrative system that flourished. This encouraged officialdom to rule with arrogant high-handedness and the security apparatus to insinuate itself back into the control of daily life, accompanied by a high level of corruption. Personal freedoms for the mass of the population are at an unprecedented level, including the right to travel abroad, acquire property, and choose their own careers and lifestyles. However, for intellectual, political, and business elites, the suffocating hand of the administrative regime weakens initiative and the freedoms proclaimed in the constitution. Elements of the atmosphere of the late Soviet years has returned, known as the period of stagnation. Although Putin in his third term achieved his goal of improving the business climate, recognized by Russia's sharp rise in the World Bank's ease of doing business index, the economic environment remained hazardous because of the weakness of the rule of law and the general indefensibility of property rights against the regime. This encouraged capital flight and inhibited inward investment, accompanied by an epidemic of "raiding" against companies. It also degraded the quality of governance, with the so-called vertical of power requiring a high degree of personal intervention to get anything done.[4] Even the president's word was far from law.

Some 1,800 policy-relevant decrees issued by Putin during his first eight years as president were not implemented. This was the price to pay for the attempt to manage everything from a single center.

Medvedev was committed to advancing the constitutional state, above all by strengthening the rule of law and tackling corruption, but he was afraid to openly challenge the prerogatives of the administrative regime. At the heart of Medvedev's rhetoric was a different concept of reform, fearing that Putin's commitment to stability was also a recipe for stagnation. Medvedev shared many of Putin's concerns, but his program of liberal reform and openness to the outside world offered the prospect of an evolutionary passage out of the limitations of the Putin system. Medvedev was committed to continuing the broad outlines of "Putin's plan" (the term used in the 2007–2008 electoral cycle to describe Putin's policy agenda, later called Plan 2020)[5]—economic modernization and the creation of a more competitive and diversified economy, international integration, social modernization, and effective political institutions—but he changed the emphasis from "manual" management toward greater trust in the self-managing potential of the system. In his Civic Forum speech on January 22, 2008, he called for the struggle against corruption to become a "national program," noting that "legal nihilism" took the form of "corruption in the power bodies."

In a keynote speech to the Fifth Krasnoyarsk Economic Forum on February 15, 2008, Medvedev outlined not only his economic program but also his broad view of the challenges facing Russia. He focused on an unwieldy bureaucracy, corruption, and lack of respect for the law as the main challenges facing the country. He insisted that "freedom is better than lack of freedom—this principle should be at the core of our politics. I mean freedom in all of its manifestations—personal freedom, economic freedom, and, finally, freedom of expression." He repeated earlier promises to ensure personal freedoms and an independent and free press. He repeatedly returned to the theme of "the need to ensure the independence of the legal system from the executive and legislative branches of power" and once again condemned the country's "legal nihilism" and stressed the need to "humanize" the country's judicial system.[6] However, as so often in Russian history, it was outside factors that derailed the program of gradual political decompression. Renewed confrontation with the United States and the West in general was evident in the Five-Day War of August 2008 with Georgia, which threatened to derail Medvedev's aspirations as the country once again, as in Soviet times, was faced with a choice between modernization and militarization.

The dilemmas were reflected in Medvedev's programmatic article "Forward, Russia!" which was published in September 2009.[7] The article articulated Medvedev's growing conviction that continued political drift was no longer an option, but it also suggested uncertainty over what was to be done. The article was presented as a discussion document for the president's annual state-of-the-nation address to the Federal Assembly, but the harshly critical tone went beyond what would be acceptable on such a formal occasion. He characterized Russian social life as a semi-Soviet social system, "one that unfortunately combines all the shortcomings of the Soviet system and all the difficulties of contemporary life." The underlying thinking was that the rent-extraction model of Russian political economy was unsustainable in the long run. This model had been sustained by windfall profits from a booming natural resources sector, above all high oil prices, but this only inhibited diversification away from excessive reliance on raw materials toward a more sophisticated service-led and high-tech manufacturing economy. The fundamental question was whether Russia, with its "primitive economy" and "chronic corruption," has a future. Medvedev attacked not Putin but the system that Putin represented, a balancing act that blunted his message.

"Forward, Russia!" listed a devastating series of problems, although it did not offer much in the way of a program to remedy the situation. First, Medvedev argued that the country was economically backward and distorted by dependence on extractive industries. Who would act as the modernizing force, however, was not clear: the state or private enterprise? Second, corruption had long been one of Medvedev's bugbears, and here he once again condemned the phenomenon. It would require a wholly impartial and independent judiciary to achieve a breakthrough, yet, as the endless cases of judges working closely with business "raiders" demonstrated, little progress was made in the Medvedev years. Third, Medvedev condemned the "paternalist mind-set" prevalent in Russian society, with people looking to the state to solve their social problems.

At the Fifteenth St. Petersburg Economic Forum on June 17, 2011, Medvedev once again set out his goals. He insisted that

> modernization is the only way to address the many issues before us, and this is why we have set the course of modernizing our national economy, outlined our technology development priorities for the coming years, and set the goal of turning Moscow into one of the world's major financial centers.

The fruits of this, he admitted, were small, "but they are there." He went on to condemn overcentralization:

> It is not possible in the modern world to run a country from one single place, all the more so when we are talking about a country like Russia. In fact, we have already gone through the kind of system when everything operates only on the Kremlin's signal, and I know from my own experience that this kind of system is not viable and is always adjusted to suit the particular individual. We therefore need to change it.

He also stressed that reform of the judicial system would continue and the struggle against corruption would be intensified.[8]

Medvedev's program has been described at length because it remains relevant to this day. As prime minister from 2012 to 2018, he remained loyal to this vision, although he was constrained by Putin's return to the top position. Nevertheless, it was a chastened Putin who returned to the Kremlin in 2012. The whole system had been rocked by the mass demonstrations against electoral fraud, and Medvedev's reformism was now reinforced by clear popular demands for change. The usual charge against Medvedev is that he was loud in rhetoric but achieved very little. There is some substance to this, since undoubtedly there was a mismatch between what he promised and what he was actually able to do. However, the major achievement was to have outlined something different from what had preceded his presidency; but since this modified program was rooted in the system shaped by his predecessor, it was caught in a logical trap that prevented a radical breakthrough. Although the list of reforms begun by Medvedev is impressive, none were carried through to any sort of logical completion.

In part this was because of his inherently cautious approach, but it was also characteristic of Putin's style of governance as a whole. Putin never uses the word "modernization," and he avoids the term "reform." In Putin's view, the experience of the disintegration of the perestroika years between 1985 and 1991 and then the chaos of the 1990s acted as a salutary warning of what happens if liberalization is too radical and speedy. Hence, under his leadership there would be no "perestroika 2.0," no repeat of Mikhail Gorbachev's runaway reform process from 1985, which ended up with the dissolution of the communist system and the disintegration of the country in 1991. Nevertheless, Putin's third term was marked by sluggish economic growth and then a recession as the oil price plunged from late 2014, and growth was only restored in 2016. The imposition of sanctions by the Western powers in response to Russia's actions in Ukraine following the overthrow of President Viktor Yanukovych in February 2014 worsened the economic climate, although encouraging the further diversification of the economy and the development of such sectors as the agri-food complex. Nevertheless, as Putin entered his fourth term in 2018 it was clear that the economy needed to be rejuvenated, and although he enjoyed enormous personal popularity, the institutions of governance also needed to be revived.

Four main themes emerge from this. The first is the remedial element. Putin's policy agenda emerged not only out of the legacy of seventy-four years of communism and the way it was overcome, notably the disintegration of the Soviet Union in 1991, but also out of the need to overcome the perceived excesses of the 1990s, above all the development of inequality, mass poverty, oligarch domination of the media, and the excessive ambitions of the new business elite. The second feature is the type of developmental program that Putin ultimately favored, with a strong role for the state to ensure that the business of business remained business, not politics, and to remain firmly in control of economic policy making, accompanied by support for national champions in the energy, military defense, and manufacturing sectors. The third feature is the political managerialism designed to counter what was perceived to be the irresponsibility engendered by an untutored democratic process, a theme that provoked an obsession with security by the *siloviki* (representatives of the security and military) in Putin's team. These three elements combined to create a profoundly tutelary regime that was in some ways reminiscent of the "trustee" democracy practiced in Singapore.[9] However, the fourth theme should not be forgotten: the ability of the regime itself to generate plans for reform. In fact, reform plan followed reform plan, but fearing the social dislocations and potential political instability that would accompany structural reform, the administration played for time.

There is a profound historical reality behind the emergence of the guardianship system. As in so many other "third wave" countries that have embarked on the path toward greater political openness since 1974,[10] democracy in Russia was forced to create the conditions for its own existence. This is a type of giant bootstrapping operation described by Ernest Gellner in his work on the development of civil society in Russia and other postcommunist countries.[11] The social subjects of capitalist democracy were being created in the process of establishing capitalist democracy, a circular process that engendered numerous contradictions. The relationship between the various subsystems of a dynamic democracy, notably a functioning multiparty system, still has to be devised. Instead, the tutelary role of the administrative regime tended to become an end in itself, and its developmental functions came to substitute for and impede the development of autonomous structures in society. Thus, there is a profound ambivalence about Putin's leadership and the nature of his developmental agenda, an ambivalence that is characteristic of Russia's long-term modernization in which adaptation to the technological and economic standards of the West has been accompanied by resistance to political Westernization.

All these contradictions were evident in Putin's leadership.[12] His presidency from 2012 was shaped by a combination of domestic and external factors. The political reforms launched by Medvedev were not repudiated, although they lost their transformative edge. It now became much easier to form parties and to participate in elections. By 2014 there were some 170 registered parties, and about a dozen were represented in regional legislatures. Some opposition figures were elected as mayors (notably in Ekaterinburg, Petrozavodsk, and Novosibirsk), but overall the regime maintained its firm grip on political life. This was reflected in the process known as the nationalization of elites, forcing top officials and legislators to withdraw their assets from abroad (a process known as "deoffshorization") and to commit themselves to Russia. Trumpeted as a measure to reduce corruption, this reduced their political independence. Plans to introduce pluralism from below were derailed by the sharply deteriorating external environment. The Ukraine crisis from November 2013 that led to the overthrow of Yanukovych in February 2014 provoked Russia to intervene. In highly controversial circumstances, Putin supported a referendum in Crimea that on March 18, 2014, saw the territory returned to Russian jurisdiction (it had been part of Russia until 1954, when it had been transferred to Ukraine). Shortly thereafter, an uprising in two of Ukraine's regions, Donetsk and Lugansk (together known as the Donbas), against the nationalistic Kiev government provoked a further deterioration in relations with the West. Various waves of sanctions were imposed on Russia, affecting individuals close to Putin, and the banking and oil sectors. Putin's domestic popularity soared, but the poisonous relations with the West reinforced the process that had long been in train of building links with the East, above all China. Putin's plan to achieve deeper Eurasian integration continued in rather less ambitious forms than originally envisaged, and on January 1, 2015, the Eurasian Economic Union (EEU) was born. Finally, the personalization of Russian politics was intensified, with Putin reelected in 2018 and set to serve his final presidency to 2024. There was no one who came close to challenging his preeminence. A whole epoch in Russian history is stamped by this man.

PROBLEMS OF POWER CONCENTRATION

Democracy in Russia is faced with the task of creating the conditions for its own existence; to this postulate, Putin has implicitly added that this cannot be done by following the logic of democracy itself. Therein lay a further level of duality—between the stated goals of the regime and its practices, which permanently subvert the principles that it proclaims. Putin's team dismantled the network of business and regional relationships that had developed under Yeltsin, and although in policy terms there was significant continuity between the two periods, where power relations are concerned a sharp gulf separates the two leaderships. Putin recruited former associates from St. Petersburg and the security forces, and on this he built a team focused on the presidential administration in the Kremlin that drove through the new agenda.[13] The power of the most egregiously political oligarchs was reduced, and in exile they plotted their revenge, further stoking the paranoia of the *siloviki*. With the fear of the oligarchic Jacobites abroad, continuing insurgency across the North Caucasus, and the specter of color revolutions, it is not surprising that the regime exhibited all the symptoms of a siege mentality, and its legitimism took an ever more conservative hue.

The Putin administration initially drew on staff from the Yeltsin team, notably Alexander Voloshin at the head of the presidential administration and Mikhail Kasyanov as prime minister. At the same time, a parallel administration was built up in the Kremlin, and gradually it dispensed with the services of Yeltsin's old guard. This was accompanied by a shift in policy priorities in the middle period of Putin's leadership. The "overmighty subjects" had been tamed, and now the Kremlin went on the offensive, not only to ensure its own prerogatives in economic policy and political life but also to forge a new model of political economy where the state's preferences predominated. The Yukos affair represented a major disciplinary act, not only ensuring that the business leaders stayed out of politics, but also bringing the state back into the heart of business life.[14] This was achieved not so much by renationalization as by "de-privatization." Economic policy was no longer a matter for autonomous economic agents but had to be coordinated with the state, while the state itself became a major player in the economic arena (in particular in the energy sector) through its "national champions," above all Gazprom and Rosneft. A number of state corporations were created, including the giant "Russian Technologies" (Rosstekh) holding company owning hundreds of factories and plants, including the giant "Avtovaz" motor company in Togliatti.

The equivalent of de-privatization in the political sphere was "de-autonomization." The ability of political actors to act as independent agents was reduced through a not-so-subtle and at times brutal system of rewards and punishments, while the economic bases of independent political activity were systematically dismantled. The "imposed consensus" of Russia's elite, as Gel'man notes, was achieved through the Kremlin's use of "selective punishment of some elite sections and selective co-optation of others."[15] As long as the Kremlin had adequate resources, in material, political capital, and authority terms, to rein in potentially fractious elites, the system could continue, but there was an ever-present threat of defection. In Putin's first two terms, an unprecedented decade-long economic boom, accompanied by windfall energy rents, reinforced the position of the power elite. This allowed a new type of "neo-Stalinist compromise" to be imposed: a type of "social contract" whereby the government promised rising standards of living in exchange for restrictions on independent popular political participation, a pact that could only be sustained, as Gorbachev discovered to his cost in the late 1980s, as long as the economy could deliver the goods. The country weathered the economic crisis of 2008–2009 because of the healthy financial reserves it had built up in the good times, and these reserves would once again help the regime survive the fall in oil prices and sanctions from 2014.

Putin also reengineered the domestic political system. Yeltsin had tried several times to create a "party of power" that would serve to push through the regime's legislative agenda in parliament, but it was Putin who succeeded in this task. In 2001 he forced the merger of a number of political parties to create United Russia (UR), which increasingly dominated the party system but was not allowed to challenge the prerogatives of the executive. The establishment of UR created a structure in whose name a government could be formed.[16] Fear of the autonomous development of an independent political force in the past ensured that no party of power managed to make a credible showing in a second election, but UR's triumph in the December 2003 elections demonstrated that a new type of politics had been created. This was confirmed by its even more convincing victory in the December 2007 Duma elections, and although it lost its constitutional majority in 2011, it remained by far the single largest party. Amendments to the law on parties in the wake of that election made registration of new parties extremely easy, but the emergence of numerous small parties did not threaten the party's dominance. In the September 2016 parliamentary election, UR was returned with an even larger constitutional majority.

Putin headed the party from April 2008, but he demonstratively did not join it. In May 2012 Medvedev became UR's leader, and he also became a party member. The creation of the All-Russia People's Front (ONF) in May 2011 was a typical Putin move, creating a nonparty body whose work paralleled that of UR but in core respects does not duplicate its electoral and parliamentary functions. The ONF rallied public activists and social organizations to Putin's banner, while not sharing in the opprobrium that became attached to UR's name. In 2011 the anticorruption campaigner Aleksei Naval'ny famously dubbed UR as "the party of thieves and swindlers."

The system survived the economic shocks of 2008–2009 and 2014–2016, but in the long term a decline in primary commodity prices threatened the support basis of the regime. Even before this, it was clear that the Putinite social contract—stability, security, and regular wages in exchange for political exclusion and passivity—was vulnerable to internal and external shocks. Medvedev as president was well aware of the problem but failed to negotiate a new social contract, and this remained on the agenda when he became prime minister. The fundamental problem of a concentrated power system is to ensure adequate renewal to avoid rendering itself so inward looking as to become dysfunctional. The reliance on a small coterie of trusted followers and the resulting weakness of competent personnel leads to reduced governmental capacity and poor policy performance. The Putin years were marked by a remarkable "stability of cadres," with some cabinet ministers serving for nearly the whole period. Medvedev promised "substantial renewal" when he became prime minister in May 2012, and over two-thirds of the cabinet was changed. Many of these ministers simply moved over to the Kremlin to serve as advisers to Putin or went on to occupy top posts in the system. It was this team that remained in power until 2018, although at the regional level a new generation of younger and more technocratic governors was appointed.

THE CHARACTER OF LEADERSHIP

Nearly three decades after the fall of the Soviet regime there is no consensus about the nature of the Russian political system. A whole arsenal of terms has been devised in an attempt to capture the hybrid nature of Russian reality, including "managed democracy," "managed pluralism," "electoral authoritarianism," and "competitive authoritarianism."[17] Following the Orange Revolution in Ukraine in late 2004, Russia's presidential administration launched the term "sovereign democracy" based on the idea that Russia would find its own path to democracy and that democracy in the country would have Russian characteristics. This was a theme Putin stressed in his state-of-the-federation speech on April 25, 2005. He took issue with those who suggested that Russia was somehow not suited to democratic government, the rule of law, and the basic values of civil society: "I would like to bring those who think like that back to political reality. . . . Without liberty and democracy there can be no order, no stability and no sustainable economic policies." Responding to Western criticism, however, Putin stressed that the "special feature" of Russia's democracy was that it would be pursued in its own way and not at the price of law and order or social stability: "Russia . . . will decide for itself the pace, terms and conditions of moving towards democracy."[18] In other words, while the content of policy would be democracy, its forms and the tempo of development would be a directed and managed process, a division that helped to sustain the dual state in Russia. It was in this speech that Putin argued that the collapse (*krushenie*) of the Soviet Union was a "major geopolitical catastrophe of the twentieth century," but he certainly did not mean that the USSR could be recreated. The phrase has been misinterpreted and taken out of context.

Under Medvedev the notion of sovereign democracy was dropped from public discourse, although it remained in the background as the general sentiment that Russia would have to do things in its own ways and would not take kindly to foreign interference in its domestic politics. With Putin's return, the theme of Russia's autonomy in domestic and foreign policy was reinforced in a policy that could be called neorevisionism—the attempt to reshape the practices of the major powers in the international system while strengthening the institutions of international society, notably the United Nations and other instruments of global governance. Putin's return to power in 2012 and his new resolve to challenge the advance of the Atlantic system (NATO and the European Union) provoked a sharp deterioration in relations with the West. Putin was demonized, and Russia was characterized as an authoritarian country.[19] If Russia had indeed taken an unequivocal turn toward authoritarianism, then this only reinforced the need to explain why this was the case. Did the cause lie in the political culture of the people, who perhaps needed to be guided by an external authority in the absence of developed traditions of self-reliance, active citizenship, and civil society? Was it the "natural resource curse" that was to blame, whereby energy rents allowed the political system to insulate itself from popular control? Or did the problem lie in a flawed institutional design, namely, the excessive powers granted the presidency by the 1993 constitution?[20]

No doubt a combination of these factors contributed to the crisis of Russian democracy. However, this chapter argues that it is still too early to write off Russia's development as a democratic state. It is too easy simply to label the country as an "autocracy." Instead, the dual-state model suggests that the Russian polity is multilayered and dynamic, with a constant interplay between the constitutional and administrative levels that prevents Russia from becoming a full-fledged democracy, but by the same token there are systemic obstacles to Russia becoming an outright dictatorship. The two systems operate in parallel, with the regime needing the legitimacy derived from the constitutional order to survive, while the regime defends the state from capture by powerful social and regional forces.

A further factor is Putin's own personality. Russia's development as a democracy was already stunted under Yeltsin in the 1990s, but Putin's charismatic personality and extraordinary rapport with the Russian people undermined the autonomy of the institutions of democracy (notably parliament and elections) while allowing a complex and dynamic system to emerge. Putin constantly emphasizes the need for evolutionary development, renouncing the "revolutionary" jumps that in his view inflicted so much damage on Russia in 1917 and 1991. This was one of the key points of his "Millennium Manifesto" issued just before he took over the presidency in December 1999.[21] Evolutionary politics are by definition contradictory, since instead of trying to resolve contradictions by the revolutionary methods, gradualism means that contradictions remain as constitutive elements of the political system. Hence the fundamental contradiction identified in this chapter between the constitutional and the administrative state remains unresolved and imbues the system with a chameleonlike character. Some people see authoritarianism, others democracy, but in fact the system is an unresolved combination of the two.

Is the country still in "transition" to an arguably more democratic system, despite numerous detours and reverses, a perspective that can be dubbed the "democratic evolutionist" view? Or is what has emerged under Putin more or less "it," stuck in some postcommunist syndrome where democratic accoutrements adorn a society and polity that mimic the authority patterns of the earlier order, although aware that there can be no return to the previous system, the "failed democratization" approach?[22] In the latter camp, Steven Fish is unequivocal: "By the time of Vladimir Putin's reelection as president of Russia in 2004, Russia's experiment with open politics was over."[23] One of the main reasons in his view for the recreation of a monocratic system was

the failure to free the economy from the grip of the bureaucracy. This inhibited the development of a vibrant economy, notably in the small and medium
business sector. Contrary to what critics of the privatization of the 1990s
argue,[24] Fish insists that more liberalization was required. The stunted development of an independent business sector deprived political life and the
media of sources of independent support, accompanied by widespread corruption and a corrosive venality in public life. The Yukos affair was a clear
manifestation of the attempt to achieve economic goals by administrative
means, using the law to achieve political purposes. While Putin's administration was clearly in favor of the creation of a capitalist market integrated into
the world economy, it feared the free operation of market *forces*. In his 1997
doctoral dissertation, Putin had argued for the creation of national champions, and this long-standing policy goal was reinforced by the concerns of
the *siloviki* in Putin's team.[25] This allowed healthy economic growth in the
good years, but from 2013 it was clear that the economy was beginning to
stagnate, while sanctions from the following year threatened living standards
as a whole.

The institutional choices embedded in the 1993 constitution, above all the
establishment of a "super-presidential" system, are considered by many to
have driven Russia toward monocracy. On the basis of his Parliamentary
Powers Index, Fish finds that Russia is a super-presidential system, although
technically it is a semi-presidential system (in which executive power is
shared by a president and a prime minister). Only the right of the lower house
to approve the president's nominee as prime minister gives it a tenuous claim
to be semi-presidential, but the costs of rejecting the nomination three times
are so high, namely dissolution and all the risks associated with a new election, that parliament would have to be suicidal to exercise its formal powers.
However, defenders of the constitution, such as one of its authors, Viktor
Sheinis, counter by arguing that the letter of the constitution has little to do
with the issue; the key problem is that the spirit of constitutionalism is
lacking. Democratic evolutionists see plenty of potential for the development
of a more robust adherence to the spirit of legality, despite present setbacks.
Although the word "democracy" is not all that popular in Russia after the
traumas of perestroika and the 1990s, its fundamental characteristics are—
free and fair elections, civic dignity, the rule of law, defensible property
rights, and accountable government.[26]

The tutelary role of the regime helped stabilize the state, but the quality of
democracy suffered. The system in formal institutional terms is a liberal
democracy, and this is what endows the present system with its legitimacy,
but practice clearly often falls short of declared principles. The constitution
of 1993 is a liberal document enshrining fundamental human rights, the rule
of law, separation of powers, federalism, and accountable governance, but
the powers of the executive are enormous and allow the emergence of a

relatively autonomous power center unconstrained either vertically or horizontally. The dual-state model calls this power center the administrative regime, to a degree unlimited by the constitutional constraints of the formal state order from above and relatively unaccountable to the representative system from below.[27] Nevertheless, the administrative regime can only survive in its present form by drawing on the normative and practical resources of the constitutional order. Without at least formal obedience to liberal constitutional norms, the regime would be exposed as little more than a dictatorship. The Constitutional Court remains an authoritative body, and there have been sustained attempts to give muscle to the independence of the judicial system, including the widespread introduction of jury trials. However, in practice the various Putin administrations, while certainly remaining within the letter of the constitution, undermined the motivating spirit of democracy, political pluralism, and judicial impartiality. There is thus rich ground for disagreement, since partisans of both the democratic evolutionist and failed democratization camps can always find evidence to support their case.

A number of countries can be described as "para-democracies," where real power lies not with the constitutionally vested authorities but with groups outside the formal power system. This was the case, for example, in Greece following the end of the civil war in 1949 up to the military coup of 1967, with the formal democratic procedures vulnerable to interference from forces not subservient to the democratic process. Local bosses were able to carve out fiefdoms, and the central government was prey to endless crises, with more than thirty governments between the end of the German occupation and 1967, and at all levels patronage relations prevailed. As in Russia, this system of controlled democracy was characterized by weak political parties, which were based on personalities rather than coherent programs. However, a fundamental difference with Russia is that in the latter there is no equivalent to repeated interventions by the military and the monarchy. Instead, in Russia the interventions come from within the dual system itself, and this endows both the formal institutions of the state and the administrative regime with a softness that inhibits either the constitutional or the administrative systems from hardening into more or less autonomous structures. Instead, the two pillars of the dual state are in a condition of permanent tension. This degrades the coherent operation of both and undermines effective long-term strategic governance, but it does provide space for ambiguity and resistance. The inner logic of the operation of the constitutional state cannot be given free rein, but at the same time, the authoritarian and corrupt inclinations of the administrative system are kept in some sort of check.

The logic of duality is reinforced by the international context in which Russia finds itself. The geopolitical dilemmas facing Putin have a strong historical resonance. Frustrated by the failure to achieve a viable framework for political relations between the post-Soviet states in Eurasia, the resolute geopolitical struggle with external great powers (America, the European Union, and China) in the region, and his exasperation with domestic liberal and democratic forces, Putin became ever more a conservative legitimist of the type that Alexander I turned into in his final years before his death in 1825.[28] Putin's innate antirevolutionism was revolted by the emergence of social movement "network" revolutions, which adopted a number of colors (rose, orange, and tulip), but which in all cases threatened his sense of the proper order of things. It is for this reason that he failed to recognize the underlying credibility of the demands of the "white" movement in the winter of 2011–2012 (the white ribbon became the symbol of the protest movement) and suggested that the demonstrators were in the pay of foreign governments. As befitting a person from the security apparatus who had witnessed the chaotic fall of communism in the German Democratic Republic in 1989, he had a deeply conservative view of how political change should take place. At the same time, Putin was unable to understand why Russia was not treated as just another of the great powers; since in his view there was no longer anything to fear from Russia, he assumed that the West would have "the serenity of spirit to understand her more."[29] Putin believed, with justice, that Russia was developing according to the same universal laws as the West, but at its own pace. The combination of disasters and achievements of the Soviet years continued into the Yeltsin period, and now Putin sought to stabilize the system to allow civil society to develop, the industrial and service economy to get back on its feet, and in general for civic and political life to regain its texture. The decline in ideological hostility of the communist sort made possible a qualitatively better relationship with the West, but instead the Cold War spirit on both sides intruded. The breakdown of relations with the West following the Ukraine crisis was only the culmination of the long-term failure to create an inclusive and mutually equitable security system since 1991.[30]

Fears of external intervention and the continuing competitive dynamic to relations with the West is one of the reasons for the enduring "extraordinary" elements in Russian politics. Another is the cultural problem of adaptation to contemporary modernity. We can briefly characterize this as a process of partial and dual adaptation.[31] Political adaptation is necessarily a partial process, since only in postcolonial and postwar contexts can one country try to copy wholesale the institutions of another. It is the nature and parameters of this difference that is important. Traditionalists of all stripes, including neo-Eurasianists, neo-Soviet imperialists, and Russian nationalists (as well as many of the *siloviki*), insist that the gulf separating Russia from the West is enormous and therefore favor yet another *Sonderweg* (own path) that would affirm Russia's distinctive native traditions (*samobytnost'*). The security-focused part of the elite points to the danger to national security and national interests from full adaptation to external models. For economic liberals, the elements of difference are precisely dysfunctional, and hence in their view Russia should adapt fully and unreservedly to the global economic order. These two worldviews are in rough balance, allowing a centrist authority to consolidate itself in the middle. The essence of Putin's leadership is the attempt to negotiate a new balance between adaptation and affirmation. Over time a system of "partial adaptation" emerged, appealing to Russian political culture and shaped by security concerns while at the same time integrating into the international economy (notably, by joining the World Trade Organization in 2012). The partial nature of Putin's adaptation strategy was derived in part from the belief that excessive adaptation could be as dangerous as too little. While committed to a certain type of democratization, the Putin leadership insisted that democracy needs to be rooted in, and congruent with, national conditions.

The strategy of partial adaptation is therefore a balancing act torn by its inherent dualism. On the one hand it looks to the norms and standards prevalent in the countries of advanced modernity; on the other, it seeks to root the adaptive process in a native discourse (managed and interpreted, of course, by the regime) while refusing to succumb to traditionalist insularity. This dualism characterizes most democratic institutions and processes in Russia and provides the framework for the dual state. The Putin strategy for political and economic modernization could not depend on the strata or institutions traditionally relied on by modernizing regimes, such as the army or Western-educated elites, and while forced in part to adapt to the social milieu in which it finds itself, it feared above all being absorbed by that milieu, in particular the social forces created by the transition process itself (notably, the oligarchs), as well as the unleashing of populist and nationalist sentiments. Nevertheless, it is clear that new forces are emerging, notably a more active class of citizens who demand inclusion in the political system on an equal and universal basis. Even before the political protests of 2011–2012, there had been clear manifestations that the Putinite system of tutelary politics was being challenged by groups who demanded more unequivocal adaption to Western patterns of modernity. However, these in turn were challenged by the traditionalists, who argued that the process of adaptation had gone too far. Putin steered a middle course but, with the wave of patriotic enthusiasm released by the return of Crimea to Russia, he was in danger of becoming hostage to the very forces that he had unleashed.

In the end, Putin was able to contain the nationalist sentiments unleashed by the Ukraine crisis, but to what purpose? Putin's centrist, modernizing, technocratic regime was in danger of becoming isolated, bereft of substantive support from abroad and unable to rely on the emerging sociopolitical structures domestically (above all, the rising class of entrepreneurs, intelligentsia, and service workers). Instead, it became reliant on traditional sources of power, above all the security apparatus and the bureaucracy, both of which were oriented to the power system itself. The existence of this bureaucratic mass provides some scope for innovation since it furnishes critical support to the modernizing leadership, but at the same time it subverts the development of the autonomous agents of a genuinely modern society. The striving for regulation and control by the securitistas threatens liberty itself. The room for maneuver of the centrist regime is rapidly declining. As he entered office for his fourth presidency, Putin once again had to choose between strengthening the constitutional state and with it enhanced political pluralism, free and fair competitive elections, and the consolidation of independent courts, or whether to maintain administrative regulation, the micromanagement of politics, manipulation of the state-owned media, and a combative foreign policy. In the classic Putinite manner, he will continue to balance between the two, drawing authority from both but failing to give either victory over the other. Whether such a stance is viable in the long run is unclear, especially since this in all likelihood will be his last presidential term, and Putin will be looking to secure his legacy as a great Russian leader.

CONCLUSION: THE POWER OF CONTRADICTION

Putin appealed to the principles of stability, consolidation, evolutionary development, and the reassertion of the prerogatives of the state. However, the concepts of consensus, centrism, and the idea of "normal" politics were beset by a number of fundamental contradictions. The central problem facing any analysis of Putin's leadership is to assess the nature of his statism. Putin came to power promising to restore the state after the depredations of earlier years, yet his focus was on building the resources of the administrative regime. He did not entirely neglect the state, undertaking a liberal reform of the judicial system in his early years and ensuring that government workers were paid on time and that the army and security apparatus received increased funds. But instead of letting the state, together with its broader representative institutions such as parliament, get on with its business, his leadership constantly intervened in manual mode to ensure that his centrist administration could govern and perpetuate its power. The regime sought to insulate itself as far as possible from ideological and popular pressure, but by the same token it was in danger of losing touch with popular aspirations.

Putin's centralism carried both a positive and a negative charge. The normative resources of the constitutional state were balanced against the arbitrariness of the administrative regime managed by a security-minded centrist authority. Putin emphasized "the dictatorship of law" and thus encouraged the development of a genuine rule-of-law state, but it did not subordinate itself to the pluralistic political process enshrined in the constitution. Once again traditions of the "revolution from above" were perpetuated, and patterns of lawlessness and arbitrariness were replicated. Putin insisted that the 1993 constitution established a viable framework for the development of a new governmental order, but his leadership was characterized by the absence of the spirit of constitutionalism, and this in turn undermined faith in the evolutionary potential of the constitution. There were few restraints on presidential power, and parliament and society were unable to call the authorities to account. Medvedev sought to overcome the gulf between the constitutional (normative) state and the administrative regime, but his half-hearted (although far from negligible) reforms were unable to achieve not rule by law but the rule of law.

There are many contradictions in the "project" espoused by Putin, but, paradoxically, these tensions themselves are the source of much of his power. Putin was able to appeal to a variety of constituencies, many of whom would be exclusive if his ideas were enunciated more clearly. The essence of Putin's centrism is the ability to reconcile antagonistic and contradictory social programs. He transcended narrow party politics and affiliation with either left or right not by evasion but by a distinct type of political praxis that was itself transcendent of the classic political cleavages of the modern age. It would be hard to label Putin's policies as president, prime minister, and once again president as either "left" or "right." Putin has been described as a "liberal conservative," an oxymoron that typifies the contradictory nature of his leadership. In an age when politics is based less on interests or ideologies than on identities and values, Putin reconciled policies and groups that in an earlier period would have been in conflict. Putin's style is antipolitical, although as a leader confronted by the need to reconcile conflicting interests and views, he proved a highly adept politician. The self-constitutive character of democracy in Russia imbued its politics with a contradictory dynamic. These contradictions became increasingly exposed, forcing Putin in his fourth presidential term to find new ways of ruling.

The characteristic feature of modernity is the emergence of autonomous civic actors accompanied by attempts by the state to manage various transformative projects that entail the management and reordering of society. In this respect Putin reflected the larger contradiction within modernity. It is a contradiction exacerbated in Russia by the clear tension between liberal democratic aspirations and the state's inability to act as a coherent vessel in which these aspirations can be fulfilled. It is for this reason that a strong state is often seen as an essential precondition for the development of liberalism,[32] while others continue to see it as the greatest threat to those liberties. However, it is more dangerous when the state is challenged by an administrative system that it can barely constrain and when power is exercised by a technocratic, but often corrupt, elite that sees its own perpetuation as synonymous with stability, security, and development. At that point, only the evolutionary but rapid consolidation of the constitutional state may avert the onset of a renewed era of revolutionary upheavals. There is a natural cycle to leadership—of rise, consolidation, decline, and fall—but Putin so far appears to have been able to defy the laws of political gravity. It will be a supreme test of his leadership to maintain the balancing act while retaining vision and purpose for the country.

DISCUSSION QUESTIONS

1. What is the dual state and how does it affect the dynamics of Russian politics?
2. To what degree do external factors shape the evolution of the Russian polity?
3. If drawing up a balance sheet of Putin's leadership, list the features that would go into the pro and contra columns.

SUGGESTED READINGS

Gill, Graeme. *Building an Authoritarian Polity. Russia in Post-Soviet Times.* Cambridge: Cambridge University Press, 2015.

Ledeneva, Alena V. *Can Russia Modernise?* Sistema, *Power Networks and Informal Governance.* Cambridge: Cambridge University Press, 2013.

Monaghan, Andrew. *The New Politics of Russia: Interpreting Change.* Manchester: Manchester University Press, 2016.

———. *Power in Modern Russia.* Manchester: Manchester University Press, 2017.

Robinson, Neil, and Gareth Schott. *Russian Politics: An Introduction.* Cambridge: Polity, 2018.

Sakwa, Richard. *Russian Politics and Society.* 4th ed. London: Routledge, 2008.

———. *The Crisis of Russian Democracy: The Dual State, Factionalism and the Medvedev Succession.* Cambridge: Cambridge University Press, 2011.

———. *Putin Redux: Power and Contradiction in Contemporary Russia.* London: Routledge, 2014.

Sakwa, Richard, Henry Hale, and Stephen White, eds. *Developments in Russian Politics 9.* Basingstoke: Palgrave Macmillan; Durham, NC: Duke University Press, 2019.

Treisman, Daniel. *The Return: Russia's Journey from Gorbachev to Medvedev.* London: Simon & Schuster, 2011.

White, Stephen. *Understanding Russian Politics.* Cambridge: Cambridge University Press, 2011.

NOTES

1. Martin Malia, *Russia under Western Eyes: From the Bronze Horseman to the Lenin Mausoleum* (Cambridge, MA: Belknap, 2000), 411–12.

2. Ernst Fraenkel, *The Dual State: A Contribution to the Theory of Dictatorship*, trans. from the German by E. A. Shils, in collaboration with Edith Lowenstein and Klaus Knorr (New York: Oxford University Press, 1941; repr., Clark, NJ: Lawbook Exchange, 2006).

3. Andrew Wilson, *Virtual Politics: Faking Democracy in the Post-Soviet World* (New Haven, CT: Yale University Press, 2005).

4. Andrew Monaghan, "Defibrillating the Vertikal? Putin and Russian Grand Strategy" (research paper, Russia and Eurasia Programme, Chatham House, London, October 2014).

5. The "Plan" encompassed all eight of Putin's state-of-the-nation addresses, as well as his "Russia at the Turn of the Millennium" article of December 30, 1999; his February 10, 2007, speech to the Munich security conference; and some other key speeches. They are in *Plan prezidenta Putina: Rukovodstvo dlia budushchikh prezidentov Rossii* (Moscow: Evropa, 2007).

6. "Vystuplenie na V Krasnoyarskom ekonomicheskom forume 'Rossiia 2008–2020: Upravlenie rostom,'" http://www.medvedev2008.ru/live_press_15_02.htm.

7. Dmitry Medvedev, "Rossiia, vpered!," http://www.gazeta.ru/comments/2009/09/10_a_3258568.shtml.

8. "Dmitry Medvedev Spoke at the St Petersburg International Economic Forum: The President Gave an Assessment of the Current State of Russia's Economy and Outlined the Main Modernization Priorities," June 17, 2011, http://eng.kremlin.ru/news/2411.

9. See, for example, Mark R. Thompson, "Whatever Happened to 'Asian Values,'" *Journal of Democracy* 12, no. 4 (2001): 154–63.

10. Samuel P. Huntington, "Democracy's Third Wave," *Journal of Democracy* 1, no. 2 (1991): 12–34. The argument was developed at length in Samuel P. Huntington, *The Third Wave: Democratization in the Late Twentieth Century* (Norman: University of Oklahoma Press, 1991).

11. Ernest Gellner, *Conditions of Liberty: Civil Society and Its Rivals* (New York: Viking, 1994).

12. For a detailed analysis, see Richard Sakwa, *Putin Redux: Power and Contradiction in Contemporary Russia* (London: Routledge, 2014).

13. On the size and role of the *siloviki* in Putin's administration, see Ol'ga Kryshtanovkaya and Stephen White, "Putin's Militocracy," *Post-Soviet Affairs* 19, no. 4 (2003): 289–306; and for later figures, Ol'ga Kryshtanovkaya and Stephen White, "Inside the Putin Court: A Research Note," *Europe-Asia Studies* 57, no. 7 (2005): 1065–75.

14. See William Tompson, "Putin and the 'Oligarchs': A Two-Sided Commitment Problem," in *Leading Russia: Putin in Perspective*, ed. Alex Pravda (Oxford: Oxford University Press, 2005), 179–202; and William Tompson, "Putting Yukos in Perspective," *Post-Soviet Affairs* 21, no. 2 (2005): 159–81.

15. Vladimir Gel'man, "Political Opposition in Russia: A Dying Species?," *Post-Soviet Affairs* 21, no. 3 (2005): 242.

16. Pavel Isaev, "Ob'edinennaia partiia vlasti vystraivaet svoiu regional'nuiu vertikal' so skandalom," *Rossiiskii regional'nyi biulleten'* 4, no. 6 (2002).

17. For an overview, see Harley Balzer, "Managed Pluralism: Vladimir Putin's Emerging Regime," *Post-Soviet Affairs* 19, no. 3 (2003): 189–227.

18. See http://kremlin.ru/text/appears/2005/04/87049.shtml; *Rossiiskaia gazeta*, April 25, 2005.

19. For example, Masha Gessen, "The Dictator," *New York Times*, May 21, 2012.

20. For a comparative analysis, see Henry E. Hale, *Patronal Politics: Eurasian Regime Dynamics in Comparative Perspective* (New York: Cambridge University Press, 2015).

21. Vladimir Putin, "Russia at the Turn of the Millennium," in *First Person: An Astonishingly Frank Self-Portrait by Russia's President Vladimir Putin*, by Vladimir Putin, with Nataliya Gevorkyan, Natalya Timakova, and Andrei Kolesnikov, trans. Catherine A. Fitzpatrick (London: Hutchinson, 2000), 212. The text was originally published as Vladimir Putin, "Rossiya na rubezhe tysyacheletiya," *Rossiiskaya gazeta*, December 31, 1999.

22. See Richard Sakwa, "Two Camps? The Struggle to Understand Contemporary Russia," *Comparative Politics* 40, no. 4 (2008): 481–99.

23. M. Steven Fish, *Democracy Derailed in Russia: The Failure of Open Politics* (New York: Cambridge University Press, 2005), 1.

24. For example, Peter Reddaway and Dmitri Glinski, *The Tragedy of Russia's Reforms: Market Bolshevism against Democracy* (Washington, DC: United States Institute of Peace Press, 2001).

25. See Harley Balzer, "Vladimir Putin's Academic Writings and Russian Natural Resource Policy," *Problems of Post-Communism* 53, no. 1 (2006): 48–54; and Vladimir Putin, "Mineral Natural Resources in the Strategy for Development of the Russian Economy," *Problems of Post-Communism* 53, no. 1 (2006): 49–54.

26. For an early study making this point, see Ellen Carnaghan, *Out of Order: Russian Political Values in an Imperfect World* (University Park: Pennsylvania State University Press, 2007).

27. For earlier discussions, see Richard Sakwa, "The Regime System in Russia," *Contemporary Politics* 3, no. 1 (1997): 7–25; Richard Sakwa, *Russian Politics and Society*, 3rd ed. (London: Routledge, 2002), 454–58; Richard Sakwa, *Putin: Russia's Choice* (London: Routledge, 2004), 86–88.

28. Malia explains Alexander I's position as follows: "Hemmed in by his position as one of the chief architects and guarantors of the Vienna system, and increasingly frustrated by his failures to effect reform at home, [Alexander] became ever more preoccupied with preserving 'legitimacy' and the established order throughout Europe." Malia, *Russia under Western Eyes*, 91.

29. Malia, *Russia under Western Eyes*, 167.

30. Richard Sakwa, *Russia against the Rest: The Post–Cold War Crisis of World Order* (Cambridge: Cambridge University Press, 2017).

31. The theme of partial adaptation is explored in my "Partial Adaptation and Political Culture," in *Political Culture and Post-Communism*, ed. Stephen Whitefield (Basingstoke: Palgrave Macmillan, 2005), 42–53, from which this paragraph draws.

32. For example, Marcia A. Weigle, *Russia's Liberal Project: State-Society Relations in the Transition from Communism* (University Park: Pennsylvania State University Press, 2000), 458, where she talks of the need for a "state-dominated liberalism."

Chapter Two

Regional Politics

Nikolai Petrov and Darrell Slider

When Vladimir Putin was first elected president in 2000, one of the first areas he identified for attention was the relationship between Russia's regions and the central government. Former president Boris Yeltsin, in the face of political and financial weakness, was forced to make considerable concessions to the regions. Regional leaders increasingly took on responsibilities that would normally be carried out by federal agencies, and they used these opportunities to entrench themselves in power while often willfully flouting federal laws and presidential decrees.

Putin came to the Kremlin after having spent the early part of the 1990s as a regional government official. He witnessed the extent of regional-center problems from a different perspective when he supervised Russia's regions for Yeltsin from March 1997 to July 1998. At that time Putin was head of the department within the presidential administration (called the Main Oversight Department, or *glavnoe kontrol'noe upravlenie*) that gathered evidence on violations of federal laws and policies in the regions. Putin's predecessor as head of the department was Aleksei Kudrin, who was later Putin's minister of finance and deputy prime minister, and his successor was Nikolai Patrushev, who became head of the Federal Security Service (FSB), which had replaced the KGB, and was later promoted to head the Kremlin's Security Council in 2008. Both men were key figures in implementing elements of Putin's policy toward the regions. All three, not coincidentally, were from Russia's second city, St. Petersburg.

This chapter examines the policies toward regional leaders. Center-region relations continued to be a key area of concern in Putin's second term and during the Medvedev presidency. Instead of attempting to develop or refine federalism in the Russian context, Putin aggressively pursued an antifederal policy designed to take away or circumscribe many powers exercised by regional leaders. His goal was to establish a unitary, centralized state under the guise of "restoring effective vertical power in the country," to use Putin's own description of his intentions. In keeping with Putin's background in the KGB (the secret police in Soviet times and early post-Soviet Russia), the main emphasis was on discipline and order. These institutional and personnel choices, however, produced a number of negative consequences. As early as 2005, some Russian officials began to propose what might be described as "re-decentralization" in order to correct some of the deficiencies in a centralized model. To date, however, centralized rule remains the defining principle in Russian regional politics.

BEFORE PUTIN: FEDERALISM BY DEFAULT

Even after the other fourteen former Soviet republics became independent, Russia remained the world's largest country; thus, it is perhaps inevitable that there would be serious problems in administering its far-flung territories. This was true both before and after the establishment of the Soviet state. The traditional approach of Russian rulers was to tighten control from the center. Despite some outward trappings of federalism (the Russian republic, for example, was called the RSFSR—Russian Soviet Federative Socialist Republic), the Soviet Union was a unitary state supplemented by parallel hierarchies: the Communist Party of the Soviet Union (CPSU) and an extensive state bureaucracy. Even under Stalin, however, "family circles" or cliques based on personal relations and patronage ties arose in the regions, insulating local politics from Moscow and allowing regional elites a free hand in many matters.[1]

In several of the former communist states of Eastern Europe—particularly in countries whose leaders embarked on a reformist agenda—a comprehensive redrawing of subnational administrative boundaries took place. In Poland, the Czech Republic, the former German Democratic Republic, Hungary, and Croatia, communist-era regional entities were eliminated or replaced by new ones. In part this was done to meet European Union (EU) entry requirements, but often another important motivation was to break up political and economic power at the regional level that had emerged under communist rule.[2] No radical redrawing of the political boundaries took place in Russia, and communist-era elites retained their power at the regional level. Russia's administrative structure closely mirrored that of the Russian republic under communism. Republics within Russia, designated "autonomous republics" in the Soviet period, received elevated status because they were home to a non-Russian ethnic group. Most often, though, Russians were the largest ethnic group even in republics; the exceptions were Dagestan, Chuvashia, Chechen-Ingushetia (divided into two separate republics in 1992),

Tuva, Kabardino-Balkaria, North Ossetia, Tatarstan, and Kalmykia. The most numerous administrative entities were *oblasts* (provinces) and *krais* (territories). The cities of Moscow and St. Petersburg also had the status of "subjects of the federation." Smaller autonomous *okrugs* (districts) located within the territory of other entities were merged with larger entities to simplify control from the center. As a result, Russia went from having eighty-nine administrative entities in 2000 to eighty-three by 2008. Adding Crimea and Sevastopol brought the total to eighty-five in 2014, a number that has remained constant into 2018.

Russian and Soviet history had never seen an attempt to apply a federal model as the basis for organizing the relationship between national and regional authorities. The policies of President Boris Yeltsin represented a revolutionary break from past methods of rule. The constitution adopted in 1993 made federalism a core component of the Russian political system. Article 71 of the constitution defines the areas of federal jurisdiction, Article 72 defines joint jurisdiction, and Article 73 grants all other functions to the regions. Many of these relationships remained to be defined by legislation, however, and Yeltsin did not take the goal of developing federal principles seriously. What prevented Yeltsin from building a more balanced system of federalism was the center's political and economic weakness. This weakness was exploited by republic presidents and governors to carve out substantial autonomy. By the time Yeltsin resigned from office at the end of 1999, Russia's federal system remained a work in progress, the result of an improvised series of compromises.

In the late Soviet period, the regions became an arena for political struggle. In 1990–1991 both Gorbachev and Yeltsin sought the support of regional elites, particularly those in the ethnically based autonomous republics within the fifteen union republics that became independent in late 1991. It was in this context that Yeltsin in 1990 famously encouraged republic leaders to "take as much sovereignty as you can swallow." In most of the republics, local leaders followed Yeltsin's lead and created the popularly elected post of president.

After the collapse of the Soviet Union in late 1991, Yeltsin faced a new and lengthy conflict—this time with the Russian legislature. Their disputes centered on the relative powers of the parliament versus the president and economic reform strategy. In this struggle, Yeltsin sought the support of regional executives—the governors whom he then had the right to appoint and dismiss—and the elected republic presidents. Ruslan Khasbulatov, the speaker of the Russian parliament who became Yeltsin's nemesis, appealed to the regional legislatures to build an alternative national power base. Since republic leaders had more independence than governors, Yeltsin rewarded the republics with larger budget subsidies and greater relative autonomy.[3] These concessions were often codified in the form of bilateral agreements signed by Yeltsin and individual leaders. The most generous terms were granted to Tatarstan, Bashkortostan, and Yakutia, the republics with the most potential leverage because of their natural resource wealth (oil and diamonds).

This battle culminated in the events of September–October 1993, when Yeltsin issued a decree dissolving the parliament. When Khasbulatov and Alexander Rutskoi, Yeltsin's appointed vice president, resisted and attempted to seize power by force, Yeltsin responded by having tanks shell the building. The new political context led to fundamental changes in regional politics.

First was the drafting of the 1993 constitution that enshrined the concepts of federalism, including the creation of a new legislature with an upper house to represent the regions—the Federation Council—with the right to veto laws passed by the lower house, the State Duma. A second consequence of the 1993 events was the dissolution of regional legislatures (though not in the republics) that had been elected in 1990. Political power in the regions shifted dramatically toward the executive branch of government, and this would be further strengthened when Yeltsin gave in to the demand by regional executives for popular elections of governors. Yeltsin's last set of appointments to the post of governor took place in late 1995–early 1996, when he appointed thirteen.[4] After that, all governors were elected to office. This gave governors added legitimacy and made their removal by Yeltsin almost impossible.

In 1994–1995, new regional legislatures were elected. The new assemblies were smaller in size than the soviets of 1990, and their powers were substantially reduced. With just a few exceptions, the new deputies tended to be local officials, employees from sectors funded by the government (education and health care), or the regional economic elite—all groups that were dependent on the executive. Only a small proportion of deputies were full-time legislators, and in their legislative role they were both unwilling and unable to challenge the region's governor or president. Very few legislatures had more than token representation by national political parties.[5]

A year after the October 1993 attack on parliament, Yeltsin once again attempted to use force to solve a political problem—this time in Chechnya. Unlike other republics, Chechnya refused to enter into a dialogue with the Kremlin and pressed for full independence. Under the leadership of General (and President) Dzhokhar Dudaev, Chechnya created its own military forces and expelled representatives of virtually all central Russian ministries, including the FSB and the Ministry of Finance. The Russian leadership did not make a serious attempt to achieve a negotiated solution to Chechnya's complaints, which strengthened the Chechens' resolve to secede. In December 1994, Yeltsin ordered Russian Army and Interior Ministry troops into Chechnya in hopes of a quick military victory. The result was a disaster: the army was ill prepared for a guerrilla war and suffered many casualties while directing much of its military might against the civilian population.

The war in Chechnya and ineffective policies in other areas threatened defeat for Yeltsin in the 1996 presidential election, and he again turned to regional leaders (as well as the business elite) for help. With the help of regional "administrative resources," such as control over the local press, government workers, and simple vote fraud in some cases, Yeltsin came from behind to win reelection in 1996. Following his victory, Yeltsin further strengthened the status of regional leaders by changing how the Federation Council was formed. From 1996 to 2000, governors and speakers of regional legislatures would automatically have seats in the Federation Council.

These serial political crises took place against a background of persistent economic emergencies that were stabilized in the mid-1990s only by resorting to "virtual" economics and financial trickery. These schemes eventually collapsed in the August 1998 devaluation and default. One common mechanism to formally balance tax receipts and expenses, which was used both by central agencies and regional governments, was sequestering funds—in other words, reducing expenditures by not paying salaries and not meeting obligations to suppliers of goods and services. In this way, the federal government effectively lost control of many of its agencies in the regions. Shortfalls in tax collection and nonpayment meant that regional leaders were almost forced to step in to provide funds or in-kind payments (office space, transportation, heat, hot water, electricity, and even food) in order to support the continued operation of federal institutions such as the criminal police, tax police, prosecutors, courts, and even Yeltsin's presidential representatives (created in 1991 to serve as his "eyes and ears" in the regions). Inevitably, federal entities in the regions shifted their loyalty from the center to the regions. Even the Russian military became increasingly dependent on regional leaders. The result was "a sustained trend towards increasing compartmentalization and regionalization of military structures, driven primarily by the shortage of resources and underfinancing."[6] This was not a power play by regional leaders. In the face of the failure by the Kremlin to carry out its responsibilities, the regions were simply trying to cope. The result was federalism by default.

Another feature of Yeltsin's policies toward the regions was the personalized and bilateral nature of center-region relationships. This was a continuation of the informal operation of regional lobbying of the central institutions during the Soviet era; both Yeltsin and most regional leaders had practical experience in this dating back to the Brezhnev era. Bilateralism was formally institutionalized in treaties negotiated between the Yeltsin administration and regional leaders. The first of these agreements was with republics; it provided a set of exceptions and exemptions that went far beyond what other regions were allowed. In the mid-1990s, over twenty new bilateral treaties with *oblasts* and *krais* were signed. These agreements made Russian federalism extremely asymmetrical, but in ways that were unsystematic and nontransparent.[7] Much of the enabling documentation at the ministerial level was kept secret. Later, most *oblasts* and *krais* also negotiated bilateral treaties with the center, though under less favorable terms. The personalization of politics meant that Yeltsin often turned a blind eye to violations of federal laws and the constitution if regional leaders demonstrated loyalty to him in federal elections.

Overall, the institutional framework and dynamics of "federalism, Russian style," had many dysfunctional elements and allowed regions control over areas of federal responsibility that were atypical of a normal federal system.[8] The nature of federal relations also undermined efforts to democratize the political system and create a market economy. Governors and republic presidents obstructed the development of a national party system and used their powers to harass political opponents and independent media. To protect local industries and markets, regional leaders created barriers to free trade between regions. They also preserved an economic climate that was hostile to outside investment and the rise of small business.[9]

PUTIN'S RECENTRALIZATION

Unlike Yeltsin, Vladimir Putin began his first term with the advantages of both firm control over central political institutions and an economy that was beginning to prosper. The improvement of the Russian economy after the August 1998 crisis cannot be overestimated in this regard. Growing oil revenues, the result of skyrocketing prices on the world market, provided Putin with resources to remold Russian government structures. This led to enhanced tax collection and greater budgetary resources that could be used to pay off past debts and to finance federal institutions. Putin's election to the presidency was closely linked to the Second Chechen War (1999–2004), which eventually restored federal control over that region by brute force. At the same time, he began a more sophisticated, multipronged strategy to restore central control over all Russian regions. One early change was in budgetary policy. Since the center had easy access to a larger revenue stream, it revised the tax code to increase the center's share, from roughly a 40/60 split in favor of the regions to 60/40 in favor of the center. As a result, regions became much more dependent on the central authorities for budgetary allocations—a factor that greatly increased their vulnerability to pressure from the Kremlin.

Federal Districts and Presidential Representatives

The first major institutional change adopted by Putin was the creation of a new level of administration between the center and the regions in the form of seven federal administrative districts (*federal'nye okruga*) headed by specially appointed presidential representatives. Each of these "super-regions" was headed by a presidential envoy, called the plenipotentiary presidential representative—*pol'nomochnyi predstavitel' prezidenta*, or *polpred* for short. The ultimate purpose of this new structure was not to replace existing regions, but rather to increase the ability of the center to coordinate the operation of federal agencies in the regions through a framework that was totally controlled by the Kremlin. The federal districts and their administrative headquarters corresponded completely to the regional command structure of the Soviet/Russian Interior Ministry troops.[10]

The term *polpred* had been used by Yeltsin in 1991 to designate his personal representative in each region. Putin abolished this post in the regions, replacing them with "chief federal inspectors" who would be directly subordinate to (and appointed by) the presidential representative for the corresponding administrative district. The decree creating presidential envoys provided for their direct accountability to the president. Yeltsin had initially given the same degree of access to his representatives, but later they were subordinated to a department within his administration.[11] While Putin appointed each of his representatives, they did not report solely to the president. The *polpreds* were still part of the presidential administration, which meant they were supervised by the head of Putin's staff. This was a source of consternation among the presidential representatives, since they wanted to be closer to the ultimate source of authority at the top of the administrative ladder. The *polpreds* were also allowed to participate in regular meetings of the president's Security Council and the Russian government cabinet chaired by the prime minister.

Putin's "magnificent seven," as they were initially referred to with some irony in the media,[12] were drawn for the most part from the *siloviki* or "power ministries": FSB, military, police, and prosecutors. The contrast with the early Yeltsin period could not be more vivid. Many of Yeltsin's *polpreds* were drawn from the ranks of radical democrats who had worked with Yeltsin in the Soviet and Russian parliaments. In effect, the early Yeltsin appointees to this post were the type of people that several of the Putin appointees had worked to put in prison camps or psychiatric wards! (Later, though, Yeltsin replaced his initial appointees with career bureaucrats, including several FSB officials.)

Presidential envoys were denied many of the instruments of real power to control developments in the regions—the right to direct financial flows from the center, for example, or the power to appoint federal officials in the regions. Depending on their skills and resourcefulness, many presidential representatives increased their leverage by expanding their links with important regional actors, such as the business community. *Polpreds* influenced personnel decisions by federal agencies and the president in their district through their recommendations for promotions. Over time, they helped create a web of cadres in the district that facilitated the center's "penetration" of the regions.

Much of the work performed by presidential representatives was secret; as a result, their actual role remained hidden. [13] The functions of the office changed over time. They devoted considerable effort initially to overseeing the process of bringing regional legislation (including republic constitutions and regional charters) into conformity with federal law and the constitution. Given that Russia has yet to address seriously the problem of establishing the rule of law, a massive effort to improve the content of laws appeared to be premature. Russia, and this is even truer of the regions, is a country where the letter of the law often counts for little in the face of arbitrariness, incompetence, politicization, and corruption in the judicial system and the bureaucracy.

Another task the Kremlin assigned the *polpreds* was to facilitate centralized control over policy making. The bilateral treaties that had been signed between regions and Yeltsin were eventually phased out. Cities and rural districts, the third level of government, were subjected to increasing restrictions on their autonomy in the interest of restoring top-down control. Under Yeltsin, the constitution had proclaimed "local self-management," which meant that popularly elected mayors enjoyed considerable powers, often leading them into conflicts with governors. Putin's 2003 Law on Principles of Organizing Local Self-Management increased the control of regional authorities over local officials, gradually pushing mayors into the "vertical of authority." Many mayors of big cities resigned their posts, frustrated both by these changes and inadequate budgetary resources. For those who didn't get the message, prosecutors began targeting mayors with corruption charges in an apparent campaign of intimidation. Another innovation introduced under Putin replaced elected mayors in favor of "city managers" chosen by city councils—bodies that were more easily manipulated by governors and the Kremlin. By 2011 the capital cities of over half of all regions had shifted from popularly elected mayors to appointed city managers. In 2014 a new "reform" of local government permitted regional parliaments (all of which by then had United Russia majorities) to eliminate the popular election of mayors of large cities, replacing them with city managers appointed by regional assemblies. Governors and the ruling party now determine who will become the mayors of cities in their regions.

Over time, the Kremlin introduced additional institutional changes in an attempt to grapple with persistent regional problems. Continued instability in the North Caucasus led former president Medvedev to create a new, eighth federal *okrug* in January 2010 that encompassed the non-Russian republics of the North Caucasus along with the predominantly Russian Stavropol region. The *polpred* was made a member of the Russian cabinet at the vice premier level, thus giving him additional powers to coordinate federal policy toward the region. Later, this morphed into a new Ministry for Economic Development of the North Caucasus. Another problematic region, the Russian Far East, was stagnating economically and losing population. In May 2012 the Kremlin sought to deal with the problem by creating a new federal ministry, the Ministry for Development of the Far East. In September 2014, the federal Ministry of Regional Development that had been created ten years earlier was abolished, in part because its functions in key problem regions had been taken over by the new, specialized ministries.

Parallel Vertical Structures

Centralization was accomplished by strengthening federal agencies' activities in regions and making sure that their chain of command was "from above" and not from regional governors. Regaining control over appointing and monitoring personnel in federal agencies in the regions was a key element. This process of centralization was accompanied by a massive expansion in the number of federal officials in the regions. Between 2001 and 2006, the number of federal executive branch employees in the regions (not including law enforcement agencies) grew from 348,000 to 616,000, according to the Russian Statistical Agency.

New territorial structures were established in the federal districts by the most important federal agencies and ministries—in all, about twenty federal agencies. To illustrate, within a year of Putin's reform, there were nineteen federal agencies represented in the Volga federal district. These included the prosecutor's office, the Ministry of Justice, the Tax Police, the Federal Tax Service, the Federal Agency on Governmental Communication, the Ministry of the Interior for Internal Troops, the Federal Criminal Police, the Federal Service on Financial Restructuring and Bankruptcy, the State Courier Service, the Committee on State Reserves, the Federal Securities Commission, the Property Ministry, the Federal Property Fund, the Ministry on Publishing and TV and Radio Broadcasting, the Ministry of Natural Resources, the Pension Fund, the Ministry of Transportation, the Health Ministry, the State Committee on Statistics, and the Ministry of Anti-Monopoly Policy (the latter two had other regional branches within which they established federal district departments).[14]

Priority was given to returning central control over military, police, and security organs. This had been largely accomplished by 2002. Central control rapidly increased over other federal organs in the regions, including courts, prosecutors, election commissions, and even the mass media. Some of the most important changes in administrative subordination took place in the Ministry of Internal Affairs (MVD). When Putin came to power, there was a symbiosis between police generals and regional leaders that seemed to be unbreakable. Putin employed chess-like maneuvers to reassert dominance over this key lever of control. In June 2001 governors lost their effective veto on appointments of regional MVD chiefs. Instead of immediately appointing his own men as the top police official in each region, he began by establishing a new intermediate level of seven MVD district directorates, each headed by high-ranking police officials who were directly subordinate to the minister of internal affairs and appointed by decrees issued by Putin. It took only a year of personnel transfers at the regional level to disentangle existing networks of relationships, restoring control by the central ministry over regional police chiefs. In subsequent years, Putin maintained these gains by forcing high rates of turnover among regional police heads, regularly moving officials from region to region.

None of the heads of the new district agencies were subordinate to the *polpred*. While such a change would make sense from the standpoint of a clear and single vertical chain of command, it would represent a major assault on the prerogatives of the Moscow-based ministries. Ever since Khrushchev's attempt to undermine the ministries and transfer their powers to regional economic councils (the *sovnarkhozy*), the ministries have effectively fought reorganizations that would decentralize power to the district or regional level. The *polpred* typically could not order the federal agencies in his district to do anything, though he could complain to Putin if they ignored his advice.

The FSB was one of the few federal ministries that did not create a new territorial structure based on the federal districts. However, in February 2006, Putin announced the creation of a new federal structure, the National Anti-Terrorism Committee, headed by the FSB chair. Each region's antiterrorism committee (none were created at the federal district level) would be headed by the governor or president of the region. The result was a new "antiterror vertical." On matters concerning terrorism and its prevention, which can be broadly construed, governors were subordinate not just to Putin but also to the chairman of the FSB. In each region, the local FSB head (also subordinate to the FSB chief, not the regional leadership) served as the head of the operational staff for antiterror operations and preparations.

Another vertical hierarchy established to increase central control over the regions was the new political party that Putin helped found, United Russia. While it got off to a slow start in many regions, United Russia rapidly expanded its regional party structures after 2004. Following the pattern of its predecessor "parties of power," United Russia was spread into the regions by recruiting key officials at all levels. It was not accidental that the party was called United Russia. The party was highly centralized, always under the control of Putin loyalists, and designed as a kind of straitjacket to bring under control what had been autonomous or governor-controlled regional political institutions. There was virtually no intraparty democracy; major party personnel decisions were made by the party's curators in the Kremlin. Putin himself served as chairman of the party from 2008 to 2012 while serving as prime minister. Medvedev took over as party leader in May 2012 when he returned to the post of prime minister.

Political parties that had significant support among regional elites were undermined or forced from the playing field. The 2001 law on political parties effectively banned regionally based parties, thus reducing the role of governor-dominated political organizations. In 2003, the Kremlin changed the rules on electing regional legislatures to require that at least half the deputies be chosen by a proportional representation system—by party list. The same advantages given to United Russia at the national level allowed it to establish a dominant role in most regional legislatures by 2006 and in all regions by 2010.

Controlling Regional Governors

The popular election of governors gave them a status that was difficult for the Kremlin to overcome. Before 2005, the Kremlin succeeded in preventing some incumbent governors from winning reelection. Methods included exerting influence on elections by instructing or pressuring the election commission or the local courts to remove a candidate from the ballot. In some cases, *kompromat* (compromising material) gathered on regional leaders was employed to persuade them not to seek another term in office. In 2003–2004, for the first time, serious criminal investigations were launched against a number of sitting governors, most typically those the Kremlin labeled as weak and ineffective. While none of these cases were brought to trial, they helped Putin establish his primacy in the period before he began appointing regional leaders. Over one-third of Russia's regional leaders were replaced during Putin's first term.

A critical component of Putin's policy restoring central control over regions was the decision to end direct popular elections of regional leaders. This occurred in the aftermath of the terrorist attack in Beslan, North Ossetia, in September 2004. Rebels, mostly from the neighboring republic of Ingushetia, took over a school on the opening day of classes, and the poorly coordinated effort to save the hostages resulted in over three hundred deaths. Elected governors must justify their reelection to voters; appointed governors have an electorate of one: Vladimir Putin.

To deflect criticism that Russia was abandoning democratic principles, the appointment process was fitted with a veneer of democratic choice. Three candidates had to be nominated, initially by the presidential envoy in the federal district in which the region was located, and they were expected to consult with major political forces in the region. From the beginning the authenticity of the process was brought into question when outsiders who were unknown in the region ended up as nominees and then governors. Another element of formal democracy was that the president's choice, once nominated, had to be approved by the regional legislature. In every case, however, regional legislatures ratified the president's choice. If they did not, the law provided for the dissolution of the legislature and new elections. After Putin began appointing governors, most of those who had not yet become members of United Russia rushed to join. By the time of the 2007 Duma elections, almost all governors had become members of the party, and they had a direct interest in ensuring the best possible performance for United Russia in subsequent regional and national elections. Governors who organized massive vote fraud were rewarded for their actions and never faced punishment.

Perhaps because of his dependence on regional leaders who could produce the electoral results he needed, Putin was extremely cautious in his dealings with strong, popular regional leaders. During his second term, governors and republic presidents who had been elected to their posts prior to 2005 and were perceived to be "loyal" were allowed to remain in power. A procedure was adopted that allowed governors to seek Putin's "vote of confidence," most often through a personal meeting with him, prior to the end of their term in office. In the vast majority of cases, Putin responded favorably without even considering other candidates and submitted the current governor's name to the regional assembly for reappointment. An important consequence of the end of elections was the de facto suspension of term limits for Russia's regional leaders. There was some speculation that this was the main purpose of the change: it would permit the reappointment of leaders viewed by the Kremlin as hard to replace.

As president, Dmitry Medvedev introduced a change in the system for nominating candidates for governor that provided further gloss to the democratic veneer. Starting in 2009 the nomination of the three candidates was transferred from the *polpred* to the largest party in the regional assembly. This meant turning the nomination process over to United Russia, since it had become the largest party in every regional parliament. Given the Kremlin's leverage over all these political actors, the charade that unfolded was obvious to all. Each of the actors in the spectacle would dutifully follow the Kremlin's script, and nominees became candidates who became governors. As a rule, the decisions about who would be nominated and who would be approved were made by the internal politics department of the presidential administration in the Kremlin.

It was Medvedev who presided over the most significant change in the corps of Russia's regional leaders. The so-called regional heavyweights who had won election many years earlier and had consolidated control over regional political and economic institutions were systematically targeted for removal starting in 2009. The victims included some of the most prominent figures on the Russian political scene, such as Mintimir Shaimiev, who had led Tatarstan since 1989, and Murtaza Rakhimov, head of Bashkortostan since 1989. Most governors saw the writing on the wall and agreed to resign quietly. The exception was the powerful mayor of Moscow, Yury Luzhkov, who resisted efforts to force him out in October 2010. Luzhkov, who had been mayor since 1992, was relieved by Medvedev with the formulation that he had "lost confidence" in Luzhkov. Later, Medvedev would claim that several of the governors had been removed because of evidence against them of corruption, though none were subjected to criminal prosecution. Many had held leadership positions in United Russia until the end and had repeatedly demonstrated their loyalty to the Kremlin.

Massive popular protests in Moscow in the aftermath of elections to the Duma in December 2011 led Putin and Medvedev to reverse themselves on the issue of popular elections of governors. Only a couple of years earlier, Medvedev had said that gubernatorial elections would not be reinstated even in "a hundred years." A law was quickly passed in early 2012 that again made the post an elected one. Almost immediately, though, steps were taken to minimize the impact of the new law. One provision, the "municipal filter," required that candidates get signatures of support from as many as 10 percent of the deputies in local legislatures. Given the high percentage of local deputies affiliated with United Russia, the chances for opposition candidates to qualify were severely limited. In most regions, only a candidate supported by the Communist Party could pass through this "filter." Several regions were allowed to opt out entirely from gubernatorial elections starting in 2013 in order to preserve ethnic harmony or "stability." These regions retained the post-2004 system of regional legislature approval of governors. Initially, republics in the North Caucasus were the only ones to opt out, and the de facto presidential appointment process remained in place in Dagestan, Ingushetia, and Kabardino-Balkaria. The elimination of popular elections for governor was later extended to three autonomous *okrugs* "nested" within the Tiumen' and Arkhangel'sk *oblasts*, all of which are rich in oil and natural gas—Khanty-Mansi, Yamalo-Nenetsk, and Nenetsk. Between 2012 and 2017, there were 106 elections of governors, and only once did a candidate nominated by Putin not win. Usually the margin of victory was between 50 and 70 percent, made possible by the efforts of the Kremlin and regional leaders to prevent strong opposition figures from running. The only exception was in Irkutsk in 2015, where a candidate from the Communist Party did well enough to force a runoff election and then won the second round against an unpopular governor.

Beginning in 2015, the Kremlin decided that governors, who now owed their positions to Putin personally, needed additional stimuli to guarantee their loyalty. A new campaign of arrests of sitting or recently replaced governors unfolded, with charges of abuse of authority and corruption. Governors were arrested and put on trial from Sakhalin, Komi, Kirov, Mari El, and Udmurtia. Deputy governors were also targeted for prosecution in some regions, a clear signal to the governors who appointed them that they could be next. While these arrests were presented in the media as evidence that in Russia "no one is above the law," in fact this was a highly selective campaign against governors who were targeted apparently because they had encroached on the interests of officials with stronger Kremlin connections. Decisions about whom to investigate (and plant evidence on, if needed) were made in the Kremlin's Domestic Politics Department, then carried out by the FSB's "Department K."[15] Overall, since 2015, criminal cases are brought each year against roughly 2 percent of high regional officials, including governors, deputy governors, and mayors of regional capitals.

KRYM—NASH (CRIMEA IS OURS)

When Maidan protesters and demonstrations forced Ukrainian president Viktor Yanukovych to seek asylum in Russia in February 2014, Putin took advantage of the disorder. Russian state television stoked fears of a new, anti-Russian regime in Kiev, and the predominantly ethnic Russian region of Crimea was encouraged to separate from Ukraine. A pro-Russian government was installed, and a hurried referendum was held, both aided by the presence—denied at the time—of Russian special forces. In a surprise move, Putin decided that Crimea should be immediately incorporated into Russia without any negotiations and without regard to Ukrainian law. Ukraine had had jurisdiction over Crimea since 1954, and the Russian argument was that annexing the region constituted the righting of a historical injustice.

The incorporation of Crimea added 2.2 million people to the Russian population and resulted in two new subjects of the federation, Crimea and the "federal city" of Sevastopol. (Previously, only two cities had this status, Moscow and St. Petersburg.) The process of integrating Crimea into Russia resembled the postwar redrawing of Soviet borders to encompass the Baltic states and western Ukraine, as well as parts of Romania (Moldova) and Tuva. Stalin telescoped the implementation of Soviet policies that had taken decades into a few years in these newly acquired territories, stirring local resentment that is still tangible seventy years later.

Incorporation of Crimea into Russia presented a whole series of unantici-pated difficulties for the Kremlin. Kiev ruled Crimea under a set of laws and institutions that were substantially different from those operating in Russia, and virtually every institution needed to be restructured to conform to Russian standards.

The international community—most vocally the United States and the European Union—rejected the annexation of Crimea as a violation of international norms governing the sovereignty of established states and their territorial integrity. Sanctions and future legal action vastly complicate the process of integrating the new entities. Crimea's airports, critical to the region's tourist economy, cannot accept international flights, since they are formally under the jurisdiction of Ukraine in the eyes of international aviation authorities. The flow of tourists from outside of Russia dropped dramatically; ironically, the largest number come from the now hostile neighbor, Ukraine. Russian banks and companies avoid the region out of fear of possible Western sanctions. Even Crimea's football (soccer) teams are in limbo, not allowed to compete in Russian leagues: the major world soccer organizations have agreed with complaints by Ukraine that these teams remain Ukrainian. Crimea has required significant new economic investment, inevitably at the expense of other Russian regions and other priorities. Water, fuel, and electricity must all be supplied from Russia, and past infrastructure—including the railroad—came through Ukrainian territory. A bridge for automobile and rail traffic across the Kerch Strait, when opened in 2018, solves many problems, but it has turned into the most expensive bridge ever constructed. Meanwhile, the economy of Crimea requires substantial Russian financial support, including pensions promised at the rate paid to Moscow residents, which is significantly higher than the Russian average. Currently, Crimea and Chechnya are by far the most heavily subsidized regions in Russia.

Following the same pattern previously outlined, the annexation of Crimea was accompanied by administrative changes as Putin placed overall supervision of Crimean developments in the hands of Dmitry Kozak, the presidential troubleshooter who had previously been tasked with overseeing the North Caucasus and the Sochi Olympics. Following the example of the North Caucasus and the Far East, a new Ministry for the Economic Development of Crimea was created—but then after a year the ministry was disbanded. A new, ninth federal district for Crimea and Sevastopol was also created and disbanded, and the two new regions were added to the Southern Federal District.

Russia gained not just Crimea but two new, potentially restive minorities: Ukrainians living in Crimea who did not want to become Russian citizens and Crimean Tatars. Repression and intimidation were the initial responses by Russia's newly appointed regional leaders. Prominent leaders of the Tatar

Mejlis, or people's assembly, were banned from the region, and protest demonstrations were prohibited.

CONCLUSION: IS REFORM POSSIBLE UNDER PUTIN?

The state of center-region affairs under Yeltsin was not sustainable—the regions had become too strong at the expense of the center. But Putin swung the pendulum too far in the opposite direction. His policies curtailed both federalism and democratic development in Russia.

The methods used by Putin and his team were in large part derived from the standard operating procedures of the KGB and its successor organization, the FSB. These included gathering compromising materials against "targets," using this information to blackmail the targets in order to gain their cooperation, planning and carrying out extralegal operations with a maximum degree of secrecy, and using diversions and feints to direct attention away from the real purpose of an operation. In the case of the shift of powers to the federal districts, a part of Putin's strategy seemed to be to create new institutions that at first seem merely to duplicate functions of existing institutions but that could later take their place. The emphasis on discipline, carrying out orders without question, and strict hierarchical relations also reflects the internal ethos of the KGB. The Putin approach to the regions seemed to suffer from a set of limitations that reflected his life experiences and background. There is a Soviet-era joke about a machinist from a defense plant who made Kalashnikovs (machine guns). When he retired from the factory, he decided to make toys for the children in his neighborhood. But whatever he tried to make, whether it was a rocking horse, a doll, or a model ship, it always came out looking like a Kalashnikov! Putin's choice of instruments and personnel made it almost inevitable that his policies for dealing with the regions would end up "looking like a Kalashnikov," a recentralized, unitary system.

Russia's leaders from the outset had only a hazy notion of what constitutes federalism or liberal democracy. To an extent this paralleled Soviet-era misunderstandings about the nature of a market economy. The absence of a planned or command system for allocating resources was equated with chaos and anarchy. Democracy and an effectively operating federal system rely on political institutions for resolving disputes with an emphasis on transparent, lawful action and the use of methods such as negotiation, persuasion, and compromise. If one sets aside the obvious exception of Chechnya, the Yeltsin presidency relied heavily on compromise and negotiation to achieve settlements with the regions. Putin, with much higher levels of public support, an effective working majority in the Duma, and a much more favorable economic and budgetary situation, could dispense with democratic procedures and still get results. Putin preferred to use his strength to force the changes he wanted largely without bargaining and without employing consti-tutional mechanisms.

How did Putin's policies work in practice? The new policies did restore central control over the military, police, and federal agencies that rightfully belonged under federal jurisdiction. But there was little recognition among Putin's inner circle that this strategy could go too far, or that excessive centralization was one of the weaknesses of the Soviet system. It is clear from Putin's statements on "restoring" vertical power that his main reference point was the USSR. To someone who was a product of the Soviet system, the elimination of checks and balances appears to increase the manageability and effectiveness of the political system. This may have been true in the short run, but there was a serious downside. A highly centralized system runs the risk of collapsing in the face of a crisis or rapidly changing conditions.

A high degree of centralization is problematic in any political system, but this was especially true of a country as diverse as Russia. Natal'ya Zubare-vich has argued that there are four different Russias.[16] First there is the Russia of big cities (from 21 to 36 percent of the total population), where the middle class is concentrated and where skilled, white-collar professions dominate. Second is what remains of industrial Russia (around 25 percent of the population), where regions are dominated both by blue-collar workers and *budzhetniki*—pensioners, teachers, and others dependent on the federal and regional budgets. This Russia includes an important subset of "mono-cities," dominated by one large factory or industry, that are especially vulner-able to changes in state contracts or subsidies. The third Russia (about 38 percent of the population) is poor, peripheral, and mostly rural. It is less dependent on government policy and survives on the natural economy. Final-ly, a fourth Russia is made up of the poorest republics of the North Caucasus and southern Siberia (Tuva, Altai). Dominated by clans, these regions are highly dependent on direct transfers from the federal budget.

Putin's 2012 "May Directives" (*ukazy*) show how excessive centraliza-tion can impact regions. After his inauguration to a third term, Putin set specific policy targets that every region would be expected to meet in a variety of areas. Targets were set for demographic and health indicators such as life expectancy, birth rate, infant mortality, and cardiovascular deaths. Economic and business targets included growth in real wages, lower mort-gage interest rates, and ease of doing business ratings. Special importance was assigned to underpaid *budzhetniki* in education and health care, who were to have their salaries increased to exceed the average income in their region. Funding from the center only partially covered the new demands on regional budgets, and the results were predictable: regions' debt levels in-creased, and they were forced to divert discretionary funds from high-priority problems to show progress on fulfilling the presidential directives. Whenever Putin met with governors one-on-one, he expected an update on how his policy goals were being met. The budget squeeze led to various tricks by regional bureaucrats to report achievements that existed only on paper. For example, to increase pay for medical personnel, some nurses and orderlies were put on part-time contracts not subject to the decree, or their jobs were reclassified as "cleaning staff." To show progress in reducing deaths from cardiovascular disease, doctors were ordered to report other maladies or "unknown" as the cause of death.

The difficulties produced by the May Directives did not help Putin grasp the limits of centralization. After his 2018 inauguration, Putin issued another (this time in a single document) "May Directive" containing a long list of ambitious policy goals with no visible means to carry them out at the regional level. About a dozen federal programs designed to implement portions of the directive were planned, with uncertain implications for regional budgets.

The default option for a Kremlin that insisted on centralized decision making was to design policies that corresponded to the worst-case scenario in the regions; in practice, this meant the North Caucasus republics. This region suffered from serious economic and political difficulties, such as low levels of development, high unemployment, inequality, and poor governance. One could make the case that Putinism in regional policy was an attempt to bring to the entire country the "successful" lessons learned from dealing with Chechnya after the war there.[17] Putin put in place a handpicked regional leader (Ramzan Kadyrov) who restored order by dealing ruthlessly with his opponents, demonstrated total loyalty to the Kremlin, shamelessly manipulated election results to the advantage of United Russia and himself, and implemented a state-dominated reconstruction program financed both from central and local resources. Yet centralized policy making was not capable of formulating policies that would be effective in the varied settings that comprise the Russian Federation. Chechnya-type policies applied in Moscow in 2010 and 2011 alienated a significant stratum of the population, producing massive anti-Putin demonstrations starting in December 2011. The protest mood changed dramatically in the aftermath of the Crimean annexation, and even the populations of large Russian cities came to view protests through the lens of Ukrainian events—as a factor that could precipitate instability or even civil war.

What are the prospects that Putin could adopt policies that would begin the process of returning the pendulum in center-region relations back toward the regions? There were several signs that a reassessment was under way in 2011. Working groups headed by two of the most important officials tasked with regional policy, deputy prime ministers Dmitry Kozak and Alexander Khloponin, headed commissions to develop proposals that would reallocate government functions and budgetary resources from the center to the regions. Nothing of substance resulted from this effort. Similarly, efforts to reform the Federation Council in ways that would increase regional interest representation also produced nothing. In the end, Putin's desire to maintain centralized control exceeds his willingness to pursue reforms that would allow regions to govern themselves more effectively. The lack of regional representation in central government decision making makes the political system vulnerable to unexpected shocks, crises, and future street protests, a consequence of policies that fail to meet regional needs.

DISCUSSION QUESTIONS

1. How did the basic institutional framework of region-center relations change from Yeltsin to Putin?
2. What elements of Russian federalism were incompatible with Putin's approach to governing?
3. Why is it that administrative complications arose after Russia annexed Crimea in 2014?
4. How likely is it that Russia will attain true federalism under Putin? Give evidence to justify your answer.

SUGGESTED READINGS

Evans, Alfred B., and Vladimir Gel'man, eds. *The Politics of Local Government in Russia.* Lanham, MD: Rowman & Littlefield, 2004.

Gill, Graeme, and James Young, eds. *Routledge Handbook of Russian Politics and Society.* London: Routledge, 2011.

Reddaway, Peter, and Robert W. Orttung. *The Dynamics of Russian Politics: Putin's Reform of Federal-Regional Relations*, vols. 1 and 2. Lanham, MD: Rowman & Littlefield, 2004 and 2005.

Reisinger, William M., and Bryon J. Moraski. *The Regional Roots of Russia's Political Regime.* Ann Arbor: University of Michigan Press, 2017.

Reuter, Ora John. *The Origins of Dominant Parties: Building Authoritarian Institutions in Post-Soviet Russia.* Cambridge: Cambridge University Press, 2017.

Ross, Cameron. *Local Politics and Democratization in Russia.* London: Routledge, 2009.

———, ed. *Russian Regional Politics under Putin and Medvedev.* London: Routledge, 2011.

Ross, Cameron, and Adrian Campbell, eds. *Federalism and Local Politics in Russia.* London: Routledge, 2009.

Zubarevich, Natal'ya. "Four Russias: Human Potential and Social Differentiation of Russian Regions and Cities." In *Russia 2025: Scenarios for the Russian Future*, ed. Maria Lipman and Nikolai Petrov. London: Palgrave, 2013.

NOTES

1. See Graeme Gill, *The Origins of the Stalinist Political System* (Cambridge: Cambridge University Press, 1996); and Gerald Easter, *Reconstructing the State: Personal Networks and Elite Identity in Soviet Russia* (Cambridge: Cambridge University Press, 1996).

2. Peter Jordan, "Regional Identities and Regionalization in East-Central Europe," *Post-Soviet Geography and Economics* 42, no. 4 (2001): 235–65.

3. Daniel Triesman, "The Politics of Intergovernmental Transfers in Post-Soviet Russia," *British Journal of Political Science* 26, no. 3 (1996): 299–335; and Daniel Triesman, "Fiscal

Redistribution in a Fragile Federation: Moscow and the Regions in 1994," *British Journal of Political Science* 28, no. 1 (1998).

4. Michael McFaul and Nikolai Petrov, *Politicheskii Al'manakh Rossii 1997*, vol. 1 (Moscow: Carnegie Center, 1998), 149.

5. Darrell Slider, "Elections to Russia's Regional Assemblies," *Post-Soviet Affairs* 12, no. 3 (1996): 243–64.

6. Pavel K. Baev, "The Russian Armed Forces: Failed Reform Attempts and Creeping Regionalization," *Journal of Communist Studies and Transition Politics* 17, no. 1 (2001): 34.

7. Steven Solnick, "Is the Center Too Weak or Too Strong in the Russian Federation?," in *Building the Russian State*, ed. Valerie Sperling (Boulder, CO: Westview, 2000).

8. Alfred Stepan, "Russian Federalism in Comparative Perspective," *Post-Soviet Affairs* 16, no. 2 (2000): 133–76.

9. Darrell Slider, "Russia's Market-Distorting Federalism," *Post-Soviet Geography and Economics* 38, no. 8 (1997): 445–60.

10. Nikolai Petrov, "Seven Faces of Putin's Russia: Failed Districts as the New Level of State Territorial Composition," *Security Dialogue* 33, no. 1 (2002): 219–37.

11. Mathew Hyde, "Putin's Federal Reforms and Their Implications for Presidential Power in Russia," *Europe-Asia Studies* 53, no. 5 (2001): 719–43.

12. The reference is to the movie *The Magnificent Seven*, which was one of the first American films to be widely shown in the Soviet Union during the Cold War. The film, a western about seven gunslingers hired by a poor Mexican village to protect it from bandits, was extremely popular in the 1960s when Vladimir Putin was growing up.

13. The most detailed examination of the early role of the federal districts and *polpreds* is Peter Reddaway and Robert W. Orttung, *Putin's Reform of Federal-Regional Relations*, vol. 1, *The Dynamics of Russian Politics* (Lanham, MD: Rowman & Littlefield, 2004). The second volume of this study (2005) shows the impact of Putin's federal reforms on law enforcement, the courts, the Federation Council, local government, political parties, and business.

14. An additional eighteen federal agencies had regional offices in another location, while forty-three had no intermediate structures between their central headquarters and regional branches. "Federal Agencies on the Territory of Nizhniy Novgorod *Oblast*," chart prepared by the Volga federal district administration (2001).

15. Confirmation of this came in the form of a YouTube video posted in April 2018 by Alexander Shestun, the mayor of Serpukhov in Moscow *oblast*. He secretly recorded threats made to him by the FSB general in charge of prosecuting regional officials and the head of the Kremlin's Domestic Politics Department. See http://www.youtube.com/watch?v=whPAGmeE6O4.

16. Natal'ya Zubarevich, "Four Russias: Human Potential and Social Differentiation of Russian Regions and Cities," in *Russia 2025*, eds. Maria Lipman and Nikolay Petrov (London: Palgrave Macmillan, 2013), 67–85.

17. See Robert Ware, "Has the Russian Federation Been Chechenised?," *Europe-Asia Studies* 63, no. 3 (2011): 493–508.

Chapter Three

The Role of Law

Kathryn Hendley

Law has had a checkered history in Russia. The rule of law, as evidenced by an independent judiciary that applies the law in an evenhanded manner to all who come before it, has been mostly absent. During the Soviet era, the leaders of the Communist Party used law in a blatantly instrumental fashion, a situation that began to change in the late 1980s when Gorbachev put forward the goal of a *pravovoe gosudarstvo*, or a "state based on the rule of law."[1] The leaders of post-Soviet Russia have reiterated this goal, yet their actions reflect ambivalence. The heavy-handed prosecutions of political opponents of the Kremlin suggest that the willingness to use law as a weapon to achieve short-term goals is a vestige of Soviet life that lives on in post-Soviet Russia. Though these prosecutions have become the most well-known feature of the Russian legal system, both domestically and internationally, they do not tell the whole story. They have occurred within a legal system that has undergone remarkable institutional reforms over the past three decades.

The contemporary Russian legal system is best conceptualized as a dual system, under which mundane cases are handled in accordance with the prevailing law, but when cases attract the attention of those in power, outcomes can be manipulated to serve their interests.[2] To put it more simply, justice is possible and maybe even probable, but it cannot be guaranteed. This lack of predictability is unfortunate, but it does not make Russia unique. Law is inherently messy. Many countries aspire to the rule of law, but none has yet achieved it in full measure. Articulating the rules is always easier than applying them to concrete circumstances. Some gap between the law on the books and the law in practice is inevitable. The efforts to bridge this gap in Russia are the subject of this chapter.

HISTORICAL OVERVIEW

The role of law in any society is not dependent solely on written law and formal legal institutions, but is also influenced by how these laws and institutions are understood and by how they are used (or not used) by both the powerful and the powerless within that society.[3] These attitudes, often referred to as legal culture, are neither uniform nor consistent. They are influenced by many factors. Primary among them are the common perceptions of the responsiveness of law and legal institutions to the interests of society. For some, these perceptions are shaped by their own experiences. But in Russia, much as in the rest of the world, the vast majority of citizens have had no firsthand encounters with the formal legal system. For them, their attitudes toward the legal system are influenced by beliefs about how law has worked in the past as well as by mass media accounts about how the legal system is presently functioning and/or anecdotal accounts of the experiences of friends or family. As a result, making sense of the role of law in contemporary Russia requires some knowledge of what came before.

The Soviet Union is often referred to as a lawless society. Taken literally, this was not true. The Soviet Union possessed all the elements of a typical legal system.[4] It had a complex body of statutory law as well as a series of constitutions. It had a hierarchy of formal courts that mirrored what would be found in any Western democracy, as well as a well-developed system of alternative dispute resolution that allowed for neighborhood mediation in so-called comrades' courts. But all of these institutions were firmly under the thumb of the Communist Party. Though the constitution prominently proclaimed their commitment to the principle of judicial independence, the absence of judicial review made the constitution largely symbolic. The legislature, though composed of representatives who were ostensibly popularly elected, operated as a rubber stamp for decisions made by party leaders. Likewise, judges tended to follow the party line.[5] All understood that anyone who diverged would not be invited to stand for reelection, and the short five-year terms ensured that judges were kept on a short leash. At the same time, this should not be taken to mean that party officials dictated the outcomes of all cases. Judges were left alone to resolve many (perhaps most) of the cases they heard in accord with the law and their consciences.[6] But judges knew that at any moment the telephone might ring and they might be told how to decide a specific case. The specter of "telephone law" hung over all cases and gave rise to a culture of dependency within the judiciary. Over time, fewer and fewer calls were needed as judges developed an instinct for what the party wanted. Not surprisingly, ordinary citizens grew skeptical of the power of the law to protect their interests. This legal culture of distrust persists to some extent to the present day and has stymied efforts to reform the legal system. A 2017 public opinion poll shows that Russians are evenly divided on the question of whether courts should be independent or should be controlled by the executive branch. [7]

Gorbachev was the first Soviet leader to make a systematic effort to change the role of law. [8] He regularly invoked the goal of creating a rule-of-law-based state or *pravovoe gosudarstvo* in his public statements. Moreover, he took concrete actions to that end. His reforms to the electoral system brought an end to the era of rubber-stamp legislatures. Under his tenure, the judicial selection system was overhauled, eliminating the Communist Party's stranglehold and granting judges life tenure. Though these reforms were certainly necessary to achieving judicial independence, they were far from sufficient. Judges could not shake off the mantle of dependency so easily. Citizens were likewise slow to abandon their skepticism regarding the capacity of judges to rule in an evenhanded manner without clear proof of a shift in judicial behavior. Along similar lines, Gorbachev introduced the principle of judicial review to Russia for the first time. He created the Committee on Constitutional Supervision, which, while not a full-fledged constitutional court, was empowered to review acts of the executive and legislative branches, making it an early (albeit feeble) attempt at checks and balances. Its impact was largely symbolic. How far Gorbachev would have pushed the legal reform had he not lost power is unknowable.

Reform to the legal system was less of a marquee issue under Boris Yeltsin but continued throughout the 1990s. In some ways, the challenges were mitigated by the disintegration of the Soviet Union. No longer did reformers have to concern themselves with how reforms would play out in all the republics, which became independent countries in 1992, but the immense size of Russia as well as the wholesale nature of the transformation left reformers with their hands full. Yeltsin's decision to abandon the halfway reforms that characterized perestroika and to embrace the goals of creating a democracy and a market economy meant that comprehensive reforms were needed. The institutional infrastructure for both democracies and markets is grounded in law. Much of the Soviet-era legislation and legal institutions were inadequate to the task. Russian reformers turned to Western advisers for assistance in writing the new laws and creating the necessary institutions. Many of these advisers approached Russia as if it was a tabula rasa, disregarding what existed on paper as well as the prevailing legal culture. Almost no area of law was left untouched by the legislative whirlwind of the 1990s. The top-down nature of these reforms and the unwillingness to pay attention to the needs of those who would be impacted felt familiar to Russians, who recognized the modus operandi from their Soviet past, albeit under a new banner. [9] The result was a continued skepticism toward the usefulness of law; a sentiment that was only deepened as the new institutions were rocked by a series of corruption scandals.

Snapshots of the judicial system taken at the beginning and end of the 1990s would reveal dramatically different pictures. Though the basic court system remained intact and continued to handle the bulk of cases, other more specialized courts were introduced. The most well known is the stand-alone Constitutional Court, which represented a dramatic break with Russia's autocratic tradition. Through its power of judicial review, the court could declare legislative and executive acts unconstitutional, thereby making the judicial branch an equal partner for the first time in Russian history. In its early days, the court took some highly controversial positions, most notably siding with the legislature against Yeltsin in the lead-up to the October Events of 1993.[10] Yeltsin disbanded the court during this crisis and, when it was reconstituted in early 1994, the justices, having learned their lesson, shied away from disputes with political overtones. Less well known, but essential to the development of a market economy, was the emergence of the *arbitrazh* courts in 1992. These courts were not created out of whole cloth but were built on the foundation of the Soviet-era system for resolving disputes between state-owned enterprises. Critical changes were made in terms of the status of the decision makers (raised from arbiters to judges) and jurisdiction (expanded to include disputes involving private firms as well as bankruptcy), but the *arbitrazh* courts represent a creative adaptation of Soviet-era institutions to serve the needs of the new Russia.[11]

In addition to the structural innovations, the depoliticization of the judicial selection process was consolidated under Yeltsin.[12] The constitution, approved by popular referendum in December 1993, provides that judges be appointed by the president, with the proviso that nominations to any of the top courts be confirmed by the Federation Council. The seemingly unchecked power of the president to select lower-level judges might seem to be an example of the expansive powers granted to the president by this constitution. In reality, however, it constituted the final step in a system designed to preference competence over political reliability, a noteworthy reversal from the previous system in which judges served at the pleasure of the Communist Party. Under the reformed system, which persists to the present day, open positions are publicized, and anyone with a law degree who is at least twenty-five and has five or more years of work in the legal profession can apply. Their applications are assessed by judicial qualification commissions (JQCs), who forward their recommendations up the bureaucratic chain, culminating in a presidential appointment. All Russian judges, other than justices of the peace, enjoy life tenure, subject to a mandatory retirement age of seventy. Justices of the peace have five-year terms, which can be served consecutively until they reach seventy. Allegations of judicial corruption and other malfeasance are handled by the JQCs, which have the power to sanction and remove judges.

Yeltsin's successors, Putin and Medvedev, came to the presidency with legal training. Their attitude toward law was undeniably shaped by their work experiences. Putin's years in the KGB seemed to have taught him the importance of discipline and predictability. Not surprisingly, he has consistently espoused a philosophy of "supremacy of law" (*gospodstvo zakonnosti*) that complements the "power vertical" and emphasizes the importance of law and order over the protection of human rights. [13] Medvedev, by contrast, spent several years on the law faculty at St. Petersburg State University and has a subtler view of law. While president, he proved more willing to meet with rights activists, and his rhetoric was notably less bombastic than Putin's. In terms of action, however, Medvedev rarely challenged Putin, either when he served as president or prime minister.

LEGISLATIVE REFORMS

Putin's consolidation of power within the Duma and his emasculation of the Federation Council allowed for legislative reforms that eluded Yeltsin. During the 1990s, a number of key pieces of legislation stalled due to opposition within the Duma. As a result, those affected had to hobble along using either the stopgap presidential decrees or Soviet codes, which had been amended so many times that they had come to resemble a patchwork quilt. Not only did this undermine the predictability of law by making it difficult to discern what the rules were, but it left the guiding principles of the Soviet era in place, at least on paper. During Putin's first two terms, this legislative logjam was broken. The manner in which laws were passed seemed to signal a return to the Soviet style of rubber-stamp legislatures. Under both Putin and Medvedev, United Russia (the Kremlin-affiliated party) was able to take advantage of both its majority and the ability of its leaders to enforce party discipline and build coalitions to enact the Kremlin's legislative agenda.

The criminal procedure code in effect when Putin took office was originally passed under Khrushchev. A new code, which enhanced the rights of judges at the expense of the police, got bogged down in the Duma in the latter years of Yeltsin's tenure. This new code was finally passed and came into effect in 2002. [14] Under its terms, the police are required to obtain warrants for investigative activities that previously could be carried out without judicial supervision. The code also limits the circumstances under which the accused may be kept in pretrial detention. Whether all of these procedural niceties are being observed in practice is a different question. The question of whether judges do a better job of safeguarding individual rights has also come into question. The Khodorkovsky case, in which the Yukos chief was jailed while awaiting trial on fraud charges despite not meeting the prerequisites of the code, shows that the rules regarding pretrial detention can and will be disregarded when convenient for the Kremlin.[15] Judging a system solely on high-profile cases can be dicey. The extent to which the state lives up to its obligations in more mundane cases is unclear, but the strong culture of backdoor dealings between judges and procurators (or prosecutors) creates grounds for suspicion.[16] The procuracy is a uniquely Russian component of the legal system that is not only charged with prosecuting crime but also with supervising justice more generally. It has stubbornly held out against numerous reform efforts aimed at making its activities more transparent.[17]

Since 2000, a Soviet-era tactic of drafting laws with intentionally vague language has reemerged. Such legislation offers maximum flexibility to officials and minimal predictability to citizens. Examples of this practice include amendments introduced in 2012 to the law governing Russian nongovernmental organizations (NGOs), which required them to register as "foreign agents" if they received financial support from outside Russia. NGOs resisted identifying themselves as "foreign agents," finding the Cold War connotations of the label to be distasteful. Authorities used the law as a pretext to conduct unscheduled audits of the records of NGOs that were not supportive of Kremlin policies. Although activists challenged the law, the Constitutional Court upheld its constitutionality.[18] Likewise the law on extremism, which was passed in 2002 to fight terrorism, has been used to outlaw political parties not in sync with the Kremlin and to ban Jehovah's Witnesses. The seemingly innocuous requirement that candidates submit the petitions supporting their candidacy as well as for permits authorizing demonstrations have been used to stymie opponents of the Kremlin. These actions demonstrate the Kremlin's willingness to use law instrumentally.

JUDICIAL POLITICS

The dualistic nature of the present-day Russian legal system can undermine the independence of the courts. "Telephone law" did not disappear with the Communist Party and continues to hold sway in cases with political resonance as well as in cases where the economic stakes are high.[19] When such cases arise, court chairmen take care to assign them to pliant and politically reliable judges. Judges who fail to heed the signals tend to get hauled before the JQC on vague charges of having dishonored the courts and are typically removed from the bench.

Judicial Selection and Supervision

The method of selecting judges and supervising them once they are on the bench has profound implications for the independence of the judicial system. Ideally, judges should look only to the law in resolving disputes; politics should not factor into their decisions. But when judges feel beholden to a political benefactor for their appointments, their impartiality can be compromised. Lifetime tenure is a potential solution, but it runs the risk of creating a judicial corps detached from society, answerable to no one. Judges, even those with lifetime appointments, must be held accountable for misbehavior. Some oversight is necessary. Yet it requires a delicate touch; otherwise it risks undermining independence. As this suggests, the mechanics of maintaining an independent judicial system are excruciatingly difficult and highly political. Striking an acceptable balance between independence and accountability can be elusive.

Locating this equilibrium point in post-Soviet Russia has proven to be particularly vexing. Under Putin's leadership, concerns about the lack of judicial accountability gave rise to subtle but important changes in the selection system.[20] The composition of the JQCs was altered. Judges no longer enjoyed a monopoly but still made up two-thirds of the membership of the JQCs at all levels. In theory, opening JQC membership to nonjudges might seem to be democratic, in that it creates an avenue for societal concerns to be expressed. Judges saw it differently, fearing an effort by the Kremlin to exert more control over the courts. While it is true that the change allows other voices into the decision-making process, it is also true that most other European countries with organs analogous to the JQCs include a mixture of judges and laypeople. Russian civil society activists have complained bitterly about their lack of influence in the judicial selection process.

In addition to selecting judges, the JQCs have sole responsibility for disciplining judges. This brings some level of accountability into the mix. Possible sanctions range from private reprimands to dismissals. Although litigants raised over fifty-three thousand complaints before JQCs in 2015, this represented less than 0.2 percent of the cases brought before Russian courts.[21]

In contrast to the judicial system in the United States, where legal professionals go onto the bench after a fairly lengthy career in some other legal arena, becoming a judge in Russia is a career choice made at a much earlier stage of life. There are two basic career paths for those interested in becoming a judge. Judges who handle criminal cases are drawn from the ranks of criminal investigators and prosecutors, whereas judges who handle noncriminal cases typically go to work for the courts as an assistant to a judge immediately after completing their legal education in order to gain the necessary experience to apply for a judicial post. Once they get onto the bench, most stay for their entire work life. Women constitute two-thirds of the judicial corps.[22] Though the prestige of the judiciary has risen considerably since the demise of the Soviet Union, it remains lower than in the United States. As in other countries with a civil law legal tradition, Russian judges view themselves as civil servants, not as policy makers.[23] Recognizing that status is linked to salary and workload, both Putin and Medvedev consistently pushed for increased funding for the courts. Even so, recruiting a sufficient number of judges to staff the courts remains difficult. Institutional efforts aimed at enhancing the status of the judiciary represent a starting point but are effective only if accompanied by societal trust. This has been slow to develop, as evidenced by public opinion polls indicating that most Russians approach the courts with skepticism. [24]

As part of an effort to build legitimacy for the courts, a law was passed mandating that, as of July 2010, all courts create websites on which judicial decisions as well as schedules for hearings are posted. Such websites have been created, though their quality varies widely. [25] Notwithstanding the fact that lower-court decisions do not constitute binding precedent, some litigants have made active use of the information posted to investigate how the judges assigned to their cases have ruled in previous analogous cases. They believe that compiling this information helps them to persuade judges to be consistent in their rulings.

Constitutional Court

The Constitutional Court is a post-Soviet innovation. Its purpose is to ensure that the constitution remains the preeminent legal authority in Russia. To that end, it is empowered to invalidate legislative and/or executive acts as unconstitutional. From a technical legal point of view, the Constitutional Court stands on equal footing with the Supreme Court (see figure 3.1), but it is unlike the Supreme Court in several important respects. First, it does not stand at the apex of an elaborate hierarchy of courts that stretch across Russia. It is a stand-alone court. [26] Second, it is a much smaller court, with only nineteen judges. The background of these judges is quite different from that of their counterparts on the Supreme Court, most of whom have worked as judges for their entire careers. By contrast, many members of the Constitutional Court are drawn from the top ranks of legal scholars and come to the bench only after several decades of working in universities or research institutes. This means that they are free of the legacy of dependence that hangs over the rest of the Russian judiciary. Because they mostly come from a scholarly background, their opinions are longer and more literate, providing a clearer window into their thinking than is possible with opinions from the other courts. This is facilitated by the fact that only this court enjoys the right to write dissenting opinions. Finally, the decisions of the Constitutional Court constitute a source of law and, as such, are binding on the other branches of government as well as on other courts.

Between 2008 and 2016, the number of petitions sent to the Constitutional Court ranged between fourteen thousand and nineteen thousand per year. [27] Almost all come in the form of individual complaints centering on alleged violations of constitutional rights. The remaining cases stem from claims

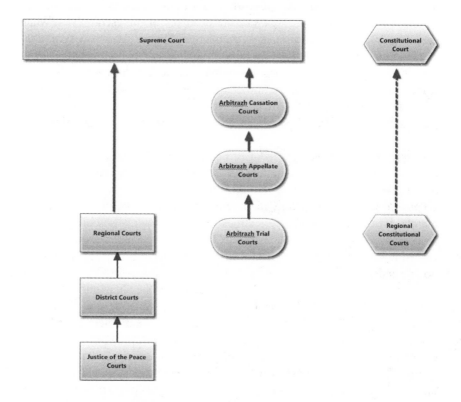

Figure 3.1. The Russian Court System

initiated by the president, a group of legislators (at least 20 percent of the members of either chamber), or regional governments. Its decisions take several forms. Not all involve an up-or-down vote on the constitutionality of a particular law or regulation. Many of its rulings lay out the justification for the constitutionality of legal norms. These so-called "authoritative interpretations" can have the effect of rewriting the law under the guise of ensuring its constitutionality. They have given the court tremendous influence in many areas of law (including taxes, contracts, and social benefits) that would not appear to fall under its jurisdiction. The court has further expanded its jurisdiction by issuing rulings that declared contested legal norms "noncontradictory to the constitution," but their interpretations of these laws are considered binding on all Russian courts.[28]

Since its reconstitution following the October Events of 1993, the Constitutional Court has been reluctant to immerse itself in political controversy. Its ability to do so has been institutionally constrained by the decision to limit its jurisdiction to cases brought to it; the court can no longer take up cases on its own initiative. The court has also adopted a more deliberative pace for resolving cases. In contrast to the chaotic practices of the early 1990s, when decisions were sometimes issued on an overnight basis, cases now take eight or nine months to wind their way through the system, allowing time for the sorts of back-and-forth discussions among the judges that are familiar to students of the US Supreme Court.[29] In terms of the substance of its decisions, the Constitutional Court has consistently been supportive of Putin's agenda to curtail regional power, including the elimination of popular elections for governors.[30] Even when the regions prevail, as in the March 2003 case brought by the legislatures of Bashkortostan and Tatarstan, the court is careful to note that regional governments are entitled to expand their powers only to the extent that they do not infringe on the federal system. The court seemed to feel emboldened by the Kremlin to bring the regions to heel. One member of the court noted, "We struck down the key clauses of 7 constitutions of the republics in June 2000 only after President Putin announced his crackdown on recalcitrant regions; we would not have been brave enough to do this under Yeltsin."[31]

Getting its decisions enforced is a problem that the Constitutional Court shares with the courts of general jurisdiction and the *arbitrazh* courts. Enforcing judgments is not just a problem in Russia; it is a problem that plagues courts everywhere. For the most part, litigants are expected to live up to the obligations imposed by the courts out of a combination of respect for the institution and a fear of being identified as noncompliant and shamed. The lack of societal trust in courts turns these assumptions upside down in Russia. Flouting judicial orders brings no disgrace. The Constitutional Court has attempted to remedy the problem by creating a department charged with monitoring its decisions. But the small size of the department (four people) and intransigence of the underlying political issues have hampered efforts at improving the record on implementation.

The Courts of General Jurisdiction

The courts of general jurisdiction are the workhorses of the Russian judicial system. Any case that is not specifically allocated to the Constitutional Court or the *arbitrazh* courts lands in their lap. In 2016, the workload of these courts, constituting over twenty-four million cases, was over twelve times greater than that of the *arbitrazh* courts. They handle all criminal cases as well as any civil or administrative case that affects an individual (rather than a firm). The number of cases heard by these courts almost quadrupled between 1995 and 2016.[32] The increase has been driven by civil cases; the number of criminal cases has actually decreased in recent years. The rise in civil claims is particularly intriguing, given that these are cases brought by individuals. Whether this reflects a fundamental shift in attitudes toward the legal system, namely a greater willingness on the part of Russians to use the courts to protect their interests, is unclear.[33]

The courts of general jurisdiction can be found in every administrative district, making them the most accessible of the Russian courts. This has only increased under Putin with the introduction of a new layer of courts, the justice of the peace (JP) courts (see figure 3.1). The JP courts were first authorized in late 1998 and were intended to provide a way to siphon off simple cases, thereby alleviating the burden on the already existing courts.[34] Creating thousands of new courts proved to be easier said than done. When Putin took over in 2000, none existed, but by 2009, JP courts could be found in every part of Russia. From an institutional perspective, they have lived up to their promise. In 2016, 72 percent of civil and administrative cases and 48 percent of criminal cases originated in these courts.[35] Thanks in large measure to this, delays throughout the entire system have been lessened.[36] The JP courts have also benefited litigants by making courts more accessible, both geographically as well as in terms of simplified procedures. As figure 3.1 indicates, those dissatisfied with the JP courts are entitled to appeal the judgment to a higher court.

Most cases that have not been diverted to the JP courts originate in the district courts, which are located in each rural or urban district. More serious matters are heard for the first time by the regional courts (which also serve as courts of appeal for the district courts).[37] The court of last resort is the Supreme Court of the Russian Federation. Like the Constitutional Court, the decisions of this court serve as binding precedent. In addition to its pure judicial function of reviewing individual cases, the court is also charged with overseeing the general development of judicial practice. To this end, it periodically issues guiding explanations of legislation that has been interpreted in contradictory fashion by lower courts. These explanations are binding on the lower courts. Ironically this gives the Russian Supreme Court greater institutional latitude than that enjoyed by the US Supreme Court, though few would argue that the political clout of the Russian court approaches that of its American counterpart.

Putin's control of the legislature allowed for thorough reforms of the three procedural codes (administrative, civil, and criminal) that govern the day-to-day operations of the courts of general jurisdiction. Some of the innovations of the new criminal procedure code have been discussed above. The code also changed the operation of the courts by institutionalizing jury trials throughout Russia. Defendants charged with certain serious felonies can opt for a jury trial and have been doing so with increasingly frequency. Jury trials accounted for 15.3 percent of such trials in 2016, compared with 8.3 percent in 2003.[38] Defendants tend to fare better with juries than with judges. While less than 1 percent of defendants are acquitted in bench (nonjury) trials, about 16 percent of defendants in jury trials are acquitted.[39] Jury verdicts, including acquittals, have been subject to appeal from the outset. After the Kremlin was embarrassed when juries acquitted defendants in several politically sensitive cases, the law was changed in 2008 to eliminate the right to a jury trial in cases of espionage, treason, terrorism, and other crimes against the state.

The broader impact of the availability of jury trials on Russians' attitudes toward the legal system is unclear. Elsewhere, juries have been justified on the grounds that they allow defendants to be judged by their peers and that they provide jurors with hands-on experience in how a democratic system operates. The relatively small number of Russians who have served on juries undermines any argument that they are building support for democracy. Public opinion polls confirm Russians' ambivalence about their merits. Around 30 percent of those surveyed in 2006 and 2017 said they trusted juries more than judges. About 20 percent said juries were less trustworthy. The only significant shift between the two surveys was in those who saw no significant difference between verdicts issued by judges and juries. This percentage increased from 19 in 2006 to 27 in 2017.[40]

The *Arbitrazh* Courts

The jurisdiction of the *arbitrazh* courts is threefold: (1) disputes between firms (irrespective of ownership structure), (2) disputes between firms and the state, and (3) bankruptcies. At the outset, almost all cases fell into the first category, but over time the docket has shifted. Comparing the case distributions in 1997, 2005, and 2016 illustrates the point well. In 1997, disputes between firms dominated the docket, constituting over 80 percent of the cases decided by these courts. By 2005, these disputes accounted for about a quarter of the cases decided, and the number of cases involving the state made up 74 percent of the docket. The picture had shifted again by 2016. Once again, interfirm debt dominated, constituting 78 percent of all cases. Disputes involving the state had receded, making up less than 20 percent of the docket. Bankruptcy cases, fueled by the introduction of personal bankruptcy in 2015, made up almost 10 percent of all cases.[41] These shifts are the result of the changing economic fortunes of Russia as well as changes in the underlying law.

The number of cases brought to the *arbitrazh* courts grew fivefold from 1996 to 2016. The willingness of economic actors to submit their disputes to the court is driven by the comparatively low costs and the speed of the process. This is not to say that litigation is the only or even the preferred mechanism of resolving disputes. For Russian managers, much as for their counterparts elsewhere, turning to the courts is a last resort, used only when efforts at negotiation have failed. Rather, the point is that litigation is a viable option for commercial disputes in Russia.

The continued viability of the *arbitrazh* courts came into question with the decision to merge what had been the top court of this system, the Higher *Arbitrazh* Court, with the Supreme Court (see figure 3.1). Putin announced this plan in mid-2013, prompting immediate protests from the business community, who had come to respect the competency of the *arbitrazh* courts. Disregarding these protests, the legislature moved with lightning speed to achieve Putin's goal, pushing through changes to the procedural codes and initiating the necessary amendments to the constitution. By August 2014, the Higher *Arbitrazh* Court was only an institutional memory. The Supreme Court now serves as the court of last resort for the *arbitrazh* courts. To accommodate this institutional reform, separate chambers have been created to handle final appeals from the courts of general jurisdiction and the *arbitrazh* courts. At present, the *arbitrazh* courts continue to operate according to their own procedures.

The European Court of Human Rights

With Russia's accession to the Council of Europe in 1996 and its ratification of the European Convention on Human Rights in 1998, it falls within the jurisdiction of the European Court of Human Rights (ECHR) in Strasbourg. Were Russians as nihilistic about law as is typically assumed, this would have made no difference. But Russians have flocked to the ECHR when their domestic courts have failed them. A 2010 survey confirmed that two-thirds of Russians are aware of the ECHR. Indeed, Russians were the fourth most common petitioner in 2016.[42] This tells us that Russians still believe justice is possible and that they are searching out ways of holding their courts and government to account. At the same time, the fact that over 80 percent of these Russian petitions are declared inadmissible reveals that Russians remain unclear about the precise function of the ECHR.

The Russian government has a mixed record at the ECHR. When damages have been assessed against it, they have generally paid without question. But when the court calls for changes in policy, Russia's record is less impressive. A 2015 law grants discretion to the Constitutional Court to override ECHR decisions.[43] To that end, when the ECHR ruled in 2017 that Russia's so-called "gay propaganda" law was discriminatory and encouraged homophobia, imposing damages of over €43,000, one legislator said that the decision would not be honored "because it contradicts the Russian Constitution."[44] On the other hand, the availability of recourse to the ECHR has undoubtedly affected judicial behavior. Russian judges, worried that their opinions will become the subject of appeals to the ECHR, are taking more care to live up to their procedural obligations. Though it might be more gratifying if such behavior stemmed from a commitment to the rule of law, fear of public humiliation can be a powerful stimulant, and perhaps the behavior will become habitual over time. Regardless of the incentive for the behavioral change, it inures to the benefit of litigants and the legal system.

THE POLITICS OF THE LEGAL PROFESSION

In many countries, lawyers are potent catalysts for legal reform. Their comprehensive knowledge of the law makes them well qualified to identify where changes are needed. Such changes may be either iterative or fundamental. Their willingness to embrace these changes and to operationalize them through their clients can have a profound impact. Merely passing a law is only a first step. More difficult is integrating new norms into daily life. Lawyers can be integral in this process.

The legal profession in Russia has not traditionally performed this sort of role. The reasons are complicated. As in other countries with civil law traditions, lawyers tend to act more as technicians than as social activists. The divided nature of the profession in such countries also contributes to its political passivity. In Russia, for example, there is no single organization that speaks for lawyers, nor is there any uniform system for licensing lawyers. This inevitably gives rise to a fragmented profession. The Soviet heritage, under which lawyers were heavily regulated and their independence was constrained, only deepened this natural instinct.

In the post-Soviet era, young people have been increasingly drawn to legal education. The number of law schools has increased from fewer than 100 in the 1980s to more than 1,200 today. The market for legal services doubled in size between 2003 and 2015.[45]

Most of the Soviet-era regulations governing lawyers have been eliminated and/or ignored in practice. The traditional distinction between litigators (*advokaty*) and business lawyers (*iuriskonsul'ty*) broke down during the 1990s. Private law firms, which had been outlawed during the Soviet era, sprang up and included both varieties of lawyers. Courts treated them similarly. This permissiveness was viewed with dismay by many *advokaty*, who had long viewed themselves as the elite of the legal profession. Becoming an *advokat* had always required persevering through a rigorous and selective process, in contrast to becoming a *iuriskonsul't*, which simply required advanced legal education. *Iuriskonsul'ty* have taken advantage of the laxness of the regulatory regime to establish themselves as experts in business law, a specialization that had been more-or-less nonexistent during the Soviet era and an area of law not much exploited by *advokaty* (who tended to focus on criminal defense work). Prosecutors and judges are separate categories of lawyers. The disaggregated nature of the legal profession makes it impossible to determine the total number of Russian lawyers. The number of *ad-*

vokaty has been increasing by 1,300 per year. By 2014, there were over seventy thousand Russian *advokaty*.[46]

Drafts of a law that would restore the *advokaty* to their preeminent role were floated but never passed during the 1990s. Under Putin, this state of affairs changed. His legislative dominance allowed for the passage of a law dealing with the legal profession in 2002. Though the law did not create a monopoly on courtroom practice, as desired by *advokaty*, it certainly made them the default option. In criminal cases, for example, defendants must use an *advokat* unless being represented by a family member. The law also established a standard process for becoming an *advokat*. Much like judges, prospective *advokaty* must satisfy the requirements of a qualifications commission, which include an oral exam. Though the questions come from a preapproved list, some have argued that the subjective nature of evaluation leaves the door open for preferential treatment and discrimination.[47] The law takes an important step toward institutionalizing the independence of the legal profession by establishing a privilege for attorney-client communications.[48]

CONCLUSION

This review of the role of law in contemporary Russia illustrates that easy conclusions are not possible. The reasons for criticism of his regime on this score are obvious. Under both Putin and Medvedev, the Kremlin's legislative agenda was pushed through with a heavy hand and often had the result of curtailing human rights. Putin's willingness to use the courts as a weapon for punishing his political opponents quite rightly calls their independence into question. Such policies would be troubling in any context but are particularly disquieting in post-Soviet Russia. They are disturbingly reminiscent of problem-solving tactics employed by Soviet leaders that would seem to have been renounced as part of the transition to a rule-of-law-based state (*pravovoe gosudarstvo*). On the other hand, the post-Yeltsin era brought critical institutional innovations. The introduction of the JP courts increased the responsiveness of courts to citizens and eased the strain on the district and regional courts. The use of courts has continued to grow, suggesting a societal willingness to turn over disputes to the courts.

These seemingly contradictory indicators make sense only when the Russian legal system is analyzed as a dualistic system. The institutional progress cannot be dismissed as mere window dressing. After all, the vast majority of the millions of cases heard each year within the Russian judicial system are resolved on the basis of the law on the books, as interpreted by the judge, and without any interference from political authorities. Justice is not out of reach in Russia; it is the likely outcome in most cases. But the continued willingness of those with political power to use law in an instrumental fashion to achieve their short-term goals means that justice can sometimes be out of reach. It also means that the commitment to the basic principle of the rule of law, namely that law applies equally to all, irrespective of their power or connections, is not yet complete. A gap between the law on the books and the law in practice exists in Russia, as in all countries. Surely it has receded from the chasm it was during the Soviet era. But whether it will increase or decrease as time goes on remains to be seen.

DISCUSSION QUESTIONS

1. What are the advantages to the Putin regime of vaguely worded legislation?
2. How has the institutional structure of the courts changed since the collapse of the Soviet Union? What impact have these changes had on citizens' access to justice?
3. What efforts have been made to enhance judicial independence in post-Soviet Russia? Is judicial independence possible in present-day Russia?

SUGGESTED READINGS

Burnham, William, and Jeffrey Kahn. "Russia's Criminal Procedure Code Five Years Out." *Review of Central & East European Law* 33, no. 1 (2008): 1–93.
Gessen, Masha. *Words Will Break Cement: The Passion of Pussy Riot.* New York: Riverhead Books, 2014.
Henderson, Jane. *The Constitution of the Russian Federation: A Contextual Analysis.* Portland, OR: Hart Publishing, 2011.
Hendley, Kathryn. *Everyday Law in Russia.* Ithaca, NY: Cornell University Press, 2017.
Maggs, Peter B., Olga Schwartz, and William Burnham. *Law and Legal System of the Russian Federation.* 6th ed. New York: Juris Publishing, 2015.
Paneyakh, Ella. "Faking Performance Together: Systems of Performance Evaluation in Russian Enforcement Agencies and Production of Bias and Privilege." *Post-Soviet Affairs* 30, nos. 2–3 (2014): 115–36.
Solomon, Peter H., Jr., and Todd S. Foglesong. *Courts and Transition in Russia: The Challenge of Judicial Reform.* Boulder, CO: Westview, 2000.
Trochev, Alexei. *Judging Russia: Constitutional Court in Russian Politics, 1990–2006.* Cambridge: Cambridge University Press, 2008.

NOTES

1. For background on the meaning of *pravovoe gosudarstvo*, see Harold J. Berman, "The Rule of Law and the Law-Based State (*Rechsstaat*)," *Harriman Institute Forum* 4, no. 5 (May 1991): 1–12.
2. The conceptualization of the Russian legal system as dualistic was first suggested by Robert Sharlet with regard to the Stalinist system. "Stalinism and Soviet Legal Culture," in *Stalinism: Essays in Historical Interpretation*, ed. Robert C. Tucker (New York: Norton, 1977),

155–56. He, in turn, was drawing on the ideas of Ernst Fraenkel, *The Dual State: A Contribution to the Theory of Dictatorship* (London: Oxford University Press, 1941). For more on the dualistic nature of the contemporary Russian legal system, see Kathryn Hendley, *Everyday Law in Russia* (Ithaca, NY: Cornell University Press, 2017).

3. For an overview of the rule of law, see Lon L. Fuller, *The Morality of Law* (New Haven, CT: Yale University Press, 1965); and Phillipe Nonet and Philip Selznick, *Law and Society in Transition* (New York: Harper and Row, 1978).

4. Harold J. Berman, *Justice in the U.S.S.R: An Interpretation of Soviet Law* (Cambridge, MA: Harvard University Press, 1963).

5. George Ginsburgs, "The Soviet Judicial Elite: Is It?," *Review of Socialist Law* 11, no. 4 (1985): 293–311.

6. George Feifer, *Justice in Moscow* (New York: Simon & Schuster, 1964).

7. "Reputatsiia sudov i sudei," Fom.ru, March 13, 2017, http://fom.ru/bezopasnost-i-pravo/13239 (accessed March 3, 2018).

8. Kathryn Hendley, *Trying to Make Law Matter* (Ann Arbor: University of Michigan Press, 1996), 34–45.

9. Kathryn Hendley, "Legal Development in Post-Soviet Russia," *Post-Soviet Affairs* 13, no. 3 (July–September 1997): 228–51.

10. In addition, the court famously took on the question of the legality of the Communist Party, giving rise to a lengthy and rather bizarre trial. David Remnick, *Lenin's Tomb: The Last Days of the Soviet Empire* (New York: Vintage, 1994), 494–530. The text of the court's decision is available in *Vestnik Konstitutsionnogo Suda*, nos. 4–5 (1993): 37–64.

11. Kathryn Hendley, "Remaking an Institution: The Transition in Russia from State Arbitrazh to Arbitrazh Courts," *American Journal of Comparative Law* 46, no. 1 (1998): 93–127.

12. Peter H. Solomon Jr. and Todd S. Foglesong, *Courts and Transition in Russia: The Challenge of Judicial Reform* (Boulder, CO: Westview, 2000).

13. There are two words for "law" in Russian: *pravo* and *zakon*. The former conveys a notion of law that incorporates human rights, while the latter invokes a more positivistic notion of statutory law. Although the phrases used to capture the goals of legal reform in Russia used by Gorbachev (*pravovoe gosudarstvo*) and Putin (*gospodstvo zakonnosti*) seem similar on the surface, they actually capture very different notions of the role of state and society.

14. William Burnham and Jeffrey Kahn, "Russia's Criminal Procedure Code Five Years Out," *Review of Central & East European Law* 33, no. 1 (2008): 1–93.

15. Mikhail Khodorkovsky was arrested in the fall of 2003 on charges of fraud, tax evasion, and theft of state property in the course of privatization. At every stage of the process, the authorities skirted on the edge of legal proprieties, typically obeying the literal letter of the law (though not always), but trampling on its spirit. His case became a cause célèbre among the international human rights community, acting to confirm the common wisdom about the dysfunction of the Russian legal system. In December 2013, Putin pardoned Khodorkovsky and released him from prison. For background on this case, see Richard Sakwa, *Putin and the Oligarch: The Khodorkovsky-Yukos Affair* (New York: Palgrave Macmillan, 2014).

16. Ella Paneyakh, "Faking Performance Together: Systems of Performance Evaluation in Russian Enforcement Agencies and Production of Bias and Privilege," *Post-Soviet Affairs* 30, nos. 2–3 (2014): 115–36.

17. Gordon B. Smith, "Putin, the Procuracy, and the New Criminal Procedure Code," in *Public Policy and Law in Russia: In Search of a Unified Legal and Political Space*, ed. Robert Sharlet and Ferdinand Feldbrugge (Leiden: Martinus Nijhoff, 2005), 169–85.

18. Vladimir Ryzhkov, "Putin's War on NGOs Threatens Russia's Future," *Moscow Times*, July 29, 2014, https://themoscowtimes.com/articles/putins-war-on-ngos-threatens-russias-future-37786 (accessed March 3, 2018). Rebuffed by Russian courts, affected NGOs have taken their claims to the European Court of Human Rights. Charles Diggins, "Russia to Answer for Its 'Foreign Agent' Law in European Court of Human Rights," *Bellona*, October 5, 2017, http://bellona.org/news/russian-human-rights-issues/russian-ngo-law/2017-10-russia-to-answer-for-its-foreign-agent-law-in-european-court-of-human-rights (accessed March 3, 2018).

19. Alena Ledeneva, *Can Russia Modernise? Sistema, Power Networks and Informal Governance* (New York: Cambridge University Press, 2013).

20. Alexei Trochev, "Judicial Selection in Russia: Towards Accountability and Centralization," in *Appointing Judges in an Age of Judicial Power: Critical Perspectives from Around the World*, ed. Peter H. Russell and Kate Malleson (Toronto: University of Toronto Press, 2006).

21. "Obzor rezul'tatov deyatel'nosti za 2015 god," n.d., http://www.vkks.ru/publication/39178 (accessed March 3, 2018).

22. Vadim Volkov, Arina Dmitrieva, Mikhail Pozdniakov, and Kirill Titaev, *Rossiiskie sud'i: sotsiologicheskoe issledovaniie professii* (Moscow: Norma, 2016), 87.

23. On the differences between common law and civil law legal traditions, see John Henry Merryman, *The Civil Law Tradition: An Introduction to the Legal Systems of Western Europe and Latin America*, 2nd ed. (Stanford, CA: Stanford University Press, 1985).

24. In a series of polls conducted between 1994 and 2016, Russians were asked whether they trusted state institutions, including courts. Over that time, the percentage of those surveyed who completely trust the courts fluctuated between from 8 to 25 percent, settling at 22 percent in 2016. A plurality of respondents have taken a middle-of-the-road position, while those who distrust the courts has held steady at about 20 percent. See http://www.levada.ru/2016/10/13/institutsionalnoe-doverie-2 (accessed March 3, 2018).

25. Infometr, "Voprosy opublikovaniia sudebnykh aktov na saitakh sudov obshchei iurisdiktsii," http://infometer.org/analitika/voprosyi-opublikovaniya-sudebnyix-aktov-na-sajtax-sudov-obshhej-yurisdikczii (accessed March 3, 2018).

26. The fifteen regional constitutional courts are not institutionally linked to the Russian Constitutional Court. Alexei Trochev, "Less Democracy, More Courts: The Puzzle of Judicial Review in Russia," *Law & Society Review* 38, no. 3 (September 2004): 513–38.

27. http://www.ksrf.ru/ru/Petition/Pages/NewReference.aspx (accessed March 3, 2018).

28. Trochev, *Judging Russia: Constitutional Court in Russian Politics, 1990–2006* (Cambridge: Cambridge University Press, 2008), 122–23.

29. Trochev, *Judging Russia*, 120–21.

30. Trochev, *Judging Russia*, 139–59.

31. Alexei Trochev, "The Zigzags of Judicial Power: The Constitutional Court in Russian Politics, 1990–2003" (PhD diss., Department of Political Science, University of Toronto, 2005), 177.

32. See http://www.cdep.ru/index.php?id=79 (accessed March 3, 2018).

33. Kathryn Hendley, "The Puzzling Non-Consequences of Societal Distrust of Courts: Explaining the Use of Courts in Russia," *Cornell International Law Journal* 45, no. 3 (Fall 2012): 527–58.

34. Kathryn Hendley, "Assessing the Role of Justice-of-the-Peace Courts in the Russian Judicial System," *Review of Central and East European Law* 37, no. 4 (2012): 373–93.

35. "Osnovnye operativnye statisticheskie pokazateli sudov obshchei iurisdiktsii za 2016 g.," http://www.cdep.ru/index.php?id=79 (accessed March 3, 2018).

36. Solomon and Foglesong report that in the mid-1990s, the statutorily imposed deadlines for resolving cases were not met in more than 25 percent and 15 percent of criminal and civil cases, respectively. *Courts and Transition in Russia*, 118–19. The 2016 data collected by the courts indicate that over 98 percent of civil and 91 percent criminal cases are resolved within the deadlines established by law, http://www.cdep.ru/index.php?id=79 (accessed March 3, 2018). Even so, delays remain a serious concern. Litigants are entitled to seek compensation from the court when cases are unreasonably delayed. In extreme instances, parties can take their complaints to the European Court of Human Rights.

37. In 2016, only about 1 percent of cases originated in the regional courts.

38. "Obzor deiatel'nosti federal'nykh sudov obshchei iurisdiktsii i mirovykh sudei za 2010 god," *Rossiiskaia iustitsiia*, no. 9 (2011): 56; "Obzor deiatel'nosti federal'nykh sudov obshchei iurisdiktsii i mirovykh sudei v 2004 godu," *Rossiiskaia iustitsiia*, no. 6 (2005): 29. When taken as a percentage of the total criminal cases, the share of cases heard by juries is infinitesimal.

39. The low acquittal rate in nonjury trials is a bit misleading. In 2016, two-thirds of criminal cases were resolved through the Russian version of plea bargaining without a full-fledged trial. "Osnovnye operativye statisticheskie pokazateli sudov obshchei iurisdiktsii za

2016 g." On plea bargaining, see Olga B. Semukhina and K. Michael Reynolds, "Plea Bargaining Implementation and Acceptance in Modern Russia," *International Criminal Justice Review*, 19, no. 4 (2009): 400–432.

40. There was a corresponding decrease in those who refused to express an opinion. "Reputatsiia sudov i sudei."

41. "Osnovanye pokazateli raboty arbitrazhnykh sudov v 1996–1997 godakh," *Vestnik Vysshego Arbitrazhnogo Suda*, no. 4 (1998): 21–23; "Spravka o rassmotrennykh delakh arbitrazhnymi sudami sub'ektov Rossiiskoi Federatsii v 2012–2013 gg.," "Sudebno-arbitrazhnaia statistika o rassmotrennykh delakh arbitrazhnymi sudami Rossiiskoi Federatsii v 2002–2005 godakh," *Vestnik Vosshego Arbitrazhnogo Suda*, no. 5 (2006): 22–23; "Otchet o rabote arbitrazhnykh sudov sub'ektov Rossiiskoi Federatsii v 2016," http://www.cdep.ru/index.php?id= 79&item=3833 (accessed March 3, 2018).

42. "European Court of Human Rights: Analysis of Statistics 2016," http://www.echr.coe. int/Documents/Stats_analysis_2016_ENG.pdf (accessed March 3, 2018). See generally Freek ven der Vet, "Protecting Rights in Strasbourg: Developing a Research Agenda for Analyzing International Litigation from Russia," *Laboratorium* 6, no. 3 (2014): 105–18.

43. "O vnesenii izmenenii v Federal'nyi konstitutsionnyi zakon 'O Konstitutsionnom Sude Rossiiskoi Federatsii,'" Federal'nyi zakon ot 14 dekabria 2015 g. No. 7-FKZ, *Rossiiskaia gazeta*, December 16, 2015, https://rg.ru/2015/12/15/ks-site-dok.html (accessed March 3, 2018).

44. Sewell Chan, "Russia's 'Gay Propaganda' Laws Are Illegal, European Court Rules," *New York Times*, June 20, 2017, https://www.nytimes.com/2017/06/20/world/europe/russia-gay-propaganda.html (accessed March 3, 2018). On Russia's record for implementation, see Rene Provost, "Teetering on the Edge of Legal Nihilism: Russia and the Evolving European Human Rights Regime," *Human Rights Quarterly* 37, no. 2 (2015): 289–40.

45. Ekaterina Moiseeva and Dmitrii Skugarevskii, "Rynok iuridicheskikh uslug v Rossii: chto govorit statistika," Seriia "Analiticheskie obzory po problemam pravoprimeneniia (St. Petersburg: IPP EUCPB, 2016), http://enforce.spb.ru/images/lawfirms_report_e_version.pdf (accessed March 3, 2018).

46. See http://fparf.ru/documents/council_documents/council_reports/13947 (accessed March 3, 2018).

47. Eugene Huskey, "The Bar's Triumph or Shame? The Founding of Chambers of Advocates in Putin's Russia," in *Public Policy and Law in Russia: In Search of a Unified Legal and Political Space*, ed. Robert Sharlet and Ferdinand Feldbrugge (Leiden: Martinus Nijhoff, 2005), 149–67.

48. For an analysis of the challenges associated with inculcating professional ethics among Russian lawyers, see Katrina P. Lewinbuk, "Perestroika or Just Perfunctory? The Scope and Significance of Russia's New Legal Ethics Laws," *Journal of the Legal Profession* 35, no. 1 (2010): 25–80.

Chapter Four

Civil Society and Protest

Alfred B. Evans Jr.

Scholars in the social sciences think of civil society as the sphere of activity that is initiated, organized, and carried out primarily by citizens and not directed by the state. Larry Diamond, for example, characterizes civil society as "the realm of organized social life that is voluntary, self-generating, at least partially self-supporting, autonomous from the state, and bound by a legal order or set of shared rules."[1] Scholarly writings on civil society in Russia bear the imprint of two different perspectives. Those scholars whose perspective is shaped by the "democratization framework" argue that a robust civil society would contribute to the growth and consolidation of democratic political institutions in Russia.[2] That point of view, which is rooted in British and American historical experiences, raises the hope that civil society will serve as a counterweight to the power of the state and thus expects that there will be continuing conflict between social organizations and the state.[3] Another group of writings on civil society has a more pragmatic orientation,[4] primarily addressing the question of whether nongovernmental organizations (NGOs) in Russia "help people solve their problems."[5] Scholars of that school of thought emphasize the usefulness of partnership between NGOs and agencies of the state in providing services to groups of people,[6] though those scholars note that NGOs that collaborate with the state may still try to preserve a degree of independence.

HISTORICAL BACKGROUND

The political regime of the Soviet Union was hostile toward the idea of civil society because its leaders saw any independence of organized groups as threatening their monopoly of power. Russian historians have confirmed that even during the earliest years of the Soviet system, the Communist Party wanted to eliminate independent groups, and that the party intensified its control of social organizations from the 1920s to the 1930s.[7] During the 1950s and 1960s a variety of informal and unofficial social groups did come into existence quietly, and there are reports that the number of groups that were not sponsored by the Communist Party increased during the 1970s and early 1980s.[8] A dissident movement voiced open criticism of the Soviet regime by the 1960s, often at great personal cost for its members, but the active participants in that movement were a tiny minority. It is likely that most people in the Soviet Union who had heard of the dissenters were indifferent or even hostile toward them, so that dissidents "failed to strike a responsive chord among the masses at large."[9]

After he came to power in 1985, Mikhail Gorbachev opened the way for a major shift in the relationship between the state and society. Part of his program of radical reform allowed citizens to create "informal" groups (*neformalye*), which were not controlled by the Communist Party. The number of those groups grew very rapidly; in 1989 the party newspaper, *Pravda*, said that around sixty thousand informal groups had come into existence.[10] Those groups were devoted to a wide range of activities, but many of them asserted demands for change in the policies of the state, and some called for change that was more basic than Gorbachev had wanted. Soon some Western scholars spoke very optimistically about the emergence of civil society in the Soviet Union, even suggesting that the shift in power between society and the state could not be reversed.[11]

CIVIL SOCIETY IN POST-SOVIET RUSSIA

Assessments of civil society in Russia several years after the collapse of rule by the Communist Party and the breakup of the USSR painted a largely negative picture. Among scholars there was a consensus that the boom in civil society organizations under Gorbachev had been followed by a slump in post-Soviet Russia in the 1990s.[12] The legacy of the Soviet system in political culture was a source of problems for organizations that sought to unite groups of Russians for the pursuit of common interests. Ken Jowitt contends that the experience of living under communist rule led citizens to see a dichotomy between the official realm and the private realm.[13] In the unofficial culture of such citizens, the sphere of political life was regarded as "suspect, distasteful, and possibly dangerous,"[14] and as sharply distinct from the sphere of private life, the only area where intimacy could be found and ethical conduct was possible.[15] Nongovernmental organizations were seen as part of the public sphere. On the basis of data from surveys, Marc Morjé Howard concluded that "most people in post-communist societies still strongly mistrust and avoid joining any kind of formal organizations,"[16] and he showed that the rate of membership in voluntary associations is lower in postcommunist countries than in the older democracies, or in post-authoritarian countries that had not been under communist control.[17]

Another serious problem for Russian social organizations in the post-Soviet period was the deep dislocation in that country's economy during the 1990s. Because of interruptions in the payment of wages and pensions and a high rate of inflation, most people in Russia were preoccupied with the struggle for economic survival and did not have the means to offer financial support for nongovernmental organizations, even if they had wanted to do that. Thus it is not surprising that most of those organizations did not even attempt to raise funds by expanding the ranks of their members or soliciting donations from potential supporters.[18] In surveys, the leaders of nongovernmental organizations in Russia often said that their biggest problem was a lack of financial support for their activities.[19] During the 1990s a few of those organizations received grants from foreign sources,[20] but that kind of support had mixed effects, on the one hand raising the level of professional competence of the leaders of the organizations, but on the other hand discouraging the leaders of such groups from seeking to build a base of support in their society.[21] In summary, civil society in Russia was weak, on the whole, by the end of the 1990s, and the two main reasons for the marginal condition of most of the organizations in civil society were the distrust of the public sphere and the unfavorable economic circumstances for social organizations.

CIVIL SOCIETY UNDER PUTIN

After Vladimir Putin became president of Russia in 2000, he consolidated control over the political system, subordinating the parliament, regional governments, political parties, and television networks to domination by the national executive leadership. Within a few years Putin turned his attention to bringing civil society into an integrated system of support for the centralized state.[22] While his speeches frequently mentioned the importance of civil society, they made it clear that he envisioned social groups as assisting the state in addressing tasks that serve the needs of the whole nation.[23] Putin is suspicious toward nongovernmental organizations in Russia that receive funding from abroad, especially if those organizations are at all involved in politics. In 2006 the parliament passed changes in the regulations for NGOs. Some groups complained that the requirements for registration and reporting under the new laws were onerous, but it is not clear whether the new procedures forced any genuinely active organizations to close down.[24]

Putin also enhanced positive incentives for organizations in civil society to provide the kinds of services that the state considered most valuable. In

2006 the federal government began to award grants to Russian NGOs through a competitive process, offering an alternative to Western funding.[25] The political regime also took the initiative in forming groups that some scholars have called "government-organized nongovernmental organizations," or GONGOs. Perhaps the most prominent of these were a series of state-sponsored youth groups, but the fact that each of these groups has been replaced or has become inactive[26] implies that none has been very successful. Another innovation of the Putin leadership that was intended to ensure a closer relationship between the state and civil society was the Public Chamber of the Russian Federation.[27] In 2004 Putin proposed the establishment of a public chamber, "as a platform for extensive dialogue, where citizens' initiatives could be presented and discussed in detail,"[28] and a law adopted by the parliament made it possible for that body to begin functioning in early 2006. The president plays a major role in appointing the members of the Public Chamber, who are said to be representatives of organizations in civil society. Though some of the members of that body have spoken out as individuals on controversial issues, over time there has not been enough of a consensus among the members to make it possible for them to attempt to exert influence on the resolution of any major controversial question. Similarly, public chambers at the regional and local levels do not seem to have played a significant role in resolving issues raised by citizens.[29]

THE ANTI-MONETIZATION PROTESTS OF 2005

Although there were protests in Russia during the 1990s, scholars disagree on the level of protest activity in the country during that decade. Most observers have depicted the population of Russia as politically passive in that period,[30] but some scholars assert that relatively large numbers of Russians took part in protests in the 1990s, mostly in connection with strikes by workers in reaction to wage arrears.[31] Graeme Robertson has found that there was a sharp decline in protests in Russia in 1999 and that the level of protest in the country remained low during Vladimir Putin's first term as president, from 2000 to 2004.[32]

The situation was to change dramatically in early 2005. The protests that erupted on a startling scale at that time arose in response to change, or "reform" in certain social benefits, or *l'goty*, for large numbers of Russians. Those *l'goty* guaranteed their recipients certain services, such as public transportation, medicines, housing, and utilities, either free of charge or at reduced rates.[33] Those benefits were provided for people in certain categories, including pensioners, veterans, the disabled, single parents, and orphans, altogether comprising about one-quarter of the population of the country. The Putin administration proposed to eliminate those entitlements and replace them with cash payments to those who had been eligible for the *l'goty*. The legislation instituting that change was adopted by the federal parliament in August 2004 after little debate and came into effect on January 1, 2005.[34] Those who had been eligible for such entitlements lost their access to free transportation and medications and lost the subsidies for housing and utilities on the first day of 2005, but they would not receive cash payments until the end of January. In addition, the funding that the federal government allocated for assistance to the regional governments was only a fraction of what would have been sufficient to compensate individual recipients for expenses they would now have to pay.

The result was an explosion of discontent and anger, coming mainly from elderly Russians, which rapidly took on alarming proportions. Protest meetings were held in and around Moscow and St. Petersburg on January 9 and 10 and almost immediately took place in other cities. The first protests were largely spontaneous, organized by elderly citizens themselves, and political parties were caught by surprise by those protests.[35] Within a few weeks, similar protests had broken out in eighty of Russia's eighty-nine regions. The number of Russians who took part in those protest actions cannot be known, but it consisted at least of tens of thousands of people, and probably hundreds of thousands. There is a consensus that the demonstrations of discontent against the replacement of entitlements were by far the largest protests to take place since Putin had become president,[36] and the first on a nationwide scale under Putin.[37] In many places the protesters blocked traffic on streets or highways, and in some cities there were physical clashes with bus drivers who refused to allow pensioners to ride for free.[38]

The intensity of the reaction to the replacement of *l'goty* seemed to catch the authorities by surprise. Generally, local police forces responded passively to the protests, as they did not attempt to hinder the movements of protesters or to break up their demonstrations.[39] In his first speech after the protests began, President Putin defended the benefits reform in principle, but he criticized the government for allegedly mishandling the reform and tried to shift the blame to regional and local leaders.[40] He also began to offer concessions to the opponents of the reform, calling for the acceleration of an increase in pensions and the allocation of additional funds to regions for compensation payments.[41] Many regional leaders also offered concessions that were intended to placate the protesters. Officials of the federal government and broadcasts on national television networks alleged that a few "instigators" or "provocateurs" had been behind the demonstrations and had manipulated the masses in the streets to serve particular political objectives.[42] Though police refrained from using force to disperse demonstrations, after some protests, indictments for administrative violations were issued to the organizers of the events.[43] The political elite also mobilized thousands of its followers to march in the streets in support of the monetization of social benefits. By the middle of March 2005, the wave of protest actions had largely subsided.[44]

The spontaneous protests of citizens in January and February of 2005 did not leave a substantial organizational legacy.[45] Nonetheless, those demonstrations did leave a distinct imprint in the memory of members of Russian society. Many thousands of ordinary people had risen up boldly to confront the political authorities. The regime had not carried out massive repression of the protesters; most of those who took part in public rallies returned safely to their homes afterward. In addition, when it was confronted with vehement discontent, the political leadership had backed down, making concessions in an effort to placate those who expressed their rage in public protests. The example of the protests against the monetization of social benefits in early 2005 has served as a model for many groups that have resorted to public protests to urge changes in policies on various levels in Russia since that time.

NARROWLY FOCUSED, DEFENSIVE PROTEST MOVEMENTS

The importance of public protests has grown in Russia in recent years, reflecting a trend that has been evident roughly since 2005.[46] It appears that the protest movements that have been most successful in gaining broad bases of popular support have been influenced by the protest movement of early 2005.[47] When citizens in Russia have been moved to protest against a decision, they usually have objected to a change that threatened to disturb a situation that had seemed to be stable and acceptable. In each case the demands of the protesters with respect to government policies have been concrete and specific, and in each case the orientation of the protest movement has been essentially defensive, in the sense that the movement sought to return to a state of affairs that had existed before a change was initiated and to restore benefits that people had assumed they enjoyed as a matter of right.

Typically, such groups have not called for the radical transformation of Russian political institutions. We should be aware, however, that some other movements that have engaged in public protests in Russia in recent years have supported goals that would entail fundamental changes in their country's political system in accordance with liberal democratic values. Yet experts on Russian society and politics point out that the organizations that have carried out demonstrations on behalf of broad, abstract political principles, such as freedom of speech or the right to assemble, have a very narrow base of support among the people of Russia. Maria Lipman acknowledges that in Russia "today there is a shortage of public demand" for such principles as freedom of the press and the accountability of government, and she reports that the majority in the country "does not care much about human rights violations or compromised democratic procedures."[48] The organizations that have not accepted the general outlines of the master frame of protest movements that emerged from the anti-monetization movement of early 2005 have not really sought a broad base of support within Russian society.[49]

In contrast, most of the groups engaging in protests have focused on issues that are relevant to the everyday lives of most people and usually are grounded in the self-interest of average citizens. Samuel Greene and Graeme Robertson confirm that "the greater part of protests are connected with much more localized dissatisfaction, both physical and material, and therefore their ideational basis has a much less abstract character."[50] The 2012 annual report from Russia's Public Chamber affirmed that the mass inclusion of citizens in protests "is observed when restrictions or infringements of rights directly touch on their lives or interests."[51] Typically, such protests over specific issues do not openly challenge the legitimacy of the national political regime but appeal to the authorities at the highest level to intervene to solve problems.[52] The examples of many protest movements show that Russians can be moved into action when they feel the direct impact of changes that damage their interests.[53]

LARGE PROTESTS IN THE WINTER OF 2011–2012

In December 2011 protests in Russia rose to a new level of magnitude in terms of the number of people taking part in them. The demonstrations that began right after the parliamentary elections of December 4, 2011, attracted several thousand participants, focused on the charge of election fraud, and demanded new elections.[54] Then, on December 10, tens of thousands took part in a demonstration in favor of "honest elections" (*chestnye vybory*) on Bolotnaya Square, which is not far from the Kremlin.[55] Even larger crowds gathered for protest rallies in the capital on behalf of the same cause on December 24, 2011, and February 4, 2012.[56] From forty thousand to one hundred thousand people attended each of these three protests in Moscow in favor of fair elections, with smaller numbers of people taking part in protests by that movement in other cities across Russia on the same days. After the presidential election was held in early March 2012, the number of people taking part in demonstrations decreased until a large crowd came together in Moscow again for a protest on May 6, 2012, on the eve of Putin's inauguration.[57]

The "honest elections" movement gave voice to the frustration that a feeling of powerlessness had generated among a substantial segment of the population of Russia. Many of those who took part in protests said that they had been reminded of their lack of control over the future of their country in

September 2011 when it was announced that Vladimir Putin would run for president in 2012, on the basis of an arrangement that had been made with Dmitry Medvedev. In an instant it was clear that the crucial decision about the selection of a president had already been made. So even before the parliamentary elections were held, a substantial number of citizens of Russia felt that they had been treated with implicit contempt. During the parliamentary election in early December 2011, many people believed that irrefutable evidence of fraud had been shown, in large part through the use of digital cameras and smartphones at polling places, furnishing visual images that spread rapidly through the internet. A critical mass of resentment had gathered enough force to send tens of thousands of Russians into the streets to express their anger over the perceived violation of their sense of dignity.

Surveys reported in the Russian press showed that a majority of those who took part in the protests in favor of honest elections were young or middle-aged adults who had higher education, lived in large cities, and worked as professionals.[58] Most of the participants in the large-scale protests also used the internet, which gives them access to information that does not come from the national television networks, which are controlled by the government and are the main source of news for most Russians. Many of the protesters were also plugged into social media such as Facebook and VKontakte, which makes it possible to inform large numbers of people instantaneously about planned events and makes it easier to assemble large crowds for protests.[59] As this information implies, another large segment of the population of Russia is quite different in terms of its sources of information and its attitudes, and the base of support for Putin is found mainly in that part of the people of Russia that consists particularly of those with lower levels of education and those who live outside the largest cities in the country.

THE DECLINE OF OPPOSITIONAL POLITICAL PROTESTS

In 2013, Olga Kryshtanovskaia, a Russian sociologist, noted that the number of people taking part in protests against the political regime in Russia had decreased sharply after the presidential election in March 2012.[60] She argued that the commitment of some of the people who had participated in earlier protests had wavered, and it seems likely that fear of persecution by the state may have had an effect on those people. Another problem that may have discouraged participation in political protests was the widespread perception that such demonstrations have not produced any concrete accomplishments. A survey of those taking part in a protest in Moscow by the Levada Center in January 2013 found that few of those people thought that such actions had obtained concessions from the state.[61]

The Putin leadership responded to the large-scale protests that began in December 2011 by further tightening the regulation of NGOs in a way that is designed to eliminate or marginalize organizations that associate with opposition to the political authorities. In 2012, a new law required organizations receiving financial support from abroad and engaging in political activities to register as "foreign agents." In 2013, the Ministry of Justice began to examine the records of NGOs that were suspected of having received grants from abroad. In some cases, along with inspectors from that ministry, officials from other divisions of the state descended on the offices of an organization at the same time, in force. In 2014 that law was amended so that the Ministry of Justice could classify an NGO as a foreign agent without that organization's involvement or consent.[62] The definition of "political activity" in the law is highly ambiguous and has been interpreted very broadly in practice.

Funding from abroad for organizations in civil society in Russia has dwindled in recent years, partly because laws adopted by the Russian state have discouraged international donors from trying to assist groups in Russia, and also because interest in Russian civil society among most foreign governments and foundations has waned in recent years.[63] The current scarcity of funding from abroad has created serious problems for some NGOs in Russia, such as those devoted to the protection of human rights, but it has not had much impact on organizations that never received grants from foreign sources. As the political regime took steps to close opportunities for political opponents, laws of 2012 and 2014 sharply increased the fines for individuals and organizations that take part in protests without permission from local authorities and added a penalty of prison time for repeat offenders.[64]

While money from sources outside their country has slowed to a trickle, funding in grants to NGOs in Russia from the state has grown.[65] The total of presidential grants to NGOs in Russia has increased greatly during the last several years, and there are grants from regional and municipal governments to social organizations. Well-informed sources say that there also has been a growth in philanthropy from large companies, which has benefited some NGOs.[66] Although some grants have been awarded to organizations that have criticized the central leadership, the general effect of discouraging foreign support for groups in Russian society and encouraging greater reliance on money from the Russian state is to ensure that most NGOs in that country will work within the boundaries of a consensus.

Since the time of the largest demonstrations in the winter of 2011–2012, Putin has depicted those taking part in political protests as a minority drawn from the urban intelligentsia and has sought to isolate that vocal minority from the rest of Russian society. He has appealed to the "silent majority" of Russians to reject the criticism that is voiced by the political opposition and to rally around his political regime. The regime has used the mass media, especially national television networks, to depict the protesters in the most negative terms possible. At the same time, Putin has praised the majority of Russians for their patriotism and devotion to traditional values. Widely publicized incidents like the performance in a cathedral in Moscow by the punk rock group Pussy Riot, which was protesting support for Putin by the Russian Orthodox Church, have played into the hands of the regime by reinforcing the impression that the opponents of the leadership are mocking the values of the majority. The government of Russia and the hierarchy of that denomination have had a close relationship from the beginning of the post-Soviet period, but Putin has extolled the merits of the Orthodox religion even more enthusiastically since the protests of late 2011 and early 2012, insisting that the Orthodox Church is one of the main sources of Russia's national identity.

RECENT TRENDS AMONG NGOs

The leaders of some NGOs in Russia have found that they are more effective in addressing the needs of groups in their society when they collaborate closely with officials in local or regional government.[67] Such collaboration implies that the NGO leaders will work within the established "rules of the game," which reportedly will provide more opportunities to influence policies than acting in opposition.[68] It is said that cooperation with local officials creates the opportunity for the growth of informal relationships, which are of primary importance.[69] Meri Kulmala observes that NGOs that are concerned with child welfare in Russia have served as agents of change in policy by providing expertise for decision making.[70] We should be aware that social organizations are able to play a role in shaping policies only if their goals are compatible with the main values of Russia's national political leadership. That consideration does not create problems for NGO leaders who can credibly interpret the priorities of the central authorities as consistent with newer methods of assisting groups who need better services.

In the period of over a quarter of a century since the Soviet system came to an end, there has been remarkable change in the means of communication with the growth of the internet and the proliferation of mobile devices. In Russia, the dramatic increase in access to the internet and the rise of social media, blogs, and a variety of websites have created new opportunities for nongovernmental organizations and social movements. Communication through social media was an important factor in attracting people to the large-scale protests in Russia in the winter of 2011 and 2012.[71] Some NGOs that were already operating in the country in earlier years have lately taken advantage of the newer means of communication. Other groups, including some environmentalists, have sprung up recently, creating "network" organizations that operate almost exclusively online.[72] Sometimes the role of leadership is not important for such networks, as they have little formal organization and are highly decentralized.[73] For some other networks, however, such as that created by Aleksei Naval'ny, the personality of an individual leader is very important. We also should be aware that the internet and social media make it possible for groups such as those of feminist activists to reach a much larger audience while they also carry out demonstrations on the streets.[74] Valerie Sperling points out that such groups seek to get their messages not only to state officials but to "a broader range of citizens,"[75] which was not as true of Russian feminist groups in the 1990s. The Blue Buckets Society, which defends the interests of the owners of automobiles, is another example of a decentralized organization that links many people by electronic means such as social media, blogs, and email messages, and also encourages Russian citizens to be more assertive in dealing with the state and exerting pressure on motorists of the elite.[76]

RECENT PROTESTS

At the local level, protests against actions by local governments and businesses have continued. The largest protests in defense of concrete interests in Russia during the last several years were those in Moscow in 2017 in reaction to the city government's "renovation" (or "demolition") program. In February 2017, Sergei Sobianin, the mayor of Moscow, unveiled a plan to replace a large number of old apartment buildings with new ones, and he publicly received approval from President Putin.[77] In the initial version of that plan, in the draft of a law that was introduced in the lower house of the national legislature (the Duma), the residents of an apartment could have been ordered to move from it and would have had very limited grounds for contesting that order in court. Though many people who lived in old apartments that were in poor condition probably welcomed the opportunity to move, many others raised an outcry, charging that their right of ownership of property would be violated. Thousands of Muscovites were aroused to oppose that proposal as they gathered in their buildings, in their neighborhoods, and in demonstrations in the center of Moscow. Feverish communication through social media linked people of districts all around the city and made it possible to form groups such as Moskvichi Protiv Snosa (Muscovites against Demolition).

There was also open and exceptionally frank criticism of the proposed law from individuals and institutions at the elite level. Most dramatically, in late April, President Putin announced that he would not sign a law that did not respect people's right of ownership. After that, representatives of the national government worked with officials of the city of Moscow and leading members of the Duma to revise the law. The changes in the draft law included a guarantee that almost all of the residents who moved would be offered new apartments near their old buildings. Another change specified that the people who decided to take part in the program could choose between getting an apartment with floor space equal to that in their old one, an apartment with market value equal to that of their old one, or a cash payment determined by the value of their old apartment. After many revisions were accepted, the law was approved by both houses of the national legislature and signed by President Putin on July 1, 2017. Once again, protests by large numbers of people were followed by concessions from the state. And once again, people who were dissatisfied with the actions of a lower level of authority had appealed to the country's highest leadership to intervene. Yet even though the law on the renovation of housing was amended extensively, some Muscovites still distrust the government of their city and do not believe that it will keep its promises during the implementation of the program.

The most recent protests that have attracted a great deal of attention in Russia and have put intense pressure on local and regional officials have been provoked by problems created by landfills in the region outside Moscow. The number of those dumps has decreased during the last several years, while the amount of garbage coming from the city of Moscow and the surrounding area has increased. When the accumulation of garbage in a landfill has gone beyond its intended limits, environmental problems for nearby towns have intensified. In June 2017, Vladimir Putin held one of his televised shows in which Russians can call him to ask questions or make requests. On that occasion, one of the calls that he fielded came from people in the town of Balashikha in the region outside Moscow, who complained about the pollution coming from a garbage dump near their homes. After Putin promised to look into the problem, the addition of garbage to that landfill ceased almost immediately.

That was good news for the residents of Balashikha, but people in some other towns in the same region worried that even more trash would be directed to dumps near them. People in those towns showed themselves to be increasingly uneasy about gases such as methane and hydrogen sulfide that were seeping out of those landfills until discontent reached the boiling point in the town of Volokolamsk.[78] On March 21, noxious fumes from a nearby landfill made it necessary to provide medical treatment for dozens of children in that town who showed symptoms of poisoning. Thousands of people in that town took part in a protest meeting, where they demanded immediate action. When the governor of the region visited Volokolamsk, a large crowd of local residents vented their anger at him, forcing him to retreat from the scene while he was pelted with snowballs. Some people in the crowd roughed up the chief executive of the local district, who had come with the governor. Soon the governor relieved that official of his duties, though that did not satisfy the local people. In a chain reaction, protests broke out in several other towns in the region that are near garbage dumps. Again average people were appealing to the central political leadership to rescue them from bad decisions by officials on lower levels. A simple solution to the problem in this area is not likely because of years of inadequate investment in infrastructure to keep pace with commercial construction in Moscow and its suburbs, but the regional government has said that measures are being taken to decrease the air pollution from landfills.[79] The police have carried out arrests and searches of the homes of the leaders of the protests in Volokolamsk and the mayor of that town.[80] The protests against pollution from landfills fit the pattern of demonstrations calling for specific changes in policies and not demanding the transformation of the political regime.[81] Yet, when citizens charge that policies have negative effects, they almost always complain that their rights have been violated, which implies flaws in the process of governing.[82] And if lower-level officials accuse protesters of aiming for a revolt and serving foreign powers, and if they try to intimidate the leaders of protests with the threat of violence or imprisonment, a confrontation between citizens and the authorities may take on broader ideological overtones.[83]

CONCLUSION: MULTIPLE NARRATIVES

We have traced three different trends among organizations in civil society in Russia since the early years of this century. First, the NGOs that depended primarily on funding from abroad and were most critical of the Putin regime have found it more difficult to function, since foreign funding has decreased sharply, harassment by officials has intensified, and there is not widespread support for such organizations in Russian society. Also, as Laura Henry has observed, no new generation of environmentalists is coming onto the scene to replace the older generation of experts who have had strong links with Westerners.[84] Second, a number of nongovernmental organizations are in a more advantageous position now because of increased financial assistance from the state, a rise in support (for some of them) from individual contributors and businesses, and (for some of them) the cultivation of opportunities to collaborate with decision makers in shaping policies. Third, some organizations, many of which have come into existence in recent years, make extensive use of the internet to appeal to their target audiences, which in some cases are small and in other cases are large. Most of those organizations are highly decentralized, but any one of them that has struck a responsive chord in a substantial group of Russian citizens has a base of support that makes it a force for policy makers to consider. Some of those organizations do not seek funding either from international sources or the Russian state. Some of them would like to see fundamental change in their country's political regime, others are independent in their advocacy but are willing to engage in dialogue with decision makers, and still others are service oriented and largely nonpolitical but welcome opportunities to cooperate with the authorities. In summary, there is a high degree of diversity in civil society in contemporary Russia, with different types of organizations going down different paths.

Any evaluation of the condition of civil society in Russia today is inevitably influenced by its underlying framework of interpretation. The opening section of this chapter gave an overview of two perspectives on civil society, and the influence of each of those has been evident in scholarly writings about organizations in Russian society. For those who consider the growth of civil society to be important mainly as a basis for a transition to democracy, the results of the trends in civil society in Russia since the collapse of the Soviet system have been disappointing. In the 1990s most of the "informal" groups that had formed while Gorbachev was in power disappeared, while the social organizations that the Communist Party had previously controlled proved largely ineffective. After Vladimir Putin came to power, the state gradually made it more difficult for the organizations that had been its most outspoken critics to operate, and those NGOs that had depended most on foreign funding found it difficult to survive. The hopes that were revived for a short time by the large-scale protests in the winter of 2011–2012 faded away as participation in demonstrations demanding far-reaching political change dwindled after having evoked a negative reaction from the state. All the while Russia's political regime took on an increasingly authoritarian character.

On the other hand, the more pragmatic approach that asks how much the organizations in civil society are capable of solving people's problems leads to a different set of conclusions about trends in Russia in recent years. Scholars who take that approach point out that domestic funding for nongovernmental organizations in Russia has increased, as the national leadership has invited socially oriented NGOs to help it address problems and donations to NGOs from individuals and businesses have become more common. Some researchers have highlighted the experiences of NGOs that have cooperated with government officials and have achieved successes in reshaping policies. Also, the growing use of the internet and the increasing availability of mobile devices have created opportunities for social activists to reach larger audiences. Though protests explicitly calling for a new national leadership usually do not attract many participants, protests that arise in reaction to events that have an impact on people's everyday lives often mobilize average Russians into vigorous action. Sometimes such protests exact concessions from the central authorities, and sometimes they do not, but new protest movements arise every year. The more pragmatic perspective on civil society heightens the awareness of positive developments in some areas of interaction between society and the state. In summary, in view of the variety of experiences of organizations in civil society in that country, perhaps we should borrow terms from Kathryn Hendley's study of law in Russia and admit that no single "monolithic narrative" can adequately comprehend the trends among all those organizations, and we should acknowledge the need to employ "multiple narratives" about their struggles, limitations, and achievements.[85]

DISCUSSION QUESTIONS

1. How were the problems faced by organizations in civil society in the Soviet Union different from those that civil society organizations have faced in Russia since the collapse of the Soviet Union in 1991?

2. The author describes two types of protests in Russia in recent years: those protesting against perceived violations of political principles, and those related to issues that have an impact on the everyday lives of groups of citizens. What are the similarities and differences between those two types of protests? Which type of protest are more Russians likely to support, and why?

3. There are two general perspectives on civil society in Russia, one of which is within a "democratization framework" and the other of which has a more pragmatic orientation. What questions does each of these perspectives lead us to ask as we study civil society in contemporary Russia? How much have organizations in civil society in post-Soviet Russia satisfied the expectations of each of these perspectives?

SUGGESTED READINGS

Argenbright, Robert. *Moscow under Construction: City Building, Place-Based Protest, and Civil Society.* Lanham, MD: Lexington Books, 2016.

Bindman, Eleanor. "The State, Civil Society and Social Rights in Contemporary Russia." *East European Politics* 31, no. 3 (2015): 342–60.

Evans, Alfred B., Jr. "Protest and Civil Society in Russia: The Struggle for Khimki Forest." *Communist and Post-Communist Studies* 45, no. 3 (2012): 233–42.

———. "Protests in Russia: The Example of the Blue Buckets Society." *Demokratizatsiya* 26, no. 1 (2018): 3–24.

Johnson, Janet Elise, Meri Kulmala, and Maija Jäppinen. "Street-Level Practice of Russia's Social Policymaking in Saint Petersburg: Federalism, Informal Politics, and Domestic Violence." *Journal of Social Policy* 45, no. 2 (2016): 287–304.

Kulmala, Meri. "Post-Soviet 'Political'? 'Social' and 'Political' in the Work of Russian Socially Oriented CSOs." *Demokratizatsiya* 24, no. 2 (2016): 199–224.

Østbø, Jardar. "Between Opportunist Revolutionaries and Mediating Spoilers: Failed Politicization of the Russian Truck Drivers' Protest, 2015–2016." *Demokratizatsiya* 25, no. 3 (2017): 279–304.

NOTES

1. Larry Diamond, *Developing Democracy* (Baltimore, MD: Johns Hopkins University Press, 1999), 221.

2. Meri Kulmala, "Post-Soviet 'Political'? 'Social' and 'Political' in the Work of Russian Socially Oriented CSOs," *Demokratizatsiya* 24, no. 2 (2016): 208. An example of a scholarly analysis that is shaped by the democratization framework is Mark R. Beissinger, "'Conventional' and 'Virtual' Civil Societies in Autocratic Regimes," *Comparative Politics* 49, no. 3 (2017): 351.

3. Sarah L. Henderson, "Shaping Civic Advocacy: International and Domestic Politics toward Russia's NGO Sector," in *Advocacy Organizations and Collective Action*, ed. Aseem Prakash and May Kay Gregory (Cambridge: Cambridge University Press, 2010), 255; Janet Elise Johnson, Meri Kulmala, and Maija Jäppinen, "Street-Level Practice of Russia's Social Policymaking in Saint Petersburg: Federalism, Informal Politics, and Domestic Violence," *Journal of Social Policy* 45, no. 2 (2016): 290.

4. Henderson, "Shaping Civic Advocacy," 255.

5. Johnson, Kulmala, and Jäppinen, "Street-Level Practice," 296–97.

6. Henderson, "Shaping Civic Advocacy," 255.

7. Alfred B. Evans Jr., "Civil Society in the Soviet Union?," in *Russian Civil Society: A Critical Assessment*, ed. Alfred B. Evans Jr., Laura A. Henry, and Lisa McIntosh Sundstrom (Armonk, NY: M. E. Sharpe, 2006), 30.

8. Evans, "Civil Society in the Soviet Union?," 42.

9. Walter D. Connor, *Socialism's Dilemmas: State and Society in the Soviet Bloc* (New York: Columbia University Press, 1988), 45. See also Evans, "Civil Society in the Soviet Union?," 43.

10. Evans, "Civil Society in the Soviet Union?," 45.

11. Evans, "Civil Society in the Soviet Union?," 45.

12. Alfred B. Evans Jr., "Recent Assessments of Social Organizations in Russia," *Demokratizatsiya* 10, no. 3 (2002): 322–42.

13. Ken Jowitt, *New World Disorder: The Leninist Extinction* (Berkeley: University of California Press, 1992), 287. Jowitt believes that his generalization applies to all countries that have been under "Leninist," or communist, rule.

14. Jowitt, *New World Disorder*, 293.

15. The annual report of Russia's Public Chamber for 2011 confirmed that Russians typically see the "circle of trust" as extending only to family members and close friends. Obshchestvennaia Palata Rossiiskoi Federatsii, *Doklad o sostoianii grazhdanskogo obshchestva v Rossiiskoi Federatsii za 2011 god* (Moscow: Obshchestvennaia Palata Rossiiskoi Federatsii, 2012), 9.

16. Marc Morjé Howard, *The Weakness of Civil Society in Post-Communist Europe* (Cambridge: Cambridge University Press, 2003), 26.

17. Howard, *The Weakness of Civil Society*, 63.

18. Valerie Sperling, *Organizing Women in Contemporary Russia: Engendering Transition* (Cambridge: Cambridge University Press, 1999), 46, 171–72.

19. In 2012 the annual report of Russia's Public Chamber said that NGOs in Russia "for the most part are extremely weak economically and often are barely surviving." Obshchestvennaia Palata, *Doklad o sostoianii grazhdanskogo obshchestva*, 18.

20. Debra Javeline and Sarah Lindemann-Komarova, "Indigenously Funded Russian Civil Society" (PONARS Eurasia Policy Memo No. 496, November 2017), 1, report that the proportion of all NGOs in Russia receiving funding from Western donors reached a high of 7 percent in 2009.

21. Sarah L. Henderson, *Building Democracy in Contemporary Russia: Western Support for Grassroots Organizations* (Ithaca, NY: Cornell University Press, 2003), 154–55, 165; Lisa McIntosh Sundstrom, *Funding Civil Society: Foreign Assistance and NGO Development in Russia* (Stanford, CA: Stanford University Press, 2006), 99–101.

22. Alfred B. Evans Jr., "Putin's Design for Civil Society," in *Russian Civil Society: A Critical Assessment*, ed. Alfred B. Evans Jr., Laura A. Henry, and Lisa McIntosh Sundstrom (Armonk, NY: M. E. Sharpe, 2006), 149.

23. Evans, "Putin's Design," 149; Sarah L. Henderson, "Civil Society in Russia: State-Society Relations in the Post-Yeltsin Era," *Problems of Communism* 58, no. 3 (2011): 18.

24. Henderson, "Civil Society in Russia," 21; Debra Javeline and Sarah Lindemann-Komarova, "A Balanced Assessment of Russian Civil Society," *Journal of International Affairs* 63, no. 2 (2010): 173–75.

25. Henderson, "Civil Society in Russia," 20; Javeline and Lindemann-Komarova, "A Balanced Assessment," 176–80; Johnson, Kulmala, and Jäppinen, "Street-Level Practice," 15.

26. Ol'ga Churakova and Elena Mukhametshina, "'Edinaia Rossiia' sozdast gruppy bystrogo reagirovaniia dlia uchastiia v ulichnykh aktsiiakh," *Vedomosti*, March 19, 2018.

27. Alfred B. Evans Jr., "The First Steps of Russia's Public Chamber: Representation or Coordination," *Demokratizatsiya* 16, no. 4 (2008): 345–62; James Richter, "Putin and the Public Chamber," *Post-Soviet Affairs* 25, no. 1 (2009): 39–65. Public chambers also have been established in most regions of Russia and in some cities.

28. Evans, "Putin's Design," 151.

29. Abbas Galliamov, "Obshchestvennye palaty okazalis' vredny v krizisnykh situatsiiakh," *Novye izvestiia*, April 16, 2018.

30. Debra Javeline, *Protest and the Politics of Blame: The Russian Response to Unpaid Wages* (Ann Arbor: University of Michigan Press, 2003), 2, 7, 8, 50; Linda J. Cook, *Postcommunist Welfare States: Reform Politics in Russia and Eastern Europe* (Ithaca, NY: Cornell University Press, 2007), 71.

31. Graeme B. Robertson, *The Politics of Protest in Hybrid Regimes: Managing Dissent in Post-Communist Russia* (Cambridge: Cambridge University Press, 2011), 41.

32. Robertson, *The Politics of Protest*, 128, 148.

33. Cook, *Postcommunist Welfare States*, 179; Susanne Wengle and Michael Rasell, "The Monetization of *L'goty*: Changing Patterns of Welfare Politics and Provision in Russia," *Europe-Asia Studies* 60, no. 5 (2008): 740.

34. Cook, *Postcommunist Welfare States*, 179; Wengle and Rasell, "The Monetization of *L'goty*," 740.

35. Robertson, *The Politics of Protest*, 180; Wengle and Rasell, "The Monetization of *L'goty*," 745.

36. "Russians Continue to Protest Social Reforms," *RFE/RL Report*, January 16, 2005.

37. Cook, *Postcommunist Welfare States*, 181.

38. Wengle and Rasell, "The Monetization of *L'goty*," 745.

39. Vladimir Aleksandrov, Ol'ga Gorbunova, and Viktor Troianovskii, "Glas naroda: Vresh', l'gota, ne uidesh'!" *Gazeta*, January 31, 2005.

40. Steven Lee Myers, "After Wide Protests, Putin Softens on His Policy of Cutting Benefits," *New York Times*, January 18, 2005.

41. Cook, *Postcommunist Welfare States*, 182; Wengle and Rasell, "The Monetization of *L'goty*," 746.

42. Robertson, *The Politics of Protest*, 179.

43. Robertson, *The Politics of Protest*, 179.

44. Ol'ga Nikitina, "Playing the Blame Game: Reforms Leave Officials and the Public Looking for a Scapegoat," *Russia Profile*, March 28, 2005.

45. That is, they did not produce many new organizations that continued to exist after the first few months of 2005. Of course, a number of organizations that had already existed and that had allied themselves with the protesters in early 2005, including political parties, labor unions, and other social organizations, survived after that time.

46. Robertson, *The Politics of Protest*, 186; Alfred B. Evans Jr., "Protest and Civil Society in Russia: The Struggle for Khimki Forest," *Communist and Post-Communist Studies* 45, no. 3 (2012): 233–42; Paul Goble, "Window on Eurasia: Russian Protests, Sanctioned and Not, Increase Dramatically in 2010, Interior Ministry Says," *Johnson's Russia List*, no. 106 (June 1, 2010); Vitalii Slovetskii, "Mnogo vystupaiut," *Novye izvestiia*, November 11, 2014.

47. Of course, there are also other measures of the success of a movement, in addition to winning popular support. For instance, another measure that most movement organizations with political goals consider important is bringing changes in a government's policies. Whether a movement is successful in reaching that goal will depend on a number of factors, including the nature of the issue that is involved and the interests that have a stake in that issue.

106 Alfred B. Evans Jr.

48. Maria Lipman, "Freedom of Expression without Freedom of the Press," *Journal of International Affairs* 53, no. 2 (2010): 163–64.

49. Jason M. K. Lyall, "Pocket Protests: Rhetorical Coercion and the Micropolitics of Collective Action in Semiauthoritarian Regimes," *World Politics* 58, no. 3 (2006), describes a movement in Russia whose organizational culture "dictates the use of tactics and slogans that have little mass appeal" (379) and whose "patterns of protest reinforce group solidarity but do not appeal to a broader audience" (400).

50. Samuel Greene and Graeme Robertson, "Sposobnost' k protestu sokhraniaetsia," *Kontrapunkt*, no. 3 (April 2016): 11. See also Jardar Østbø, "Between Opportunist Revolutionaries and Mediating Spoilers: Failed Politicization of the Russian Truck Drivers' Protest, 2015–2016," *Demokratizatsiya* 25, no. 3 (2017): 282.

51. Obshchestvennaia Palata, *Doklad o sostoianii grazhdanskogo obshchestva*, 62.

52. Østbø, "Between Opportunist Revolutionaries," 283.

53. For some examples of recent protest movements that are not discussed in this chapter, see Alfred B. Evans Jr., "Many Russians Aren't Protesting against Putin—They Want His Help," The Monkey Cage, *Washington Post*, August 21, 2017.

54. Alexander Bratersky, "50,000 Protest Duma Election Results," *Moscow Times*, December 6, 2011; Fred Weir, "Chanting 'Russia without Putin,' Flash Mobs Roil Moscow," *Christian Science Monitor*, December 7, 2011; Kseniia Zav'ialova, "Ne zabyli vkiuchit' televizor," *Kommersant*, December 10, 2011.

55. Ellen Barry, "Rally Defying Putin's Party Draws Tens of Thousands," *New York Times*, December 10, 2011; Kseniia Zav'ialova, "Dukh perepostmodernizma," *Kommersant*, December 10, 2011.

56. For large crowds, the estimates of the number of participants have differed every time, with the police estimating the number as much smaller than that stated by those who organized the event. "Tens of Thousands Gather in Fresh Russia Vote Protest," *Moscow News*, December 24, 2011; Fred Weir, "Huge Protest Demanding Fair Russian Election Hits Moscow," *Christian Science Monitor*, December 24, 2011; Ellen Barry, "Young and Connected, 'Office Plankton' Protesters Surprise Russia," *New York Times*, December 24, 2011; Andrei Kozenko, "Pokhody vykhodnovo dnia," *Kommersant*, February 4, 2012; Dmitrii Vinogradov, "Poklonnaia prevzoshla Bolotnuiu na 18 tysiach chelovek," *Moskovskie novosti*, February 4, 2012; Eileen Barry and Andrew E. Kramer, "Protesters Throng Frozen Moscow in Anti-Putin March," *New York Times*, February 4, 2012.

57. Kseniia Zav'ialova, "'Marsh millionov' zakonchilsia massovoi drakoi i zaderzhaniiami," *Kommersant*, May 6, 2012; Ezekiel Pfeifer, Jonathan Earle, and Rachel Nielsen, "On Eve of Inauguration, Mass Protest Ends in Violence," *Moscow Times*, May 7, 2012.

58. Alina Lozina, "Yuppies Comprise Core of Election-Rights Protesters," *Moscow News*, December 27, 2011; Iuliia Khomchenko, "Zrelyi protest," *Moskovskie novosti*, December 27, 2011; *Novaia gazeta*, "Kto vyshel na prospekt Sakharova 24 Dekabria?," December 28, 2011; Viacheslav Riabykh, "Portret gospodina Demonstranta," *Novye izvestiia*, December 28, 2011; Boris Dubin, "Iakimanka i Bolotnaia 2.0. Teper' my znaem, kto vse eti liudi!," *Novaia gazeta*, February 9, 2012.

59. Roland Oliphant, "Social Networks Strained at Rallies," *Moscow Times*, December 28, 2011; Georgii Il'ichev, "Dekabrist-2011. Sotiologi izmerili kachestvo protestnogo dvizheniia," *Novaia gazeta*, December 28, 2011.

60. O. V. Kryshtanovskaia, V. I. Shalak, M. Iu. Korostikov, and N. S. Evengeeva, "Analiticheskii otchet o provedenii sotsiologicheskogo issledovaniia 'Dinamika protestnoi aktivnosti: 2012–2013,'" *Gefter*, August 2, 2013, 12.

61. Levada Center, "Opros na 'Marshe protiv podletsov,' 13 Ianvaria," http://levada.ru (accessed February 7, 2013).

62. Grigorii Tumanov, "K NKO primenili silu zakona," *Kommersant*, June 10, 2014.

63. Eleanor Bindman, "The State, Civil Society and Social Rights in Contemporary Russia," *East European Politics* 31, no. 3 (2015): 351; Johnson, Kulmala, and Jäppinen, "Street-Level Practice," 15; Laura A. Henry, "Russian Environmentalism and the Foreign Agent Law" (paper presented at the 49th Annual Meeting of the Association for Slavic, East European, and Eurasian Studies, Chicago, IL, November 2017), 14.

64. Robert W. Orttung, "Nations in Transit 2013: Russia," in *Nations in Transit 2013: Authoritarian Aggression and the Pressures of Austerity* (Washington, DC: Freedom House, 2013), 464; Ivan Nechepurenko, "New 'Anti-Maidan Law' Lets Russian Authorities Come Down Harder on Protesters," *Moscow Times*, July 22, 2014.

65. Javeline and Lindemann-Komarova, "Indigenously Funded Russian Civil Society," 2.

66. Javeline and Lindemann-Komarova, "Indigenously Funded Russian Civil Society," 3.

67. Meri Kulmala, Markus Kainu, Jouko Nikula, and Markku Kivinen, "Paradoxes of Agency: Democracy and Welfare in Russia," *Demokratizatsiya* 22, no. 4 (2014): 547; Bindman, "The State, Civil Society and Social Rights," 350; Elena Bogdanova and Eleanor Bindman, "NGOs, Policy Entrepreneurship and Child Protection in Russia: Pitfalls and Prospects for Civil Society," *Demokratizatsiya* 24, no. 2 (2016): 156.

68. Bogdanova and Bindman, "NGOs," 167.

69. Meri Kulmala and Anna Tarasenko, "Interest Representation and Social Policy Making: Russian Veterans' Organisations as Brokers between the State and Society," *Europe-Asia Studies* 68, no. 1 (2016): 159.

70. Meri Kulmala, "Paradigm Shift in Russian Child Welfare Policy," *Russian Analytical Digest*, no. 200 (2017): 7.

71. Beissinger, "'Conventional' and 'Virtual' Civil Societies," 359, 360.

72. Henry, "Russian Environmentalism," 26.

73. Henry, "Russian Environmentalism," 30.

74. Valerie Sperling, *Sex, Politics, and Putin: Political Legitimacy in Russia* (Oxford: Oxford University Press, 2015), 244.

75. Sperling, *Sex, Politics, and Putin*, 244.

76. Alfred B. Evans Jr., "Protests in Russia: The Example of the Blue Buckets Society," *Demokratizatsiya* 26, no. 1 (2018): 3–24.

77. Alfred B. Evans Jr., "Protests against the Demolition and Replacement of Housing in Moscow: The Defense of Property Rights" (paper presented at the Annual Meeting of the Western Political Science Association, San Francisco, CA, March 2018).

78. Ivan Nechepurenko, "When a City of 40,000 People Gets Poisoned, They Don't Care," *New York Times*, April 5, 2018; Fred Weir, "Russian Consumerism May Be Poisoning This Town. But Nascent Civil Society Is Pushing Back," *Christian Science Monitor*, April 12, 2018.

79. "Musor perestanut vvozit' na staryi uchastok svalki 'Iadrovo' s subboty," Newsmsk.com, April 13, 2018.

80. "Politsiia prishla c obyskami k mery i v administratsii protestnogo Volokolamska," Newsmsk.com, April 13, 2018.

81. Andrei Kolesnikov, "Moral Protests: How Citizens Are Born in Russia," Carnegie Moscow Center, April 18, 2018, https://carnegie.ru/commentary/76100.

82. Sarah Lindemann-Komarova, in a message to this author on August 2017, said that in the protests with which she is familiar, "people are protesting not just policy but process and fairness and their rights." But she added that "many organizers" of protests insist that they must "keep politics out of it" and not let politicians and political parties "exploit them" and take credit for their efforts.

83. Greene and Robertson, "Sposobnost' k protestu," 14, observe that as a result of such tactics, protests in some parks in Moscow have taken on "an ideological character." So far, such examples are more the exception than the rule, but if that were to change greatly, the situation would have troubling implications for Russia's political leaders.

84. Henry, "Russian Environmentalism," 13.

85. Kathryn Hendley, *Everyday Law in Russia* (Ithaca, NY: Cornell University Press, 2017), 4, 226.

Chapter Five

The Media

Maria Lipman

Shortly after Vladimir Putin became the president of the Russian Federation, the Kremlin took control of all news and political broadcasting on national TV networks. Smaller-audience outlets, however, could exercise relative freedom of expression and pursue nongovernment editorial lines. During the "tandem rule" of 2008–2011, the government grew a bit more permissive, and the nongovernment media took advantage of a more auspicious environment.

Since Putin's return to the Kremlin in 2012, and especially following the political crisis in Ukraine and the annexation of Crimea in 2014, Russia has been going through a dramatic transformation both on the world stage and domestically. Internationally, it has shifted toward ever deepening confrontation with the West. Domestically, Putin's regime has opted for a conservative,[1] radically anti-Western course; the regime has become more authoritarian, deeply deinstitutionalized, and more personalistic. The Kremlin has pursued a zero-tolerance policy toward political activism opposing the state; constraints on the public realm including nongovernment media have been further tightened. Those nongovernment outlets that remain defiant are at risk. It should be noted, however, that while the Kremlin has resorted to violence as it applies to political activists, in its effort to harness the press it still relies on softer, manipulative means.

This chapter focuses mostly on media outlets operating in, or broadcasting from, Moscow. Moscow is the center of Russia in more ways than most national capitals: it is a powerful magnet for anyone with ambition, whether it be making money, a career in government or management, or academic or artistic pursuits, in literature or in fashion. Media is no exception.

PUBLIC/PRIVATE SPHERES IN POSTCOMMUNIST RUSSIA

After the collapse of Soviet communism and the establishment of Russia as a postcommunist state, President Boris Yeltsin's reforms created new opportunities for independent political, social, and economic activities. The 1990s witnessed a largely unconstrained press, though the causes of this freedom were many. During the political turmoil of the last years of the Soviet Union, Yeltsin evolved as a fierce anticommunist, and this turned him into a proponent of an independent press and a natural ally of new Russian journalists who also saw the Communist Party as a grave threat to Russia's democratic development.[2] His government almost never intervened to mute criticism of Yeltsin himself or his policies. Very early in his tenure, Yeltsin's government succeeded in passing a very progressive law on mass media.[3] But the Yeltsin government was also weak. Fighting many political and economic battles simultaneously, the Russian state simply did not have the capacity to control the media even if policy makers had wanted to.

THE RISE OF PRIVATELY OWNED MEDIA

Market reforms initially helped to stimulate the growth of media outlets not controlled by the government, including, first and foremost, television.[4] NTV, the first private television network, was launched in 1993 by one of Russia's major first-generation business tycoons, Vladimir Gusinsky.[5] NTV quickly earned its credentials as a serious news organization when it provided critical coverage of the First Chechen War (1994–1996). Every day, the horrible scenes from Chechnya appeared on television screens in Russian homes and generated broad antiwar sentiments, not unlike the way the coverage of the Vietnam War had shaped opinions of the US audience. Partly as a result of media coverage, Yeltsin was forced to initiate a peace process with Chechnya; otherwise, he had no chance for reelection in 1996. NTV also produced the puppet show *Kukly* (Puppets), a political satire that spared no one. NTV quickly achieved a new level of post-Soviet professionalism, quality, and style that the rival state channels Ostankino and RTR lacked. Evgeny Kiselev, NTV's cofounder and host of *Itogi* (Results), a Sunday night wrap-up show on politics, became a national celebrity.

Before starting NTV, Gusinsky had already launched his own daily newspaper, *Segodnia* (Today). He also bought a stake in a popular radio station, Ekho Moskvy (Echo of Moscow), that began broadcasting in 1990 and gained prominence during the days of the attempted communist coup in August 1991. In 1995 he founded a weekly magazine, *Itogi*, published in partnership with *Newsweek*, making his company, Media-Most, a media powerhouse. Other financial tycoons followed Gusinsky, believing that the media, especially television, was an important political tool. Through an inside deal arranged by the Kremlin, Boris Berezovsky acquired part owner-ship and de facto control of Ostankino, Russia's largest television network, which was renamed ORT (*Obshchestvennoe Rossiiskoe Televidenie*, Russian Public Television).[6] This "public" status, however, hardly meant anything, except the emergence of another powerful media tycoon and another national television asset under private control.

In the Russian media environment of the 1990s, adherence to the high principles of editorial independence professed by editors and journalists soon grew problematic. Russia's media tycoons who emerged during Yeltsin's presidency were hardly consistent advocates of a free and independent press. Rather, they were profit seekers with questionable business ethics and con-troversial political agendas. As a result, media outlets were frequently biased, as the new tycoons would use them to pursue their own political and business goals. Yet the very fact that they were owned or controlled by non–state actors endowed those post-Soviet media with immense importance: after the decades of tight ideological control by the communist state, they could offer alternative coverage, not guided by the interests of the government. Besides, those early tycoons permanently engaged in fierce rivalries, so if the media environment of the 1990s did not meet high democratic and ethical princi-ples, at least it ensured pluralism of coverage and opinion.

The emerging media tycoons proved as susceptible as others to what one Moscow-based Western diplomat called the "incestuous" relationship be-tween business and government.[7] This made them potentially vulnerable to government oversight. The state—or more aptly in Russian, *vlast'* (the pow-er)—may have been dramatically weakened after the political turmoil fol-lowing the collapse of the USSR and the ensuing economic meltdown, but it retained some leverage in different strategic sectors, including the national broadcast media. For example, while Berezovsky effectively controlled ORT, the Russian federal government remained its majority shareholder. The government also owned 100 percent of the state radio and TV company, even as its regional subsidiaries were de facto controlled by local governors. As the Kremlin was preparing for the election cycle of 1999–2000, the govern-ment began to slowly reclaim its media territory. The first major step was the creation of a government agency in charge of the media and a consolidation of state broadcasters under federal auspices. In 1998, regional TV subsidiar-ies were brought together and subordinated to VGTRK (All-Russian State Radio and Television Company). Its main asset was the national channel RTR, renamed Rossiia in 2001.

RECONSOLIDATION OF THE STATE

When Vladimir Putin became Russia's new president in 2000, his primary goal was to reassert the power of the state. In *First Person*, Putin's book of interviews, he said, "At some point many people decided that the president was no longer the center of power. I'll make sure that no one ever has such illusions anymore."[8] During his presidency, Putin effectively fulfilled his pledge. Since the outset of his rule, all political power has been steadily concentrated at the top of the executive branch, and government decision making was sealed from the public eye; gradually Putin emerged as Russia's uncontested and unchallenged leader.

As for the media, state-owned television was strengthened organizationally and financially for the upcoming election cycle of 1999–2000. The oligarchic media played a very significant role in that political campaign. But unlike the 1996 presidential election when the media tycoons Gusinsky and Berezovsky combined their TV resources in the effort to get Yeltsin reelected,[9] this time they ended up on different sides. Berezovsky committed his channel, ORT, to support the Kremlin.[10] Gusinsky's channel, NTV, however, would not support the Kremlin's hastily masterminded party Edinstvo (Unity) in the parliamentary race, nor would it back Putin, Yeltsin's anointed successor, in the March 2000 presidential election.

In the December 1999 election, the pro-Kremlin Edinstvo outperformed its main challenger—the party of the Moscow mayor Yury Luzhkov and former prime minister Evgeny Primakov, and in March 2000 Putin was elected president. The Kremlin thus defeated its rivals. This made Berezovsky the winner (and Putin's kingmaker) and Gusinsky the loser. But the consequences for their media properties, as well as for themselves, were similar. Soon thereafter, both were stripped of most of their media assets and forced into exile.

THE CAMPAIGN AGAINST OLIGARCHIC MEDIA

Expanding state control over national TV media was a major element of Putin's policy of reasserting state power. Within days of Putin's inauguration in May 2000, Gusinsky and his media holdings came under massive attack.[11] The Kremlin, however, carefully avoided harassing or persecuting journalists or editors. Instead, the campaign was mostly disguised as business litigation against Gusinsky's businesses. In late 2000, Gusinsky was forced to flee abroad and never returned to Russia. In the spring of 2001, Gusinsky's media company was taken over by the media subsidiary of the state-controlled giant Gazprom, Gazprom-Media. Media-Most, once the biggest privately owned media group in Russia, was dismantled. Eventually, though not immediately, the new management of NTV transformed the channel's editorial policy to keep it firmly in line with the Kremlin's political goals.

Putin's task of bringing under state control all national television channels with political broadcasting was greatly facilitated by the fact that the majority of the Russian public would not see the attack at NTV/Media-Most as a threat to freedom of the press and, more generally, was not opposed to the reinstatement of government control undertaken by Putin.[12] Neither would the journalistic community show solidarity with their Media-Most colleagues.

ORT, the channel controlled by Berezovsky, was reclaimed by the state at about the same time as NTV. Regaining control over ORT took much less time than the takeover of NTV and was mostly hidden from the public eye. It was not until the 2011 litigation in the High Court of London between two major Russian tycoons, Berezovsky and Roman Abramovich, that the story was finally revealed to the public. According to testimony at the hearings, Berezovsky had been pressured to sell his 49 percent stake in ORT to a Kremlin-chosen buyer, Roman Abramovich, who had earlier done special, secret, and costly favors for Putin. Secretly buying ORT on Putin's, or the Kremlin's, behalf was one such favor. Abramovich never claimed control over the channel, and the Kremlin has since used it as its political resource.[13]

In 2001–2002, there were two failed attempts to launch new, privately owned, national television channels. Through various techniques, the Kremlin made sure that both projects would be short-lived.[14] In 2002 NTV's highly popular *Kukly* show was canceled. By the middle of 2003, all three federal TV channels, whose outreach far surpassed all other Russian media, were turned into political tools of the Kremlin.

MANAGED TELEVISION COVERAGE

The coverage of three tragedies—the 2000 sinking of the submarine *Kursk*, the 2002 terrorist siege of a Moscow theater, and the 2004 terrorist attack on a school in Beslan—illustrates the Kremlin's expanded control over television broadcasting. Back in 2000, the media, including national television, tried their best to cover the *Kursk* catastrophe, which took the lives of all 118 sailors on board. While the officials, both uniformed and civilian, sought to cover up the inefficiency of the rescue operation and the poor condition of the Russian navy, Russian journalists undertook thorough investigations to report what the government sought to hide. Putin was furious: he lashed out at "people in television" who "over the past ten years have destroyed that same army and navy where people are dying today."[15] Soon thereafter, the state assumed control over ORT.[16]

In October 2002, a group of terrorists seized a Moscow theater with over eight hundred people inside. In a badly bungled rescue operation, at least 129 hostages were killed, almost all of them by the poisonous gas used by the rescuers. This time, federal television was mostly tame, but the journalists of NTV, though taken over by Gazprom the previous year, still retained their professional instincts. They tried to produce detailed reportage of the tragic developments, even as government officials instructed the channel's top manager to temper the journalists' investigative zeal. Once again, Putin was infuriated.[17] Within three months of the event, the top NTV manager was replaced by a more amenable figure.

In September 2004, over 1,100 people, most of them children, were taken hostage in a school in Beslan in the Caucasus region of North Ossetia–Alania. During the siege and subsequent storming of the school building, at least 334 hostages were killed. The rescue operation left serious doubts about the competence of those in charge. By 2004, however, the government had secured full control over all three major federal television channels. For their top managers, cooperation with the government had become a higher priority than professional skills or ethics.[18] This time, Putin made no remarks about the coverage or TV reporters' performance.

TIGHTENED CONTROL OVER
POLITICAL AND PUBLIC SPHERES

The government used the tragedy at Beslan as a pretext to tighten controls, launching what eventually amounted to full-blown political reform that endowed the Kremlin with a virtually unlimited capacity to bar unwelcome forces or figures from Russian political life.[19]

The end of 2004 was also marked by the Orange Revolution in Ukraine, which the Kremlin saw as a Western plot to install a pro-Western regime on Russia's border with the help of foreign-funded nongovernmental organizations (NGOs). The "orange scare" pushed the Kremlin to further tighten its grip on power. The NGOs sponsored from abroad became the primary target of this campaign. State-controlled media, first and foremost national TV channels, engaged in smearing foreign-funded NGOs as agents of the West seeking to do damage to Russia.[20]

By the middle of his second term, Putin presided over a deeply deinstitutionalized and personalized political system; he did not have to worry about political competition or public accountability. National TV channels steadily and effectively generated a sense that there was no alternative to Putin's leadership. The high and rising price of oil enabled the government to generously deliver to the people; Putin's approval rating hovered above 80 percent,[21] and the dominant public mood was that of quiescence.

Any political action or organization opposing the government was strongly discouraged, and the remaining independent political groups and activists were scarce, fragmented, and generally reduced to irrelevance. In this environment, the government could afford a modicum of permissiveness toward smaller-audience or niche liberal media so that the more modernized and critically minded minority would have an opportunity of expression.

CONTROLLED TELEVISION AS THE KREMLIN'S POLITICAL RESOURCE

Control over national television networks constituted a major element of the political system and the pattern of state-society relations that Putin built. State control over TV is by no means a coercive operation: top TV managers are staunch loyalists who have committed their skills and their organizations' capacities to advancing the government's goals. The mass-audience channels, especially Channel One (ORT was renamed Channel One in 2002) and Rossiia, as well as NTV, have been effectively used as tools to shape public perceptions by boosting certain developments, playing down others, or ignoring them altogether, and by praising or smearing certain figures or groups (the above-mentioned media campaign against foreign-funded NGOs is but one example).[22]

The 2003 State Duma election, which further consolidated the Kremlin's control, was criticized by the Organization for Security and Cooperation in Europe (OSCE) monitoring mission, which pointed to biased media coverage favoring the incumbent.[23] Putin's reelection in 2004 was a heavily manipulated affair with a preordained result: Putin won handily, with 71 percent of the vote.[24]

Before Putin left the presidency in 2008, he had handpicked a successor, his protégé Dmitry Medvedev. As a presidential candidate, Medvedev was featured on television almost as prominently as Putin and gained 70 percent of the vote. Putin became the prime minister in Medvedev's government; though technically his position was inferior to Medvedev's, in fact Putin remained the most powerful man in Russia. The coverage of the three major TV channels was deftly adjusted to what came to be referred to as the "tandem rule" and helped maintain high approval ratings for both leaders.[25]

The role of TV as the Kremlin's indispensable political resource is inseparable from its business aspect. While the three federal broadcasters did not compete in news coverage—generally bland and hardly different from channel to channel—they fiercely competed for advertisers' rubles by offering the audience a broad choice of entertainment shows and TV series, at least some of them of highly professional, state-of-the-art quality. Advertisers attracted by the channels' broad outreach eagerly committed their budgets to government-controlled TV. On top of that, the federal TV channels, as a key element in the structure of state power, were also assured of government subsidies.[26] Further, entertainment programming performs an important sociopolitical function by keeping people pacified and demobilized; glued to the TV screens by their favorite shows, viewers stay on the same channels for the pro-Kremlin news coverage.

ECONOMIC RISE

In the 1990s there was still hope—or a dream—that the Russian media would evolve as a public institution holding the government to account. During the first decade of the 2000s the Kremlin thoroughly eliminated any chance that the media would fulfill this public mission. But as an industry and as a lucrative business, media flourished. The rising price of oil boosted economic growth and contributed to a steady rise of the advertising market (it reached R131 billion in 2011),[27] making media a promising and prestigious business venture. Russian media groups perfected their business models and expanded to include movie production, printing and distribution businesses, and telecommunications.

In the course of the 2000s the Kremlin continued to redistribute and consolidate media holdings. After getting rid of the two major media tycoons, Gusinsky and Berezovsky, the Kremlin approved or orchestrated deals in which media assets ended up in the hands of loyal owners. While Putin's government took pride in ridding Russia of oligarchic media, media assets amassed during Putin's own tenure are enormous and substantially exceed those held by Gusinsky or Berezovsky in the 1990s. Besides, now loyalty to the president became the order of the day, and big business in general as well as holders of media assets in particular pledged full allegiance to the man in the Kremlin.

The largest-audience media outlets, the Kremlin's essential political resource, have been entrusted to magnates who made their fortunes in the 2000s in the energy sector or banking. By the late 2000s, National Media Group (NMG), controlled by business structures associated with Yury Kovalchuk, broadly reported to be a member of Putin's inner circle of old friends,[28] emerged as one of three major media holdings alongside state-owned VGTRK and Gazprom-Media, a subsidiary of the state-controlled giant Gazprom. NMG includes two national media channels with news coverage (REN TV and Channel Five) and an entire range of other TV, print, and internet resources. In early 2011, NMG vastly increased its holdings by purchasing a 20 percent share in Channel One.[29] In 2016, the value of NMG was estimated at R150 billion ($2.2 billion).[30] In addition to media assets, Kovalchuk's Bank Rossia bought shares in Russia's largest advertising sales house, VI (formerly Video International).[31] The concentration of media properties eventually produced a "media oligopoly"[32] with huge media holdings (including nearly all of the two dozen federal TV channels, some with news coverage, some purely entertainment) concentrated in the hands of just the three entities mentioned above. Other major media owners included metal tycoon Alisher Usmanov, whose media assets include the publishing house Kommersant and vast internet holdings.[33]

BEYOND DIRECT CONTROL, BUT AT THE KREMLIN'S DISCRETION

By 2008 it became common among the critically minded, modernized, and liberal minority in Russia to dismiss news coverage of national TV broadcasters as heavy-handed and boring propaganda. This constituency drew instead on a range of alternative sources of information—print, radio, internet, and smaller-audience television channels—that pursued editorial independence of varying degrees. The list of such outlets included dailies such as *Kommersant, Vedomosti* (a business daily, until 2015 published jointly by the *Wall Street Journal* and the *Financial Times*), or *Novaia Gazeta*; weeklies, such as *The New Times, Kommersant-Vlast'*, or *Russian Newsweek* (closed on the initiative of its German publisher in 2010); and radio stations, first and foremost, Ekho Moskvy (this list is not exhaustive). A variety of websites offered a combination of news, analysis, and opinion unconstrained by censorship or other modes of state control (the internet in Russia still remained free). REN TV, a channel with a sizable audience, had at least one show called *Nedelia* (The Week) with an independent voice (the show was a weekend wrap-up of news hosted by Marianna Maksimovskaia). Some journalists even engaged in investigative reporting and exposed abuses of offices by high-ranking government officials. The picture of Russia that emerged from those outlets was entirely different from the image offered by federal TV channels.

In a more open political environment, some of the stories reported by the above-mentioned relatively independent media would become the subject of a parliamentary discussion or probe; others would generate political scandals. But in Putin's Russia competitive politics had been thoroughly eliminated, the legislature had been turned into an arm of the Kremlin executive, judicial rulings were bent to the Kremlin's will whenever needed, and autonomous political activism was thoroughly marginalized. In these conditions, existing elements of free media remained politically irrelevant, unable to make a difference in policy making.[34]

While the Kremlin tolerated a degree of free expression, it made sure that the nongovernment media stay marginal and restricted to their "niche" of converted audience. And if marginalization was not enough, the Kremlin had an array of administrative, legal, and other tools to use against excessively audacious media. Those instruments were infrequently applied and served to intimidate defiant media outlets and remind them that they are at the Kremlin's discretion: if they go too far and inflict the anger of the powerful upon themselves, there will be nothing to protect them. [35]

Unlike the Soviet Union where a system of preliminary censorship ensured that every word on paper or on air conformed with the Communist Party line, Putin's Kremlin did not seek to stifle every voice. In fact, the media that pursued editorial independence could even be useful for the Kremlin as a safety valve that helped the critically minded to let off steam. The problem with media freedom in Putin's Russia was, therefore, not the absence of alternative sources of information. Rather, it was the tightly controlled political system and the social environment in which a vast majority showed no interest in alternative sources of information. Both factors made nongovernment media irrelevant and defenseless in the face of state power. Though nongovernment media continued to operate, the atmosphere grew increasingly inauspicious. Some journalists felt discouraged and opted for nonpolitical beats or even other occupations; some adjusted to the controlled political environment and engaged in self-censorship. [36]

TANDEM RULE: VERBAL LIBERTIES AND THE "DIGITAL DIVIDE"

The environment of general public quiescence began to change with the transition to "tandem rule." The more cynical may have regarded Dmitry Medvedev's presidency as merely a public relations trick—putting a "soft face" to Putin's authoritarian regime. But Medvedev's liberal rhetoric (he famously said that "freedom is better than nonfreedom"; the word "modernization" became the mantra of the tandem period), his younger age, and his enthusiasm for gadgets and the digital world appealed to certain constituencies, especially younger urban Russians. Besides, the very fact that there were two men at the top instead of just one loosened the system a bit and emboldened some of the marginal opponents of the regime. The phrase "political thaw" entered the political lingo of the tandem's early period. [37]

The new permissiveness unleashed more criticism by the media. Though federal television channels remained fully under state control, beyond the everyday operation on federal TV a mild degree of audacity could be found in the television community. For instance, annual TV awards were repeatedly granted to "non grata" TV journalists who had been barred from television, or to those from smaller-audience TV channels who had retained a relatively independent voice. At the awards ceremony in 2010, Leonid Parfyonov, a top

TV star forced out of NTV in 2004, gave a speech in which he harshly denounced federal broadcasters:

> For a correspondent of federal television the top government executives are not newsmakers, but the bosses of their bosses . . . a correspondent is not a journalist, he is a bureaucrat guided by the logic of allegiance and subordination. . . . Nothing critical, skeptical or ironic about the president or the prime minister can be aired on federal channels.[38]

Tandem rule was also marked by the emergence of new media outlets or the politicization of those that theretofore had remained largely nonpolitical. Kommersant, which since its inception back in 1990 had been a well-established print media holding, in 2010 launched Kommersant FM, well-informed news and analysis radio. *TV Dozhd* (TV Rain) was launched in 2010 as an almost unique example of (medium-scale) entrepreneur Alexander Vinokurov and his wife Natalia Sindeeva openly funding a media outlet that pursued nongovernment editorial policy. TV Rain was able to substantially broaden its outreach after it was included in cable packages. Several thick glossies, such as *GQ*, *Citizen K*, or *Esquire*, also turned to political themes (*Esquire* made this choice even earlier), apparently responding to an emerging interest in social and political matters among their reasonably prosperous, well-traveled, Westernized audiences. *Bolshoi Gorod* (*Big City*), a biweekly magazine about Moscow city life, was reformatted and offered strongly politicized, sometimes angry coverage. *Afisha* (*Billboard*) magazine, originally focused on culture and leisure, now developed a defiant political voice.

The newly energized nongovernment media realm was filled with reportage, critical policy analysis by experts, as well as angry opinions and poisonous jokes. The tandem period was also marked by rapidly growing internet penetration; most major print and radio outlets developed internet platforms; and web, print, audio, and video were also merging. Though television remained the main source of news for a majority of Russians (and the only one to those living in remote places), a growing number of people in large urban centers drew on the internet. In 2012, 24 percent of Russians in a national poll said they relied on the internet for news,[39] up from 11 percent less than one year earlier. Advanced web users in greater numbers switched to Facebook, where they found references to media publications made by their like-minded liberal "friends." The number of social network users was growing faster in Russia than anyplace else in Europe.

The penetration of the web was not yet universal, yet broad enough to generate a "digital divide," with more sophisticated users being generally more critically minded and drawing on alternative, nongovernment sources of information. The internet was awash with reports, submitted by professional journalists and ordinary citizens writing about lawlessness, injustice, or abuse by government or police authority. The number of bloggers increased, some of them gaining huge popularity and becoming voices of authority for tens of thousands of loyal followers. The popularity of social networks facilitated the exchange of information, strengthened social linkages, and promoted interest in civic causes. Civic activism was on the rise.[40] The fragmented "islets" of nongovernment media seemed to be merging into something of an archipelago. Then Putin announced that he was returning to the presidency.

PUTIN'S RETURN TO THE KREMLIN: HARDENED AUTHORITARIANISM

By the end of the tandem period, Russia's economy began to slow down, so even before he returned to the Kremlin, Putin arguably knew he would no longer be able to maintain his regime's legitimacy by generously delivering to the people. This in itself called for a change of policy away from permissiveness toward tighter controls.

The shift toward harder and more authoritarian policy was triggered by the mass street protests that broke out in December 2011 and continued in 2012. The outrage over the "castling" trick—with Putin and Medvedev announcing that Putin, not Medvedev, would run for president in 2012 and Medvedev would take the office of prime minister—was further deepened by egregious rigging during the parliamentary election of December 2011. Mass protest rallies brought out tens of thousands in the Russian capital (reaching one hundred thousand at some point in Moscow) and other large urban centers; the protesters chanted "Putin, Go!" or "Russia without Putin." Many among the new generation of journalists were at the very center of the protest.[41] The new media provided enthusiastic coverage of the protests, while the internet and social networks were also excellent tools to organize rallies and disseminate information among the protest community.

The Kremlin showed tolerance toward the protests up until Putin's successful election for a third term. After his inauguration in May 2012, the Kremlin launched a counteroffensive against the newly politicized and defiant Russian citizenry. The state-controlled TV networks played a major role in this onslaught: the political coverage was viciously pitting the conservative majority against their excessively modernized compatriots. The TV smearing campaigns and "documentaries" attacked the anti-Putin protesters, civic and political activists, and liberal journalists. Terms such as "national traitors" and "fifth column" entered the language of the TV news and talk shows.

CRACKDOWN ON NONGOVERNMENT MEDIA

Nongovernment media that theretofore had enjoyed relative freedom of expression came under pressure around the time of the 2011 parliamentary election. The fact that most major media had been redistributed to loyal owners greatly facilitated the Kremlin's task. Business tycoons concerned about their vast holdings in nonmedia spheres could be fully relied on to adjust the editorial line of their outlets to the Kremlin's interests and get rid of unwanted writers or editors, sometimes even preempting the Kremlin's requests. This spared the Kremlin the trouble of direct interference, harassment, or persecution of individual journalists.

Beginning in late 2011, quite a few leading editors were fired by or forced to resign by the owner. In December 2011 the editor in chief of *Vlast'*, the *Kommersant* weekly magazine (owned by billionaire Usmanov), was forced to resign after publishing a photograph of a voting ballot with an expletive applied to Putin.[42] Then the general director of the Kommersant publishing house was replaced, as well as the editor in chief of Kommersant FM radio. In short order, *Kommersant*, until then a high-quality mainstream daily, lost several other prominent journalists, grew much tamer, and fell below its earlier editorial standards. The editor in chief of *Bolshoi Gorod* had to go, and since then the magazine has generally avoided sensitive political subjects. In 2014, Marianna Maksimovskaia's weekly show *Nedelia* was closed by the REN TV network.

One of the major blows in the media realm was radical reformatting in late 2013 of the Russian state news agency RIA-Novosti (this decision was taken by Putin personally).[43] RIA-Novosti had been a successful operation headed by a highly professional and respected manager, Svetlana Mironyuk, who was now replaced by Dmitry Kiselev, a TV host known for his raving attacks on air at anyone whom the Kremlin regarded as an enemy of Russia: Ukrainian politicians, gays, Americans, and so on. One month later TV Rain fell under pressure. Under the pretext of an unethical question to the viewers posted on TV Rain's website, one after another, all cable operators terminated their contracts with the channel (there is every reason to believe that the operators' decisions were prompted by the Kremlin).[44] TV Rain's audience, which had reached about seventeen million, dramatically dropped to under one hundred thousand when the channel was forced to reduce its distribution to paid internet subscription.

The next to fall under attack was Galina Timchenko, the editor in chief of Lenta.ru, a political website owned by billionaire Alexander Mamut, a major owner of internet media. Timchenko and her team had turned their outlet into a must-read for those interested in high-quality news coverage. The fact that Timchenko's audacious and independent website was rapidly gaining popularity was probably enough reason for the owner to fire her in order to avoid (or preempt) the Kremlin's discontent.[45] Almost all members of her team quit as a sign of protest. With a group of her former *Lenta* staffers, Timchenko launched a new website called Meduza.io.[46] *Meduza*, however, is operating from Latvia.

The forced redistribution of media assets that had been practiced since the early 2000s was applied again in 2014: Pavel Durov, the founder of Russia's most popular social network, VKontakte, was forced to sell his network to a partner of billionaire Usmanov[47] and subsequently left Russia. In 2016, three top editors at media-holding RBC (owner billionaire Mikhail Prokhorov) were dismissed or quit after publishing reports and investigations on politically sensitive subjects. One of the three, Yelizaveta Osetinskaya, who had turned RBC into a highly professional and successful holding, left Russia and, with a group of RBC journalists who had quit in solidarity, has launched The Bell, a Russian-language website focused on business news and commentary operating out of the United States.[48]

The Kremlin increasingly regards the internet as a challenge to centralized government control; pressure on news websites is but one out of many new constraints. According to Andrei Soldatov, Russia's leading internet expert, in recent years the Russian authorities made substantial progress in imposing legal, technological, and other constraints on the web.[49] But while the government's effort to control the internet may be intense, it is "more of an emergency measure than a realistic attempt to regulate the internet on a day-to-day basis."[50] The operation aimed at blocking the messenger Telegram in spring 2018[51] appears to prove Soldatov's point.

Following the political crisis in Ukraine and the annexation of Crimea in 2014, a highly intense campaign of jingoistic propaganda appeared on Russian national television. Mass-audience TV channels have descended upon Ukrainian "fascists" and their Western "masters." The TV news shows became much longer than usual and almost entirely focused on Ukraine, with only a small fraction of airtime devoted to Russia proper. This propaganda onslaught further boosted Russian nationalism and the rally-around-the-leader effect generated by the annexation of Crimea; Putin's approval rating, which had dropped to 60 percent before his return to the Kremlin, jumped up to over 80 percent and has remained at this level through the end of his third term and his reelection in 2018.

In 2014–2015 the pleasurable emotion was national pride: Putin demonstrated that Russia, which had been long taken for granted after the collapse of the Soviet Union, could act without asking anyone's permission; it was now the West that was weak, forced to accept the annexation of Crimea as a fait accompli.

The high-pitch TV propaganda was toned down around mid-2015, but patriotism and national pride remained at historic highs.[52] Those Russians who may distrust TV as a source of *information* do not defect to alternative sources that provide critical coverage of government policies and may under-mine the sense of national pride and belonging to the patriotic majority. The strong dominance of the state over the media realm creates an atmosphere that helps to reduce demand for the opposition press and deepen distrust and resentment for any troublemakers who seek to challenge the government. The demand for alternative, that is, nongovernment, media is limited to a narrow stratum of urban Russians, most of them in Moscow. The "digital divide" that emerged in the late 2000s is gone. As internet use has grown to 60 or 70 percent of the population—80 percent among eighteen- to thirty-year-olds—the profile of users has come to resemble Russian society at large.[53]

CONCLUSION: NOT SCORCHED EARTH

It would be wrong, however, to describe the Russian media scene as scorched earth. Even as the number of "islets" providing independent news has been shrinking as a result of the Kremlin's crackdown, new ones contin-ue to emerge.[54] Despite the obvious risks, some young Russians still see independent journalism and investigative reporting as inspiring and exciting pursuits. For those in Russia who make a point of seeking out nongovern-ment sources of information (6 percent nationally and 16 percent in Moscow, according to the Levada Center),[55] a substantial number of news reports, analyses, and opinion pieces are still readily available on various websites, including Facebook, on a daily basis. A new, independent media award, called Redkollegia, was recently established by a private Sreda Foundation. Redkollegia grants two or three awards every month to those who "keep up high professional standards at a time when free, high-quality journalism is under state pressure."[56] About seventy journalistic works have been awarded in less than two years, most of them published in Moscow outlets, but about one-third appeared in the local, provincial media. All the awarded materials are republished on the Redkollegia website; this way the award-winning reporters are introduced to an audience beyond their publications.

In today's world, civic journalism, bloggers, or websites of informal pub-lic initiatives or nonprofit organizations (referred to in Russia as nongovern-ment organizations, or NGOs) not infrequently attract larger audiences than "conventional" media, and Russia is no exception. For instance, Aleksei Naval'ny, Russia's most prominent opposition activist and antigraft crusader, has repeatedly published videos in which he and his colleagues expose the wrongdoings of high-ranking government officials. His YouTube video makes allegations of corruption against Prime Minister Dmitry Medvedev.[57] It was posted in March 2017 and was viewed more than twenty-five million times before the end of that year. Other projects also exist.[58]

The Kremlin's tight control is extended first and foremost to the largest-audience media, most important among them being major national TV channels with regular news broadcasts. Beyond that controlled realm, there lies a broad range of media with diverse scope, quality, content, and genre whose operation is shaped not so much by directions from above as by various degrees of loyalty and self-censorship. Their editorial policies are determined by the heavily centralized political system and the Kremlin's intolerance toward independent political activism. A very high concentration of media assets in the hands of the state and Putin's loyalists further reinforces media loyalty to the state and its leader.

The remaining realm of nongovernment media and online civic journalism is small. The work of independent journalists and civic activists does not enjoy high public demand or appreciation and they can't expect to influence government policies, but they still aspire to make a difference by informing their niche audiences and stimulating political discussion, and sometimes helping those in need or in trouble.

DISCUSSION QUESTIONS

1. What constitutes media freedom, and what are its safeguards? Why did media freedom in the early postcommunist period prove to be so easy to suppress?
2. How was the oligarchic media of the 1990s different from the concentration of media assets in the late 2000s–early 2010s?
3. The two major crackdowns on media in Putin's Russia are ten years apart. What are the causes, targets, methods, and results of these two campaigns?
4. How and why did the media scene change during Dmitry Medvedev's presidency? Do you see a problem with journalists being at the forefront of the mass protests of 2011–2012?
5. How and why has the media scene changed since Putin's return to the Kremlin in 2012?

SUGGESTED READINGS

Baker, Peter, and Susan Glasser. *Kremlin Rising: Vladimir Putin's Russia and the End of Revolution*. New York: Lisa Drew/Scribner, 2005.

Federman, Adam. "Moscow's New Rules." *Columbia Journalism Review*, January–February 2010. http://www.cjr.org/feature/moscows_new_rules.php?page=all.

Hoffman, David. *The Oligarchs: Wealth and Power in the New Russia.* New York: Public Affairs, 2002.

Idov, Michael. "The New Decembrists." *New York Magazine*, January 22, 2012. http://nymag.com/news/features/russian-revolutionaries-2012-1.

Lipman, Maria. "Freedom of Expression without Freedom of the Press." *Journal of International Affairs* 63, no. 2 (2010): 153–69.

———. "Russia's Nongovernmental Media under Assault." *Demokratizatsiya: The Journal of Post-Soviet Democratization* 22, no. 2 (2014): 179–90.

Lipman, Maria, Anna Kachkaeva, and Mikhail Poyker. "Media in Russia: Between Modernization and Monopoly." In *The New Autocracy: Information, Politics, and Policy in Putin's Russia*, ed. Daniel Treisman. Washington, DC: Brookings Institution, 2018.

Ostrovsky, Arkady. *The Invention of Russia: The Journey from Gorbachev's Freedom to Putin's War*. London: Atlantic Books, 2015.

Soldatov, Andre, and Irina Borogan. *The Red Web: The Struggle between Russia's Digital Dictators and the New Online Revolutionaries*. New York: Public Affairs, 2015.

NOTES

1. For an analysis of the conservative shift following Putin's return to the Kremlin and annexation of Crimea, see Marlene Laruelle, "Putin's Regime and Ideological Market: Difficult Balancing Game," March 16, 2017, http://carnegieendowment.org/2017/03/16/putin-s-regime-and-ideological-market-difficult-balancing-game-pub-68250.

2. On the anticommunist "united front" of Yeltsin's administration and the postcommunist media, see Michael McFaul, *Russia's 1996 Presidential Election: The End of Polarized Politics* (Stanford, CA: Hoover Institution Press, 1997).

3. The Russian law on mass media, adopted in December 1991, was preceded by a Soviet media law framed the previous year by the same group of liberal experts inspired by a desire to provide legal safeguards of media independence from the state. See http://www.medialaw.ru/e_pages/laws/russian/massmedia_eng/massmedia_eng.html.

4. Ellen Mickiewicz, *Changing Channels: Television and the Struggle for Power in Russia* (Oxford: Oxford University Press, 1997).

5. See the chapter about Vladimir Gusinsky in David E. Hoffman, *The Oligarchs: Wealth and Power in the New Russia* (New York: Public Affairs, 2002), 150–74.

6. Russian Public Television (ORT) gained control of the first national television channel in Russia through presidential decree no. 2133 on November 29, 1994, and began broadcasting on April 1, 1995. Several private companies purchased 49 percent; Berezovsky's Logovaz owned 8 percent of the shares, while the share of the state owners totaled more than 50 percent. Nonetheless, Berezovsky used side payments and bribes to gain control of the company's operations and editorial policy. See Paul Klebnikov, *Godfather of the Kremlin: Boris Berezovsky and the Looting of Russia* (New York: Harcourt, 2000), 159–61.

7. Glenn Waller, an Australian diplomat quoted in Hoffman, *The Oligarchs*, 322.

8. Nataliya Gevorkyan, Natalya Timakova, and Andrei Kolesnikov, *First Person: An Astonishingly Frank Self-Portrait by Russia's President Putin, Vladimir Putin*, trans. Catherine A. Fitzpatrick (New York: Public Affairs, 2000).

9. Hoffman, *The Oligarchs*, 325–64.

10. The 1999 parliamentary election turned out to be Russia's last truly competitive national election, and the competition was fierce and at times ugly. The operation of Berezovsky's television was shocking even by Russian standards. The use of television as a tool for smearing the Kremlin's political rivals was driven to grotesque proportions by TV journalist Sergei Dorenko, hired to fulfill this mission by Boris Berezovsky. See Hoffman, *The Oligarchs*, 464–70.

11. For more detail about the campaign against Gusinsky and his media, see Maria Lipman and Michael McFaul, "Putin and the Media," in *Putin's Russia: Past Imperfect, Future Uncertain*, 2nd ed., ed. Dale R. Herspring (Lanham, MD: Rowman & Littlefield, 2005), 59–64; and Hoffman, *The Oligarchs*, 442–85.

12. Though the campaign against NTV caused public protest and two large protest rallies were held in Moscow, national polls suggested that "only 4 percent of the public regarded the NTV takeover as a government attempt to limit media freedom." Floriana Fossato, "The Russian Media: From Popularity to Distrust," *Current History* 100, no. 648 (2001): 343.

13. "Tainaia zapis': Abramovich i Berezovsky o Putine," BBC Russian, November 9, 2011, http://www.bbc.co.uk/russian/russia/2011/11/111108_abramovich_berezovsky_tape.shtml; "Berezovsky vs Abramovich: Abramovich kupil ORT za $10 mln," http://www.gazeta.ru/business/2011/11/07/3825378.shtml1/2.

14. The fates of two channels, TV-6 and TVS, are discussed in more detail in Lipman and McFaul, "Putin and the Media," 64–67.

15. Peter Baker and Susan Glasser, *Kremlin Rising: Vladimir Putin's Russia and the End of Revolution* (New York: Lisa Drew/Scribner, 2005), 89. Putin's even more emotional statements were quoted in *Kommersant-Vlast'*, "Vstrecha s rodnymi," August 29, 2000, https://www.kommersant.ru/doc/17499.

16. According to the testimony in the above-cited litigation between Abramovich and Berezovsky, the coverage of the *Kursk* disaster by ORT was the final reason why Putin demanded that Berezovsky relinquish control of the largest national TV channel. Putin was cited as saying that he would be personally in charge of ORT.

17. Baker and Glasser, *Kremlin Rising*, 174–75.

18. Baker and Glasser, *Kremlin Rising*, 34–35.

19. For a detailed description of the electoral reform, see Nikolai Petrov, "Kakaia vlast'—takie i vybory, kakie vybory—takaia i vlast' (ob itogakh izbiratel'nogo tsykla 2007–2008 gg.)," *Carnegie Moscow Center Briefing Paper* 10, no. 2 (2008).

20. Putin personally set the tone for this campaign by emphasizing that "he who pays the piper calls the tune." See "Vstrechi s predstaviteliami razlichnykh soobshchestv," July 5, 2005, http://archive.kremlin.ru/appears/2005/07/20/1801_type63376type63378type63381_91644.shtm.

21. According to the Levada Center's polls, Putin's approval rating in 2007–2008 ranged between 79 and 88 percent. See http://www.levada.ru/indeksy.

22. For example, in recent years, Russian television fomented anti-Ukrainian, anti-Georgian, and anti-American sentiments. It ran "documentaries" smearing Mikhail Khodorkovsky, once Russia's richest man, deemed a dangerous rival by Putin and some in his close circle. Khodorkovsky was prosecuted, served ten years in jail, and eventually was forced out of Russia. In 2010 it vilified Moscow mayor Yury Luzhkov, who wouldn't resign at the Kremlin's request. Following the annexation of Crimea, federal TV channels became a tool of raw anti-American and anti-Ukrainian propaganda.

23. In its final report on the Russian 2004 presidential election, the OSCE/ODIHR Election Observation Mission stated, "the State-controlled media comprehensively failed to meet its legal obligation to provide equal treatment to all candidates, displaying clear favoritism towards Mr. Putin," March 14, 2004, https://www.osce.org/odihr/elections/russia/33101?download=true.

24. Maria Lipman, "In Russia It's No Contest," *Washington Post*, December 1, 2004, http://www.carnegieendowment.org.

25. "Rankings of Russian Leaders and the Situation in the Country," Levada Center, March 4, 2010, http://www.levada.ru/press/2010030404.html. See also Mikhail Fishman and Konstantin Gaaze, "Efir dlia dvoikh," *Russian Newsweek*, August 4, 2008; Maria Lipman, "Freedom of Expression without Freedom of the Press," *Journal of International Affairs* 63, no. 2 (2010): 153–69.

26. On various forms of government subsidies to media see Vasily Gatov, "How the Kremlin and the Media Ended Up in Bed Together," March 11, 2015, https://themoscowtimes.com/articles/how-the-kremlin-and-the-media-ended-up-in-bed-together-44663. For instance, the state subsidizes signal transmissions to smaller cities (under two hundred thousand residents).

27. Channel One and Rossiia were by far the largest in terms of capitalization and were the largest recipients of advertising revenues. In 2010 these two major federal television channels received about 40 percent of all the TV advertising revenues in Russia.

28. An investigation conducted in 2014 by the internet resource rbc.ru produced a fairly complex chart illustrating the ownership structure of the National Media Group. Since the companies and individuals mentioned in the publication refused to comment, the authors opted for evasive phrases, such as "companies controlled by Yury Kovalchuk." The investigation maintains that three other major tycoons belonging to Putin's inner circle—the Rotenberg

brothers and Gennady Timchenko, as well as Putin's friend of many years musician Sergei Roldugin—also have stakes in NMG. Igor Terentiev, "Iashchik Rotenbergov: kak milliardery sviazany s Natsional'noi media gruppoi," November 17, 2014, http://top.rbc.ru/business/17/11/2014/5468ae40cbb20f2878362373#xtor=AL-%5Binternal_traffic%5D--5Brbc.ru%5D-%5Bmain_body%5D-%5Bitem_2%5D. See also Maria Lipman, Anna Kachkaeva, and Michael Poyker, "Media in Russia: Between Modernization and Monopoly," in *The New Autocracy: Information, Politics and Policy in Putin's Russia*, ed. Daniel Treisman (Washington, DC: Brookings Institution, 2018), 159–90.

29. Konstantin Gaaze, "Otdel'no vziatiy telekanal," February 9, 2011, http://www.forbes.ru/ekonomika-opinion/vlast/63087-otdelno-vzyatyi-telekanal. According to one estimate, by the end of 2013 the NMG media empire de facto controlled eleven of the largest Russian TV channels, 60 percent of the television audience, and 80 percent of the television advertisement revenues. Dmitry Kamyshev, Olga Beshlei, and Zhanna Ul'ianova, "Kooperativ 'Ozero': efir vziat," *New Times*, December 2, 2013, http://www.newtimes.ru/articles/detail/74981?sphrase_id=237051.

30. Polina Rusiaeva and Yelizaveta Surganova, "Mediakompanii Kovalchuka i Mordashova otsenili v 150 mlrd rublei," March 31, 2016, http://www.rbc.ru/technology_and_media/31/03/2016/56fcf20c9a7947dd35dbd00f?from=main.

31. Bank Rossiia acquired VI in 2010. Kseniya Boletskaya, "'Video International' smenil khozyaev," June 28, 2010, http://www.vedomosti.ru/business/articles/2010/06/28/video-interneshnl-smenil-hozyaev.

32. About "media oligopoly," see Maria Lipman et al., "Media in Russia."

33. BBC Russian, "Milliarder Alisher Usmanov sobiraetsia uiti iz biznesa," September 28, 2012, http://www.bbc.co.uk/russian/business/2012/09/120928_usmanov_business_finish.shtml.

34. Maria Lipman, "Constrained or Irrelevant: The Media in Putin's Russia," *Current History* 104, no. 684 (2005): 319–24.

35. For example, radio *Ekho Moskvy* was repeatedly threatened when its coverage angered Putin. See David Remnick, "Echo in the Dark," *New Yorker*, September 22, 2008, https://www.newyorker.com/magazine/2008/09/22/echo-in-the-dark. In 2012, *Ekho Moskvy* was threatened once again. See Maksim Ivanov, "My vsegda na kriuchke," *Kommersant*, March 30, 2012, https://www.kommersant.ru/doc/1903903.

36. Aleksandr Gorbachev and Ilya Krasil'shchik, eds., *Istoriia russkikh media 1989–2011* (Moscow: Afisha, 2011), 295–97.

37. One of Medvedev's moves that inspired hopes of liberalization was his meeting with the top editor of *Novaia gazeta* (his first to a print outlet), a paper known for its exposure of the government's wrongdoings and its criticism of the Kremlin policies.

38. See Parfyonov's address at "Vlast' predstaet dorogim pokoinikom: o nej tol'ko khorosho ili nichego," November 25, 2010, http://www.kommersant.ru/doc/1546420. The coverage of the TV awards ceremonies censored out the unwanted lines.

39. Levada Center, March 20, 2012, http://www.levada.ru/20-03-2012/chislo-polzovatelei-interneta-rastet.

40. See, for instance, Masha Lipman, "Quashing Rallies May Not Stave Off Discontent in Russia," *Washington Post*, August 9, 2010, http://carnegie.ru/2010/08/09/quashing-rallies-may-not-stave-off-discontent-in-russia-pub-41366.

41. Michael Idov, "The New Decembrists," *New York Magazine*, January 22, 2012, http://nymag.com/news/features/russian-revolutionaries-2012-1.

42. "Koval'sky uvolitsia iz Kommersanta po soglasheniyu storon," December 16, 2011, https://lenta.ru/news/2011/12/16/kovalsky.

43. "Putin Orders Overhaul of Top State News Agency," RT, December 9, 2013, https://www.rt.com/news/ria-novosti-overhaul-putin-960.

44. Masha Lipman, "Asking the Wrong Question on Russian TV," *New Yorker*, February 5, 2014, http://www.newyorker.com/news/daily-comment/asking-the-wrong-question-on-russian-tv.

45. David Remnick, "Putin Moves against the Press," *New Yorker*, March 12, 2014, http://www.newyorker.com/news/daily-comment/putin-moves-against-the-press.

46. Anna Nemtsova, "Russia's Freest Website Now Lives in Latvia," November 29, 2014, http://www.thedailybeast.com/articles/2014/11/29/russia-s-freest-website-now-lives-in-latvia.html?via=desktop&source=facebook.

47. Nickolay Kononov, "The Kremlin's Social Media Takeover," *New York Times*, March 10, 2014, http://www.nytimes.com/2014/03/11/opinion/the-kremlins-social-media-takeover.html. In 2018 Pavel Durov found himself at the center of attention when the government moved to block his messenger Telegram.

48. Masha Lipman, "The Demise of RBC and Investigative Reporting in Russia," *New Yorker*, May 18, 2016, https://www.newyorker.com/news/news-desk/the-demise-of-rbc-and-investigative-reporting-in-russia. The editors hired to replace those who were dismissed or quit made it clear to the RBC team that their editorial policy would be more cautious. See https://meduza.io/feature/2016/07/08/esli-kto-to-schitaet-chto-mozhno-pryamo-voobsche-vse-eto-ne-tak.

In another episode of media redistribution in favor of staunch loyalists, in June 2017 Prokhorov sold control of his troublesome media asset to energy tycoon Grigory Berezkin. Berezkin is not a major media holder, but he owns the pro-Kremlin tabloid *Komsomolskaya Pravda*, Russia's largest circulation daily; his loyalty to the Kremlin is not in doubt. See Max Seddon, "Mikhail Prokhorov sells control of Russian media outlet RBC," June 16, 2017, https://www.ft.com/content/37fd60b8-66b4-3b38-9286-4e7062c45229.

49. Andrei Soldatov, "Why We Should Care about Russia's Stance on the Internet," March 10, 2014, http://www.cyberdialogue.ca/2014/03/why-we-should-care-about-russias-stance-on-the-internet-by-andrei-soldatov.

50. Emily Parker, "Russia Is Trying to Copy China's Approach to Internet Censorship," Slate.com, December 16, 2011, http://www.slate.com/articles/technology/future_tense/2017/04/russia_is_trying_to_copy_china_s_internet_censorship.html.

51. Aaron Mak, "What's Happened since Russia Banned Telegram," Slate.com, April 25, 2018, https://slate.com/technology/2018/04/russian-internet-in-chaos-because-of-telegram-app-ban.html.

52. In November 2015, 68 percent said they were proud of Russia's political influence in the world, up from 46 percent in October 2012, and 85 percent were proud of the country's armed forces, up from 59 percent three years earlier. Levada Center, "Pride and Patriotism," September 12, 2015, http://www.levada.ru/eng/pride-patriotism.

53. Fond Obshchestvennoe Mnenie, "Interes k novostiam v Internete," July 23, 2015, http://fom.ru/SMI-i-internet/12247.

54. See *Esquire* on new young journalists Margarita Zhuravleva, "10 molodykh zhurnalistov, za kotorymi nuzhno sledit' v 2018 gody," March 6, 2018, https://esquire.ru/articles/44772-10-journalists-2018. And see *Meduza* on new projects and trends in 2014–2017, with a special mention of the emergence of interesting media projects in the provinces, "Russkie media 2014–2017: chto s nami proizoshlo za eti tri goda," October 20, 2017, https://meduza.io/slides/russkie-media-2014-2017-chto-s-nami-proizoshlo-za-eti-tri-goda.

55. Denis Volkov and Stepan Goncharov, "Rossijsky medialandshaft-2017," August 22, 2017, https://www.levada.ru/2017/08/22/16440.

56. *Redkollegia* is Russian for "newsroom," http://redkollegia.org.

57. Aleksey Naval'ny, "Don't Call Him 'Dimon,'" March 2, 2017, https://www.youtube.com/watch?v=qrwlk7_GF9g.

58. For example, hotline/media project Ovdinfo (https://ovdinfo.org) collects and reports information about police detentions at street rallies and other public gatherings; Ovdinfo also records various forms of political pressure and coordinates legal assistance for those detained. Takie dela (https://takiedela.ru) is a charitable and media project that publishes stories about people with various problems and needs and helps collect charity donations. Mediazona (https://zona.media) covers courts, law enforcement, and prisons with a primary focus on political persecutions.

Part II

The Economy and Society

Chapter Six

Economic Inequality and Social Policy

Thomas F. Remington

Since Vladimir Putin assumed Russia's presidency in 2000, the share of households living in poverty has decreased, but economic inequality has risen. Real incomes have increased for all segments of society, but they have grown fastest for those at the top. Broadly speaking, when incomes rise in Russia, they have risen more for the rich than for the poor, but when growth slows down, so too does inequality. The differentiation of incomes across the regions has leveled off, but the disparities are still high by international standards. Meantime, inequality in the distribution of wealth under Putin has climbed even faster than for income. The level of inequality in the distribution of wealth in Russia is among the highest in the world.

Economic inequality is rising throughout the world, but there is no one single cause. In any society, inequality is the aggregate outcome of many forces, including those affecting labor incomes at the low, middle, and upper ends; the accessibility and quality of public services such as education, health care, and safety; and government tax and social policies. Moreover, poverty and inequality are different phenomena. Both are important issues, but poverty is a condition affecting individuals and households, whereas inequality is an aggregate property of a community or a society. A country's poverty rate can decline at the same time that inequality is rising. As in Russia, this happens when incomes overall are rising, but a greater share of the gains goes to those at the high end of the distribution than to those at the bottom or in the middle. In that case, average incomes are rising, but the mean income level is rising faster than the median—which is the level of income at which there are as many people above it as below it. One reason why inequality matters is that high and rising economic inequality can worsen the quality of governance even when poverty is declining.

Economists use several different measures of inequality in the distribution of incomes and wealth. Among these is the Gini index (see below). Another is the share of national income going to particular quantiles (such as the top quintile or 20 percent, the top decile or 10 percent, or the top percentile or 1 percent). A related measure is the ratio between top and bottom quantiles, for example, the ratio of the ninetieth percentile to the tenth percentile. These measures can be used for income or for wealth, but inequality in the distribution of income is different from inequality of wealth. Wealth, such as real estate and stock shares, is not income until it is sold, when it realizes income for the seller. And inequality has many dimensions. In addition to differences between rich, middle, and poor households in a society, there can also be wide differences across regions, as well as across social categories, such as between women and men, racial and ethnic groups, and rural and urban populations.[1]

This chapter poses four questions about economic inequality in Russia: How high is it? What is driving it? What are its consequences for politics and society? And how are Putin's policies affecting it? In answering these questions, we compare Russia with the United States in order to view Russian inequality in the light of a more familiar case.

HOW HIGH IS INEQUALITY IN RUSSIA?

No one measure of inequality gives us a complete answer to the question of how high inequality is in Russia. The Gini coefficient is a widely used summary score that measures how much the distribution of income or some other material quantity across households in an actual society deviates from a perfectly equal distribution. If every household receives an equal share of income, for example, then whether the average income is low or high, the Gini coefficient for that society would be zero. If, however, one household received all the income, and the others none, the coefficient would be one (or 100 percent). Therefore, Gini coefficients vary between 0 percent and 100 percent. Real-world societies with very high levels of inequality (such as South Africa) have a Gini index in the sixties. Those with low inequality (such as Sweden) score in the twenties. Russia, the United States, and China all have Ginis in the mid- to high forties. Brazil's Gini coefficient is in the fifties. Global inequality—treating every household as if it was part of a single economy—is in the sixties.[2]

Gini coefficients, like most measures of inequality that are reported by national statistical bureaus, are based on household surveys. Interviewers survey a representative sample of households in the country, asking how much income each household received in the last thirty days or year. They then extrapolate from the sample to calculate the Gini index for the whole society, as well as the shares going to each quintile, decile, and so on. Although they are widely used, there are a few problems with using household sample surveys. For one, household surveys tend to undersample people at the highest and lowest ends of the income distribution. Moreover, surveys will lump all the households reporting that they receive more than some threshold into a top-end group, making it impossible to know how income is distributed *within* that group. For another, people are often reluctant to reveal their actual incomes, a problem made worse when a large share of their incomes comes from semilegal or illegal activities. In general, the larger the share of such unreported, "gray" income, the higher the actual level of inequality. Therefore, countries with a great deal of corruption or black market activity have considerably higher actual inequality than is reported using household surveys.

For this reason, in recent years social scientists have measured inequality by using income tax returns supplemented with other data, a method that allows for much more precise measurement of the shares of national income going to people in each bracket, particularly at the top end. But of course this method requires that the national income tax office make available millions of records with individual names removed. Assuming that the tax records are detailed and reasonably accurate, tax data yield a much more fine-grained picture of the actual level of inequality in a given country than do household surveys. In the case of the United States, the pioneering research of Emmanuel Saez, Thomas Piketty, Gabriel Zucman, and their colleagues has shed powerful new light on the dramatic increase in the concentration of incomes at the top of the ladder. Analyzing IRS data, they found that inequality in the United States is much higher and rising more quickly than anyone had realized. For example, they found that between 1993 and 2015, the top 1 percent of income earners in the United States saw almost a doubling of their real incomes, whereas the bottom 99 percent saw a gain of only 14.3 percent.[3] Overall, the top 1 percent receives about 22 percent of total income.

The same team of researchers has also been able to gather income tax and other data to draw up estimates of inequality for many other countries, including Russia.[4] For Russia they have estimated that the top 1 percent receives between 20 and 25 percent of all income, making Russia's level comparable to or higher than that of the United States.[5] (For China, it is estimated that the top 1 percent receives about 14 percent of income; in South Africa, almost 20 percent; and in Brazil, almost 28 percent.) Below, we review some of the figures about inequality of wealth in Russia as well. First, though, let us look at the trends in how income inequality has changed over the last two decades. For this we will use official Russian statistical bureau figures. Figure 6.1 shows trends in inequality, income, and poverty from 1995 to 2016.

The figure shows that inequality rose steadily with economic growth until the great recession of 2008, when it began to decline as economic growth declined. Meantime, following a sharp uptick in poverty in the late 1990s, poverty declined substantially until around 2013. Then when real incomes began to fall again in 2014, poverty began rising and inequality falling.

We can get another and more fine-grained perspective on inequality by analyzing the data from the Russian Longitudinal Monitoring Survey, a large-scale, long-term survey project run by the University of North Carolina and the Higher School of Economics in Moscow. This large annual survey of Russian households is designed to represent the entire Russian population and is intended to gather information about the economic and demographic circumstances of households and individuals in Russia.[6] Although it suffers from the same problems of representativeness and accuracy as do other household surveys, it does show a steady trend in the direction of widening income gaps between the top decile and the rest of the population, as do other studies (see figure 6.2).

Incomes at the bottom and middle of the distribution have risen under Putin, but it is the incomes at the top that have risen fastest (the ninetieth percentile is the point in the distribution separating the top decile from the

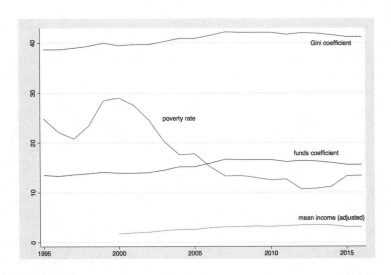

Figure 6.1.   Trends in Income, Inequality, and Poverty, 1995–2016
Source: Rosstat.
Note: The "funds coefficient" is the ratio of the total income of the top decile to the total income of the bottom decile. Mean income is expressed as a ratio of nominal mean income to the subsistence minimum for the given year.

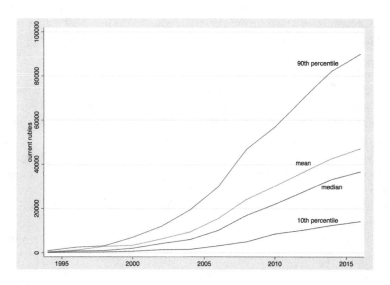

Figure 6.2.   Income Growth by Income Level
Source: RLMS.

other 90 percent of the population, so the sharp rise in the ninetieth percentile reflects the concentration of income growth in the very highest brackets).

Wealth in Russia is even more unequally distributed than income. Unfortunately, wealth distribution is extremely hard to measure because of the tendency of rich Russians to invest their wealth in overseas assets and tax shelters. Thomas Piketty's team estimates that the total amount of personal wealth held overseas is equal to the total amount held in Russia—an amount three times larger than official net foreign reserves.[7] They also estimate that the top 1 percent of wealth holders own about 43 percent of national wealth and the top decile owns over 70 percent—levels of wealth concentration comparable to the United States.[8] Other estimates place the concentration of wealth in Russia even higher: the Credit Suisse Global Wealth Report for 2017 estimates that the top decile of wealth holders in Russia own 77 percent of all household wealth and the top 1 percent 56 percent.[9] Both of these figures are higher than in the United States and are among the highest in the world.

Poverty can fall even when inequality rises. Putin's regime has done a great deal to reduce poverty by raising low-end wages and increasing pensions. However, until recently, price inflation ate up much of these gains. Currently, however, even despite very low inflation, real incomes are falling and poverty is rising. This is keeping inequality from rising but puts pressure on consumers. One response by households has been to take on more consumer debt in order to maintain living standards. Still, a very large number of people live close to the poverty line. A 2017 survey found that 39 percent of respondents lacked enough money to buy food or clothing, and among respondents fifty-five years old or older, 54 percent could not afford food or clothing.[10] Many people who are not formally below the poverty line are nonetheless in meager circumstances.

A large share of the working population receives very low wages. According to Vice Prime Minister Tat'iana Golodets, who oversees social policy for the government, almost five million employed people receive wages at the level of the poverty line.[11] As many as another two million receive wages *below* the poverty line. Altogether around 17 percent of the employed population receive incomes too low to allow them to provide for their families.[12] Russia sets a federal minimum wage level, but it is still well under the poverty line. So those workers who receive wages at the level of the minimum wage, or even above it, often live in poverty. Within the government a debate has raged for many years over whether to mandate that the minimum wage be no less than the poverty line (this norm is in fact fixed in law, but the law is not enforced). President Putin recently told the government to ensure that the minimum wage be at least equal to the poverty line by 2019, but many government officials and economists object that raising the minimum wage will only have the effect of reducing employment—much as conservatives in the United States claim that raising the minimum wage pushes employers to lay off low-wage labor.[13]

At the other end, top managers in sectors such as banking, real estate, and energy receive incomes comparable to their "super-manager" counterparts in the United States.[14] To a large degree, their incomes are rents coming from control of lucrative assets rather than from technological innovation or entrepreneurship. In *The Wealth of Nations*, Adam Smith provided a classic definition of rents as "reaping where you did not sow." More technically, rents are the incomes obtained by keeping an income-generating asset from competition; rent seeking is the effort made by the owner of the asset to preserve monopoly control of that asset. Monopolists collect rents so long as there is no competition in their market. Owners of oil wells collect rents when the price of oil goes up even if they have done nothing to increase production. The economist Joseph Stiglitz argues that in the United States, rent seeking is responsible for a great deal of the growth of inequality.[15] For example, generous intellectual property rights protection allows monopoly rents to accrue to managers in industries such as pharmaceuticals, entertainment, and digital services. Russian companies have been much less innovative; there are many fewer successful companies building their businesses around digital technologies, for example, and the share of high-technology products is only 10 percent of total exports, while oil and gas constitute over half.[16] The huge natural resource wealth of Russia has generated enormous rents for the owners and managers of energy companies and companies tied to them, such as finance and real estate. For example, the president of Gazprom receives around $20 million per year, the chairman of Rosneft receives about the same, as does the chairman of the board of the VTB Bank; the president of Sberbank (Russia's largest national savings bank, also state owned) receives around $11 million.[17] The average monthly wage in Russia in 2016 was R36,746, or about $7,300 per year, so top CEOs receive incomes several hundred times higher than the average employee in the economy. Top government officials are also paid well. A senior official in the Russian government or presidential administration has a base salary of about six times higher than the earnings of the average employee in the economy, similar to the ratio in the United States. But Russian officials also receive a number of monetary and in-kind benefits beyond base salary, such as bonuses and access to restricted state clinics and recreational facilities.

As in the United States, Russia has seen large gains in the incomes flowing to the financial sector (FIRE—finance, insurance, and real estate). Much of the income derived from those sources has been converted into wealth, often in the form of overseas assets such as high-end real estate and offshore investment accounts. This wealth in turn generates more income for its owners, particularly when they sell an asset. In November 2017, for example, a Russian oligarch known as the "potash king" sold a painting believed to be by Leonardo da Vinci, which he had purchased for $127.5 million in 2013, for a price of $400 million.[18] The buyer was later revealed to be the government of Abu Dhabi. The high incomes of the very wealthy fuel a substantial market for luxury goods. As in the United States, the luxury market expands as the appetites of the wealthy for status consumption goods grows. As Aras Agalarov, a well-known developer of luxury housing in Russia (and friend and business associate of Donald Trump), commented, "there is a well-known joke about the clients of expensive boutiques, 'the worse things are for the country, the higher the incomes of the sellers of luxury goods.'"[19]

Because Russia's exports are heavily skewed toward natural resources rather than manufactured goods, it is less exposed to the effects of globalization and technological advancement than are high-income capitalist societies. Therefore, Russia has experienced less of the "hollowing out" of middle-income jobs than has the United States.[20] Incomes in the middle of the distribution have been rising, but this is mostly due to increasing salaries in the financial sector and government, not from a growing entrepreneurial sector. The total share of incomes from entrepreneurship, in fact, has fallen in half since 1995 (down to 8 percent in 2016). As a result, the middle-income group—what might be called the middle class—is increasingly made up of state employees, including those serving in the armed forces, the police, other state services, teachers, doctors, and those in the social services sector.

People employed in financial services, insurance, and real estate make up another sizable share of the middle-income group.[21]

Overall, the distribution of incomes in Russia among the upper-income, middle-income, and lower-income segments of the population is very similar to that of the United States, despite the much higher level of income in the United States. The median income for individuals in Russia for 2016 is equivalent to about $4,500 per year (US), an amount a little over twice the poverty line. If we define the middle-income category as all those receiving at least two-thirds of the median but less than twice the median, about 55 percent of Russians are in the middle-income group, 19 percent are above that, and 26 percent below it. These proportions are very similar to the United States, where median individual income in 2016 was $31,000. About 59 percent of Americans are in the middle-income group, 15 percent above it, and 26 percent below it. Russia and the United States both have smaller middle-income groups and larger lower-income groups than the countries of Western Europe.[22]

WHAT DRIVES INEQUALITY?

As we have seen, some of the reasons inequality is high and rising are the same as those in the United States, while others reflect the strong natural resource orientation of the Russian economy and the legacy of the transition from communist rule. The fact that so much of Russia's wealth is tied up in natural resource assets has several consequences. One is that regions with large natural resource assets tend to have considerably higher average incomes. The state budget uses revenues from the export of natural resources to redistribute to the public sector and to social programs such as pensions. Because the share of income from entrepreneurship is declining, this means that more and more groups of the population are becoming more dependent on state sources of income. Finally, like other countries afflicted with the "resource curse," Russia has neglected to develop other sources of economic growth, such as technological innovation and entrepreneurship.[23] Whether the resource assets themselves are state or privately owned matters much less than does the ability of the managers of the assets to protect the high rent-based incomes they receive from managing them. Because owners and managers of large private companies depend so heavily on state favor, knowing that they can be removed at any time or even arrested and their assets confiscated, each individually tries to stay compliant with the regime's demands.[24] Yet at the same time, as a *collective* body, they exercise a good deal of *indirect* influence. If the government were to consider raising income or payroll taxes significantly, for example, the wealthy would find ways to hide even more of their income overseas. That is one reason that every time the idea of higher payroll taxes or a progressive income tax scale comes up, the government rules against it. As a result, the state's tax and social policies are only mildly redistributive, leaving a large share of the population at living standards not far above the poverty line and a much smaller segment of the society at the top enjoying very high incomes. Therefore, the high inequality of wealth and income in Russia stems to a larger extent from the country's dependence on natural resources and the rent seeking and corruption this fosters than from the degree to which wealth is publicly or privately owned. [25]

In the early years of the transition from communist rule, economists argued that income inequality would first rise and then fall. It would rise in the initial phase of the transition as more of the productive assets of the country, capital and labor, shifted out of the planned and state-owned sector and into the private and market-driven sector. Since the latter would be more productive, it would generate higher profits than the state sector and would pay higher wages to those who were productive. Wages would become "de-compressed" as wages came closer to reflecting actual productivity. Some workers would lose out, but even more workers would end up benefiting from the higher wage levels paid to more skilled and productive workers. Later, these economists argued, wage levels would become more equal as more and more workers obtained the skills needed for a dynamically growing economy and moved out of unproductive state enterprises and into the more productive market sector. [26]

However, this scenario did not play out in Russia. Although other post-communist countries evolved along this path, in Russia, in part because of the heavy resource orientation of the economy and in part because of poor state institutions, the markets for capital and labor remained heavily distorted by political and social pressure. The simplistic transition theory overlooked the fact that Soviet state enterprises were far more than simply units for economic production. They were crucial nodes of social provision for most of the population. Not only did they supply secure lifetime employment and social benefits such as housing, but they also often provided health care, recreation, child care, and consumer goods to their employees and their families. In many cities in fact, big state enterprises were—and still remain—the only source of livelihood for large proportions of the community. Enterprises were therefore basic units of social welfare and not merely locations of economic production. Without some means to shift the great bulk of social responsibilities from enterprises to towns and regions, therefore, turning state enterprises into profit-seeking, market-oriented firms was impossible without provoking a vast social upheaval. [27]

WHAT ARE THE EFFECTS OF INEQUALITY?

Above I argued that high and rising inequality corrodes the quality of government. This is true regardless of whether the government is democratic or autocratic. The reason is that when there is high polarization between rich and poor (just as is the case when there is high polarization between racial and ethnic groups), any public policy implicitly becomes a test of the government's willingness to tax some in order to redistribute to others. Scholars have shown that in highly polarized societies, the provision of public goods such as education, health care, sanitation, security, and the like is lower than in more economically or socially homogeneous societies.[28] However, when incomes in the middle are rising faster than incomes at the top, middle-class groups are more likely to favor expanding access to and quality of public goods and services.[29]

When inequality is high and rising, the wealthy tend to retreat into their own enclaves of privately provided goods and services. For example, they opt to live in gated communities with private security and other services. They send their children to private schools and get medical care in private clinics. They use private means of transportation. They enter smaller and more select insurance pools for retirement income and medical care. They have little interest in paying more in taxes for public schools, clinics, roads, sanitation, pension insurance, and the like. In a society where racial or ethnic divisions reinforce economic divisions—as in much of the US South or South Africa under apartheid—the wealthy resist sharing the benefits of better education with the poor because this would threaten their racial or ethnic domination. In a society dominated by a large and growing middle class, more people tend to see their circumstances as similar and are more willing to share the cost of public goods and services.

Russia does not have the sharp racial divisions that the US South or South Africa have. Nevertheless, there is a clear bifurcation between public and private provision of services such as education and health care. Although Putin's government has greatly expanded spending on improvements to education, health care, infrastructure, and social insurance benefits, these have not succeeded in stimulating broad-based economic growth of the kind that would reduce inequality. Fiscal and social policy is caught in a dilemma. Raising taxes (both income taxes and social insurance contributions) in order to redistribute incomes from rich to poor strata and regions would probably result in a large-scale flight of incomes into the shadows, that is, into unreported, under-the-table cash payments and informal employment. It would also stimulate more capital flight. On the other hand, the government cannot increase spending on productive investment in human capital and physical infrastructure unless it cuts spending elsewhere.

Under Putin, even though state spending has risen substantially, the share of private spending in total outlays on health care has been relatively constant, ranging between about 35 and 40 percent.[30] State spending and private spending on health care have both risen steadily and tend to be complementary, in that regions with higher state spending per capita also have higher private spending. Private spending also rises with income; people in higher income brackets spend a higher share of their income on health care. Yet even though the state substantially increased spending on health care in the 2000s, equalizing health care across regions and widening access for poorer strata, state health-care spending on a per capita basis is lower than most OECD countries.[31]

There is a similar parallelism of public and private spending on education, although the share of private spending is lower than for health care and is declining. For higher education, private spending is about one-quarter of total spending; for preschool, it is about 11 percent; and for vocational secondary education, it is about 9 percent. Overall, the private share of spending on education is about 14 percent.[32] As with health care, people in higher income brackets spend a higher share of their income on education. The fact that richer people are able to, and do, spend higher shares of their incomes on education and health care for themselves and their families means that they are able to transmit their advantages to the next generation. As in the United States, this means that inequality of incomes today tends to reproduce inequality across generations.

Former finance minister Aleksei Kudrin has been proposing a major shift in budget priorities, away from military and security spending and toward human capital and infrastructure. He argues that, with the population aging and demanding more in the way of old-age pension payments and health spending, Russia will face a growing fiscal squeeze, with a widening budget deficit and slowing growth in the coming decades. Kudrin points out that, as a share of the budget, the government spends less on health and education than do Western European countries, but more on defense and security. He recommends increasing overall government spending but cutting spending on defense and security and raising it on public infrastructure (by a third) and on education and health care (by as much as 1 percent of GDP on education and 0.7 to 0.8 percent of GDP on health care). The objective would be to shift Russia's model of growth away from its dependence on natural resource exports and toward more sustained and faster economic growth based on technological innovation. In this model, broad-based economic growth rather than redistributive spending would bring about a long-run reduction in economic inequality.[33] However, similar proposals in the past have largely gone unheeded.

HOW DOES SOCIAL POLICY AFFECT INEQUALITY?

Much of the structure of Russian social policy is a legacy of the Soviet system. The Soviet system made broad use of in-kind benefits and exemptions (*l'goty*). These included subsidized goods and services such as free transportation, discounts on medications, and subsidized housing and utilities. The Soviet system also used direct cash payments, such as cash supplements for children. For the most part, these social benefits were provided categorically, that is, to everyone who met the eligibility requirements regardless of need. Contemporary Russia continues this system. Indeed, Russia makes extremely wide use of these categorical benefits. There are around eight hundred federal-level benefits and cash subsidy programs. In addition, regional governments run their own benefits programs, averaging around one hundred such programs in each region.[34] Because these benefit programs are not needs-tested, most of the spending goes to people above the poverty line. Even poverty programs wind up benefiting the poor less than the nonpoor—only one-quarter of the spending designated to assist the needed actually reaches the needy. Two-thirds of the populace receives some form of social assistance. Although 84 percent of the poor receive some form of social assistance, on average it only makes up 2 percent of their income. Only about one-quarter of social assistance spending by the state goes to reducing poverty.[35] In short, Russian social spending is highly inefficient in reducing poverty.

Although government social spending is not particularly redistributive, the share of government social spending in the population's income has risen. This means that for more and more people, an increasing share of their income comes from federal social programs. The share of social income in total income has risen from about 13 percent in 2005 to almost 20 percent in 2016.[36] This includes pensions, but many other forms of social spending as well. According to the World Bank, pension spending is almost 9 percent of GDP and 23 percent of total government spending. Pensions, like nearly all other forms of social spending, are not means-tested.[37] But for the bottom 40 percent of the population, pensions are the main driver of the growth of incomes, and for overall income growth, government spending is the main driver of income growth. Overall, about half of total income comes from the public sector, either as salary for public employees or as social transfers.[38] Therefore, as a World Bank report concludes, although Russia's fiscal and social policies are not particularly redistributive (they are more so than in the United States but less so than in Europe), they have resulted in a substantial increase of dependence on state spending for income even at the same time that inequality has risen.

As noted above, within the government there are strong proponents of introducing a progressive income tax that would exempt low-income groups and raise the rate for higher-income earners. Each time this is discussed, however, opponents within the government and the State Duma object that a higher tax rate would drive more incomes into the shadows. They also note that a progressive income tax would be administratively difficult to collect. Income taxes require considerable bureaucratic capacity, which is one reason that weak governments tend to rely on easier-to-collect revenue sources such as sales and excise taxes. In effect, tax policy acknowledges that wealth income earners are able to thwart the government's capacity to collect income taxes by shifting their incomes off-book or into overseas assets. Therefore, even though Russia does not have well-organized lobbies opposing a progressive tax system, the wealthy in Russia exercise an indirect influence over government by being able to threaten to hide a substantial share of their incomes and assets from the tax authorities.

At present the individual income tax is set at a flat 13 percent rate. This makes the tax relatively easy to collect. Nearly all revenues from the income tax, however, go to the regional governments rather than the federal government, and for most regions they are the principal source of revenue.[39] The federal government depends primarily on taxes from the sale and export of oil and gas, so the federal authorities have much less at stake in making the income tax a more effective source of revenue. More important for social policy is the set of payroll taxes that go into the country's main social insurance funds: the Pension Fund, Mandatory Medical Insurance Fund, and Social Insurance Fund. The payroll tax is set at 30 percent of wages up to a certain ceiling, above which the rate is 10 percent. Therefore, like payroll taxes in the United States, Russia's social insurance tax falls more heavily on those paid at lower wage levels.

Of the social insurance funds, the Pension Fund is by far the largest. It pays out old-age pensions and other social benefits to more than forty million people. Because the contributions from employed people only fund about two-thirds of the amount needed to pay current pensioners, the federal government each year must transfer a sizable amount of money out of the budget to make up the difference. Because of the growing strain on federal budget resources of meeting current pension obligations, as of 2015 the government changed the system for paying out pensions from a defined benefit to a defined contribution system. It adopted a complicated formula for calculating each pensioner's benefits based on the years the person had worked, how much they had contributed, and the current balance of the Pension Fund budget. As a result, a person's benefits can vary from year to year. This adjustment eased some of the strain on the Pension Fund budget, but it also meant that pension payments remain low. They are currently running at the equivalent of about one-third of the average wage. Although pensions have raised many older people to a living standard above the poverty threshold, almost two-thirds of pensioners are in the bottom half of the income distribution.[40] Because Russia's population is aging, as the share of elderly people is increasing relative to the number of people in the work-force, the financial strain of the pension system is rising. Experts and policy makers agree that Russia will need to raise the age of eligibility for pensions from the current sixty years of age for men and fifty-five for women first set in 1932. But because retirement age is a politically sensitive issue, the government keeps postponing official approval of the change. The author-ities are also trying to reduce the number of people who evade payroll taxes by receiving part of their pay in unreported cash, but their success has been limited. At least 20 percent of the employed population are unregistered and not paying into the social funds.[41] The government faces a stark choice: if it raises payroll tax rates, it risks provoking a further flight of wages into the shadows, but if it does not, the social insurance funds will continue to run a deficit.

CONCLUSION

Real incomes in Russia have been shrinking, with occasional brief reversals, since 2014. Real incomes were down 0.7 percent in 2014, 3.2 percent in 2015, 5.8 percent in 2016, and 1.7 percent in 2017.[42] So far Russians have coped without much protest, adjusting to their reduced circumstances by tightening their belts and increasing their use of consumer credit. The government has been particularly attentive to the needs of the poorest seg-ments of the population and has raised the minimum wage level and pension payments. Nevertheless, over this period, the poverty rate has increased. At the same time, inequality has fallen slightly, demonstrating that when in-comes rise, it is the groups at the top that benefit the most, and when incomes fall, high-end income growth levels off. In part this is because when the economy slows down or shrinks, firms pay lower bonuses to their employees (bonuses can often comprise as much as half of an employee's total compen-sation). When times are hard, more workers seek employment off-book or shift some of their wages into under-the-table cash payments. These adjust-ments in turn starve the government of tax revenue and the social insurance funds of resources needed to pay pension insurance and other social benefits. The solution to this problem would be a higher rate of economic growth that expanded the share of middle-income households.

Occasionally, senior Russian leaders call attention to the problem of in-equality. In an address to the State Council on February 8, 2008, President Putin declared,

> We must see to it that all citizens of our country, using their knowledge and abilities, and, where needed, the help of the state, have the opportunity to receive a high-quality education, support their health, obtain housing, and

receive a worthy income. That is, to have a standard of living defining their belonging to the so-called middle class. And I believe that the minimum threshold for the share of the middle class in the social structure by 2020 must be no less than 60 percent and perhaps even 70 percent. And the differentiation in family incomes must be reduced from the current absolutely unacceptable 15-fold gap to one more reasonable.[43]

Four years later, in an article published shortly before the 2012 presidential election, he wrote, "The differentiation of incomes is unacceptable, outrageously high. . . . Therefore the most important task is to reduce material inequality."[44] However, once he was reelected president in 2012, Putin ceased to draw attention to the problem of inequality as such, focusing instead on problems of poverty and the need to bring up the salaries of public-sector employees.

As in the United States, tackling economic inequality would be an enormous challenge for the political system because it would significantly alter the balance of control over rent-producing resources. As we have seen, despite the enormous differences in the political, social, and economic systems between Russia and the United States, economic inequality in the two countries is comparable in scale, causes, and effects. Russian economic inequality is a far more recent phenomenon, having been given its impetus by the transition from communist rule and then getting locked in by the continuing dependence of the economy on its natural resource wealth and the strongly oligarchic character of its politics.

Prime Minister Medvedev declared that "technological progress creates other challenges as well, among them social, such as the growth of inequality. Here we mean not only inequality in people's incomes, but also inequality in territorial development. The speed of technological changes in the megapolises and large cities may increase the gap between them and small cities and rural areas."[45] But this misses the mark. Inequality in Russia is less a function of technological change than the fact that an economy based on resource extraction and financial activity, with weak and corrupt state institutions, allows a small segment of wealthy individuals to capture large streams of rents. Economic growth based on technological innovation and entrepreneurship would equalize opportunity across strata of the population and across regions. Unless the economy shifts to a more diversified, innovation-based model of growth, therefore, the likeliest scenario for Russian development is an alternation between economic policies favoring oligarchic control over resources and policies increasing state control. The former will favor rising inequality and a shrinking middle class, while the latter will choke off the sources of self-sustaining economic growth. Diversifying the basis of the economy and upgrading the technological level of production, however, would require a substantial investment not only in human capital, but also in the effectiveness and probity of state institutions.

DISCUSSION QUESTIONS

1. In what ways are the trends in income distribution in Russia similar to those in other countries, and in what ways are they different?
2. How do the legacies of the Soviet era affect the distribution of incomes and wealth today?
3. How has the transition from a planned, state-socialist economy affected social welfare policy?
4. What policies has the Putin regime pursued to address the issues of inequality and poverty?
5. How does Russia's reliance on oil and gas exports affect economic inequality?

SUGGESTED READINGS

Cook, Linda J. *Postcommunist Welfare States: Reform Politics in Russia and Eastern Europe.* Ithaca, NY: Cornell University Press, 2007.

Ellman, Michael, ed. *Russia's Oil and Natural Gas: Bonanza or Curse.* London: Anthem, 2006.

Remington, Thomas F. *The Politics of Inequality in Russia.* New York: Cambridge University Press, 2011.

Treisman, Daniel. "Is Russia Cursed by Oil?" *Journal of International Affairs* 63, no. 2 (2010): 85–102.

NOTES

1. On inequality in rural Russia, see Stephen K. Wegren, *Rural Inequality in Divided Russia* (New York: Routledge, 2014).

2. A useful overview of global inequality and how it is measured is Branko Milanovic, *Global Inequality: A New Approach for the Age of Globalization* (Cambridge, MA: Harvard University Press, 2016).

3. Emmanual Saez, "Striking It Richer: The Evolution of Top Incomes in the United States," June 2016, https://eml.berkeley.edu/~saez/saez-UStopincomes-2015.pdf.

4. They have made their data available at http://wid.world.

5. Filip Novokmet, Thomas Piketty, and Gabriel Zucman, "From Soviets to Oligarchs: Inequality and Property in Russia, 1905–2016" (NBER Working Paper Series, No. 23712, August 2017), 4.

6. The Russia Longitudinal Monitoring Survey of the Economic Situation and Population Health of the National Research University–Higher School of Economics, conducted by the National Research University–Higher School of Economics and Demoscope, in collaboration with the Carolina Population Center of the University of North Carolina at Chapel Hill and the Institute of Sociology of the Russian Academy of Sciences, http://www.cpc.unc.edu/projects/rlms, http://www.hse.ru/rlms.

7. Novokmet, Piketty, and Zucman, "From Soviets to Oligarchs," 5.

8. See http://wid.world/data.

9. Credit Suisse Research Institute, *Global Wealth Report 2017*, https://www.credit-suisse.com/corporate/en/research/research-institute/global-wealth-report.html.

10. Mariia Zheleznova, "Bednost' optimistov," *Vedomosti*, June 29, 2017.

11. "Ol'ga Golodets: V Rossii est' unikal'noe iavlenie—rabotaiushchie bednye," *Kommersant*, March 14, 2017.

12. "Rabotaiushchie bednye v Rossii i za rubezhom," *Sotsial'nyi biulleten'*, no. 10 (October 2017): 7–8.

13. Anatolii Komrakov, "Pravitel'stvu prikazano povysit' dokhody grazhdan," *Nezavisimaia gazeta*, September 12, 2017.

14. On "super-managers," see Thomas Piketty, *Capital in the Twenty-First Century* (Cambridge, MA: Harvard University Press, 2014), chap. 9.

15. Joseph E. Stiglitz, *The Price of Inequality: How Today's Divided Society Endangers Our Future* (New York: Norton, 2013).

16. Ol'ga Kuvshinova, "Kudrin predstavil napravleniia reform dlia Rossii," *Vedomosti*, April 11, 2017.

17. "Reiting samykh vysokooplachivaemykh top-menedzherov v Rossii vozglavili Miller i Sechin," *Vedomosti*, November 24, 2016.

18. https://www.forbes.com/sites/angelauyeung/2017/11/15/at-auction-russian-billionaire-sells-da-vinci-painting-for-the-most-money-ever-in-history/#185fc35c7124.

19. Quoted in Bulat Stolyarov, "Malen'kie sekrety biznesa dlia bogatykh," *Vedomosti*, August 27, 2002.

20. The "hollowing out" of middle-income jobs as a consequence of technological change and globalization has been discussed by many economists. See, for example, Claudia Goldin and Lawrence F. Katz, *The Race between Education and Technology* (Cambridge, MA: Harvard University Press, 2010).

21. E. M. Avraamova, "Novye vyzovy rasshireniiu rossiiskogo srednego klassa," April 2017, http://www.ranepa.ru/images/insap/Avraamova-srednii-klass.pdf.

22. Rakesh Kochhar, "Middle Class Fortunes in Western Europe," Pew Research Center, May 25, 2017. Russian figures are derived from the Russian State Statistical Office (Rosstat), http://www.gks.ru/bgd/regl/b17_14p/Main.htm.

23. On the resource curse, see Macartan Humphreys, Jeffrey Sachs, and Joseph Stiglitz, *Escaping the Resource Curse* (New York: Columbia University Press, 2007); Terry Lynn Karl, *The Paradox of Plenty: Oil Booms and Petro-States* (Berkeley: University of California Press, 1997); Michael Ross, "The Political Economy of the Resource Curse," *World Politics* 51, no. 2 (1999): 297–322; Michael Ross, "Does Oil Hinder Democracy?," *World Politics* 53, no. 3 (2001): 325–61; Michael Ross, "The Natural Resource Curse: How Wealth Can Make You Poor," in *Natural Resources and Violent Conflict: Options and Actions*, ed. Ian Bannon and Paul Collier (Washington, DC: World Bank, 2003), 17–42.

24. David Szakonyi, "Governing Business: The State and Business in Russia," Foreign Policy Research Institute, January 2018, https://www.fpri.org/wp-content/uploads/2018/01/Szakonyi-Final-Version.pdf.

25. In this respect, Russia illustrates the theory of inequality in the United States offered by Joseph Stiglitz more than the theory advanced by Thomas Piketty, which is centered on the rising share of private wealth in the economy.

26. See, for example, Philippe Aghion and Simon Commander, "On the Dynamics of Inequality in the Transition," *Economics of Transition* 7, no. 2 (1999): 275–98.

27. Thomas F. Remington, *The Politics of Inequality in Russia* (Cambridge: Cambridge University Press, 2011), chap. 2.

28. William Easterly, "The Middle Class Consensus and Economic Development," *Journal of Economic Growth* 6, no. 4 (2001): 317–35; Alberto Alesina, Reza Baqir, and William Easterly, "Public Goods and Ethnic Divisions," *Quarterly Journal of Economics* 114, no. 4 (1999): 1243–84.

29. Benjamin M. Friedman, *The Moral Consequences of Economic Growth* (New York: Knopf, 2005).

30. N. A. Avksent'ev, V. M. Baidin, O. A. Zarubina, and N. N. Sisigina, "Chastnye raskhody na zdravookhranenie v regionakh Rossii: faktory i posledstviia," *Finansovyi zhurnal/Financial Journal*, no. 2 (2016): 20–35.

31. S. V. Shishkin et al., *Zdravookhranenie: sovremennoe sostoianie i vozmozhnye stsenarii razvitiia* (Moscow: Higher School of Economics, 2017), https://www.hse.ru/data/2017/04/21/1168819633/Zdrav_2017.pdf.

32. L. M. Gokhberg et al., eds., *Indikatory obrazovaniia 2016: statisticheskii sbornik* (Moscow: Higher School of Economics, 2016), https://www.hse.ru/primarydata/io2016.

33. A. Kudrin and I. Sokolov, "Biudzhetnyi manevr i strukturnaia perestroika rossiiskoi ekonomiki," *Voprosy ekonomiki*, no. 9 (2017): 5–27.

34. Tat'iana Lomskaia and Elizaveta Bazanova, "Lish' chetvert' sotsial'nykh vyplat i l'got v Rossii dokhodit do nuzhdaiushchikhsia," *Vedomosti*, July 18, 2017.

35. Ol'ga Kuvshinova, "Sistema sotspodderzhki ne podderzhivaet bednykh—issledovanie," *Vedomosti*, November 28, 2016.

36. Author's calculations from Rosstat data.

37. World Bank Group, *Russia Economic Report*, no. 36 (November 2016), http://www.worldbank.org/en/country/russia/publication/rer.

38. World Bank Group, *Russia Economic Report*, 34.

39. Tat'iana Grishina, "Regionam NDFL dorozhe pribyli," *Kommersant*, October 5, 2016.

40. E. Gurvich and Iu. Sonina, "Mikroanaliz Rossiiskoi Pensionnoi Sistemy," *Voprosy ekonomiki*, no. 2 (2012): 41–43, tables 14–15.

41. Alexandra Prokopenko and Ol'ga Kuvshinova, "Vlasti khotiat obiazat' nerabotaiushchikh grazhdan oplachivat' sotsial'nye uslugi," *Vedomosti*, October 23, 2016.

42. *Informatsiia o sotsial'no-ekonomicheskom polozhenii Rossii 2017 god*, no. 12 (Moscow: Rosstat, 2017), 104.

43. Vystuplenie Vladimira Putina na rasshirennom zasedanii Gosudarstvennogo sovet, "O strategii razvitiia Rossii do 2020 goda," February 8, 2008, https://regnum.ru/news/954426.htm.

44. Vladimir Putin, "Spravedlivoe ustroistvo obshchestva, ekonomiki—glavnoe uslovie nashego ustoichivogo razvitiia v eti gody," *Komsomol'skaia pravda*, February 13, 2012.

45. Medvedev speaking at the Gaidar Forum, "Progress tekhnologii sozdaet risk rosta neravenstva, zaiavil Medvedev," January 16, 2018, http://quicknews.eu/ru/articles/695001.

Chapter Seven

Economic Policy

Laura Solanko and Pekka Sutela

The decade of the 1990s was not kind to the Russian economy. According to official statistics, during the decade the economy contracted up to 50 percent in industrial output, and another 40 percent of agricultural production was lost. In all, from 1990 to 1995, Russia's GDP declined by an estimated 50 percent, although some analysts argue that the true decline may have been somewhat less. Unemployment and labor unrest spiked. Russia experienced mass poverty. Inflation peaked at 2,509 percent in 1992, when most consumer prices were freed, and declined thereafter but failed to reach single digits during the remainder of the decade. The Russian government ran up enormous debt. The federal budget deficit fluctuated between 5 and 10 percent of GDP. As the decade wore on, budget deficits were financed by issuing short-term ruble-denominated government debt (GKOs). Due to the size of the financial need, together with political and economic uncertainty, the GKOs could only be sold with very high yields, which ultimately reached 100 percent annually. The debt spiral was clearly unsustainable. Worse, about one-third of GKOs were held by foreigners, which added to exchange rate risk. The litany of economic troubles culminated in the ruble crisis of August 1998, when the state had to announce a partial default on its debt, and the ruble collapsed against foreign currencies. The ruble crisis had two main effects. First, Russia's credibility as a borrower was lost. Second, the crisis changed the framework for Russia's macroeconomic policy. A political consensus for macroeconomic stabilization had been reached in principle by 1995, but turning the consensus in principle into consistent practical policies had proven impossible.

The 1998 crisis marked an end to one phase in Russia's economic transformation. Thereafter, a new and stronger consensus emerged on economic policy. The new approach was introduced by the leftist Primakov-Masliukov government in 1998–1999 (against their early announcements) and continued to the end of the Yeltsin period. The new economic consensus had several ingredients, which defined the political economy of Putin's Russia.[1] The purpose of this chapter is to examine the elements of the post-1998 economic stabilization consensus and the new challenges in the post-2008 world.

TASKS FOR THE 2000s

The first task facing the new Putin regime in 2000 was balancing the budget. Continued accumulation of debt was not only potentially destabilizing but also in conflict with the goal of attaining economic sovereignty. Russia needed to do away with the need to finance its debt from external lenders. The only way to do this in the short term was to reduce expenditures, in particular the complex and nontransparent web of subsidies that had emerged behind the veil of economic liberalization in the 1990s at the federal, regional, and local levels. From 1997 to 2001 a fiscal adjustment of some 10 percent of general government balance was enacted, primarily by cutting expenditures, especially subsidies to companies.[2] In the short term there was little alternative to this fiscal shock, as a return to monetizing deficits was excluded by the bitter experiences of the early 1990s. There was still a fiscal deficit of 4 percent of GDP in 1999, but thereafter the country experienced surpluses until the financial crisis of 2008–2009. Public foreign debt shrank from 66.8 percent of GDP in 1999 to 2.7 percent in 2007; total public debt remained less than 15 percent of GDP after 2005.[3] Russia, one of the grandest fiscal failures of the 1990s, emerged as a model for fiscal conservatism in just a few years. Necessity caused by failure was turned into virtue.

Russia's quest to balance the budget was helped by traditional export commodities—oil, gas, minerals, and, later, agricultural production. Exporters reaped great benefits from the cheap ruble and later from high prices, although their export volumes were often constrained by production and transport capacity. Russia was able to increase exports of oil and some minerals while exports of pipeline-tied gas stagnated. The world had an unprecedented golden period of economic growth during 1992–2008. Russia, with its newly privatized companies, was at last able to join booming global markets. From the trough of early 1998 to the peak in summer 2008, the export price of oil increased tenfold. Prices of Russia's other export commodities also increased, though generally not as much. Evsey Gurvich and Aleksei Kudrin estimate that the oil windfall alone reached up to 15 percent of GDP annually, while economists Clifford Gaddy and Barry Ickes give even higher estimates.[4] The price of oil was important for Russian incomes and budgets, but Russia was not able to live on oil revenue alone. Distributing the revenue windfall became a key policy issue that had not existed in the 1990s because of low oil prices.

The second task was to fix the tax system. The state had fought a losing battle for more effective company taxation in the 1990s, especially under Minister of Finance Boris Fyodorov. The true state of company finances was hidden in nonmonetary exchanges and webs of implicit subsidies, especially at the regional level. It is estimated that only one-fifth of all transactions in and around the domestic energy sector were conducted in rubles. The state routinely accepted nonmonetary clearing of tax obligations. A construction company could have its tax arrears offset by contributing to a public construction project. What prices were used in calculating a proper offset remained unclear. With a ballooning export revenue windfall, this situation could no longer be accepted. Oligarchs, regional governors, and others had to be subordinated to an emerging "power vertical," to use Putin's words.

The share of the federal government in tax revenue increased, and most regions became dependent on tax transfers from the Moscow center. A stiff oil revenue taxation regime was introduced: the average tax rate rose to 60 percent, and the marginal tax rate even surpassed 90 percent.[5] The former figure is not exorbitant in international comparison, but the latter was, leaving hardly any incentives to increase upstream oil production. The confiscatory tax rate was corrected only years later. In 2014, the burden of oil-sector taxation shifted from taxing export revenue to taxing oil production.

The state also needed to decide what to do with the tax revenue from the energy sector, which had reached one-half of all federal tax revenue. Logically there were three alternatives. The first alternative was that monies could be distributed among the population, to be used for consumption or private investment as households wished. In view of the income decline and hugely increased income differentials in the 1990s, this would have been a politically popular solution, but it was abandoned by the regime as populism. Many resource-rich countries had shown evidence of the "Dutch disease" due to using high export revenue to increase money and wealth of the population, presumably for the general good, but actually leading to high inflation, an overvalued exchange rate, and lost competitiveness in nonresource production. The Putin regime was politically strong enough to avoid this option.

A second alternative had stronger political support and suggested using oil-sector tax revenue for investment in the economy at large. Though investment ratios were very high under Soviet socialism, evidence showed that much of the money used by the state had actually disappeared in hidden inflation, with little if any impact on actual production capacity. Russia thus inherited a capital stock that was smaller, older, and more worn out than official statistics claimed. What had been inherited from the Soviet Union was not what the emerging market economy needed. In addition, while official GDP had dropped by almost one-half in the 1990s, the collapse of investment was even steeper, some four-fifths. The country badly needed high real investment to grow in a sustainable way. Moreover, there was a need to close plants in and around the military sector, which produced very little of what was needed in a market economy. This side of capitalist creative destruction was, however, hardly raised in Russian debates. Protecting existing jobs has always been a priority that constrained economic choices in the Putin regime. One key question for the future is whether this basically conservative attitude will continue.

Because there was little optimism that foreign investment was sufficient to fund modernization, the argument was made that export revenue windfall should be invested into the economy, not only in roads, railways, and airports, but also in health, education, housing, innovation, and other such purposes that were seen as the responsibility of the state. This argument for development was made, not surprisingly, by the Ministry of Economic Development. Investment in the economy was to receive a major boost by the introduction of four "national programs" that took effect in 2006 with great fanfare, in health, housing, education, and agriculture. Dmitry Medvedev, as first deputy prime minister, was responsible for their implementation. Looking not at the budget plans but at their actual implementation, however, shows that the national programs' share as a proportion of all state expenditures never increased.

A final alternative proved the winner of policy debate. Russia opted for a fiscally conservative strategy of maintaining a budget surplus, paying back most public debt, and accumulating reserve funds. This course was pursued by Aleksei Kudrin, who served as the minister of finance from May 2000 to September 2011. The decisive voice for fiscal conservatism was that of Vladimir Putin. Steep taxation of oil export revenue was in place by 2004. Accumulation of a stabilization fund was started the same year. By the end of 2007 it amounted to $156.8 billion and a year later to $225.1 billion.[6] The growth was stupendous. As part of the official reserves of the country— peaking at just over $600 billion in mid-2008—these monies had a key role in combating the 2008 crisis. Just before the crisis, the stabilization fund had been divided into a reserve fund (for stabilizing fiscal revenue) and a national welfare fund (mostly for supporting the pension system).

The third task was transforming Russia from an economy based on barter to one based on rubles; in other words, the economy had to be monetized. A monetized economy increases the productivity of labor compared to an economy based on barter. In Russia, barter chains could have a number of participants, and the transaction costs involved in establishing and maintaining such chains were great. Barter has little transparency, exchange pricing could be arbitrary, avoiding taxation was easy, and the whole barter economy was prone to corruption. When barter was used in lieu of taxation, the efficiency of public finance obviously suffered. Goods obtained in barter can only be used for limited purposes. On the other hand, money facilitates risk control, saving for investment, and economic growth. There is considerable evidence that monetary and financial systems contribute to economic growth. Berkowitz and DeJong show that financial development has been the key domestic driving force for Russia's economic growth.[7]

States usually wish to have complete or at least shared (in currency unions) control over the money circulating within their borders. It is a matter of prestige—sovereign currency being one of the defining features of a state—but more important is the economic benefit. Beyond that, sovereign currency opens up the possibility of monetary policy; its scope depends on foreign trade and trade payments. Russia liberalized its foreign trade in the early 1990s, but capital mobility was officially announced as a major achievement of economic policy only in 2006 and this attitude remains to today. Russia has not introduced capital controls even in face of the macroeconomic adversity of 2014–2015.

There was some speculation in the 1990s that Russia's nonmonetary market economy was nationally specific, an outcome of the Soviet economy. However, as predicted by standard economic theory, the Russian economy monetized and de-dollarized quickly as inflation was brought under control and the exchange rate stabilized. At its peak in late 1998, barter accounted for 61 percent of manufacturing turnover. The ratio normalized to about 10 percent within a few years.[8]

The ruble had lost much of its credibility in the early 1990s, and continued high inflation made it difficult to reestablish. Savings held in rubles were lost in 1992, to some degree in 1994, and again more widely in 1998. Dollars remained for a few years rare in Russia, but the share of foreign currency deposits as a percentage of all deposits peaked at more than 40 percent after 1998.[9] From 1999 to 2007 deposit dollarization declined gradually, especially after 2003 when the ruble began to appreciate due to high export revenue. In early 2008 deposit dollarization hit a minimum of 12 to 13 percent, but the possibility of dollarization remains real. This was seen at the peak of the financial crisis and again in 2014, when lower oil prices and economic stagnation led both to a weaker ruble and avoidance of using it as a currency reserve.

MONETARY POLICY

Russia's transformation into a money-based economy was one of the major positive changes of the early 2000s. However, Russian financial markets still remain small and underdeveloped relative to the size of the economy, which has implications for the conduct of monetary policy.

Inflation

Turning first to inflation, table 7.1 indicates that inflation was on a down-ward trend, from 12 percent in 2003 to 9 percent in 2006. In 2007 and 2008 it again increased. Some of the increase may be explained by external factors: the global economy was in overdrive, global food prices increased, and though Russia is among the three biggest exporters of grain, it imports many other foodstuffs. There was also domestic overheating with excess demand for skilled city-based labor and construction materials in particular. Fiscal policy was procyclical as it targeted the budget surplus. As revenue was increased by higher export tariff incomes, expenditures increased as well. The ruble devaluation of fall 2008 raised import prices.

After 2008, inflation continued to decline to 6 percent in 2011. Many Russians blame inflation on the monopolized structure of the economy, but that is a valid explanation only if monopoly profits increase continuously or

Table 7.1. Russian Monetary Indicators, 2003–2017 (in percentages, end of year)

	CPI	M2 Growth
2003	12.0	50.5
2004	11.7	35.8
2005	10.9	36.8
2006	9.0	48.8
2007	11.9	47.5
2008	13.3	1.2
2009	8.8	16.3
2010	8.8	28.5
2011	6.1	22.6
2012	6.6	43.5
2013	11.4	0.8
2014	12.9	17.7
2015	5.4	31.1
2016	2.5	22.3
2017	2.2	11.9

Source: BOFIT Russia Statistics, https://www .bofit.fi/en/monitoring/statistics/Russia -statistics (accessed April 30, 2018).

the efficiency of monopoly producers keeps declining. Some of the stubborn level of inflation is due to needed hikes of tariffs for gas, electricity, and transportation. More importantly, before the switch to a free float in the end of 2014, fighting inflation was not the Central Bank's sole priority.

Most central banks concentrate on inflation control, perhaps together with maintaining an acceptable level of employment, as the Federal Reserve does. The Russian Central Bank has targeted both keeping inflation on a downward trend and stabilizing the ruble exchange rate. The latter has been desirable due to the continuing risk of dollarization. In practice, as long as export revenue kept increasing, the Central Bank increased the ruble supply, as shown in table 7.1.

A booming ruble supply should preferably have been sterilized, that is, withdrawn from the market by selling government or Central Bank bonds. As bond markets remained very small—and the state did not need them for financing budget deficits—this option did not work. The Central Bank did issue its bonds, but not so much to sterilize as to offer an asset in which to park excess liquidity. There has been no distinct effect on the financial markets stemming from Central Bank issuance of bonds.[10]

The Central Bank of Russia first shifted its strategy to inflation targeting and full exchange rate flexibility as longer-term goals around mid-decade. Russia finally announced that inflation targeting would take place in the beginning of 2015. As the ruble came under pressure in the currency market, the shift was brought forward to November 2014. A shift to inflation targeting implies a shift from rough policy instruments like reserve ratios to more market-based policy instruments like interest rates. A critical precondition for the shift is that the financial markets are sophisticated enough to be responsive to changes in Central Bank key rates. A country that has segmented markets, lack of trust, negative real interest rates, and excess liquidity in the banking system was not an obvious candidate.

The Central Bank had the clear backing of the political leadership in pushing through the shift. The nominal interest rate was raised to 17 percent in December 2014, making real interest rates positive. While extremely tight monetary policy discouraged bank lending, it had the desired effect on inflation. Toward the end of 2017, market participants have begun to adjust to the new monetary policy regime. Both headline inflation and inflation expectations have declined to levels never before experienced in Russia. The inflation rate fell to single digits during 2015–2017 and was below 3 percent in both 2016 and 2017 as shown in table 7.1. Low inflation is expected for the foreseeable future. Recent studies note a clear break in the Central Bank's policy rules in early 2015.[11]

Exchange Rate Policy

The Central Bank chose to maintain a stable nominal exchange rate up to 2009, first pegging to the dollar and then to a bi-currency basket that reflected the structure of Russia's foreign trade (55 percent USD/45 percent euro). Exchange rate stability was maintained by interventions in foreign exchange markets. There was pressure on the ruble to appreciate, as much of the ballooning export revenue was exchanged into rubles, thus strengthening demand for domestic currency. The Central Bank sold rubles and bought foreign currency. There is no hard evidence that the ruble was overvalued in 1998, but it was clearly undervalued after the devaluation. As no country with an open economy can choose a real exchange rate of its liking, real appreciation of the ruble was inevitable in the 2000s. As the nominal exchange rate was kept stable, real appreciation had to happen through domestic inflation that was higher than abroad.

Targeting the nominal exchange rate was understandable given Russia's history of dollarization and the goal of de-dollarization. Shifts in asset allocation between the ruble and foreign currencies have been sensitive to the real exchange rate between currencies, a matter of rational market behavior. Targeting the exchange rate may also have been inevitable as the Central Bank did not have a monetary policy channel through which to choose a suitable money supply. There was a lot of uncertainty about demand for money. Fine-tuning the money supply was also impossible as the behavioral patterns of the small but fast-growing banking sector were largely untried. The Russian Central Bank has mostly concentrated on fighting money laundering and other violations of regulation, in the process learning little of actual bank behavior. There has been a target for annual money growth, but that has been traditionally missed by wide margins, with no negative consequences for the Central Bank. Nor could the Central Bank easily use interest rates to regulate demand for money. With little market for interest-bearing assets and negative real interest rates, the interest rate channel was of little importance.

Beginning in 2009, the Central Bank gradually withdrew from foreign exchange markets, and the exchange rate policy moved to a managed float. The width of the corridor changed over time. The exchange rate was allowed to move freely within the corridor. If it approached either of the set corridor boundaries, the Central Bank intervened. If the change in markets was deemed permanent, the corridor itself was shifted. This situation changed in December 2014 when the Central Bank allowed the ruble to float freely along with the fall in the price of oil. Most central banks, including Russia's, combine inflation targeting with a floating exchange rate.

The policy task ahead was not an easy one. All economic agents had to adjust to a volatile exchange rate—not a simple task in an economy where many contracts and, for example, rental agreements in prime locations were still specified in dollars. Nevertheless, the floating ruble has brought tangible benefits for the economy. Fluctuations in oil prices in 2015–2017 had a much smaller effect on public finances and the economy as a whole as the weakening ruble took most of the hit.

FISCAL POLICY

Taxation

Before 2010 the main responsibility for fighting inflation remained with fiscal policy. Most windfall oil export revenue was and still is taxed by the state. As noted above, energy-sector taxation—including export tariffs and natural resource exploitation payments—has accounted for roughly one-half of federal fiscal revenue. Russia is dependent on energy for exports and tax revenue, but not directly for jobs. Less than 2 percent of all Russian jobs are in extracting and transporting basic energy. [12]

Taming the oil sector for taxation has been a major challenge. Oil companies have been able to minimize their taxation by using such vehicles as transfer pricing and on- and offshore tax havens. As a consequence, many analysts have concluded that official statistics grossly underestimate the energy sector's true contribution to GDP (probably somewhere between 20 and 30 percent, rather than below 10 percent as shown in official statistics). [13] Tax authorities have been unable to trust the bookkeeping values and profits of oil companies. Company taxation has therefore not been based on profits but on trade turnover.

Taxation of oil and oil companies is also complicated by the changing structure of production. As long as almost all production took place in conditions similar to those of the traditional supergiant fields of Western Siberia, the taxation system did not matter too much. Production, however, must now increasingly move into high-cost and widely differing far eastern and northern conditions. Taxation by turnover discriminates severely against investment in such fields, which are needed for maintaining national production levels. Consequently, both oil and gas producers have received tax exemptions, first in the Far East and in the North as well. Turnover-based taxation that was supposed to be similar for all has thus given way to negotiated taxation, a certain recipe for influence peddling and outright corruption in the heart of Russia's export and tax revenue. This situation helps to explain why energy-sector taxation has been in turmoil for decades. The current shift from export revenue taxation toward a key role of natural resource exploitation payments hardly changes the situation.

Contrary to most advanced market economies, Russia receives only a little revenue from the taxation of personal income, accounting for only a couple of percent of GDP; most government revenue comes from foreign trade, commodity taxes, and profit tax, as well as from social security contributions. Income tax avoidance has traditionally been rife. Russia therefore did not engage in a huge fiscal risk when it was one of the first Central and Eastern European countries to introduce a flat tax of 13 percent on all income in 2001. The goal was to decrease tax avoidance. Studies show that the impact on tax avoidance was much greater than on labor supply.[14] Russia's adoption of a flat income tax is seen as one of the major economic policy achievements of the early Putin regime. Introducing progressive income taxation regularly figures in further tax reform proposals, especially in those coming from experts with a European egalitarian value orientation. The prospects for abandoning the flat income tax, however, remain weak. It is a feature of Russian capitalism to remain.

Regional Revenue

Russia is, according to the 1993 constitution, a federation. Since 1992, relations between the center and regions have changed thoroughly. During the Yeltsin years, regions were much more independent and less beholden to the center. In the 1990s, regional revenues as a share of total state revenues increased from 40 percent in 1992 to about 55 percent in 1997–1998.[15] One might have expected the regions to do their utmost to widen the tax base by promoting new entrepreneurship. Instead, incumbent plants captured the state. Both regional and local authorities tended to protect existing jobs through taxation, regulation, and corruption.[16] This situation was partly due to the importance of several hundred one-company towns, usually based on military-industrial companies, that had little future. Simultaneously, regional expenditures as a share of total expenditures also rose from less than 30 percent to about 55 percent.

The relationship between the center and regions changed in many ways when Putin came to power. Putin took several steps to reestablish the primacy of centralized power beginning in 2000. Establishing "the vertical of power," the Putin regime aimed at controlling regional political and economic elites. The share of regional expenditures declined only slightly, to about one-half of total expenditures. In contrast, the share of regional revenues fell significantly, to about 35 percent in 2005.[17] On average, therefore, regions became dependent on transfers from the center. Even though direct elections of regional governors were reinstated in 2012, the president retained the de facto right to dismiss and nominate any candidate. Thus, regions and regional leadership remained dependent on financial support by the Kremlin. Loyalty to the party in power is awarded by promotions or financial assistance. Loyalty is measured by voter turnout and share of votes for the party in power, not by a region's economic prosperity.[18]

Budget Rules

Budget expenditures tend to increase when the economy is booming. This was clearly the case in Russia in the latter half of the 2000s, when budget expenditures contributed to overheating the economy. Current expenditure decisions often imply longer-term spending commitments. Basing expenditure decisions on temporarily high, but intrinsically volatile, oil revenue is fiscally irresponsible. For well over a decade, the International Monetary Fund has argued that fiscal policy should be based on maintaining a constant "non-oil" deficit, defined as expenditure minus revenue, assuming some "normal" oil price and ensuing revenues. While the argument for using a non-oil deficit constraint on expenditure commitments is compelling, the apparent simplicity of the non-oil deficit concept is deceptive.

In spring 2012, Russian authorities debated whether the "normal oil price" should be the average of the past ten years (as the fiscally conservative Ministry of Finance argued) or the past three years (as preferred by the high-spending Ministry of Economic Development). This seeming technicality does not have a self-evident answer but implies huge differences in expenditure levels, as the average oil price of 2010–2012 was much higher than for 2001–2012.

The revised budget rule, finally adopted in late 2012, restricted the federal budget deficit to 1 percent of annual forecasted GDP from 2013 to 2015. The collapse of oil prices in late 2014 and the subsequent recession made it impossible for the government to adhere to the rule. The newest budget rule was adopted in summer 2017. Under the current rule, the federal primary budget balance must be zero or positive with estimated budget revenues. The estimate uses a base average oil price of $40 per barrel that is increased by 2 percent each year. All budget revenue from production and export of oil and gas above the base oil price is to be transferred to the National Welfare Fund.[19] The base oil price, a very conservative estimate of future oil prices, reflects a hard-earned understanding that a world of permanently high oil prices may be illusory. The promise of a huge transfer of income to Russia's next generation no longer seems guaranteed.

THE 2008–2009 FINANCIAL CRISIS

The global financial crisis that started in late 2008 and extended through 2009 revealed how dependent the Russian economy is on swings in global markets. The first impact was on export prices, led by oil and followed by minerals and then gas. When the crisis hit, there was a lot of uncertainty about the coming pattern of the crisis. Although some expected a fast dip followed by an equally fast global recovery (a V-form crisis), the majority opinion in Russia, as elsewhere, foresaw a long recession (a U-form crisis).

Amid the uncertainty, the collapse of global commodity prices occurred faster and deeper than was justified in retrospect. When fears of a U-form recession gave way to optimism for a V-form, global oil prices also recovered quickly.

The second impact was on Russia's export volumes. For example, steel exports were cut in half practically overnight, as European construction activity was curtailed. More important for the long run, in the beginning of 2009, Russia and Ukraine got involved in another dispute over gas prices, transit tariffs, and the settlement of accumulated Ukrainian debt for gas. Four-fifths of Russian gas exports to Europe cross Ukrainian territory, and supplies to Central Europe were disrupted exactly at the time when relatively cheap liquefied natural gas (LNG) was entering markets in large amounts. Russia's reliability as gas supplier was compromised, and its gas export prices seemed inflated. The Russian-Ukrainian crisis has further devalued Europe's willingness to depend on Russia for a quarter of its gas consumption.

The third and arguably most important impact was that global investors started pulling their monies out of all peripheral markets. Russian public and private entities were not deep in debt, but existing debt was short term, it had increased quickly, and investors grew pessimistic about Russia's overall economic prospects since they tended to see them through the prism of oil prices. Foreign short-term finance had maintained what existed as interbank markets, and now that it was withdrawn, the wheels of Russian finance were fast slowing down. Another full-scale financial crisis was threatening Russia, and were financial markets to stall, the impact on production, incomes, and employment would be drastic as well.

In responding to the 2008–2009 financial crisis, Russia chose an expensive policy alternative. Some $200 billion in official reserves were used to satisfy demand for foreign currencies. But this money did not just disappear. Some of it was used to service private foreign debt, which declined by about $100 billion during the crisis.[20] The remainder of the reserves that were expended were shifted from public reserves into private assets. Most important, devaluation did not lead to a continuous spiral fed by further expectations of further devaluation as experts had expected. What had failed elsewhere somehow succeeded in Russia.

Similar to other countries, the Russian government supported both its financial sector and the real economy. A large portion of the support was channeled to huge manufacturing enterprises whose profitability was questionable at best. The crisis measures helped in keeping employment high but also cemented old and inefficient production structures for years to come. Not only did the non-oil deficit widen to almost 15 percent of GDP, but large commitments were also left as a fiscal burden for future years.

THE RECESSION OF 2015–2016

Recovery from the effects of the global financial crisis was rapid, as oil prices returned to precrisis levels by early 2011. After the rapid recovery, growth rates began to slow. Investment growth turned negative in 2013. For reasons that are unclear, domestic investors assessed that the rate of return to risk was better elsewhere. When oil prices collapsed again in the latter half of 2014, the Russian economy was hardly growing at all. Moreover, the global environment was less benign than at any time since the collapse of the Soviet Union.

The illegal annexation of Crimea and the war in eastern Ukraine led Western countries to impose economic sanctions on Russia. The sanctions severely restricted the access of several of Russia's largest corporations and commercial banks to global financial markets. Russia retaliated by banning imports of certain foodstuffs from the European Union, the United States, and other countries. These countersanctions naturally increased consumer prices and contributed to a decrease in household real incomes.

The fiscal policy reaction to the crisis was expected. The budget rule was temporarily lifted, and federal expenditures were allowed to remain intact. The monetary policy framework changed dramatically as the Central Bank shifted to inflation targeting. Suddenly the ruble was allowed to fluctuate freely, leading to a sizable devaluation. A weaker ruble made domestic production more attractive and smoothed the effect of falling oil prices on government revenue. At the same time, however, monetary policy became extremely tight. To fight ballooning inflation and support the currency, the Central Bank's key rate was raised from 5.5 to 17 percent in December 2014.

The resulting recession was milder than in 2009, wiping out less than 3 percent of Russian GDP in 2015–2016. In contrast to the previous crisis, real incomes took a serious hit. Household real incomes were almost 10 percent lower in 2016 than in 2013. Economic recession and the increasing role of the state in the economy may have seriously hampered social upward mobility, lowering the potential growth rate in the future.

NEW TASKS FOR THE 2010s AND 2020s

Toward the end of the 2000s, the critical tasks of post-1998 economic stabilization had been achieved. Thanks to rising oil prices and a greatly streamlined tax system, the federal budget was running sizable surpluses, and the economy had been successfully remonetized. As the urgency of fixing the system waned, a wide consensus emerged that Russia's economic development could not be based on oil and gas. Experts projected that oil production would increase little, if at all. Maintaining current export volumes demanded major improvement in the notoriously low energy efficiency of the economy. Gas prices in particular had to be increased to reach international levels. Households and jobs could no longer be subsidized by artificially low energy prices. Modernization and diversification were badly needed. That was the message of the first "Russia 2020" economic program that was passed in late 2008. The 2008 global crisis, however, postponed most attempts to implement the program. Its goal of making Russia an innovation-based society by 2020 was utopian at best.

The problems were real enough, and another attempt was needed. In January 2011, then prime minister Vladimir Putin gave the Russian economic expert community the task of "writing the economic program of the post–May 2012 government." The document produced by more than one thousand experts was published in March 2012.[21] At 864 pages, it is not a policy program but rather a wide-ranging survey of policy tasks, many of them complex and demanding. Within two months, this vast document had been condensed into "May Decrees" (*Maiskie ukazi*) that President Putin signed in conjunction with his inauguration address on May 7, 2012.[22] The May Decrees required the Medvedev government to fulfill a range of tasks varying from increasing the country's overall labor productivity by 150 percent to increasing the share of domestically produced critical medicine to 90 percent. Little remained of the original program document's notions of enhancing the public-private partnership or reforming the country's social policy framework.

The approach taken in the May 2012 Decrees underlines two broad issues. First, the Putin regime increasingly believes in state-led development. Private enterprise and free competition, with all the uncertainty inherent in a free market economy, is not favored. The worldview of the decrees is one of "manual control," whereby economic development occurs by establishing and fulfilling detailed targets singled out by the president. Second, the leadership acknowledges that the growth model of the 2000s is no longer relevant. Many of the drivers of past growth were transient, and the world economy can no longer be expected to provide as benign an environment for Russia as before.

In any case, the regime clearly lacks a strategic view on how Russia is supposed to prosper. This lack of vision has resulted in a multitude of narrow, sector-specific development programs that in many cases support vested interests with the aim of maintaining employment.[23] In this respect, the approach of the May 2012 Decrees was closer to reality than that of the 2008 or 2012 versions of the Russia 2020 strategy.

Following the practice of previous election cycles, preparation of new economic policy strategies for the post–May 2018 government began in late 2016. This time the task was shared by two competing groups. The first group was led by the conservative Stolypin Club, while the second aligned around the liberal-minded Center for Strategic Studies. Both groups acknowledged that Russia badly needed more investment, the pension system required reform, and the competitiveness of domestic industries had to be improved. Neither program was officially published, but the new May 2018 Decree mention many of the ideas favored by the more liberal group. The underlying approach to economic development, however, is no different from the previous decrees. The May 2018 Decree requires the Medvedev government to create twelve new national programs in areas ranging from digital economy to demography to guarantee that the country achieves "breakthroughs in science and technology and socioeconomic development."[24] The current regime clearly seems to believe in state-led economic development driven by sectoral programs and executive orders.

Hopes for serious reforms that would address the structural weaknesses of the Russian economy are not high. The regime feels no urgency to embark on necessary reforms that are by their nature complex and difficult to implement. The Russian economy is still capable of generating a tolerable standard of living for most of the population. And the incumbent industrial firms have no interest in making the economy more transparent or competitive.

This looming stagnation raises fundamental issues. How can the business environment be improved to facilitate long-term investment? Assuming that Western sanctions are not lifted, where can financial resources be raised? And where should investment be made? Currently, Russia has a competitive advantage in natural resources, agriculture, and—potentially at least—mathematics-based services. The growing importance of import-substitution policies makes it increasingly difficult to assess if any of these would be competitive in an open economy.

CONCLUSION

The economic policies of Putin's third term were based on conservative fiscal policies, a relatively independent inflation-targeting Central Bank, and increasingly protectionist trade policies. All of this has allowed the economy to weather the 2015–2016 recession relatively unscathed but has resulted in declining real incomes and a growing role of the state in the economy. For the most part the future does not look very promising, although there are sectoral exceptions, for example in agriculture, which has been growing faster than national GDP since 2013, and the value of food exports is steadily increasing.[25] Russian GDP grew on average by 7 percent annually in 2000–2008. The average growth in 2010–2017 was 1.7 percent. Most forecasters expect similar growth to prevail well into the next decade. To find new sources of growth, Russia needs a strategic view on how to prosper in the future. Such a strategic view has been completely lacking since 2012.

Pension reform, which is difficult to plan and implement, is also badly needed. The same intractability applies to many other needed reforms. The Ukrainian crisis and subsequent geopolitical tensions have made deep structural reforms much less probable than optimists wished for six years ago.

Current and future challenges are complex and difficult, and Russia is highly unlikely to match its growth performance of the 2000s. Russia's investment rate is alarmingly low for an emerging economy, its labor force is shrinking for demographic reasons, and the international environment is much less favorable than earlier. Russia has only itself to blame for most of these predicaments. Most importantly, the Putin regime has failed to make needed reforms and adjustments. The reason is not a shortage of sensible reform programs or detailed road maps. Summoning the political will to address systemic deficiencies during Putin's fourth term will be one of his key challenges.

DISCUSSION QUESTIONS

1. What were the three economic tasks that the Putin regime had in 2000 to put the Russian economy on the right track?
2. How have Russia's fiscal policies changed over time?
3. How have Russia's monetary policies changed over time?
4. What is the main economic policy challenge facing Russian leadership over the next five years?
5. Are you optimistic or pessimistic about Russia's economic future? Why?

SUGGESTED READINGS

Alexeev, Michael, and Shlomo Weber, eds. *Handbook of the Russian Economy*. Oxford: Oxford University Press, 2013.
Åslund, Anders. *Russia's Capitalist Revolution*. Washington, DC: Peterson Institute for International Economics, 2007.
Sutela, Pekka. *The Political Economy of Putin's Russia*. London: Routledge, 2012.
Treisman, Daniel. *The Return: Russia's Journey from Gorbachev to Medvedev*. New York: Free Press, 2011.

NOTES

1. Pekka Sutela, *The Political Economy of Putin's Russia* (London: Routledge, 2012).
2. David Owen and David O. Robinson, eds., *Russia Rebounds* (Washington, DC: International Monetary Fund, 2003).
3. BOFIT Russia Statistics, https://www.bofit.fi/en/monitoring/statistics/russia-statistics (accessed May 10, 2018).
4. Alexey Kudrin and Evsey Gurvich, "A New Growth Model for the Russian Economy," *Russian Journal of Economics* 1, no. 1 (2015): 30–54; Clifford G. Gaddy and Barry W. Ickes,

"Russia after the Global Economic Crisis," *Eurasian Geography and Economics* 50, no. 3 (2010): 281–311.

5. Michael Alexeev and Robert Conrad, "The Russian Oil Tax Regime: A Comparative Perspective," *Eurasian Geography and Economics* 49, no. 2 (2009): 93–114.

6. BOFIT Russia Statistics, https://www.bofit.fi/en/monitoring/statistics/russia-statistics (accessed May 10, 2018).

7. Daniel Berkowitz and Daniel N. DeJong, "Growth in Post-Soviet Russia: A Tale of Two Transitions," *Journal of Economic Behavior & Organization* 79, nos. 1–2 (2011): 133–43.

8. Russian Economic Barometer, http://ecsoc.ru/en/reb (accessed June 11, 2012).

9. Seija Lainela and Alexey Ponomarenko, "Russian Financial Markets and Monetary Policy Instruments," *BOFIT Online*, no. 3 (2012).

10. Lainela and Ponomarenko, "Russian Financial Markets," 26.

11. Iikka Korhonen and Riikka Nuutilainen, "Breaking Monetary Policy Rules in Russia," *Russian Journal of Economics* 3, no. 4 (2017): 366–78.

12. Employment share obviously grows when a wider definition of the energy sector is used, including refining, trading, and manufacturing branches that are dependent on providing energy producers with pipes, machinery, and so forth. The figure grows further if jobs dependent on low energy costs are added, but doing that makes distinguishing the energy and the nonenergy parts of the economy impossible.

13. Sutela, *The Political Economy of Putin's Russia*, 94–95.

14. Denvil Duncan and Klara Sabirianova Peter, "Does Labour Supply Respond to a Flat Tax? Evidence from Russian Tax Reform," *Economics of Transition* 18, no. 2 (2010): 333–63.

15. Migara A. De Silva, Galina Kurlyanskaya, Elena Andreeva, and Natalia Golovanova, *Intergovernmental Reforms in the Russian Federation: One Step Forward, Two Steps Back?* (Washington, DC: World Bank, 2009).

16. Ekaterina Zhuravskaya, "Federalism in Russia," in *Russia after the Global Economic Crisis*, ed. Anders Åslund, Sergey Guriev, and Andrew W. Kuchins (Washington, DC: Peterson Institute for International Economics, 2010), 59–78.

17. De Silva et al., *Intergovernmental Reforms*.

18. Thomas Remington, Irina Soboleva, Anton Sobolev, and Mark Urnov, "Governors' Dilemmas: Economic and Social Policy Trade-Offs in the Russian Regions (Evidence from Four Case Studies)," *Europe-Asia Studies* 65, no. 10 (2013): 1855–76.

19. BOFIT Weekly 17/2017, https://www.bofit.fi/en/monitoring/weekly/2017/vw201729_1 (accessed April 26, 2018).

20. BOFIT Weekly 16/2009, https://www.bofit.fi/en/monitoring/weekly/2009/venajan_ulkomainen_velka_supistui (accessed April 26, 2018).

21. "Strategiia-2020: novaia model rosta—novaia sotsialnaia politika," http://www.2020strategy.ru (accessed March 21, 2012).

22. Ukazov Presidenta Rossii ot 7 Maya 2012 No. 596–606, http://government.ru/orders/selection/406 (accessed April 26, 2018).

23. Yuri Simachev, Natalia Akindinova, et al., *Strukturnaya politika v Rossii: novie uslovia i vosmozhnaya povestka* (Moscow: Higher School of Economics, 2018).

24. "Executive Order on National Goals and Strategic Objectives of the Russian Federation through to 2024," http://en.kremlin.ru/events/president/news/57425 (accessed May 10, 2018).

25. See Stephen K. Wegren, Alexander Nikulin, and Irina Trotsuk, *Food Policy and Food Security: Putting Food on the Russian Table* (Lanham, MD: Lexington Books, 2018); and Stephen K. Wegren and Christel Elvestad, "Russia's Self-Sufficiency and Food Security: An Assessment," *Post-Communist Economies* 30, no. 5 (2018).

Chapter Eight

Crime and Corruption

Louise Shelley

More than two decades after the collapse of the Soviet Union, organized crime and corruption remain intractable problems for the Russian state. Violent crime rates are high, especially for homicide. Ethnically related violence exacerbates these rates.[1] Organized crime is no longer as visibly violent, and gang wars with numerous fatalities are no longer fought for control over the aluminum industry, as was the case in the 1990s. However, the extent of the crime problem has not diminished; its form has merely changed over time. Powerful organized crime groups are no longer as influential because the functions and activities of organized crime have been subsumed by the increasingly authoritarian Russian state and the president's political cronies.[2]

With the enormous growth of Russia's drug markets, its crime groups are now more deeply involved in the narcotics trade than in the past. Moreover, the pervasive problem of corporate raiding,[3] by which valuable businesses are taken over by force and legal manipulation, reflects the fact that organized crime often serves as the enforcers for powerful officials who seek to obtain the property of political rivals and competitors.[4]

The Russian state, because of an absence of political will and a pervasive high level of corruption within its ranks, has been ineffective in dealing with these problems. Moreover, the long-term rule of President Putin and his close associates has proven the adage that "absolute power corrupts absolutely."[5] Compounding the problem is the political-criminal nexus and the fact that politicians who assume political office have legal immunity from investigation and prosecution.[6] The specialized police units that combated organized crime were abolished in September 2008 without any alternative enforcement strategy.[7] Moreover, the problem of corruption has become a highly political issue that drove tens if not hundreds of thousands of Russian protesters to the streets. The anticorruption efforts of blogger Aleksei Naval'ny make him a popular political figure within Russian society.[8] President Putin restricted this challenger by placing Naval'ny under house arrest and trying to isolate him and would not let him participate as a candidate in the presidential election in 2018.[9]

Russia's crime problems are not just national; they are international. Russian criminals were among the first to take full advantage of globalization.[10] Some had links to officials in the Kremlin, and others came out of the security apparatus. Many criminals who initially set up operations overseas were the so-called *vory-v-zakone* (thieves-in-law), or the traditional elite of the Soviet-era criminal world who lived according to rigidly established rules.[11] In addition, many smaller groups of criminals from the former USSR are operating within Western Europe, involved in serious organized crime, tax evasion, and money laundering.[12] Russian-speaking organized crime has assumed an important role in the darknet, on which they sell products harmful to computer systems such as malware and botnets. Products such as malware can also facilitate entry into bank accounts and deprive citizens of their savings. A Russian cybercriminal was indicted in the United States for running an exchange that facilitated the use of cryptocurrency, which made large-scale criminal activity more feasible.[13]

Crime groups often combine Russian criminals with their compatriots from other post-Soviet states. Whereas their activities were once focused primarily on the acquisition of key sectors of the Russian economy, more recently they have become greater participants in the international drug trade and in computer crime, complementing their international role in the trade of women, arms, endangered species, and illegal timber.[14] Moreover, the technical capacity of the criminals has pushed them to the forefront of computer crime, with major involvement in the production of child pornography marketed through the internet, "phishing," and even wholesale coordinated attacks on the internet and on websites of foreign countries such as Estonia and Georgia, viewed as unfriendly to Russia.[15] The largest generator of spam on the internet for a period, before it shut down under pressure, was an online pharmaceutical business run by Russian criminals.[16]

In Russia, there is a unique integration of the licit and illicit economies. Key sectors of the economy are controlled by oligarchs with criminal pasts or close ties to organized crime. But the parallels that many commentators once tried to draw between the oligarchs and the robber barons have been proven invalid. Robber barons used corruption and coercion to eliminate competition and intimidate laborers. In Russia, the order was reversed. Criminality was crucial to the acquisition of key sectors in energy, aluminum, and natural resources. Then violence was used to eliminate competitors.

Russia's licit and illicit economies operate on a natural resources model, which is not surprising, as illicit business is shaped by the same cultural and historical factors that shape the legitimate economy. The illicit economy mirrors the patterns of the legitimate one. Historically, Russia was never a society of traders. Before the 1917 revolution, Russian trade was dominated by non-Russians: Armenians, Greeks, Germans, and others, who lived in distinct districts of Moscow. Russians did not trade. Instead, they sold natural resources such as fur, timber, and the natural mineral wealth of their vast empire. With the reintroduction of capitalism in 1992, old patterns of business quickly reemerged. The sale of oil, gas, and petroleum products represented about half of the federal budget in 2015.[17] Russia suffers from the natural resource curse, failing to invest in human capital, as do other oil-rich countries that lack the rule of law.[18]

The trafficking of women operates on the natural resources model. Russian criminals sell off the women like a raw commodity, selling them to other crime groups who will exploit the women in the destination countries, maximizing their profits.[19] The Russian state shows little will to protect its citizens, even though it is facing a severe demographic crisis, and the export and sale of its women of childbearing age threatens the very survival of the Russian nation. The natural resources model of both licit and illicit trade is extremely harmful to the long-term health of the Russian economy and the Russian state. Russian legislation to combat trafficking has failed to result in a significant number of prosecutions.[20]

This chapter is based on a wide variety of sources, including analyses that have been carried out in Russia by researchers affiliated with TraCCC (Terrorism, Transnational Crime and Corruption Center) centers in Russia for over fifteen years, until recent political developments in Russia made this collaboration difficult.[21] The multidisciplinary research focused on particular aspects of crime, such as human trafficking, money laundering, the role of crime groups in the process of privatization, corporate raiding, overall crime trends, and many other topics.[22]

Interviews have been conducted with large numbers of law enforcement agents in Russia and in other parts of the world concerned with post-Soviet organized crime. Legal documents of criminal cases in Russia and abroad have been studied to understand the mechanisms of organized crime activity. Civil litigation in the West among key industrial figures with criminal pasts has also been examined to shed light on the acquisition of businesses through criminal tactics.[23]

In addition, the chapter draws on the Russian press and national and regional data to understand the evolution and geography of crime in Russia. The chapter also uses Western scholarship on crime and policing in Russia, which has increased in recent years.[24] Analysis of crime data reveals striking regional differences from west to east, in part a legacy of the Soviet era where labor camps were concentrated in Siberia and new industrialized cities gave rise to particularly high rates of criminality.[25]

OVERALL TRENDS IN CRIME

The growth of crime and the absence of an effective law enforcement response[26] have affected the quality of daily life, the longevity of the population, and the economy. Beccaria, the Enlightenment thinker, wrote that the certainty of punishment is more important than its severity. In Russia, at the present time, there is no certainty of punishment, which has contributed to significant crime rates. The prosecutor general reported that there were 2.1 million crimes reported in Russia in 2014, 2.2 million in 2013, and 2.3 million in 2012. In 2015, there was a noted increase in crime rates of almost 7 percent.[27] These statistics should be treated with certain skepticism as Russian law enforcement has long understated the extent of crime to prove their efficiency. There may not be certainty, but there is severity for those who are caught and either cannot pay the bribes to get out of the criminal justice system or who are subjects of particular political concern to the government, such as the former oil magnate Mikhail Khodorkovsky.[28] Khodorkovsky was released from his second prison term in December 2013, but not pardoned.[29] The framing of political opponents on trumped-up charges continues to remain a problem. The following trends characterize Russian crime and organized crime:

- High rates of homicide
- High rates of youth crime and child exploitation
- Very high rates of drug abuse and a rapidly escalating problem of international drug trade
- High level and extensive cybercrime that can have political dimensions
- Large-scale human smuggling and trafficking from, into, and through Russia
- Corporate raiding resulting in insecure property rights and undermining entrepreneurship
- Organized crime involvement in all sectors of the economy
- Significant complicity of organized crime and law enforcement[30]
- Organized crime involvement in the foreign policy of Russia[31]

These trends are discussed in more detail below.

Homicide

In the immediate post-Soviet period, Russia had very high rates of homicide, the result both of high rates of interpersonal violence and the contract killings associated with organized crime. Increased violence was also explained by the availability of weapons, which had been tightly controlled during the Soviet period.[32] The availability of arms, facilitated by the small-weapons trade of Russian organized crime and former military personnel, made many ordinary acts of crime more violent than in the past.[33] The decline in Russian medical care meant that many individuals who were merely assault victims in the past now became homicide victims. Even though contract killings have declined, intrapersonal violence remains very high, partly explained by enduring problems of alcohol abuse. According to a scholar of Russian violence, "post-communist Russia's homicide mortality rate has been one of the highest in the world, exceeding that of European countries by a factor of 20–25, and for most of the post-communist period has also been significantly higher than that of other ex-Soviet states."[34] In 2015, the homicide rate was 11.3 per one hundred thousand, a rate that far exceeded the rates of most European countries, which are consistently in the low single digits.[35]

Youth Crime and Child Exploitation

Youth crime and child exploitation are enduring problems in Russia, explained by the high rates of abandoned children, street children, and the number of institutionalized children whose parents have left them or whose parents have been declared incompetent to raise their children.[36] Parents have been determined to be unfit because of alcoholism, drug use, domestic violence, and child sexual exploitation. The number of homeless or abandoned children is estimated to be at the same level as after World War II. There are seven hundred thousand orphans and two million illiterate youth.[37] According to the prosecutor general's office in 2010, over 2 percent of Russian children were homeless, totaling over six hundred thousand.[38] Children exposed to high levels of violence in their youth often replicate those patterns in adolescence and adulthood. Moreover, the absence of programs to help deinstitutionalized youth after eighteen return to their communities has made many of the females susceptible to sex traffickers.

Commercial sexual exploitation of children is recognized as an increasing problem, and the State Duma has not yet passed adequate legislation to combat all aspects of this phenomenon.[39] Russia only outlaws the production of child pornography starting at age sixteen. Unfortunately, there has been a rise in the production of child pornography by younger teenagers, and system administrators struggle to remove this material from websites.[40] Russians, with their increased travel, are also increasingly cited as engaged in sex tourism. The Russian mafia is allegedly highly involved in child sex tourism in Thailand.[41]

Drug Abuse

Drug addiction has skyrocketed in Russia. This increase has occurred in the number of users, the geographical reach of the problem, and the variety of drugs used. As the market has grown, there also appears to be a presence of large and more powerful organized crime groups involved, although no monopolization of markets has yet emerged. According to official figures, almost 6 percent of the total population, or some 8.5 million people, are drug addicts or regular users, and treatment programs for addiction are almost nonexistent.[42]

According to the Ministry of Internal Affairs, there are four million youth who use drugs, starting as young as age eleven. The rate of drug abuse is 2.5 times higher among youth than among adults. By 2005, mortality connected to drug abuse was forty-two times higher for youth than in the 1980s, while the comparable figure for adults was twelve times higher.[43] In 2013, there were one hundred thousand deaths attributed to the drug epidemic.[44] To provide a comparative perspective, this is 2.5 times the number of 2017 deaths from opioids in the United States, a country with more than twice the population of Russia.

Russian official statistics reveal an alarming trend in the quantity and the distribution of the drug trade. For example, in 1985, the Ministry of Internal Affairs had identified only four regions in Russia with over ten thousand serious abusers of drugs. By the beginning of the twenty-first century, that figure had climbed to over thirty regions. Today there is hardly a city in Russia in which there are not drug addicts.[45] Drug abuse is not evenly distributed.[46] Whereas 310 addicts were registered per 100,000 people in Russia as a whole in January 2004, the figure in the Russian Far East was 542 per 100,000.[47] In a very short period, Russia has developed one of the world's most serious problems of drug abuse.

The drug problem in Russia does not consist of only one commodity. Synthetic drugs including opioids have now surpassed heroin as the most common drugs abused by the population. Many of these are being sold through the dark web, which is increasingly targeted by Russian authorities.[48] Russia is a market for heroin and opium, hashish, marijuana, synthetics, and other dangerous illegal substances. A designer drug called *krokodil*, or crocodile, related to morphine, spread rapidly in Russia.[49] More recently, a powerful narcotic based on codeine, called spice, has spread across Russia.[50] Another drug called salts, referred to in the United States as PABS, or psychoactive bath salts, is consumed intravenously in Russia, with devastating consequences for Russian women who are the prime consumers.[51]

Russia is a major transshipment route for drugs out of Afghanistan.[52] According to the Russian Federal State Statistics Service, Russia was the world's largest market for heroin produced in Afghanistan, and 1.5 million users consumed seventy thousand kilograms of heroin.[53] Opiates in particular are highly problematic. The Russian domestic opiate market has been valued at $12 billion, or roughly one-fifth of the world market, explained by Russia's proximity to Central Asia and drug production in Afghanistan. Synthetic drugs enter Russia from Western Europe (coming through Ukraine, Belarus, and the Baltic states) and Asia. Cocaine enters from Latin America brought by Latin Americans to Europe for transshipment, and Russians are operating in Colombia and elsewhere.[54]

The drug business appears to be employing an ever-larger number of Russian citizens annually. Not only are crime groups more actively engaged in the drug trade, but many impoverished Russian-speaking citizens of former Soviet states serve as drug couriers. Explanations for the growth lie in the political-criminal nexus and the links that Russian organized crime has formed with crime groups in many other parts of the world.

Russia is also increasingly a transit country for drugs from Afghanistan, Pakistan, and Iran into European markets.[55] The so-called Northern Route of heroin smuggling has a market value of approximately $13 billion per year. This route has linked Afghanistan via Central Asia (Tajikistan and Kyrgyzstan or Uzbekistan and Turkmenistan) to Russia and Europe.[56] Finally, Russia's initial importance to the global heroin trade was as a transshipment country. But Russia is now an important consumer. Many of the consumers are young, and some were former military personnel previously deployed on the borders in Central Asia and in the Chechen conflict.

The actors in this illicit economy range from Russian military personnel, law enforcement, and ordinary criminals to Soviet ethnic crime groups and illegal immigrants from Asian countries. Corrupt relationships that exist among the drug traffickers and local and regional officials allow these crime groups to operate throughout Russia, even in the capital. Furthermore, crime groups from many other countries are active in Russia. These include crime groups from not only the neighboring states of the former USSR but also Eastern Europe, Japan, China, South and possibly North Korea, Vietnam, Nigeria, and Latin America.[57]

The Russian situation also recalls the Colombian situation, where drug trafficking is used to finance nonstate violent actors, including separatist and terrorist movements.[58] Dagestan, a region adjoining Chechnya, is now a major entry point for drugs into Russia.[59] Although the links between insurgencies and the drug trade are not as strong in Russia as in Colombia, there is an important link in both drug markets between drugs and violent conflict. Organized crime, including drug trafficking, has been a factor in the proliferation of violence in the North Caucasus. There is less violence in the Russian areas close to Central Asia because the drug trade is consolidated and controlled by the leaders of some Central Asian countries.[60]

Human Smuggling and Trafficking

Human trafficking persists on a large scale. Trafficking is not just of Russian women exported for sexual exploitation abroad; there is also a large importation of trafficked women from poorer states of the former Soviet Union. There is also the exploitation of North Korean workers for forced labor in camps.[61] Moreover, there is a significant illegal migrant population. Many of the workers are exploited. There is also an increasing problem of the exploitation of the children of illegal migrants who have no legal status and cannot attend school.[62]

Even as the Russian economy has grown and the middle class has expanded, the problem of sex trafficking of Russian women persists on a large scale because of poverty, vulnerability, and hopelessness.[63] Adolescents are also affected, as many youth live in poorly supported children's homes. Others are living in the streets, having been abandoned by their parents or having run away from drunken and violent parents.

With its increasing affluence, labor shortages, and a male population reluctant to do hard physical labor, a rapid influx of illegal immigrants into Russia occurred, primarily from impoverished countries in Central Asia such as Tajikistan and Kyrgyzstan, comprising approximately 21 percent of the ten million foreigners who are estimated to be residing in Russia.[64] Russia estimates that there are five to ten million illegal migrants in Russia. This figure is in addition to legal migrants, a category of worker introduced in Russia to provide temporary work permits for up to three months. Despite this new category of legal migrants, 80 percent of all migrants are employed in the informal or "shadow" economy, receiving a fraction of the wages paid to Russian workers. Survey research reveals that one-quarter of those surveyed knew migrants who had been enslaved: their passports were taken away, their wages were withheld, and the migrants were kept in confinement. The number of those subject to labor trafficking is now estimated to exceed the number of victims of sex trafficking.[65] Despite this massive exploitation, aiding these people is not a priority for either Russian citizens or the state. Significant numbers become victims of labor and sex trafficking, although some Russian businesses are trying to set up and abide by labor standards.[66] There is very little concern for individual rights, a legacy of the Soviet period and even prerevolutionary traditions.

Corporate Raiding

Corporate raiding combines the use of illegal acts and the misuse of criminal law to deprive business owners of valuable property. It exists on a broad scale in Russia. The problem of corporate raiding is not merely a problem of insecure property rights but also involves significant threats to the life and welfare of individuals whose property is sought by highly protected and connected individuals. *Reiderstvo* (raiding) is often initiated at the behest of powerful government people and is often executed by law enforcement officials. Therefore, its victims are not just threatened by private citizens but are persecuted with the full force of the state. Tom Firestone, a long-serving US Department of Justice prosecutor assigned to the American embassy in Moscow, explains,

> "Reiderstvo" differs greatly from the U.S. hostile takeover practice in that it relies on criminal methods such as fraud, blackmail, obstruction of justice, and actual and threatened physical violence. At the same time, though, "reiderstvo" is not just simple thuggery. In contrast to more primitive criminals, Russian "reideri" rely on court orders, resolutions of shareholders and boards of directors, lawsuits. In short, it is a new more sophisticated form of organized crime.[67]

The problem of corporate raiding remains pervasive in Russia. In 2015, two hundred thousand economic crimes were prosecuted, many associated with corporate raiding.[68] Wealthy businesspeople are subjected to corporate raiding. While the raid is proceeding, many of them are confined on trumped-up charges, and some agree to the charges to escape the brutal treatment they can expect while in confinement. If they manage to depart from Russia, some are subject to Red Notices through Interpol, which demand that the country where they reside deport them to Russia.[69]

Organized Crime

Post-Soviet organized crime is distinct from organized crime in many regions of the world because it initially focused on the legitimate economy and only more recently assumed a larger role in the drug trade and other aspects of the illicit economy.[70] Organized crime was able to grow so rapidly in the first decade of the post-Soviet period because of pervasive corruption among government officials, the incapacity of demoralized law enforcement, and the perception by criminals that they could act with near total impunity.[71] During the Soviet period, party sanctions placed some curbs on government misconduct, but with the collapse of the Communist Party, and in the absence of the rule of law, there were no limits on the conduct of government officials. The crime groups could function effectively because they corrupted or co-opted government officials and were rarely arrested and incarcerated.[72] Corruption, bribery, and abuse of power escalated rapidly, but there was a sharp diminution of prosecutions for these offenses.[73] The failure to sanction well-placed individuals as well as any officials for corruption is an ongoing problem in Russia.[74]

The law enforcement system was decimated by poor morale and dangerous work conditions, as well as by the dismissal and departure of many long-term personnel at the end of the Soviet period. For these reasons it was ill equipped to deal with the increasing number of serious crimes. Moreover, law enforcement's inexperience with investigating and prosecuting crimes in a market economy gave organized crime groups the opportunity to expand their financial reach enormously. A whole business of private protection evolved, often staffed and run by organized crime, and crime groups extracted payments from those in need of protection rather than actually providing a service. They have been named "violent entrepreneurs" by the Russian researcher Vadim Volkov.[75]

The diversity of post-Soviet organized crime is one of its hallmarks. The traditional criminal world of thieves-in-law continued and evolved to the new market conditions.[76] Crime groups are multiethnic and often involve cooperation among groups that are antagonistic outside the criminal world.[77] Foreign groups not only operate on Russian territory but also provide partnerships with Russian crime groups to carry out their activities. For example, Japanese Yakuza work with Russian organized crime in the Far East to illegally secure needed timber in exchange for used Japanese cars for the Russian market.

Organized crime groups are not involved exclusively in one area of criminal activity. Crime groups may specialize in drug trafficking, arms trafficking, or auto theft, but most crime groups are multifaceted, spanning many aspects of the legitimate and illegitimate sectors of the economy simultaneously. In any one region of the country, most forms of illicit activity will be present. There are regional differences as well; for example, organized crime involvement with environmental crime is greater in Siberia and the Far East than in the more densely populated regions of western Russia.[78] But it is a serious problem throughout Russia.[79]

The involvement of Russian organized crime in the banking sector undermined the integrity of the financial system and facilitated massive money laundering out of Russia during the 1990s. Russian money laundering, as distinct from capital flight, was so significant in the 1990s that it drained Russia of much of its investment capital.[80] Only after the Russian financial collapse in 1998, and after Russia was cited by the Financial Action Task Force for noncompliance with international money laundering standards early in the following decade, were substantial improvements made in the banking sector.[81] But there are still problems with organized crime having influence over some banks and capital flight associated with it.[82] Russians continue to launder money through countries such as Moldova, Latvia, and Cyprus. The extent of this ongoing problem was uncovered by the revelations of the Panama Papers and more recently by banking scandals in Riga. The pace of capital flight has accelerated since the imposition of economic sanctions on Russia after the Ukraine invasion, with $85 billion leaving Russia during the first nine months of 2014.[83] In 2017, Russians estimate that $31 billion left the country.[84]

THE GEOGRAPHY OF CRIME

The vastness of Russia's enormous territory results in significant variations in crime by region. Compounding these geographical differences is the fact that many regions of Russia, such as the North Caucasus, Tatarstan, and parts of the Volga region, have strong ethnic influences that also shape the characteristics of crime. Furthermore, there are certain regions characterized by particularly high rates of crime, such as the major cities of Moscow, St. Petersburg, and Ekaterinburg, as well as the regions of Siberia and the Russian Far East. The Crimea since annexation by Russia in March 2014 is also the locus of crime and smuggling. Many Russian crime groups have moved to Ukraine.[85] Crime rates escalate as one moves from the western part of the country to the east. This phenomenon is a legacy of Soviet-era policies of strict population controls, a massive institutionalized penal population that often settled close to their former labor colonies in Siberia after release, and the development of new cities east of the Urals without necessary infrastructure and social support systems.

Siberia and the Urals

During the Soviet era, new cities were established, particularly in Siberia, which were populated primarily by young men, and there was no planning to attract women to the same communities. With the existing internal passport and registration system that restricted mobility, women could not move to these communities without employment. Therefore, these new cities quickly became areas with high rates of alcohol consumption, violent crime, and other forms of criminality.

At the end of the Soviet period, these communities that were the basis of Soviet industrial production went into significant decline. The rich natural resources of the Urals and Siberia, however, provided large revenues for the corrupt bureaucrats and crime groups that appropriated this state property as their own. Furthermore, the Urals region was a major center of the Soviet Union's military-industrial complex. With the decline of Soviet military production, many of these factories ceased to function, leaving many citizens without jobs or incomes. The economic crisis that hit this region helps explain the large number of children at risk. Although economic prosperity has come to many cities in the area since 2000, serious problems endure. High levels of drug addiction characterize Siberia, especially around Irkutsk, and the narcotic known as salts is heavily abused there by women.[86]

There is an enormous diversity of organized crime groups operating in Siberia. The Trans-Siberian Railroad that traverses Russia is a key area for crime groups to operate. Moreover, the railroad's proximity to China contributes to the active presence of crime groups, facilitated by serious problems of corruption along the border. In addition to such powerful local crime groups as the Bratsk criminal society, there are groups from Central Asia and the Caucasus, including Ingush and Chechen organizations.[87]

The Russian Far East

The Russian Far East has seen a significant decline in population since the collapse of the Soviet Union. The absence of economic development in the region and its isolation from the more populous western regions of Russia have provided an enormous incentive for citizens to leave. The region had extremely high crime rates in the 1970s, and the region continues to be characterized by very high rates of crime and violent crime. Making the situation worse, criminal elements have also moved into local government. Epitomizing this problem was the former mayor of Vladivostok, Vladimir Nikolayev, an organized criminal with the *klichka*, or criminal name, of Winnie the Pooh, who was elected in 2004.[88] His ouster in 2007 was made all the more difficult because he held the second position in the United Russia Party for the Russian Far East. Sergei Darkin, the criminal governor of Primorskii *krai* in the Russian Far East, was forced out in 2012.[89] The pattern of corruption in Vladivostok and the region continues. In 2016, the mayor of Vladivostok, Igor Pushkarev, similar to his predecessors, faced corruption charges.[90] Pushkarev was taken to Moscow, and his case went to the Supreme Court of Russia.[91]

Organized crime groups from the Russian Far East work with South Korean, Japanese, Chinese, and Vietnamese crime groups. Much of the criminality is connected with the ports and the massive shipping that flows through this region. Many of the shipping and fishing companies are dominated by organized crime.[92] The impoverished military in the region has contributed to massive unauthorized arms sales to foreign governments and organized crime groups. A sale of Russian helicopters to North Koreans was averted in the late 1990s only when members of the police, who were not part of the scheme, stumbled on the helicopters just prior to delivery.[93]

Much of the crime is connected with the exploitation of natural resources. Fish and timber a decade ago represented 93 percent of the exports from the Russian Far East. Seafood from overfished waters, according to crime data from the organized crime authorities in the Russian Far East, wind up in Japanese and Korean markets.[94] Since the fall of the Soviet Union, there has been a fourfold decline in forested land.[95] Half of the hardwood in the Russian Far East is illegally harvested, either by corrupt officials or by gangs in the communities. According to the World Wide Fund for Nature (WWF) in Russia, between 10 and 35 percent of all the hardwood in Russia is logged illegally.[96]

Crime in Major Urban Centers

Moscow, as Russia's largest city and economic powerhouse, is home of the largest and most important crime groups, such as Solntsevo and Izmailovo. These groups had penetrated the most lucrative sectors of the economy, such as banks, real estate, and raw materials. But the power of these groups has diminished as they have been pushed out of the lucrative sectors as the oligarchs around Putin have acquired key sectors of the economy.

The crime groups are part of a very diverse picture of criminality in the city. Ethnic crime groups have been deeply involved in the consumer markets for food and consumer goods. Restaurants, clubs, and casinos have been centers of criminal activity and investment. But in this rich investment environment, it is often hard to differentiate where the criminality ends and the corruption of government officials begins.

Moscow has become one of the most expensive cities in the world. The absence of competition, the large sums extracted by organized crime as their share of profits, and the domination of real estate by organized crime groups in cooperation with corrupt officials help explain the extremely high cost of business and of daily life. The wife of former Moscow mayor Yury Luzhkov was a billionaire, with much of her fortune made from real estate before her husband's ouster.[97] Corruption in the real estate sector also exists in St. Petersburg, with many of Putin's associates from his St. Petersburg days benefiting.[98] The criminalization of real estate continues, even though its form has evolved over time. In the past, many citizens simply lost their apartments and disappeared without trace. No protection was available from the government to defend tenants who were threatened by high-level organized crime. High-level officials in Moscow and St. Petersburg demanded significant bribes for information about the availability of property for rent and purchase. Construction companies that built much of the new construction often have organized crime figures as major shareholders or financiers. Corporate raiding of valuable urban real estate remains a serious problem.

Moscow is still a major center of money laundering, despite enhanced controls. The close relationship between the banks and powerful individuals, the cash-reliant economy, and the lack of effective regulation of financial markets still make it relatively easy to move illicit funds from the very large shadow economy.[99] The presence of such substantial Russian money in the Panama Papers, in the UK, and in key financial centers overseas attests to this problem.

CONCLUSION

Crime rates were suppressed in the Soviet years, a consequence of its high levels of social control, high rates of incarceration, and controls over places of residence. With liberalization during the Gorbachev era, fundamental changes occurred in Soviet crime patterns. Crime rates rose rapidly, and organized crime became a formidable actor in the new economy. The 1990s were traumatic. Many Russians lost their life savings in bank failures. Unemployment rose dramatically, particularly among women. The social safety net collapsed. In the absence of effective state enforcement, organized crime filled the vacuum and became a visible force in society, not only through its displays of violence and its role in private protection but also through the key role it played in privatization and politics in the transitional period.

Although the Putin-Medvedev years have brought greater stability, Russia has not been able to eliminate the high rates of violent crime, endemic corruption, and pervasive organized crime. High levels of money laundering and export of capital have continued to deprive Russia of the capital it needs for investment, although the record profits obtained during the boom years of oil revenues masked the impact. They are now more apparent with Russia under sanctions from the West.

As Putin has assumed sole leadership, even more sinister aspects of the crime problem have emerged. Criminals are increasingly used as tools of state policy. There are also indications that Russia used criminals in its invasion of Ukraine, especially in the Crimea.[100] They are used ever more frequently by the state as hackers and cybercriminals who have been utilized to launch attacks against prominent Western targets and to interfere in Western European and American elections.

Crime problems have evolved over the years, yet crime remains an important element of the structure of the Russian economy, society, and political system. The number of homicides associated with organized crime has declined, but homicide rates remain among the highest for a country not engaged in a civil war. Conflicts over property are no longer decided by shootings but often instead by expensive litigation in the West, particularly London, where many of Russia's richest citizens have placed their assets.[101]

Despite the centrality of the crime and corruption problem, there has been no concerted state action commensurate with the size of the problem. Rather, the administration of President Putin has attempted to exploit rather than eliminate the criminal groups. Law enforcement and the courts are so corrupt and subservient to the state that they are unable to effectively address the problem. Without an effective law enforcement apparatus, an empowered civil society, or a free media, it is very difficult to curb the rise of organized crime or the pervasiveness of corruption. The criminal trajectories set in motion in the early post-Soviet period have continued. Organized criminals have so much power because they assumed critical investment positions in key sectors of the economy in the transitional period. Massive collusion with and corruption of politicians have ensured this continued ownership. In fact, many criminals have sought governmental positions to acquire immunity from prosecution and hold such positions on the national and regional level.

Crime in Russia is a major political and economic influence on society. The heavy involvement of criminals and corrupt politicians in the legitimate economy is a key explanation for the absence of transparency in Russian financial markets. This contributed to the especially precipitous decline of the Russian markets relative to other international exchanges in fall of 2008, and the massive capital flight and money laundering in recent years is further evidence that needed change has not occurred. Furthermore, the existence of widespread monopolies as a result of organized crime and oligarchic dominance of the economy has led to high prices. Pervasive criminal activity is an enormous impediment to entrepreneurship and the emergence of small and medium-sized businesses that are crucial to long-term economic development and a middle class that could be the backbone of a more democratic society.

Corruption also remains endemic. The long-term destabilizing influence of this corruption should not be underestimated. It has contributed to human brain drain, capital flight, and a disillusionment of many citizens with government, not just in Moscow but in many more remote regions as well.[102] Protests across the country in 2018 revealed that pervasive corruption is disturbing to many, including Russian youth. This may augur for a different future, but profound change is not imminent.

DISCUSSION QUESTIONS

1. What are some of the macro-characteristics of Russian crime?
2. In what forms is corruption manifest in Russia?
3. Summarize the geography of crime. In which regions is the problem of crime and corruption the worst?
4. Why is cybercrime such a serious problem in Russia? How it is linked to the political process?
5. How has the government's approach to crime and corruption changed since Putin returned to office in 2012?

SUGGESTED READINGS

Dawisha, Karen. *Putin's Kleptocracy: Who Owns Russia?* New York: Simon & Schuster, 2014.
Galeotti, Mark. *The Vory Russia's Super Mafia.* New Haven, CT: Yale University Press, 2018.
Karklins, Rasma. *The System Made Me Do It: Corruption in Post-Communist Societies.* Armonk, NY: M. E. Sharpe, 2005.
McCarthy, A. Lauren. *Trafficking Justice: How Russian Police Use New Law, from Crime to Courtroom.* Ithaca, NY: Cornell University Press, 2015.
Orttung, Robert, and Anthony Latta, eds. *Russia's Battle with Crime, Corruption and Terrorism.* New York and London: Routledge, 2008.

182 *Louise Shelley*

Stephenson, Svetlana. *Gangs of Russia: From the Streets to the Corridors of Power.* Ithaca, NY: Cornell University Press, 2015.

Varese, Frederico. *Mafias on the Move: How Organized Crime Conquers New Territories.* Princeton, NJ: Princeton University Press, 2011.

———. *The Russian Mafia: Private Protection in a New Market Economy.* Oxford: Oxford University Press, 2005.

Volkov, Vadim. *Violent Entrepreneurs: The Use of Force in the Making of Russian Capitalism.* Ithaca, NY: Cornell University Press, 2002.

NOTES

1. Natalia Yudina, "Xenophobia in Figures: Hate Crime in Russia and Efforts to Counteract It in 2017," SOVA Center for Information Analysis, February 12, 2018, http://www.sova-center.ru/en/xenophobia/reports-analyses/2018/02/d38830 (accessed May 5, 2018).

2. Hannes Adomeit, "The 'Putin System': Crime and Corruption as Constituent Building Parts," *Europe-Asia Studies* 68, no. 6 (2016): 1067–73.

3. Thomas Firestone, "Criminal Corporate Raiding in Russia," *International Lawyer* 42, no. 4 (2008): 1207–29; Louise Shelley and Judy Deane, "The Rise of Reiderstvo: Implications for Russia and the West," Reiderstvo.org, May 2016, http://reiderstvo.org/sites/default/files/The_Rise_of_Reiderstvo.pdf; Michael Rochlitz, "Corporate Raiding and the Role of the State in Russia," *Post-Soviet Affairs* 30, nos. 2–3 (2014); Ararat Osipian, "Predatory Raiding in Russia: Institutions and Property Rights after the Crisis," *Journal of Economic Issues* 46, no. 2 (2012): 470.

4. An illustration of this is the arrest of an oligarch in September 2014. See "Russian Oligarch Yevtushenkov Arrested," Radio Free Europe/Radio Liberty, September 17, 2014, http://www.rferl.org/content/evtushenko-arrested-russia-sistema-money-laundering-charge/26588656.html (accessed April 29, 2018).

5. Karen Dawisha, *Putin's Kleptocracy: Who Owns Russia?* (New York: Simon & Schuster, 2014).

6. Roy Godson, ed., *Menace to Society: Political-Criminal Collaboration around the World* (New Brunswick, NJ: Transaction, 2003); Leslie Holmes, "The Corruption-Organised Crime Nexus in Central and Eastern Europe," in *Terrorism, Organised Crime and Corruption: Networks and Linkage,* ed. Leslie Homes (Cheltenham, UK: Edward Elgar, 2007), 84–108.

7. Mark Galeotti, "Medvedev's First Police Reform: MVD Loses Specialised Organised Crime Department," http://inmoscowsshadows.wordpress.com/2008/09/11/medvedevs-first-police-reform-mvd-loses-specialised-organised-crime-department (accessed April 29, 2018).

8. See Russia's Anticorruption Foundation, https://fbk.info/english/about (accessed April 29, 2018).

9. Shaun Walker, "'Putin Is Destroying Russia: Why Base His Regime on Corruption?' Asks Navalny," *The Guardian,* October 17, 2014, http://www.theguardian.com/world/2014/oct/17/putin-is-destroying-russia-why-base-his-regime-on-corruption-asks-navalny (accessed April 29, 2018); "Russian Opposition Leader Alexei Naval'ny Barred from Running for President," *The Guardian,* December 25, 2018, https://www.theguardian.com/world/2017/dec/25/russian-opposition-leader-alexei-navalny-barred-from-running-for-president (accessed April 19, 2018).

10. They have globalized and moved to different locales to increase their business opportunities in different markets. See Frederico Varese, *Mafias on the Move: How Organized Crime Conquers New Territories* (Princeton, NJ: Princeton University Press, 2011).

11. These organized crime groups are not the product of post-Soviet society; they also flourished under the Soviet regime. Frederico Varese, *The Russian Mafia: Private Protection in a New Market Economy* (Oxford: Oxford University Press, 2001); Yakov Gilinskiy and Yakov Kostjukovsky, "From Thievish Cartel to Criminal Corporation," in *Organised Crime in Europe,* ed. Cyril Fijnaut and Letizia Paoli (Dordrecht: Springer, 2004), 181–202; Mark Galeotti, *The Vory Russia's Super Mafia* (New Haven, CT: Yale University Press, 2018).

12. Europol, *Organised Crime Threat Assessment 2011*, May 4, 2011, http://www.europol. europa.eu/content/press/europol-organised-crime-threat-assessment-2011-429 (accessed April 29, 2018); Walter Kegö and Alexandru Molcean, *Russian Speaking Organized Crime Groups in the EU* (Stockholm: Institute for Security and Development Policy, 2011), 26.

13. "Russian National and Bitcoin Exchange Charged in 21-Count Indictment for Operating Alleged International Money Laundering Scheme and Allegedly Laundering Funds from Hack of Mt. Gox," US Department of Justice, July 26, 2017, https://www.justice.gov/usao-ndca/pr/ russian-national-and-bitcoin-exchange-charged-21-count-indictment-operating-alleged (accessed April 19, 2018).

14. For trade of women, see Louise Shelley, *Human Trafficking: A Global Perspective* (Cambridge: Cambridge University Press, 2010), 174–200; G. M. Zherebkin, *Otvetstvennost' za nezakonnuiu rubku lesnykh nasazhdenii. Analuz nelegal'nykh rubok na rossiiskom Dal'nem Vostoke i metodika ikh rassledovaniia* (Vladivostok: Apel'sin, 2011); Nicholas Schmidle, "Disarming Victor Bout: The Rise and Fall of the World's Most Notorious Weapons Trafficker," *New Yorker*, March 5, 2012, 54–65.

15. "Marching Off to Cyberwar: The Internet; Attacks Launched over the Internet on Estonia and Georgia Highlight the Difficulty of Defining and Dealing with 'Cyberwar,'" *The Economist*, December 4, 2008, http://www.economist.com/node/12673385 (accessed April 29, 2018).

16. Damon McCoy, Andreas Pitsillidis, Grant Jordan, Nicholas Weaver, Christian Kreibich, Brian Krebs, Geoffrey M. Voelker, Stefan Savage, and Kirill Levchenko, "PharmaLeaks: Understanding the Business of Online Pharmaceutical Affiliate Programs," http://www.cs.gmu. edu/~mccoy/papers/pharmaleaks.pdf (accessed April 29, 2018).

17. Russian Exports 1994–2018, TradingEconomics.com, https://tradingeconomics.com/ russia/exports (accessed April 19, 2018).

18. Daniel Treisman, "Is Russia Cursed by Oil?," *Journal of International Affairs*, April 15, 2010, http://jia.sipa.columbia.edu/russia-cursed-oil (accessed April 29, 2018).

19. Shelley, *Human Trafficking*, 113–21.

20. Lauren A. McCarthy, *Trafficking Justice: How Russian Police Use New Law, from Crime to Courtroom* (Ithaca, NY: Cornell University Press, 2015).

21. The publications of these centers can be accessed through http://traccc.gmu.edu/aboutus/international-centers/study-centers-in-eurasia/russia-centers-and-projects. At their height, the websites in Saratov, Vladivostok, and Stavropol had approximately one million readers annually.

22. For some of this research, see http://traccc.gmu.edu/about-us/international-centers/ study-centers-in-eurasia/russia-centers-and-projects/russian-book-publications (accessed April 20, 2018).

23. Simon Goodley, "Oleg Deripaska Accuses Rival Bringing £1.6bn Suit of Running Protection Racket," February 13, 2012, https://www.theguardian.com/world/2012/feb/13/olegderipaska-rival-crime-claims (accessed April 29, 2018).

24. Gilles Favarel-Garrigues, *Policing Economic Crime in Russia: From Soviet Planned Economy to Privatization*, trans. Roger Leverdier (New York: Columbia University Press, 2011); Brian Taylor, *State Building in Putin's Russia: Policing and Coercion after Communism* (Cambridge: Cambridge University Press, 2011); Vadim Volkov, *Violent Entrepreneurs: The Use of Force in the Making of Russian Capitalism* (Ithaca, NY: Cornell University Press, 2002).

25. Louise Shelley and Yuri Andrienko, "Crime, Violence and Political Conflict in Russia," in *Understanding Civil War: Evidence and Analysis*, ed. Nicholas Sambanis (Washington, DC: World Bank, 2005), 87–117; Elina Alexandra Treyger, *Soviet Roots of Post-Soviet Order* (PhD diss., Harvard University, June 2011); A. Lysova, N. G. Shchitov, and W. A. Pridemore, "Homicide in Russia, Ukraine and Belarus," in *Sourcebook of European Homicide Research*, ed. M. Liem and W. A. Pridemore (New York: Springer, 2011), 451–69.

26. Lauren McCarthy and Mary Elizabeth Malinkin, "Every Day Law Enforcement in Russia," Wilson Center, September 8, 2015, https://www.wilsoncenter.org/article/everyday-lawenforcement-russia (accessed April 18, 2018).

27. "Russia Sees 2015 Crime Spike," *Moscow Times*, September 16, 2015, https://themoscowtimes.com/news/russia-sees-2015-crime-rate-spike-49597 (accessed April 18, 2018).

28. Serge Schmemann, "The Case against and for Khodorkovsky," *International Herald Tribune*, October 19, 2008, http://www.nytimes.com/2008/10/20/opinion/20mon4.html (accessed April 29, 2018); Alena Ledeneva, "Telephone Justice in Russia," *Post-Soviet Affairs* 24, no. 4 (2008): 324–50; Kathryn Hendley, "Telephone Law and the 'Rule of Law': The Russian Case," *Hague Journal on the Rule of Law* 1, no. 2 (2009): 241–64.

29. Holly Yan and Dick Wright, "Russian Dissident Mikhail Khodorkovsky Speaks Out," CNN, December 22, 2013, http://www.cnn.com/2013/12/22/world/amanpour-mikhail-khodorkovsky-interview (accessed April 29, 2018).

30. Illustrative of this is the Magnitsky case in which an individual who attempted to whistle-blow on police corruption died in prison. See http://www.bbc.com/news/world-europe-20626960 (accessed April 29, 2018). A law in honor of him was passed at the end of 2012 in the United States and other countries. In the United States, it is called the Global Magnitsky Act, https://www.state.gov/e/eb/tfs/spi/globalmagnitsky (accessed April 29, 2018).

31. This has been seen in regard to the invasion of Ukraine by Russia as well as the previously mentioned cyberattacks. See Mark Galeotti, "Crime and Crimea: Criminals as Allies and Agents," November 3, 2014, http://www.rferl.org/content/crimea-crime-criminals-as-agents-allies/26671923.html (accessed April 29, 2018).

32. Louise I. Shelley, "Interpersonal Violence in the Soviet Union," *Violence, Aggression and Terrorism* 1, no. 2 (1987): 41–67.

33. N. F. Kuznetsova and G. M. Minkovskii, *Kriminologiia: Uchebnik* (Moscow: Vek, 1998), 553.

34. Treyger, *Soviet Roots of Post-Soviet Order*, 8; see also W. A. Pridemore, "Social Structure and Homicide in Post-Soviet Russia," *Social Science Research* 34, no. 4 (2005): 732–56.

35. Russian Federation—Homicide Rate, https://knoema.com/atlas/Russian-Federation/topics/Crime-Statistics/Homicides/Homicide-rate (accessed April 19, 2018); United Nations Office on Drugs and Crime, *Global Study on Homicide 2013*, 12, https://www.unodc.org/documents/gsh/pdfs/2014_GLOBAL_HOMICIDE_BOOK_web.pdf (accessed April 19, 2018).

36. Clementine K. Fujimura, Sally W. Stoecker, and Tatyana Sudakova, *Russia's Abandoned Children: An Intimate Understanding* (Westport, CT: Praeger, 2005).

37. "V Rossii—'tretiia volna' bezprizornosti, beznadzornosti, negramotnosti, i prestupnost' podrostov (statistika)," NewsRu.com, June 1, 2005, http://www.newsru.com/russia/01jun2005/generation.html (accessed April 29, 2018).

38. Olga Khvostunova, "Russia's Invisible Children: The Unrelieved Plight of Russia's Homeless Youth," May 31, 2012, http://imrussia.org/en/society/245-besprizorniki (accessed April 21, 2018).

39. See the mission of Stellit, http://eng.ngostellit.ru (accessed April 29, 2018).

40. "The Kids Aren't Alright: Why Russian Adolescents Are Selling Self-Created Pornography Online," *Meduza*, July 27, 2017, https://meduza.io/en/feature/2017/07/27/the-kids-aren-t-alright (accessed April 21, 2018).

41. ECPAT, *Sexual Exploitation of Children in Travel and Tourism: Europe Report*, May 2016, 26–27, http://www.globalstudysectt.org//wp-content/uploads/2016/12/Region-EUROPE.pdf (accessed April 25, 2018).

42. "Over 8 Million Russians Are Drug Addicts—Government Report," RIA-Novosti, September 17, 2013, http://sputniknews.com/russia/20130917/183511725/Over-8-Mln-Russians-Are-Drug-Addicts--Govt-Report.html (accessed April 28, 2018).

43. "V Rossii—'tretiia volna' bezprizornosti."

44. Mark Galeotti, "Narcotics and Nationalism: Russian Drug Policies and Futures," 2016, https://www.brookings.edu/wp-content/uploads/2016/07/Galeotti-Russia-final.pdf (accessed April 21, 2018).

45. B. Tselinsky, "Sovremennaia Narkosituatsiia v Rossii: Tendentsii i Perspektivii," *Organizovannaia Prestupnost, Terrorizm, i Korruptsiia*, no. 4 (2003): 21.

46. A. G. Museibov, "Regional'nye praktiki po preduprezhdeniiu nezakonnogo oborota narkotikov," *Sotsiologicheskie issledovaniia*, no. 7 (2003): 125–30.

47. Based on the analysis of the Vladivostok branch of the Transnational Crime and Corruption Center, http://www.crime.vl.ru/index.php?p=1202&more=1&c=1&tb=1&pb=1 (accessed May 5, 2018).

48. US State Department, *International Narcotics Control Strategy Report*, vol. 1, March 2018, https://www.state.gov/documents/organization/278759.pdf (accessed April 26, 2018).

49. Simon Schuster, "The Curse of the Crocodile: Russia's Deadly Designer Drug," June 21, 2011, http://www.time.com/time/world/article/0,8599,2078355,00.html (accessed April 29, 2018).

50. Shaun Walker, "Spice Is Just the Latest Horror Drug to Hit Russia," October 20, 2014, http://www.theguardian.com/world/2014/oct/20/spice-synthetic-drug-gaining-griprrussia (accessed April 29, 2018).

51. Anna Nemtsova, "The Drug Decimating Russia's Women," *Daily Beast*, November 18, 2017, https://www.thedailybeast.com/the-drug-decimating-russias-women (accessed April 21, 2018).

52. Country Report: Russia, Bureau of International Narcotics and Law Enforcement Affairs, *2014 International Narcotics Control Strategy Report (INCSR)*, http://www.state.gov/j/inl/rls/nrcrpt/2014/vol1/223000.htm (accessed May 5, 2018).

53. *2014 International Narcotics Control Strategy Report*; UNODC World Drug Report 2011, http://www.unodc.org/documents/data-and-analysis/WDR2011/World_Drug_Report_2011_ebook.pdf (accessed May 5, 2018).

54. Aaron Beitman, "Perspectives on Illicit Drugs in Russia," Schar School of Policy and Government, George Mason University, December 5, 2011, http://traccc.gmu.edu/2011/12/05/perspectives-on-illicit-drugs-in-russia (accessed April 29, 2018); Oleg Yegorov, "$61 Million in Cocaine: The Mysterious Haul That Has Russia and Argentina in Cahoots," Russia Beyond, February 18, 2018, https://www.rbth.com/lifestyle/327679-61-million-of-cocaine-russia-argentina (accessed May 5, 2018).

55. Tselinsky, "Sovremennaia Narkosituatsiia v Rossii," 23; Kairat Osmonaliev, "Developing Counter-Narcotics Policy in Central Asia, Washington and Uppsala: Silk Road Paper," Central Asia-Caucasus Institute and Silk Road Studies Program, 2005; "Drug Dealers, Drug Lords, and Drug Warriors-cum-Traffickers: Drug Crime and the Narcotic Market in Tajikistan," Schar School of Policy and Government, George Mason University, http://traccc.gmu.edu/?s=drug+dealers+and+drug+lords (accessed May 5, 2018); Letizia Paoli, Victoria A. Greenfield, and Peter Reuter, *The World Heroin Market: Can Supply Be Cut?* (Oxford: Oxford University Press, 2009).

56. Nabil Bhatia, "Opioids in the Golden Crescent: Production, Trafficking and Cooperative Counternarcotics Initiatives," March 13, 2017, http://natoassociation.ca/opioids-in-the-golden-crescent-production-trafficking-and-cooperative-counternarcotics-initiatives (accessed May 5, 2018); *World Drug Report 2017*, 18, https://www.unodc.org/wdr2017/field/Booklet_1_EXSUM.pdf (accessed May 5, 2018).

57. Sergei Golunov, "Narkotorgovlia cherez Rossiisko-Kazakhstanskuiu granitsu: Vyzov i problemy protivodeistviia," http://traccc.gmu.edu/pdfs/publications/drug_trafficking/goluno01.pdf (accessed April 29, 2018); Beitman, "Perspectives on Illicit Drugs in Russia."

58. Tamara Makarenko, "Terrorism and Transnational Organised Crime: The Emerging Nexus," *Transnational Violence and Seams of Lawlessness in the Asia-Pacific: Linkages to Global Terrorism* (Hawaii: Asia Pacific Center for Strategic Studies, 2004); Kimberley Thachuk, "Transnational Threats: Falling through the Cracks?," *Low Intensity Conflict & Law Enforcement* 10, no. 1 (2001); Sabrina Adamoli et al., *Organized Crime around the World* (Helsinki: HEUNI, 1998); Barbara Harris-White, *Globalization and Insecurity: Political, Economic and Physical Challenges* (Hampshire: Palgrave Macmillan, 2002); Ian Griffith, "From Cold War Geopolitics to Post-Cold War Geonarcotics," *International Journal* 49, no. 1 (1993–1994): 1–36; R. Matthew and G. Shambaugh, "Sex, Drugs, and Heavy Metal: Transnational Threats and National Vulnerabilities," *Security Dialogue* 29, no. 2 (1998): 163–75; Louise I. Shelley, *Dirty Entanglements: Corruption, Crime and Terrorism* (Cambridge: Cambridge University Press, 2014).

59. Louise I. Shelley and Svante E. Cornell, "The Drug Trade in Russia," in *Russian Business Power: The Role of Russian Business in Foreign and Security Relations*, ed. Andreas Wegner, Jeronim Perovic, and Robert W. Orttung (London: Routledge, 2006), 200.

60. Alexander Kupatadze, "Kyrgyzstan—A Virtual Narco State?," *International Journal of Drug Policy* 25, no. 6 (2014): 1178–85; Alexander Kupatadze, "Bribe, Swindle, Steal," April 9, 2018, http://bribeswindleorsteal.libsyn.com/website/corruption-in-the-caucasus (accessed May 5, 2018).

61. US State Department, *Trafficking in Persons Report, 2017, Russia*, https://www.state.gov/j/tip/rls/tiprpt/countries/2017/271269.htm (accessed April 28, 2018).

62. See this synopsis of the work of Dmitry Poletaev in Aaron Beitman, "Addressing the Problem of Labor Exploitation of Foreign Migrant Children in Russia," Schar School of Policy and Government, George Mason University, August 21, 2013, http://traccc.gmu.edu/2013/08/21/addressing-the-problem-of-labor-exploitation-of-foreign-migrant-children-in-russia (accessed April 28, 2018).

63. McCarthy, *Trafficking Justice*.

64. Ekaterina Egorova, "Illegal Migration in Russia," in *Migration in Russia, 2000–2013*, ed. Igor Ivanov (Moscow: Spetskniga, 2013), 48–59.

65. Elena Tyuryukanova, "THB, Irregular Migration and Criminal Gains" (paper presented at OSCE-UNODC-CYPRUS Regional Meeting on Human Trafficking and Money Laundering, Larnaca, Cyprus, September 18–19, 2008).

66. Office of the Special Representative and Coordinator for Combating Trafficking in Human Beings OSCE, "Ensuring That Businesses Do Not Contribute to Trafficking in Human Beings: Duties of States and the Private Sector" (Occasional Paper Series, no. 7, Vienna, November 2014), 71–78.

67. Firestone, "Criminal Corporate Raiding in Russia," 1207.

68. Shelley and Deane, "The Rise of Reiderstvo."

69. Red Notice Abuse Report, http://rednoticeabuse.com (accessed April 28, 2018).

70. Svetlana Glinkina, "Privatizatsiia and Kriminalizatsiia—How Organized Crime Is Hijacking Privatization," *Demokratizatsiya* 2, no. 3 (1994): 385–91.

71. Louise Shelley, "Organized Crime Groups: 'Uncivil Society,'" in *Russian Civil Society: A Critical Assessment*, eds. Alfred B. Evans, Jr., Laura A. Henry, and Lisa McIntosh Sundstrom (Armonk, NY: M.E. Sharpe, 2006), 95–109.

72. G. F. Khohkriakov, "Organizovannia prestupnost' v Rossii: 60-e gody-pervaia polovina 90-x godov," *Obshchestvennye nauki i sovremennost'*, no. 6 (2000): 62–74.

73. See Louise Shelley, "Crime and Corruption," in *Developments in Russian Politics*, ed. Stephen White, Alex Pravda, and Zvi Gitelman (Houndmills: Palgrave, 2001), 239–53; Alena Ledeneva, *How Russia Really Works: The Informal Practices That Shaped Post-Soviet Politics and Business* (Ithaca, NY: Cornell University Press, 2006); Leslie Holmes, "Crime, Organised Crime and Corruption in Post-Communist Europe and the CIS," *Communist and Post-Communist Studies* 42, no. 2 (2009): 265–87.

74. Adomeit, "The 'Putin System.'"

75. Volkov, *Violent Entrepreneurs*; Vadim Volkov, "Silovoe predprinimatel'stvo v sovremennoi Rossii," *Sotsiologiecheskie issledovaniia*, no. 1 (1999): 55–65.

76. Mark Galeotti, *The Vory: Russia's Super Mafia* (New Haven, CT: Yale University Press, 2018).

77. Varese, *The Russian Mafia*; Alexander Kupatadze, *Organised Crime, Political Transitions and State Formation in Post-Soviet Eurasia* (Houndmills: Palgrave Macmillan, 2012).

78. EIA, "Liquidating the Forests," 2013, https://eia-global.org/reports/liquidating-the-forests-report (accessed April 29, 2018).

79. "Russian Polluters Evading Huge Environmental Fines," May 11, 2015, https://themoscowtimes.com/articles/russian-polluters-evading-huge-environmental-fines-46462 (accessed May 5, 2018).

80. Center for Strategic and International Studies, *Russian Organized Crime and Corruption, Putin's Challenge* (Washington, DC: CSIS, 2000), 32–39.

81. For continuing problems with Russian money laundering, see Bureau of International Narcotics and Law Enforcement Affairs, *2012 International Narcotics Control Strategy Report*

(INCSR), vol. 2, March 7, 2012, http://www.state.gov/j/inl/rls/nrcrpt/2012/vol2/184117. htm#Russia (accessed May 5, 2018).

82. N. A. Lopashenko, *Begstvo kapitalov, peredel sobstvennosti i ekonomicheskaia amnistiia* (Moscow: Iuridicheskie programmy, 2005); Anna Repetskaya, *Ekonomicheskaya Organizovannaya Prestupnost' V Rossii* (Moscow: Palmarium Academic Publishing, 2012).

83. Viktoria Votonovskaya, "Capital Flight from Russia Soars to $31.3 Billion in 2017," *Moscow Times*, January 18, 2018, https://themoscowtimes.com/news/capital-flight-from-russia-soars-to-313-bln-in-2017-60209 (accessed May 5, 2018); Luke Harding, "Panama Papers: A Special Investigation Revealed: The $2bn Offshore Trail That Leads to Vladimir Putin," *The Guardian*, April 3, 2016, https://www.theguardian.com/news/2016/apr/03/panama-papers-money-hidden-offshore (accessed May 5, 2018); Neil Buckley, "Latvia: A Banking Scandal on the Baltic," February 23, 2018, https://www.ft.com/content/e7b586c4-1883-11e8-9376-4a6390addb44 (accessed May 5, 2018); Vladimir Kuznetsov and Ksenia Galouchko, "Russia Capital Rush Extends to $13 Billion Last Quarter," Bloomberg, October 9, 2014, http://www.bloomberg.com/news/2014-10-09/russia-capital-outflows-slowed-to-13-billion-last-quarter.html (accessed May 5, 2018).

84. Votonovskaya, "Capital Flight from Russia."

85. Mark Galeotti, "How the Invasion of Ukraine Is Shaking Up the Global Crime Scene," November 6, 2014, http://www.vice.com/read/how-the-invasion-of-ukraine-is-shaking-up-the-global-crime-scene-1106 (accessed May 5, 2018).

86. The problem first identified by Anna Repetskaya a decade ago still endures. See Anna Repetskaya, "Irkutsk Organized Crime Press Review," *OC Watch* 5 (1999): 16.

87. Mark Galeotti suggests that Chechen organized crime may be seen as a franchise, as there is more Chechen organized crime than Chechens. See "'Brotherhoods' and 'Associates': Chechen Networks of Crime and Resistance," in *Networks, Terrorism and Global Insurgency*, ed. Robert J. Bunker (London: Routledge, 2005), 175; Aaron Beitman, "Organized Crime in Western Siberia," part 3, discusses Repetskaya's research on the crime groups present in Western Siberia, April 26, 2012, http://traccc.gmu.edu/2012/04/26/organized-crime-in-western-siberia-part-3 (accessed April 29, 2018).

88. "Vladivostok Mayor Stripped of Power among Corruption Investigation," Associated Press, March 1, 2007, http://www.nytimes.com/2007/03/01/world/europe/01iht-russia.4763829.html (accessed April 29, 2018).

89. "Russian Far East Governor Steps Down," RIA-Novosti, February 28, 2012, http://sputniknews.com/society/20120228/171590672.html (accessed May 5, 2018).

90. Dmitry Frolovskiy, "Vladivostok: The Many Loves of Russia's Far East Capital," *The Diplomat*, September 3, 2016, https://thediplomat.com/2016/09/vladivostok-the-many-lives-of-russias-far-eastern-capital (accessed April 29, 2018).

91. Ekaterina Arenina, "Details of Vladivostok Mayor Igor Pushkarev's Corruption Case," Russiangate, October 26, 2017, https://en.russiangate.com/society/details-of-vladivostok-mayor-igor-pushkarevs-corruption-case/?sphrase_id=372417 (accessed April 28, 2018).

92. See website of the Vladivostok Center, http://www.crime.vl.ru (accessed April 29, 2018), which has extensive material on corruption in the Far East Region.

93. V. A. Nomokonov, ed., *Organizovannia prestupnost': tendentsii, perspektivy bor'by* (Vladivostok: Dalnevostochnogo universiteta, 1998).

94. P. V. Korovnikov, "Problemy dekriminalizatsii sfery prirodopol'zovaniia Primorskogo kraiia i nekotorye puti ikh resheniia," in *Rossiia i ATR Problemy bezopasnosti, migratsii i prestupnosti* (Vladivostok: Dal'nevostochnogo universiteta, 2007), 88–89.

95. Dal'nii Vostok: Khronika organizovannoi prestupnosti (Obzor pressy 1997–August 2003), http://www.crime.vl.ru/index.php?p=2640&more=1&c=1&tb=1&pb=1 (accessed April 29, 2018).

96. WWF-Russia, "Combating Illegal Logging and Corruption in the Forest Sector," https://new.wwf.ru/en/what-we-do/forests/combating-illegal-forest-exploitation (accessed April 28, 2018).

97. Vadim Nikitin, "Feminism as Cronyism for Russia's Power Women," March 1, 2009, http://foreignpolicyblogs.com/?s=feminism+as+cronyism (accessed May 5, 2018).

98. Dawisha, *Putin's Kleptocracy*.

99. Bureau of International Narcotics and Law Enforcement Affairs, *2012 International Narcotics Control Strategy Report.*

100. Galeotti, "Crime and Crimea."

101. "Court Battle between Roman Abramovich and Boris Berezovsky Ends," *The Guardian*, January 19, 2012, http://www.theguardian.com/world/2012/jan/19/court-battle-abramovich-berezovsky-ends (accessed May 5, 2018).

102. See, for example, "Astrakhan Focus of Anti-Putin Protests," Euronews, April 14, 2012, http://www.euronews.com/2012/04/14/astrakhan-focus-of-anti-putin-protests (accessed May 5, 2018).

Chapter Nine

Gender and Politics

Janet Elise Johnson and Alexandra Novitskaya

Women have a huge presence in Russia. Women make up a higher proportion of senior management positions in small to midsize businesses in Russia—around 40 percent—than anywhere else in the world.[1] Oligarch Elena
Baturina, who built a construction business into a net worth of more than $1
billion in 2017, is Russia's richest woman and one of the richest women in
the world. Former dissidents-turned-civil-rights-activists Liudmila Aleksee-
va, the late Natalia Gorbanevskaia, and Valeria Novodvorskaia have been
championing human rights for decades. Gaining international fame after per-
forming near the Kremlin, the feminist punk band Pussy Riot became the
symbol of the 2011–2012 opposition in Russia, joining other women, such as
Evgeniia Chirikova, an environmental activist, who had dared to criticize
Putin's rule (and who fled Russia in 2015). Once seen as a dilettante because
of her career in reality TV and her connection to Putin (as daughter of his
first patron), TV journalist Ksenia Sobchak turned out to be a keen critic of
the regime and an important face of the opposition, going as far as running
against Putin in the 2018 presidential elections. Not immune to violence,
women politicians (Galina Starovoitova in 1998), journalists (Anna Politkovskaia in 2006 and Anastasia Baburova in 2009), and human rights activists (Natalia Estemirova in 2009) have been prominent among those mur-
dered for their activism.

These achievements reflect not only the extraordinary efforts of these
women but the Soviet legacy. During the Soviet Union, women had been
heavily recruited into the labor force because of Marxist ideology's promise
of equality and the imperative of catching up with industrialization in the
West. With pressure from Inessa Armand and the feminist Aleksandra Kol-
lontai, who were the first two women to head the newly formed Women's
Department of the Communist Party, the Bolshevik government created what

189

could be considered highly progressive legislation in support of women, such as paid maternity leave, subsidized day care, legalized abortion, easily accessible divorce by either spouse, and restrictions on sexual harassment. The Soviet system also advanced women into local politics, surpassing their Western counterparts.

However, women gained more duties than liberation or equal rights. After World War II—when there were twice as many women aged twenty to twenty-nine than men—women were summoned to rebuild the ruined country and to replenish its lost population, to produce and reproduce. Throughout, Soviet women faced a triple burden of work, home, and procurement of scarce basic goods. In contrast to the propaganda of women on tractors, women were restricted from around five hundred of the most lucrative jobs on the pretense of protecting their fertility. There was only one woman, Ekaterina Furtseva, who was a member of the ruling Politburo, but only for four years (1957–1961) before being shifted to the much less powerful position of minister of culture. In the Soviet Union, women's inclusion was not about gender equality but about equal mobilization of everyone in society.[2] It was faux emancipation.

In the post-Soviet period, gender equality has remained elusive and complicated. New problems—such as sex trafficking and widespread sexual harassment—emerged among the new freedoms. The shrinking of the welfare state put many women, especially single mothers and disabled women, into poverty, even as they may qualify for benefits. Even middle-class women have had trouble making ends meet, as families were put on a roller-coaster ride of economic insecurity. Most precarious have been women migrants, who often lack legal residence rights and are often not ethnically Russian, which makes them more vulnerable to crime and corruption as well as subject to virulent xenophobia.[3] Most limited in their rights are women in the North Caucasus, where male leaders have called for a revival of religious "traditions" such as bride kidnapping, female genital mutilation, and polygamy; Chechnya's leader has authorized a reign of terror, including defending brutal "honor" killings of women.[4]

Since Putin came to power in 2000, there has been the appearance of more inclusion of women in politics. Valentina Matvienko governed Russia's second city, St. Petersburg, from 2003 until 2011, when she became chair of the upper house, the highest government position held by a woman since Catherine the Great. Since 2013, Elvira Nabiullina, a longtime member of Putin's government, has headed Russia's Central Bank, the first woman to head a central bank in one of the world's biggest economies. Though still lagging behind the world average, women in the bicameral legislature reached the highest proportions in post-Soviet Russian history, with 17.1 percent in the Federation Council in 2014 and 15.3 percent in the 2016 election for the State Duma.

But these increases in women in politics have been a bait and switch, a con in which the appearance of gender equality is given while the reality is backsliding.[5] Though still a legal and provided part of state-funded health care, abortion has been increasingly restricted since 2003, for the first time since Stalin, and motherhood promoted as the best choice for women. Though there were some small reforms on domestic violence in 2016, they were reversed six months later, when Orthodox Church–sponsored groups worried that the reforms meant that it was not OK to slap your children or your wife.[6] The most prominent gender-related policy is the "maternity capital," introduced in 2007, in which the government promised a contribution to children's education, housing, or mothers' retirement to women who have more than one child.[7] Such a payment—about $7,000 in 2016—may provide a small kind of assistance to mothers but ignores the underlying problems of health care, child care, and irresponsible fathers that contribute to Russia's declining population. Three of four eligible women do not use it, either because they still wouldn't be able to afford a mortgage or because they do not trust the government-run banks to protect their pension savings.[8]

The repressive legislation passed in the aftermath of the 2011–2012 protests has had particularly negative consequences for women. The 2012 law requiring organizations engaging in political activities and receiving foreign funds to register as "foreign agents," which was expanded over the next several years, has been used against more than a dozen feminist and lesbian organizations, incurring great costs for the organizations even when they then win in court.[9] The 2013 law banning "gay propaganda" toward minors threatens LGBT mothers, legitimating attacks on and social control over all women as well as people whose gender and sexuality do not fit the standard established by the government.

This chapter explains the limitations placed on women in politics and the importance of feminism in opposition. We also make a deeper critique, arguing that gender constitutes the essential, internal supports of the edifice of the regime that has been consolidated under Putin. It is not just that, as the feminist-identified protest punk band Pussy Riot explained, "Putin is a symbol of sexism and patriarchal attitudes . . . present in every unit of the society."[10] We argue that only by seeing gender can Russian politics be understood.

MALE DOMINANCE OF POLITICS

Over the last decade, political science has moved beyond the transition paradigm with its focus on Russia's level of democratization.[11] With Putin's rise to power, observers labeled Russia as a hybrid regime but increasingly recognized that such regimes have their own particular dynamics. The attention turned toward informal politics, the informal institutions and practices that undermine the formal institutions and procedures laid out in the Russian constitution.[12] Instead of a meaningful formal political system, Russia, like other Eurasian countries, has a hybrid of empty rules and regulations mixed with the institutionalization of informal rules and practices that sometimes use the formal rules but more often subvert them. The system is neopatrimonial, characterized by personalistic relations such as nepotism (favoring relatives) and cronyism (favoring friends), even as the formal-legal sometimes matters.

This new regime dynamics paradigm is more ideologically neutral and promises much insight into how such regimes work; however, most political scientists who study Russia are blind to gender.[13] By gender, we mean rules about how men and women are to behave that operate as central organizing forces in intersection with other structures of power such as class, ethnicity, and sexuality. While the first generation of gender scholars thought more about women, more recent theorizing considers the role of masculinity and how gender gets embedded in social and political institutions in the form of male dominance.[14] Extending the scholarship showing that postcommunism is gendered, we argue that gender is embedded in and essential to Russia's informal politics.[15] Our intent is not about blaming men but to see how gender can stabilize regimes, something that is especially important for regimes like Russia, where formal constitutions cannot provide predictability.

Most obviously, the high-glossed image of Putin illustrates the power of "hegemonic masculinity," the masculine ideal for political leaders.[16] More so than in most other countries, the Kremlin has been explicit in its attempt to establish Putin as the ideal man-leader. Pictures of tough-guy Putin, often with a bare sculpted chest or illustrating his manly prowess hunting, racing, or practicing judo are propagated (with a new set of bare-chested photos released in August 2017), but they are mere phantasms, as Putin is never in real danger.[17] His image has also been sexualized to show that he is the only man that women—and the whole country—should want. As a result, his masculinity is unlike other statesmen, who must appear with their wives (and children) at their sides. Putin's former wife was virtually invisible, and most Russians saw no problem when his divorce was made public in 2013. Even his alleged long-term dalliance with a much younger former rhythmic gymnast and two-term Duma deputy Alina Kabaeva, perhaps even fathering her children, has been unremarkable. This informally constructed masculinity, not the typical symbols of constitutionalism and the flag, has been central to legitimating Putin's leadership and the post-Soviet regime.[18]

Despite the assertions that this hegemonic masculinity with its embrace of heterosexuality is traditionally Russian, this masculinity is revisionism that offers alternatives to what many saw as the powerless, emasculated Soviet man. At the same time, this masculinity is based on an old myth of the sexual innocence of Russians, a new conservatism, where homosexuality is viewed as foreign.[19] Hegemonic masculinity also uses the Soviet model of gender discourse in which sexuality was silenced and conflict within heterosexual relationships was hidden.[20] That the Kremlin has had to do this much cultural work shows that Putin's position is more precarious than most Westerner observers assume.[21]

Over the last several years, Putin's masculinity project has been bolstered by the consolidation of an alliance with the Russian Orthodox Church based on a shared critique of Western "gender ideology."[22] (The church's Patriarch Kirill openly supported Putin's return to the presidency as "God's miracle," and Putin had an official celebration for Kirill at the Kremlin.[23]) The new church-state "antigender" campaign opposes gender equality, reproductive rights, sex education, and LGBTQ rights marked by the antigay legislation.[24] These moves helped Putin claim global leadership of illiberal populism around the world and his party, United Russia, to win big in the 2016 Duma election, securing three-fourths of the seats, more than enough to change Russia's constitution. This hegemonic masculinity also helps explain Putin's warmongering in Georgia, Ukraine, and Syria, which, because of the financial costs, does not seem rational. Russia had never got rid of its imperial ambitions, but Putin's land grab in Crimea reads as a reassertion of his masculinity through imperialist lenses: history would have never "forgotten" him for failing to act, so he had to act.

Russia's regime also illustrates the informal power of "homosociality," how being of the same sex can help individuals "understand and thus [can] predict each other's behavior."[25] In most places around the world, elite networks have historically been "predominantly accessible for other men as well as more valuable when built between men." Homosociality protects networks and provides predictability, rational goals for elite men in any regime, but especially ones that do not have predictable formal institutions. In Russia, homosociality is most evident in the key elite networks that dominate Russian politics and which have included very few women. This is particularly true among the *siloviki*. The dominance of men is essential to the network: they draw personnel from the Soviet coercive structures such as the KGB that were predominantly men. In addition, the *silovik* mentality is about hegemonic masculinity and homosociality. They call for more order engineered by a strong state staffed by men, with imported cultural traditions such as secrecy that help keep women out.[26] Putin's relationship with the *siloviki* may be uneasy at times, but his idealization of the KGB culture—a homosocial experience virtually impossible for women to share—began in his early childhood.[27] Putin has even been open about the importance of homosociality, asserting at the 2011 International Women's Forum that it is easier to work with men than women.[28]

While seeing that informal elite networks—made up of those with economic and/or political power—have proven more reliable than Russia's unclear institutions and weak parties,[29] most political scientists of Russia have missed the importance of hegemonic masculinity and homosociality to the building and maintenance of the personal relationships within the networks. For example, Alena Ledeneva has pointed to the Kremlin's revival of the tradition of enforced solidarity and mutual cover-up (*krugovaiia poruka*), but failed to note the gender of this practice, as evidenced in her illustrative political cartoon: men in suits stand in a circle with guns pointed at each other.[30] Similarly, the use of compromising materials (*kompromat*) by the Kremlin has been seen as a key strategy to keep elites from stepping out of line, but this observation has missed the way *kompromat* tends to mix allegations of abuse of office, disloyalty, or incompetence with titillating questions about sexual behavior, orientation, or sufficient masculinity. For example, in 1999 when Putin was head of the Federal Security Service, or FSB, which is the post-Soviet successor to the KGB, a video of Russia's prosecutor general—or someone who looked a lot like him—in bed with two women was shown on TV, causing the prosecutor to lose his job; he had been investigating corruption in the Kremlin. Putin's job at the KGB, as the Soviet Union collapsed, was not as a spy but as a case officer who gathered information about people in order to be able to manipulate them, a skill he appears to have translated into the post-Soviet era.[31]

The threat of *kompromat* works so well now that the actual use of it against the inner circle is rare. In one recent case where *kompromat* was deployed and not just threatened, the former defense minister Anatoly Serdiukov's affair was made public in order to undermine his protection from his father-in-law (Viktor Zubkov), a former deputy prime minister and friend of Putin. Critics and opposition leaders fare worse, several of whom have been caught in a "honeypot" by a woman who offers herself up and then brings out drugs or bondage to catch them on video in compromising positions. Before the 2016 election for the State Duma, a videotape of Mikhail Kasyanov, a former prime minister and opposition leader, was played on national television, which showed him having sex with a female member of the opposition, followed by pillow talk in which Kasyanov appears to admit to skimming money, dismiss his fellow opposition leaders, and agree to make sure his lover gets a position in the Duma "with a fat paycheck."[32]

WOMEN IN POLITICS UNDER PUTIN

In addition to holding the regime together, hegemonic masculinity and homosociality establish a bulwark of male dominance that restricts women in politics. Feminist theorists point out that hegemonic masculinity comes with "emphasized femininity," ideals of women who are compliant to male dominance.[33] Emphasized femininity in Russian politics is illustrated most colorfully in Putin's comments about Hillary Clinton. In a remark understood as a derisive penis joke, he questioned her ability to lead: "At a minimum, a head of state should have a head."[34] Later, responding to Clinton's comparison between Putin and Hitler (for annexing Crimea), Putin said that "it's better not to argue with women," adding that Clinton had never been "too graceful" in her statements, and that strong accusations usually illustrate weakness, but "maybe weakness is not the worst quality for a woman."[35]

Though made about an American politician, these comments serve as oblique, public threats to women participating in Russian politics. The threat also appears in the guise of pseudo-respect for Russian women as the most beautiful and in sexist assumptions about them. For example, in the early 2000s, a party campaigned against Matvienko with the slogan "Being Governor Is Not a Woman's Business."[36] In the 2016 Duma election, *Life-News*, a tabloid with links to the Kremlin, published nude pictures of a Moscow member of the opposition and her (female) chief of staff. In her 2018 presidential bid, Ksenia Sobchak faced a barrage of sexist commentary in the media and from male politicians, including being called a "disgusting bitch."[37] This was set in the context of a plethora of images of sexualized women encouraging (male) citizens to vote for Putin, as well as an ad warning Russians that, if they did not vote, a candidate like Sobchak (who had expressed support for LGBTQ rights) would win and help gay people take over.[38] These informal rules of the gender game have been so institutionalized in Russia that they only need to be rarely enforced in order to signal the severe consequences facing women who do not stay in line.

The result is that male dominance has simultaneously empowered a small number of women to positions of some power, while severely limiting their opportunities to represent women and push for gender equality. As in other countries, women tend to be excluded from the more "powerful" positions on issues related to law enforcement, military, and international diplomacy and are relegated to what are traditionally viewed as care-related issues of family, children, health, and welfare. This has been especially true for social and health policy issues in which heads of ministries and legislative committees are informally reserved for women. But, instead of being "workhorses" on these issues, as they are in more democratic regimes, elite women in Russia serve as "stand ins . . . a demonstration without meaning," brought in during periods of status quo and then moved out when real changes are made.[39]

Outside of these "feminized" ministries, women are brought in as "cleaners" to sweep messes under the rug so that the men leaders look good. For example, to insiders, Matvienko was brought to "clean up" St. Petersburg, but she failed to keep corruption under wraps (that is, to keep up Putin's cover story of bringing order to Russia). Her final landing place, chairing the

Federation Council, is a position that provides few patronage perks. In other cases, women famous for achievements outside of politics are used as "showgirls"—to use the Russian nomenclature—to enlist support for the regime's political party. This is a feminized version of the Russian practice of "locomotives": nominating big names such as celebrities, singers, and athletes (including an opera singer, a rhythmic gymnast, and a former Playboy model) to attract voters.[40] Their roles are portrayed as being kissed on the hand by their male counterparts, putting on makeup, or acting beautiful and silly.[41] In the 2016 Duma election, nationalism was attached to the showgirl role, exemplified by the election of the "sex symbol" Natalia Poklonskaya. Poklonskaya, once a Ukrainian citizen, changed sides when Crimea was annexed in 2014 and was appointed the general prosecutor of Crimea for Russia (and then prosecuted pro-Ukrainian activists).

Other deputies, most notably Irina Yarovaia, Elena Mizulina, and Ekaterina Lakhova, have been "loyalists," known for sponsoring hastily conceived, ideological bills to signal their allegiance with Putin; Mizulina and Lakhova are particularly striking because they once identified as feminists. Mizulina, who has changed her party affiliation several times and gained notoriety during her 2008–2015 tenure as the head of what is left of the Duma Committee on Family, Women, and Children's Affairs, authored laws restricting abortion and banning gay propaganda while proposing taxing divorce, taking children away from same-sex parents, and adding Orthodoxy to the preamble of the constitution. She also spearheaded the successful campaign to undo progress on domestic violence. Lakhova, once head of the woman-only faction Women of Russia, championed the law banning adoption of Russian children by Americans, helping her to secure a move to the Federation Council in 2014. Yarovaia coauthored the "foreign agent" law that threatens nongovernmental organizations, as well as a 2016 package of legislation (known as the Yarovaia law) under the guise of "antiterrorism," which greatly increases the regime's ability to surveil citizens' online activities. Instead of having to demonstrate loyalty to the regime, male deputies are more likely to leave the Duma to go into private or state-owned enterprises, indicating their greater access to the long-term spoils of patronage and political entrepreneurship.[42]

In all these roles, women must have powerful (male) patrons or demonstrate ultimate loyalty to the regime. Even the head of the Central Bank, Elvira Nabiullina, with strong economist credentials and mostly supported by an economically liberal coalition, is the protégé of Putin's close friend and is married to a chief theorist for Putin's economic policy. All these roles come with limited power. In the best case, they are akin to throwing women off a "glass cliff" by bringing them into failing businesses.[43] The worst-case scenario is illustrated by Maria Maksakova, a prominent opera singer, who was elected in 2011 as a showgirl but later spoke out against the gay propaganda law.[44] In October 2016, she and her husband (also a deputy) fled to Ukraine, claiming they had been hounded by the FSB for their views, even to the point of Maksakova's miscarrying (her husband was then shot and killed in 2017, apparently by the FSB).

Looking at the inclusion of women in Russian political arenas also indicates the relative power of these arenas in the regime. With the introduction of competitive elections, the proportion of women in the legislatures dropped by more than half, and then continued to drop through the 1990s (see figure 9.1).

That said, there have been increases of women in the Duma, the Constitutional Court, and the Public Chamber, arenas that are showplaces of constitutionalism or representation. Even so, women continue to be underrepresented. At the top of the regime, the president and the prime minister have never been women. As of 2018, there have only been six women governors since the end of the USSR and only one super-governor (head of the federal dis-

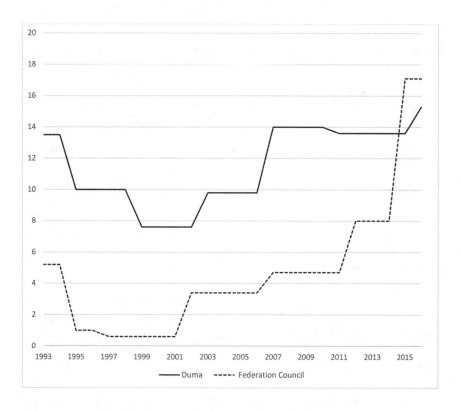

Figure 9.1.   Percent of Women in Russia's Legislatures, 1993–2016
Source: Inter-Parliamentary Union, "Women in National Parliaments," April 1, 2018, http://archive.ipu.org/wmn-e/classif.htm.

tricts), Matvienko, for six months. In other bastions of power, the Presidium
of the State Council and the Security Council, there have been very few
women. This pattern of "the higher, the fewer" women in politics is common
to most political systems, including the Soviet one, but the Russian case
helps reveal how much this pattern is now about informal politics. The most
informal gatherings—perhaps in the sauna at Putin's various homes—likely
have no space for women at all.

FEMINIST ACTIVISM RESISTING MALE DOMINANCE

Perhaps unsurprisingly given these limitations on women and representation,
the primary arena of resistance to male dominance in Russia's politics has
been outside the political system. In the first decade after the Soviet collapse,
feminism gained only a small toehold in Russia in some gender studies
centers and women's crisis centers, where the former focused on academic
apprehension of feminist theory and gender studies and the latter addressed
violence against women.[45] Feminism in Russia never became mainstream or
even properly understood by the masses. Many Russians embraced "traditional" gender roles—in theory more than practice—because of the Soviet
faux emancipation. While women tended to staff the nongovernmental organizations that proliferated after communism, many were focused on social
issues, extending women's traditional caregiving roles from their own children to the broader society, and most did not see themselves as organizing as
women, let alone as feminists.[46] Those who were interested in promoting
gender equality tended to use the weaker language of "women's rights"
common in the Western donor community rather than the confrontational
feminisms that had emerged in the 1960s and 1970s in the West.[47]

Small pockets of more radical feminism began to emerge with the growth
of social media and increased availability of internet access across the country. Russia's largest online feminist platform, Feministki (http://feministki.
livejournal.com), founded in 2006, grew to several thousand subscribers and
prompted lively debate, including over whether women should live separate-
ly from men. Other groups included the radical intersectional Moscow Feminist Group,[48] the separatist Womenation,[49] and the sexist media–tackling Za
Feminizm (Pro Feminism).[50] Although most eschew direct involvement in
politics, the democratic party Yabloko has an active "gender faction" headed
by a self-identified feminist that has provided more public visibility to the
small groups. Pussy Riot arose as part of these developments.[51] In December
2011 at the beginning of protests against electoral fraud, they took the stage
near Red Square in multicolored balaclavas that covered their faces, and
then, in February 2012, they briefly occupied Moscow's showplace church
calling on the "Mother of God [to] Drive Putin Away." As their lyrics expli-

citly took on Putin, homophobia, sexism, and the regime's alliance with the Russian Orthodox Church, Pussy Riot became the first feminist-identified group to openly and directly confront the regime.

For the first time, the regime felt threatened by feminism, arresting the three members of the group that they could find and then, after a show trial reminiscent of the Soviet period, sentencing them to two years in a labor camp. The trial of Pussy Riot also showed how the gender of the persecuted artists could be used against them (from accusations of being bad mothers to being somebody else's puppet, since such young women could not possibly have come up with all those profoundly critical ideas by themselves).[52] Putin stated that he pitied the imprisoned members, not for being incarcerated under harsh conditions, but for losing their "feminine dignity" by their protest.[53] For Putin, a woman who would participate in a demonstration or, even worse, facilitate protest action is a deviant and does not possess "real" or "proper" femininity.[54] Much of the Russian public was swayed by the show trial—leaving the group misunderstood as blasphemers more than political dissidents.[55] The prosecution gave Pussy Riot international prestige, making this feminist punk band a symbol of resistance to Russia's regime.

Since Pussy Riot's imprisonment, the repression of feminist projects has been stepped up as part of the overall restrictions on independent political expression, including on social media. After Russia's invasion of Ukraine in 2014, feminism became a specific target amid the omnipresent nationalist propaganda predicated on hegemonic masculinity and emphasized femininity. Feminist ideas challenging these norms were branded as anti-Russian. The most prominent women's crisis center, ANNA, was put on the "foreign agent" list in 2016, apparently because of its domestic violence activism during Duma debates.[56]

However, feminists resist, using both conventional and innovative forms. Feminists marched in their own column in an October 2012 protest for the first time in post-Soviet Russian history and have continued to do so, as in the 2014 May Day parade.[57] In 2012–2013, a group of feminist activists organized such exhibitions of feminist art as the *Feminist Pencil* in Moscow and in St. Petersburg, uniting women artists from various regions and artistic traditions. V-Day, an international campaign against gender violence, reached Russia in 2013–2014. In 2014, Eve Ensler's *The Vagina Monologues* play ran for three days with great success (all three performances were sold out), with all proceeds going to support crisis centers for women. These events brought gender violence and widespread sexism, both safer issues than directly challenging the regime, to the public space. When Russia's Supreme Court proposed moving the provision on battery from the criminal to the administrative code, which would make it less serious of a crime, activists wrote a brief against the change, enlisted the President's Human Rights Council, lobbied the Public Chamber, and collected signatures for a petition. (They persuaded Putin, who voiced concern about the move, leading the Duma to keep battery between "close persons" criminalized, but this moderate success was reversed six months later.) Feminists in St. Petersburg have taken sides on the sex work/prostitution divide, with Silver Rose formed by former sex workers and their allies to provide psychological and legal assistance to sex workers, versus Eve's Ribs (Rebra Evy), which advocates the abolition of prostitution. In 2018, a student in international relations at St. Petersburg State University protested on International Women's Day by making posters of sexist statements made by the faculty, such as "women do not have a place in politics," and the head of the department threatened an investigation into the student.[58] Essential resistance to hegemonic masculinity has come from LGBT groups, some of which include feminism. Side by Side, which runs an annual LGBT film festival and successfully fought a "foreign agent" allegation in the courts, has even had feminist and women's organizations come to them for advice.[59]

The members of Pussy Riot entered back into the fray right after they were released in 2014 in the lead-up to Russia's Sochi Olympics. After their attempt to film a video, *Putin Will Teach You to Love the Motherland,* was interrupted first by arrests and then by beatings by uniformed Cossacks working as security for the Olympics, their activism has mostly been performance based, using their international prestige to protect themselves. The focus of their videos is broad, including police violence against people of color and the election of Donald Trump in the United States, but central remains the corruption and violence of the male-dominated Putin regime (see their YouTube channel, wearepussyriot, which has some forty-seven thousand subscribers). For example, with a video ("Chaika") named for the general prosecutor whose sons appear to have gotten wealthy, Pussy Riot parodies the hypocrisy of the male-dominated elites claiming to be Orthodox Christian patriots but who embrace coercion and purloin resources.[60] "Be loyal to those in power, cause power is a gift from god, son," Pussy Riot's front woman Nadezhda Tolokonnikova sing-song chants, dressed as an employee with the prosecutor's office. Linking informal power to gender, Pussy Riot suggests that Russia's expansionary moves are so that there is more "mother Russia" for elites to "milk," but they are patriots because they do this in Russia, "not Europe where they have gay people." Pointing out how anticorruption campaigns are often used as part of intra-elite conflicts, not transparency, Tolokonnikova intones, "I run the war on corruption, or to be more precise, I run the corruption here," with the ultimate loyalty being to Putin.

These myriad actions have led to larger flashes of mobilization. In 2016, tens of thousands of women (and some men) organized a virtual flash mob sharing their stories of rape, sexual assault, incest, and sexual harassment on social media, started by a Ukrainian woman's Facebook post using the hashtag #Iamnotafraidtospeakout (#yaneboius'skazati/#yaneboius'skazat'). Sympathizing with those who had spoken out, Russian and Ukrainian celebrities shared their personal stories of sexual assault. More than just discourse, the online flash mob led to the resignation of a school principal for negligence and a criminal conviction of a popular teacher (for "engaging in any sexual activities with a child under sixteen years of age") at one of Moscow's most prominent public schools (No. 57, portrayed in the 2010 documentary film *My Perestroika*). Despite its similarity to the #Iamnotafraidtospeakout campaign, the Russian public's initial reaction to the US-initiated #metoo movement was a mix of skepticism and ridicule, as prominent politicians and TV personalities—including the chair of the Duma's Committee on Family, Women, and Children, Tatiana Pletneva—asserted that sexual harassment was foreign to Russia.[61] However, another online flash mob broke out in 2018 when the Duma Ethics Committee found nothing wrong with the behavior of Deputy Leonid Slutski, whom several women journalists alleged had groped them. The flash mob collected 13.9 million signatures calling for his resignation.[62] Several national media outlets started boycotting the Duma as an "unsafe space for women." Oksana Pushkina, a former TV talk show host and now the deputy chair of the Committee on Family, Women, and Children, is the sole member of the Duma to come out in support of the women and against sexual harassment.[63]

The cross-mobilization between gay rights and feminist activism has also helped foster a change in support of LGBT issues among the opposition. The once-nationalist-and-not-particularly-progressive opposition leader Aleksei Naval'ny included the possibility of solving inheritance and civil union issues and permitting pride marches on his agenda.[64] His promises, while incomplete, were strikingly different from the way Russian politicians had dealt with LGBT issues in the past. Similarly, during the 2018 presidential elections campaign, candidate Ksenia Sobchak included support not just for feminism but also for LGBT issues in her agenda, the first presidential candidate ever to do so.[65] This is a significant change in a society where both pro- and anti-regime forces readily use homophobia as a successful tactic for demeaning the political enemy.[66]

CONCLUSION

Scholars and students of Russian politics often do not see gender, a blindness that the Russian regime cultivates even as it uses gender. Gender, along with other differences such as ethnicity and nationality, is cast as natural and thus outside of politics. Bringing gender into focus helps observers grasp the operation of informal politics—bolstered by support beams of hegemonic masculinity and homosociality—underneath the increasingly thinning veneer of constitutionalism and democracy. Understanding these gendered informal politics also helps explain the increase in the number of women in formal politics since Putin came to power. As feminist political scientists have been arguing, the mere presence of women in formal political arenas does not secure gender equality because the practices and norms of male dominance remain. In Russia, the regime restricts women's positions and limits their opportunities, reserving only a few options—regime-worshipping loyalists, workhorses in fields typically understood to be feminine, temporary political cleaners in messy situations, or mere showgirls—and requires a powerful (male) patron.

Seeing gender also helps explain the emergence of Pussy Riot, with its seemingly crass lyrics designed to counter the regime's crass masculinity and homosociality in politics, as well as the regime's overreaction to these "girls" whom most Russians do not support. Contesting the regime's consolidated male dominance challenges institutionalized corruption—the issue that drove the 2011–2012 protests—much more so than anticorruption legislation, which has often been used against the regime's opponents. The regime's crackdown on feminist and LGBT protests reveals just how limited are the opportunities for any political expression in Russia today.

All these gendered informal politics help explain the paradox between increasing numbers of women in office under Putin's rule and the lack of progress in gender equality. The maternalist policies of Putin's regime, such as restrictions on abortion and maternity capital, fit with emphasized femininity, while tackling structural gender inequality (including criminalizing domestic violence) does not. Policies limiting the rights of LGBT citizens also fit the gendered informal politics of this kind of regime. The gender of informal politics also explains why the regime only cursorily attends to society's problems, while leaving most women, men, and their families on a roller coaster of financial instability. Facing traditionalist propaganda unchallenged by a strong feminist or women's movement, most women in Russia remain under the burden of not only work but also housework, childbearing, and child rearing, in conventional (if not always married) heterosexual relationships.

The informal obstacles in Russia have implications for explaining weak gender equality across postcommunist states, even as almost all have passed gender equality and domestic violence legislation. While the smaller postcommunist states needed the appearance of gender equality represented by these legislative reforms as they sought membership in European institutions, Russia is a former superpower that has focused on a reenergizing military and foreign policy and increasingly distancing itself from the West. In all postcommunist states, real equality remains elusive, a puzzle in a world with some visibly powerful strong women, such as Germany's chancellor Angela Merkel. Raising questions about how hegemonic masculinity and homosociality get institutionalized uncovers new layers in this equality paradox of formal laws but weak implementation.

DISCUSSION QUESTIONS

1. What are the main achievements of women in Russian politics?
2. What are the main obstacles to women's participation and representation in Russian politics?
3. What kinds of feminisms exist in Russia and how successful are they at challenging male dominance?
4. How does "seeing gender" clarify the way in which Russia's politics work?

SUGGESTED READINGS

Alyokhina, Maria. *Riot Days*. New York: Metropolitan Books, 2017.
Healey, Dan. *Russian Homophobia from Stalin to Sochi*. London: Bloomsbury, 2017.
Ilic, Melanie. *The Palgrave Handbook of Women and Gender in Twentieth-Century Russia and the Soviet Union*. London: Palgrave Macmillan, 2017.
Johnson, Janet Elise. *The Gender of Informal Politics: Russia, Iceland and Twenty-First Century Male Dominance*. Basingstoke: Palgrave Macmillan, 2018.
Lomasko, Victoria. *Other Russias*. Translated by Thomas Campbell. United Kingdom: Penguin, 2017.
McCarthy, Lauren A. *Trafficking Justice: How Russian Police Enforce New Laws, from Crime to Courtroom*. Ithaca, NY: Cornell University Press, 2015.
Sperling, Valerie. *Sex, Politics, & Putin: Political Legitimacy in Russia*. Oxford: Oxford University Press, 2015.
Suchland, Jennifer. *Economies of Violence: Transnational Feminism, Postsocialism, and the Politics of Sex Trafficking*. Durham, NC: Duke University Press, 2015.
Sundstrom, Lisa McIntosh. "Russian Women's Activism: Two Steps Forward, One Step Back." In *Women's Movements in the Global Era: The Power of Local Feminisms*, ed. Amrita Basu. Boulder, CO: Westview, 2010.

NOTES

1. Grant Thornton's 2014 International Business Report as reported in "Russia Is World's No. 1 Employer of Women Managers, Report Says," *Moscow Times*, June 18, 2014, http://www.themoscowtimes.com/business/article/russia-is-worlds-no-1-employer-of-women-managers-report-says/502168.html. Other reports find lower proportions of women. See OECD, "Percentage of Employed Who Are Senior Managers, by Sex," 2012, http://www.oecd.org/gender/data/proportionofemployedwhoareseniormanagersbysex.htm.

2. Gail Warshofsky Lapidus, *Women in Soviet Society: Equality, Development, and Social Change* (Berkeley: University of California Press, 1978), 200–232.

3. In 2012, anti–human trafficking activists unearthed an organized criminal group running an illegal operation in Moscow, where young women from Central Asia were lured into coming to Russia for lucrative jobs, ending instead in literal slavery, forced to work at a grocery store with their passports taken away and freedom of movement restricted. "Obyknovennoe rabstvo: Fotoreportazh," RidusNews, November 1, 2012, http://www.ridus.ru/news/51159.

4. "RJI Submits Shadow Report to UN Women's Committee on Women's Rights in the North Caucasus," Stitching Justice Initiative, October 13, 2015, https://www.srji.org/en/news/2015/10/rji-submits-shadow-report-to-un-women-s-committee-on-women-s-rights-in-the-north-caucasus/?sphrase_id=674500.

5. Janet Elise Johnson, *The Gender of Informal Politics: Russia, Iceland and Twenty-First Century Male Dominance* (Basingstoke: Palgrave Macmillan, 2018).

6. Janet Elise Johnson, "Gender Equality Policy: Criminalizing and Decriminalizing Domestic Violence," *Russian Analytical Digest*, no. 200 (March 28, 2017): 2–5, http://www.css.ethz.ch/content/dam/ethz/special-interest/gess/cis/center-for-securities-studies/pdfs/RAD200.pdf.

7. Linda J. Cook, "The Political Economy of Russia's Demographic Crisis: States and Markets, Migrants and Mothers," in *The Political Economy of Russia*, ed. Neil Robinson (Lanham, MD: Rowman & Littlefield, 2013), 97–119. Also, http://www.pfrf.ru/family_capital.

8. Ekaterina Borozdina, Anna Rotkirch, Anna Temkina, and Elena Zdravomyslova, "Using Maternity Capital: Citizen Distrust of Russian Family Policy," *European Journal of Women's Studies* 23 (2016): 60–75.

9. Johnson, *The Gender of Informal Politics*, 118.

10. Vladislav Moiseev, "Bunt Feminizma: Zachem Obrazovannye Devushki Provodyat Pank-Moleben v Khrame Khrista Spasitelya," *Russky Reporter*, February 24, 2012, http://rusrep.ru/article/2012/02/24/pussy_riot.

11. Thomas Carothers, "The End of the Transition Paradigm," *Journal of Democracy* 13, no. 1 (2002): 5–21.

12. Scott Radnitz, "Review Article: Informal Politics and the State," *Comparative Politics* 43, no. 3 (2011): 351–71.

13. Janet Elise Johnson, "Fast-Tracked or Boxed In? Informal Politics, Gender, and Women's Representation in Putin's Russia," *Perspectives on Politics* 14, no. 3 (2016): 643–59.

14. R. W. Connell and James W. Messerschmidt, "Hegemonic Masculinity: Rethinking the Concept," *Gender & Society* 19, no. 6 (2005): 829–59; Elin Bjårnegard, *Gender, Informal Institutions and Political Recruitment: Explaining Male Dominance in Parliamentary Representation* (Houndmills, Basingstoke: Palgrave Macmillan, 2013).

15. See Association of Women in Slavic Studies, "Bibliographies (Women East-West)," October 15, 2014, http://www.awsshome.org/bibliographies.html.

16. Connell and Messerschmidt, "Hegemonic Masculinity," 849.

17. Janet Elise Johnson and Aino Saarinen, "Twenty-First-Century Feminisms under Repression: Gender Regime Change and the Women's Crisis Center Movement in Russia," *Signs: Journal of Women in Culture & Society* 38, no. 3 (2013): 543–67; Helena Goscilo, *Putin as Celebrity and Cultural Icon* (New York: Routledge, 2013); Valerie Sperling, *Sex, Politics, & Putin: Political Legitimacy in Russia* (New York: Oxford University Press, 2015).

18. Sperling, *Sex, Politics, & Putin*, 13–15, 20–21.

19. Dan Healey, *Homosexual Desire in Revolutionary Russia: The Regulation of Sexual and Gender Dissent* (Chicago: Chicago University Press, 2001).

20. Anna Temkina, "Nastoyashchii muzhchina," Polit.ru, June 12, 2013, http://polit.ru/article/2013/06/12/temkina; Dan Healey, "Chto takoe 'tradizionnye sexualnie otnoshenia'?," in *Na Pereputie: Metodologia, teoria i praktika LGBT i kvir-issledovanii (sbornik statei)*, ed. Alexander Kondakov (Sankt Peterburg: Center Nezavisimyh Sociologicheskih Issledovanii, 2014), 60.

21. Temkina, "Nastoyashchii muzhchina."

22. Kevin Moss, "Russia as the Savior of European Civilization: Gender and the Geopolitics of Traditional Values," in *Anti-Gender Campaigns in Europe: Mobilizing against Equality*, ed. Roman Kuhar and David Paternotte (Lanham, MD: Rowman & Littlefield, 2017), 195–214.

23. Sperling, *Sex, Politics, & Putin*, 13–15, 273.

24. Moss, "Russia as the Savior of European Civilization."

25. Bjårnegard, *Gender, Informal Institutions and Political Recruitment*, 24.

26. Richard Sakwa, *The Crisis of Russian Democracy: The Dual State, Factionalism, and the Medvedev Succession* (Cambridge: Cambridge University Press, 2011), 118.

27. Putin: "Even before I graduated from school, I wanted to work in intelligence. It was a dream of mine, although it seemed about as likely as a flight to Mars. . . . But then books and spy movies . . . took hold of my imagination. What amazed me most of all was how one man's effort could achieve what whole armies could not. One spy could decide the fate of thousands of people. At least, that's the way I understood it. . . . I wanted to be a spy." Vladimir Putin, Nataliya Gevorkyan, and Natalya Timakova, *First Person: An Astonishingly Frank Self-Portrait by Russia's President Putin, Vladimir Vladimirovich*, trans. Catherine A. Fitzpatrick (New York: Public Affairs, 2000), 22.

28. Elena Semenova, "Continuities in the Formation of Russian Political Elites," *Historical Social Research* 37, no. 2 (2012): 74.

29. Gulnaz Sharafutdinova, *Political Consequences of Crony Capitalism Inside Russia* (Notre Dame, IN: University of Notre Dame Press, 2010), 28.

30. Alena Ledeneva, *How Russia Really Works: The Informal Practices That Shaped Post-Soviet Politics and Business* (Ithaca, NY: Cornell University Press, 2006), 105–6, 270.

31. Fiona Hill and Clifford Gaddy, "Putin and the Uses of History," *National Interest* 117 (January 2012): 30.

32. Mikhail Klikushin, "Former Russian Prime Minister Caught on Camera Having Sex with Opposition Leader: Secret Video of Mikhail Kasyanov Having Sex," *Observer*, April 5, 2016, http://observer.com/2016/04/former-russian-prime-minister-caught-on-camera-having-sex-with-opposition-leader.

33. Connell and Messerschmidt, "Hegemonic Masculinity," 848.

34. "Things You Didn't Know about Russian President Vladimir Putin," News.com.au, March 5, 2014, http:// www.news.com.au/world/europe/things-you-didnt-know-about-russian-president-vladimir-putin/story-fnh81p7g-1226845669588.

35. Jake Miller, "Hillary Clinton: Vladimir Putin May Not Like My New Memoir," CBS News, June 11, 2014, http://www.cbsnews.com/news/hillary-clinton-vladimir-putin-may-not-like-my-new-memoir.

36. Elisabeth Duban, *CEDAW Assessment Tool Report for the Russian Federation*, ABA-CEELI (Moscow, 2006), 56–58.

37. Andrei Gatinski and Yevgenia Kuznetsova, "Zhirinovski i Sobchak reshili pozhalovatsya drug na druga Chaike," March 2, 2018, https://www.rbc.ru/politics/02/03/2018/5a996d219a7947a686e1956c.

38. Mikhail Shibankov, "Ksenia Sobchak Leaves Russia's Most Recent Presidential Debate in Tears," *Meduza*, March 15, 2018, https://meduza.io/en/news/2018/03/15/ksenia-sobchak-leaves-russia-s-most-recent-presidential-debate-in-tears; "Zhirinovsky obrugal Sobchak matom vo vremya debatov na 'Rossiya 1,'" February 28, 2018, https://meduza.io/video/2018/02/28/zhirinovskiy-obrugal-sobchak-matom-na-debatah-sobchak-oblila-ego-vodoy; Amelia McBain, "Homophobic Russian Ad Warns That the Gays Will Take Over if People Don't Vote," Out.com, February 19, 2018, https://www.out.com/news-opinion/2018/2/19/homophobic-russian-ad-warns-gays-will-take-over-if-people-dont-vote.

39. Elena Kochkina, "Sistematizirovannye nabroski 'Gendernye issledovaniia v Rossii: ot fragmentov k ktriticheskomu peresmysleniiu politicheskikh strategii," *Genderenye issledovaniia*, 15 (2007):109–11, http://www.kcgs.org.ua/gurnal/15/03.pdf. For instance, MP Oksana Dmitrieva, currently of the "Just Russia" party, had proposed many times legislative initiatives that would improve social policy concerning the elderly and the poor, but all her proposals failed to be passed/approved by fellow Duma members.

40. Elena Semenova, "Ministerial and Parliamentary Elites in an Executive-Dominated System: Post-Soviet Russia 1991–2009," *Comparative Sociology* 10, no. 6 (2011): 914, 919.

41. This is illustrated in a tongue-in-cheek slide show at http://www.kommersant.ru/gallery/2140440#id=842137.

42. Semenova, "Ministerial and Parliamentary Elites," 923.

43. See Michelle Ryan and Alex Haslam, who coined this term. Michelle K. Ryan and S. Alexander Haslam, "The Glass Cliff: Evidence That Women Are Over-Represented in Precarious Leadership Positions," *British Journal of Management* 16, no. 2 (2005).

44. Anna Nemtsova, "Russian Whistleblowers Turn on Putin—But Can They Be Trusted?," *Daily Beast*, February 17, 2017, http://www.thedailybeast.com/articles/2017/02/17/russian-

spy-whistleblowers-turn-on-putin-but-can-they-be-trusted; "Lutsenko nazval zakachika ubiist-va Voronenkova," *Novoe Vremya*, October 9, 2017, https://nv.ua/ukraine/events/lutsenko-nazval-familiju-zakazchika-ubijstva-voronenkova-1995045.html.

45. Kochkina, "Sistematizirovannye nabroski," 94–97; Johnson and Saarinen, "Twenty-First-Century Feminisms under Repression," 552.

46. Kochkina, "Sistematizirovannye nabroski," 118. Three-fourths of NGO staff were women in 2004.

47. Kochkina, "Sistematizirovannye nabroski," 102.

48. Although the Moscow Feminist Group rejects participation in formal politics, its members recognize the political implications of being a feminist: "When we just started our meetings, most of us could not call ourselves open feminists. . . . [B]eing a feminist meant taking a political stand which assumed both strong resistance and strong vulnerability." Nadia, "Ychuastnitsy gruppy o sebe, o politike i o tom, chem my zanimaemsia," August 15, 2014, http://ravnopravka.ru.

49. The group's VKontakte page lists 1,724 subscribers as of March 2018, https://vk.com/womenation.

50. Nataliia Bitten, interview by Johnson, May 20, 2013, Moscow, Russia.

51. Vera Akulova, "Pussy Riot: Gender and Class," in *Post-Post-Soviet? Art, Politics and Society in Russia at the Turn of the Decade*, ed. Marta Dziewanska, Ekaterina Degot, and Ilya Budraitskis (Warsaw: Museum of Modern Art, 2013), 279–87; Masha Gessen, *Words Will Break Cement: The Passion of Pussy Riot* (New York: Riverhead Books, 2014); Janet Elise Johnson, "Pussy Riot as a Feminist Project: Russia's Gendered Informal Politics," *Nationalities Papers: The Journal of Nationalism and Ethnicity* 42, no. 4 (2014): 583–90.

52. "Pussy Riot i seksizm-chastnyi obshchego otnosheniia," October 19, 2012, http://feministki.livejournal.com/2369110.html.

53. Press Conference by Vladimir Putin, December 19, 2013, http://kremlin.ru/transcripts/19859.

54. Women protesting can even be at risk of violence from the special forces, whom Putin has labeled "healthy guys," contradicting the accounts of special forces physically assaulting women participants of protest rallies. See http://avmalgin.livejournal.com/4220864.html.

55. Marina Yusupova, "Pussy Riot: A Feminist Band Lost in History and Translation," *Nationalities Papers* 42, no. 4 (2014): 604–10.

56. "O deiatel'nosti ne kommercheskikh organizatsii: Informatsionnyi portal Ministersterstva iustitsii Rossiiskoi Federatsii," November 10, 2014, http://unro.minjust.ru/NKOForeignAgent.aspx.

57. Akulova, "Pussy Riot: Gender and Class," 280.

58. "Mozg aspirantki zatochen na zamuzhstvo: Studentka SPbGU povesila u sebya na fakultete plakaty s tsytatami prepodavatelei o zhenshchinakh," March 7, 2018, https://meduza.io/feature/2018/03/07/mozg-aspirantki-zatochen-na-zamuzhestvo-studentka-spbgu-povesila-u-sebya-na-fakultete-plakaty-s-tsitatami-prepodavateley-o-zhenschinah.

59. Manny de Guerre, interview by the authors, March 15, 2014, New York.

60. Nick Robins-Early, "Pussy Riot's New Video Sheds Light on a Major Russian Scandal," *Huffington Post*, February 3, 2016, http://www.huffingtonpost.com/entry/pussy-riot-chaika-navalny_us_56b21c1fe4b01d80b244a4ae?utm_hp_ref=pussy-riot.

61. Marina Ivanova and Stanislav Zakharkin, "Kto i zachem v Rossii blokiruyet zakon o azschite ot seks-domogatelstv," November 2, 2017, https://ura.news/articles/1036272817.

62. The number of signatures may be found at https://socialdatahub.com/ru/sluckiy_1521672047.

63. "Dlia bol'shinstva Lenia—khoroshii paren' a devki—dury," *Meduza*, March 23, 2018, https://meduza.io/feature/2018/03/23/dlya-bolshinstva-lenya-horoshiy-paren-a-devki-dury.

64. Ksenia Sobchak, interview with Aleksei Naval'ny, July 22, 2013, http://ksenia-sobchak.com/sobchak-zhivem-aleksej-navalnyj-22-07-2013.

65. Artem Landendburg, "Prezidentskie vybory-2018 i LGBT: Odna protiv vsekh," February 24, 2018, http://bok-o-bok.ru/opinion.asp?pid=28&lan=2&tid=1948.

66. Valerie Sperling, "Nashi Devushki: Gender and Political Youth Activism in Putin's and Medvedev's Russia," *Post-Soviet Affairs* 28, no. 2 (2012): 247.

Part III

Russia and the World

Chapter Ten

Relations with the United States

Andrei P. Tsygankov

Russia's relations with the United States have entered an especially tense period. The crisis in Ukraine has strengthened Russia's determination to gain Western recognition as a great power. Russia intervened in Syria, demonstrating the ability to project power in the Middle East. The election of Donald Trump as the US president generated new hopes in the Kremlin for improved relations with America. Instead the elections further strained those relations and added the issue of Russia's meddling in American domestic affairs to the already extensive list of US-Russia disagreements. US intelligence agencies concluded that Russia intervened in the US presidential election.[1] Russia's cyber activities, military strategy, and media role have come under close scrutiny, with multiple investigations, hearings, and reports seeking to uncover the Kremlin's true intentions and capabilities. The year 2017 alone witnessed the US House of Representatives adopt a new package of sanctions against Russia, alongside Iran and North Korea. The West and Russia both decided to expel diplomats and to close several diplomatic facilities. There were also new tensions over Ukraine, the Middle East, and North Korea and mutual accusations of violating nuclear obligations.

This chapter documents Russia's perception, power tools, and policy toward the United States. I proceed by describing changes in global politics and Trump's views on Russia. The next two sections analyze the Kremlin's worldview, perception of opportunity presented by the US change of power, and Russia's capabilities in military, diplomatic, information, and cyber areas. The chapter then assesses the trajectory of Russia's difficult relations with the United States following Trump's election and concludes by evaluating Russia's motives and likely future policy.

CHANGES IN GLOBAL AND INTERNAL AMERICAN POLITICS

The year 2016 signaled critically important changes in world politics. The new populist wave rejected the Western liberal consensus as reflecting the narrow preferences of global elites. In Europe, skeptical assessments of liberal globalization grew stronger, resulting in a British referendum on membership in the EU. Euroskeptics won the referendum, leading to replacement of the British government and initiation of the country's withdrawal from the EU. The voting reflected the continent's crisis of economy and migration. Europe was suffering from structural imbalances, unemployment, debt, stagnant performance, and a large inflow of migrants fleeing from Middle Eastern instability. In 2015 alone, 1.3 million people of Middle Eastern origins reached the European continent.[2] The migration crisis deepened the already existing problem of Europe's coexistence with Muslim immigrants.[3] Those in favor of British withdrawal (Brexit) received public support in part for advocating restrictive immigration policies.

Other parts of the world were also entering economic and political uncertainty. Growing economic inequality and a decline of labor markets generated new protectionist sentiments, creating conditions for populism and fragmentation of the global economy.[4] This economic uncertainty was accompanied by growing political instability. Even the traditionally stable European continents, let alone the Middle East, Eurasia, and other parts of the world, increasingly demonstrated a lack of inclusive politics, pushing toward rivalry and competition. As argued by Richard Sakwa, new political tensions in Europe between Russia and the "Atlantic" West reflected larger changes in the international system.[5] The previously strong and authoritative United States was no longer able to arrest dangerous developments.

In the United States, against overwhelming expectations, the liberal presidential candidate Hillary Clinton lost to the maverick Donald Trump. The latter advocated more nationalist policies, such as introducing stronger restrictions on immigration and trade. While campaigning for president, Trump also argued for the benefits of scaling down US commitments to allies in Europe and Asia. He promises to put America first by withdrawing from expensive military commitments abroad and leaving the World Trade Organization. Like all populists, he had simple messages for his main audiences at home: workers who feared losing their jobs to global markets, segments within the middle class who saw their pay shrinking as the rich got richer, and army servicemen who were tired of fighting wars for American hegemony. For the first time since the post–World War II era, the old internationalist consensus was questioned by someone who called for different rules for military, political, and commercial engagement abroad.

The values of reducing international obligations in the interest of the American people were on display in Trump's inaugural address in which he promised to be guided by the America First principle. In particular, the president insisted on reviving America's industry, military, infrastructure, and middle class by "transferring power from Washington, D.C. [to] . . . the American People" and promising "every decision on trade, on taxes, on immigration, on foreign affairs [to be] made to benefit American workers and American families."[6] Trump claimed that "we've made other countries rich while the wealth, strength, and confidence of our country has disappeared over the horizon."[7]

Trump's subsequent actions reflected his great power nationalism. Facing resistance from many within the political class, he acted to curb what he saw as America's overly extensive international commitments. The United States withdrew from the Trans-Pacific Partnership agreement negotiated by the Obama administration, UNESCO, and the Paris Climate Accord. It also cut the country's contribution to the United Nations budget for 2018–2019 by 5 percent. Trump announced plans to raise trade barriers, especially for Chinese and European steel and aluminum, which were introduced in mid-2018. He further proclaimed the intent to renegotiate the nuclear deal with Iran—in May 2018 he announced the withdrawal from the 2015 agreement by the United States. Trump announced an expensive program of nuclear rearmament. The Draft Nuclear Posture Review revealed what some observers viewed as America's drive for global hegemony, potentially leading toward a nuclear arms race with Russia.[8]

On Russia, Trump's views differed from those of the US establishment. The American political class had been in agreement that Russia displayed an aggressive foreign policy seeking to destroy the US-centered international order. Influential politicians, both Republicans and Democrats, commonly referred to Russian president Vladimir Putin as an extremely dangerous KGB spy with no soul. Instead, Trump saw Russia's international interests as not fundamentally different from those of America. He advocated for the United States to find a way to align its policies and priorities with those of the Kremlin on defeating terrorism in the Middle East—the same goal that Russia shared. Trump promised to form new alliances to "unite the civilized world against Radical Islamic Terrorism" and to eradicate it "completely from the face of the Earth."[9] He even hinted that he was prepared to revisit the thorny issues of Western sanctions against the Russian economy and recognition of Crimea as a part of Russia. Trump further expressed his admiration for Putin's leadership and high level of domestic support.[10]

Subsequent developments made Trump accept the dominant view of Russia advocated by his advisers and the political establishment. The US National Security Strategy and new Defense Strategy reflected the view dominant within the establishment that Russia, alongside China, Iran, and North Korea, topped the list of security threats to the United States. Trump fired several loyal supporters and reversed views on important international issues including Russia. Investigations, intelligence leaks, and critical media commentaries concerning Trump's possible "collusion" with the Kremlin made it difficult for him to act on his promises and work on strengthening ties with Russia.

RUSSIA'S WORLDVIEW AND PERCEPTION

Vladimir Putin's worldview is not incompatible with that of Trump and can be defined as pragmatic great power nationalism. Both leaders prioritize national greatness in ethnic rather than economic, political, and military terms. Putin's perspective is that of a strong state capable of exploiting liberal globalization for Russia's national interests. In economic affairs, the Kremlin has insisted on protecting a national path of development and natural resources. According to this perspective, relying on market forces is essential but insufficient: "Even in developed countries, market mechanisms do not provide solutions to strategic tasks of resource use, protecting nature, and sustainable economic security."[11] In political affairs, Russia has sought to shield itself against what it views as harmful influences of the West's global democratization pressures. Russia's officials had been among the most vocal critics of military interventions in Yugoslavia, Iraq, and Libya launched by the Western nations and justified by the West on humanitarian grounds. In response to the political instability during the 1990s and the color revolutions during 2003–2005, the Kremlin insisted on Russia's right to "decide for itself the pace, terms and conditions of moving towards democracy" and warned against attempts to destabilize the political system by "any unlawful methods of struggle."[12]

Since Putin's return to the presidency in March 2012, the official stress has been on Russia as a "conservative" power and the worldwide defender of traditional values.[13] In addition to stressing such values, Putin articulated a new idea uniting Russians and non-Russian nationalities in domestic affairs. The Kremlin presented the idea of state-civilization with a special role historically played by ethnic Russians identified as "the core [*sterzhen'*] that binds the fabric" of the country's culture.[14] The discourse of distinctiveness grew stronger in the context of the Ukraine crisis and Western sanctions against the Russian economy in response to Russia's annexation of Crimea. In attempting to stress Russia's civilizational distinctiveness, Putin sought to justify incorporation of Crimea in terms of consolidating Russia's values.[15]

Putin's view of Trump has been flexible and noncommittal. Although Russia's president described Trump as a "brilliant" (*yarkiy*) politician, he refused to be perceived as Trump's unequivocal supporter. Instead, Putin sought to stress that both presidents are motivated by their country's interests, and not personal "chemistry."[16] During a press conference at the BRICS summit in China in September 2017, the Russian president famously quipped that Trump "is not my bride. I am not his bride, nor his groom. We are running our governments."[17]

Putin's flexible perspective on Trump reflected Russia's complex internal perception of the American president and the US-dominated world order. The Russian foreign policy community has been divided between those favoring a decline of liberal, US-centered globalization and Russia's international assertiveness and those cautioning against a fundamental disruption of the international system. The latter point to limitations of Russia's power and to uncertainty with regard to the contemporary world order transition. Unlike those pushing for change, the more pragmatic voices are skeptical that such change will result in a stable and secure global order.

For example, the Council of Foreign and Defense Policy, Russia's most influential think tank, concluded in its report that "the old West will not remain the leader," yet "the rapid shift of influence toward the 'new' centers of power observable over the last fifteen years will most likely slow down, while competition for power will increase."[18] Some Russian analysts proposed to draw lessons from the late nineteenth-century rivalry of great powers that ended in World War I. Timofei Bordachev argued that economic interdependence and nuclear deterrence notwithstanding, great power relations are likely to descend further toward military confrontation if lessons are not learned from the 1871–1914 period in international relations.[19] Members of this group warn that during the period of international uncertainty, Russia should be wary of overextension and develop a strategy of internal concentration and reform.[20] Still others such as Andrei Kortunov argue that a viable alternative to US hegemony is still a Western liberal order because it remains the one that is based on rationality, openness, and institutional norms.[21]

This divide is also evident in the Russian foreign policy community's assessment of Trump. During the US presidential elections, those favoring a decline of the US-centered order did not hide their preference for Trump's presidency and celebrated his victory in the hope for a grand bargain with America.[22] Others either did not have preferences or supported Hillary Clinton as a more predictable candidate than the highly impulsive Trump.[23]

Subsequent developments in the United States complicated the world order debate inside Russia. Investigations of Trump's potential "collusion" with the Kremlin made it difficult for him to act on his promises to normalize relations with Russia. His supporters in Moscow no longer advised the Russian leadership to reach out to Trump in order to jointly negotiate a new global order. Instead, they advised continuing the assertive foreign policy, thereby strengthening bargaining power for future negotiations with the West. Others felt vindicated in their initial skepticism with respect to Trump and the United States as a potential partner and called for strategic restraint, patience, and internal concentration.[24]

The other important idea for Putin has been that of Russia's great power status. Russia's foreign policy consensus regarding the country's status has been that it remains an independent great power with global capabilities and a major voice in international institutions. Ever since the 2000 Foreign Policy Concept warned of a threat of "a unipolar structure of the world under the economic and military domination of the United States,"[25] the Kremlin has insisted on an alternative organization of the world order. It has been committed to a multipolar and multilateral world of great powers, and under no circumstances has it been prepared to settle for a status as a follower in the US-led coalition.

Multilateralism is of special significance to a Russia that seeks to compensate the weaknesses of its relative power capabilities with active diplomacy. In his speech at the Munich Conference on Security Policy in February 2007, Putin was extremely critical of US "unilateralism," accusing the United States of "disdain for the basic principles of international law" and of having "overstepped its national borders in . . . the economic, political, cultural and educational policies it imposes on other nations."[26]

The position on Russia as an upholder of international law and balance of power has encompassed material and institutional dimensions of an emerging world order reflecting the belief by the Kremlin in the strengthening of relations outside the Western world. Since his return to the presidency in 2012, Putin has advocated a world order respectful of cultural and political diversity. In a speech at the Valdai International Discussion Club in September 2013, Putin defended the notion of "the God-given diversity of the world" and principles of collective leadership and decision making by contrasting the post–Cold War world with those established following the Napoleonic Wars and World War II:

> Russia agrees with those who believe that key decisions should be worked out on a collective basis, rather than at the discretion of and in the interests of certain countries or groups of countries. Russia believes that international law, not the right of the strong, must apply. And we believe that every country, every nation is not exceptional, but unique, original and benefits from equal rights, including the right to independently choose their own development path. . . . I want to remind you that the Congress of Vienna of 1815 and the agreements made at Yalta in 1945, taken with Russia's very active participation, secured a lasting peace.[27]

Putin further stressed the importance of multilateralism and international law while speaking at the plenary meeting of the seventieth session of the UN General Assembly in September 2015 in New York, warning against "any attempts to undermine the legitimacy of the United Nations as extremely dangerous" by again drawing a positive comparison to agreements made in Yalta following World War II.[28]

The position of the United States, however, has been principally different. The Washington Consensus is centered on the idea of US global leadership and the preservation of its status as the dominant power. With respect to Russia, the consensus view has been that Russia is in no position to serve as a principal opponent of the US-centered international liberal order. The conventional wisdom has been that Russia is a declining autocratic power. Official statements from Washington reflect this perspective. Following President Obama's reference to Russia as a "regional power" that threatens others "out of weakness,"[29] other US officials expressed similar convictions, even while recognizing Russia as a top-level national security threat. Trump, too, made it clear that he was not willing to concede on power grounds and instead wanted to engage in tough bargaining with Russia by insisting on American terms. As one commentator interpreted, "President Trump may be looking for 'good deals' for the United States in working with Russia— meaning deals in which he believes that America gets what it wants and needs from Moscow at the lowest reasonable cost to Washington."[30]

RUSSIA'S POWER CAPABILITIES

Russia is not in a position to directly challenge the United States and the US-centered international order. From an economic, military, and reputational standpoint, Russia's capacity to defend its interests and project influence— by means of soft or hard power—was limited even in Eurasia. For example, Russia's conflict with Georgia in August 2008 demonstrated a need for military reform and a strategy for strengthening its reputation among its neighbors. When Moscow recognized South Ossetia and Abkhasia's independence from Tbilisi following the war with Georgia, not even Russia's closest allies, such as Belarus and Central Asia, supported the Kremlin.

The Kremlin, however, assumed the West's graduate decline and the ability to exploit it in Russia's interests. The goal was not a defeat or surrender of the other side. Rather than aiming for a conflict, Russia wanted to gain from the West cooperation and recognition of what Moscow viewed as its proper status in the international order. The purpose has been to make the West recognize Russia's status by presenting Western nations with limitations of their power and revealing their vulnerabilities on military, economic, political, and cultural dimensions. The overall objective has been to push for global changes by avoiding unnecessary antagonisms with the West and relying on low-cost methods.

Despite Russia's economic weakness, Western sanctions failed to alter the Kremlin's behavior in any meaningful way. Russian GDP growth was negative during 2015–2016 and grew by less than 2 percent in 2017. By 2017, Russian living standards had been declining for four consecutive years, while the state continued to allocate money for defense purposes.[31] However, sanctions, even when accompanied by a major decline in oil prices, saw most Russians rally behind Putin and grow anti-American. Russian elites and the larger population are not in the mood to protest against Putin or pressure him to bow to the West's pressures. The more that Western governments try to pressure the Kremlin, the more nationalist and anti-Western the Russian public becomes.

The Russian military has been debating the notion of winning wars without direct military contact by relying on technologically sophisticated covert tactics and nonstate actors.[32] Moscow viewed military preparations by NATO with growing alarm.

NATO too was increasingly worried about Russia's military goals and means. Following the crisis in Ukraine, the dominant discussion within NATO and the US Department of Defense concerned the motives and tactics of Russia's military actions using the notion of "hybrid warfare." The concept assumed Moscow's newly developed capacity to combine traditional military power with covert efforts to undermine an enemy government. Counteractions proposed by the Atlantic alliance's commanders ranged from building up defense capacity on Western borders to actively arming Kiev and preparing to confront Russia should it choose to escalate in Ukraine. The Western defense approach prevailed. In addition to consolidating the perception of Russia as a military threat, NATO pursued the movement of troops and military infrastructure, training exercises, defense spending, and the acceptance of new members. The Wales summit in September 2014 confirmed the commitment to collective defense and to developing a readiness action plan that includes a continuous rotation of air, land, and maritime forces in the region. The defense ministries of NATO countries then approved the proposed plan in December 2015 and invited Chernogoria to join the alliance. Finally, at the July 2016 Warsaw summit, NATO decided to move four battalions to Poland and the Baltic states to be stationed there indefinitely on a rotation basis. The alliance also conducted massive military exercises in Eastern Europe in 2016 and 2017.[33]

In Moscow, these actions by NATO were viewed as confirming that the alliance was a tool of Western expansion at Russia's expense. The Kremlin was convinced that the crisis in Ukraine was only a pretext for the West's open designation of Russia as the main threat. Both state officials and members of the expert community frequently articulated the view that any expectations of normalization of relations with NATO would be unrealistic. In 2015, the renewed National Security Strategy also identified NATO's military activities and attempts by the United States and the West to preserve world economic, political, and military domination as the main threats.[34]

Russia's military preparations were consistent with the identified perception and sought to contain what was viewed as further encroachment by

NATO and the West. While the Atlantic alliance was worried about protecting the Baltics from the Kremlin's potential attack, Russia feared for the security of its enclave in Kaliningrad. Responding to NATO's military build-up in Poland and Lithuania, attempts by the alliance to pull in neutral states such as Finland and Sweden, and additional missile defense deployment in Europe by the United States, Russia indicated that it considered deployment of advanced nuclear-capable missiles into Kaliningrad and Crimea by 2019.[35] During his trip to Finland in June 2016, Putin stated that he considered the NATO contingents in the Baltics as "elements of aggressive behavior" and assessed such developments as "absolutely unfair and inconsistent with reality," promising a counteraction.[36] Rather than challenging NATO in the Baltics, Russia concentrated its troops in its southern and western regions.[37] In response to what it viewed as highly provocative military exercises and air patrolling, Russia conducted massive exercises of its own and engaged in bold asymmetrical behavior testing the West's patience. In several cases, Russian planes flew unusually close to Western warships, running a high risk of casualties or direct military intervention. These were but some developments that sought to demonstrate that the Kremlin was more "determined" than NATO and in command of its perceived spheres of influence.[38]

On the diplomatic front, Russia's pragmatism assumes the growing importance of multiple models of economic and political development.[39] Russia sought to prevent future expansion of the Atlantic alliance and to relax Western pressures by issuing conciliatory statements, developing bilateral contacts with European states, and engaging the United States in joint actions in Syria and elsewhere. In particular, the Kremlin sought to reassure European non-NATO members, explaining Russia's response to the alliance's actions as defensive and calling for development of a collective security system globally and in Europe.[40] In October 2015, Russia sent troops to Syria and began to scale down its rhetoric on Ukraine in order to engage with the United States. At the St. Petersburg International Economic Forum in June 2016, Putin even called the United States the "only superpower," stating that "we want to and are ready to work with the United States."[41] He made similar statements following the election of Trump as US president.[42] Unable on its own to effectively respond to security challenges from NATO, Russia is also likely to continue to exploit non-Western institutional vehicles, such as the Shanghai Cooperation Organization, and develop bilateral ties with China, Iran, India, and Turkey, as well as selected European countries such as France, Germany, and Italy.

In the areas of cyber-information, the Kremlin for the first time in the post–Cold War era sought to influence American politics. Moscow has advocated its own version of media and information management by relying on the tools of lobbying and soft power since the early 2010s.[43] The Kremlin established an infrastructure to influence the formation of Russia's image in the world. The Russia Today (RT) television network became the TV and internet-based outlet to promote Russia's worldview globally. In addition to RT and the news agency Sputnik, Russia developed an extensive presence in cyberspace. The country is known for strong skills in mathematics and computer science, continuing to supply programmers across the world. In August 2016, unknown hackers attacked the site of the Democratic National Committee and then released confidential materials on Hillary Clinton to Wiki-Leaks. US intelligence agencies concluded that Russia intervened in the US presidential election with the objective of undermining American confidence and, possibly, even falsifying the election's results.[44] The Russia issue became central in the new internal divide in the United States because it reflected both political partisanship and the growing value division between Trump voters and the liberal establishment. Some liberal commentators even went so far as to speculate that Putin wanted to bring to power his favorite candidate, Donald Trump, in order to then jointly rule the world.[45]

To many observers, this rise of Russia's presence in the global cyber and media space seemed surprising given Russia's limited information capabilities and soft power appeal in the West. The Kremlin, however, was motivated by the limited and asymmetric deployment of its media, information, and cyber power. It sought to be recognized for its power capabilities and to strengthen its bargaining position in relations with the United States. Rather than trying to be involved in a full-scale information war with the West, the Kremlin wanted to expose limitations of the West's global dominance.[46]

MISCALCULATIONS AND PRAGMATISM

Russia's relations with Trump have evolved from initial high hopes to a considerably more restrained view. The latter assumed that cooperation with the United States, while important, can only be limited and must be based on recognition of Russia's power and interests.

Following Trump's election and subsequent inauguration, the Kremlin did what it deemed necessary to improve the relations. In response to President Barak Obama's decision to expel thirty-five Russian diplomats allegedly involved in spying and cyber-interference with American elections, Putin chose not to reciprocate. Instead, he wished Obama a happy new year and invited children of American embassy staff in Moscow to celebrate the holiday in the Kremlin. Two months after the inauguration, Putin sent his envoy to the State Department to propose the full normalization of relations.[47] The plan envisioned restoration of diplomatic, military, and intelligence contacts and laid out a road map for moving in this direction. The road map included consultations on cyber issues with Russia's top cyber official, Andrei Kruts-kikh, in April 2017 and special discussions on Afghanistan, Iran, Ukraine, and North Korea to take place in May 2017. The expectation was that by the time of Putin and Trump's first meeting, top officials of both countries' executive branches would meet and discuss areas of mutual importance.[48] The Kremlin hoped that Trump's promises during the election campaign could be fulfilled.

Instead, relations went into another crisis in April 2017 when the United States accused Syrian president Bashar al-Assad of using chemical weapons against the opposition and bombed one of Syria's military bases that was partly used by Russia. The tough responses from Russia included a statement from the Ministry of Defense that suspended an agreement to minimize the risk of flight incidents between US and Russian aircraft operating over Syria. The suspension of the agreement implied the possibility of Russia shooting down American missiles if similar cases were to take place. The Kremlin issued a statement that the risk of confrontation between the US-led coalition and Russia had "significantly increased."[49]

The incident destroyed Russia's domestic pro-Trump consensus and generated new fears of US pressures in the form of military encirclement and attempts to politically destabilize Putin's system. Shortly after the Syria incident, Secretary of State Rex Tillerson traveled to Moscow in part to alleviate these fears. Russian analysts such as Fyodor Lukuyanov warned that if Trump "keeps striking Syria to put pressure on Assad and Russia, then Russia will have no option but to escalate. . . . That opens up the possibility of war."[50] The trip was symbolically important because Tillerson refused to meet with pro-Western opposition and focused in his meetings with Russian officials on issues of mutual importance. However, the trip failed to resolve major disagreements and revive the pre-April credit of trust. The Kremlin expected proposals from Washington to normalize relations on a mutually beneficial basis. Instead, the United States assumed Russia's weakness and expected it to comply with Washington's priorities regarding Syria, Ukraine, Afghanistan, and nuclear issues, in addition to taking responsibility for and ceasing any future interference with Western elections.[51]

The Kremlin drew its conclusions from the crisis and concentrated on addressing individual issues. When Putin and Trump finally met on the sidelines of the G20 in Hamburg in early July 2017, they reached an understanding on concrete issues of cybersecurity, Syria, Ukraine, and North Korea. In particular, they proposed to form a joint group to address cybersecurity and initiated a cease-fire and the establishment of deescalation zones in Syria.

However, the newly established dialogue was soon broken by the US Congress's decision to introduce a package of new sanctions against Russia for its actions in cyberspace, Ukraine, and Syria. Under increased domestic pressure, Trump signed the new bill despite his criticisms of it as unhelpful for relations with Russia. In the second half of July, the Kremlin followed by ordering 750 members of the US embassy staff to leave Russia, justifying this by restoring "parity" in terms of numbers of diplomats working in both countries. The issue escalated further when on September 1, 2017, the United States ordered Russia to close its consulate general in San Francisco within two days. The United States also sent the FBI to inspect the offices and private residencies of the Russian consulate.

In addition to the crisis with diplomats, the United States increased pressures on Russia regarding Ukraine and North Korea. Secretary of Defense James Mattis and the newly appointed State Department envoy on Ukraine, Kurt Volker, traveled to Kiev and indicated that the United States was considering providing the Ukrainian government with lethal weapons. Trump also issued multiple threats to use force against North Korea if Russia and China failed to prevent Kim from developing a nuclear program and conducting additional missile tests.

Russia responded with a mixture of sticks and carrots on Ukraine. Putin made clear that US supplies of lethal weapons to Kiev would not alter the balance of power in the region. In addition, in September 2017 he proposed the deployment of UN peacekeepers to prevent violations of the cease-fire in eastern Ukraine and to provide conditions for implementing the Minsk agreement. On North Korea, Russia cooperated with the United States by supporting the US-proposed sanctions in the UN Security Council. Trump wanted more and stated before his trip to Asia in November 2017 that a relationship with Russia would be "a great thing" because it "could really help us in North Korea."[52] However, in exchange the Kremlin demanded that sanctions be considerably softened. Russia and China also indicated that they did not believe in sanctions as the solution to the issue.

Further developments in the two countries' relations dissuaded their leaders from unwarranted expectations. Pragmatically, as Russia sought to focus on areas of potential cooperation, it kept demonstrating its leverage in Syria, Ukraine, and other issues. In the meantime, the United States wanted to cooperate with Russia on American terms. Washington continued to increase pressures on Russia through sanctions and demanded that the Kremlin stop what Washington saw as violations of the Intermediate-Range Nuclear Forces Treaty. In order to counter Russia, the White House signaled a new nuclear buildup.[53] US officials also gave tough warnings for Russia not to meddle in the 2018 congressional elections.[54]

The Kremlin continued to deny any involvement in the US or any other foreign election, while demonstrating Russia's power capabilities. On March 1, 2018, in addressing Russia's Federation Council, Putin revealed his country's new weapons systems capable of penetrating the US missile defense system, including the hypersonic nuclear cruise missile Kinzhal and the hypersonic intercontinental ballistic missile (ICBM) Avangard. In the same speech, Putin presented the heaviest of already known ICBMs, Sarmat, designed to replace the older one, Voevoda, or the SS-18 Satan.[55] Along with several other unveiled systems, the three weapons challenged the United States' earlier decision to withdraw from the ABM treaty and the White House's new nuclear plans stated in the Draft Nuclear Posture Review. Putin's presentation further repositioned Russia as a leading force in a potential nuclear arms race.

Overall, Russia's relations with the United States entered new territory. Relations no longer followed the dynamics of cycles of cooperation and conflict that had held since the Cold War's end.[56] The Ukraine crisis and sanctions imposed by the West against the Russian economy made it impossible to implement another "reset" in bilateral relations previously tried under Barak Obama's leadership. Trump and Putin's efforts notwithstanding, US-Russia relations remained frozen in conflict, with the American political establishment blocking the White House's efforts to initiate a constructive dialogue with the Kremlin. In part, the distrust of Russia by America's political establishment was on full display following the summit between Trump and Putin in Helsinki in July 2018. That mistrust was fueled by Trump's obsequious behavior toward Putin and Trump's seemingly blanket acceptance of Putin's denial of election meddling over unanimous conclusions by the US intelligence community that Russia had meddled. The one-on-one meeting between Trump and Putin created additional mistrust because no one knew what Trump agreed to or promised. Despite the uproar that followed the summit, shortly afterward Trump invited Putin to the White House for another summit in fall 2018.

On the other hand, the two sides remained dependent on each other for resolving vital international security issues and cooperating on counterterrorism, nuclear nonproliferation, and regional stability. They had no choice but to look for possibilities to cooperate, yet from the very weak foundation of undermined trust and disagreement on each other's capabilities and intentions. From an American standpoint, cooperation with Russia therefore cannot be "anything more than compartmentalized, tactical and transactional— precisely because the core ideological and geopolitical cleavages are so pronounced."[57] The relationship, therefore, was pragmatism by default in which rivalry and elements of cooperation had to coexist in the increasingly fragmented and insecure world.

CONCLUSION

Russia's new policy toward the United States combines cooperation and asymmetric rivalry. Not able to match the United States in overall material capabilities, Moscow has built multiple economic, political, and military relations with non-Western powers, and it has strengthened its capacity to undermine US policy globally. Asymmetric methods of Russian foreign policy include selective use of media and information technology, cyber power, hybrid military intervention, and targeted economic sanctions.

As the two countries were involved in symmetric confrontation over the majority of issues during the Cold War, such confrontation often excluded any cooperation between the two nations. Today's world is different and assumes possibilities for both rivalry and cooperation depending on the issue. However difficult cooperation may be, it has taken place with respect to negotiating START, counterterrorism, and nonproliferation of nuclear weapons. In the past, Russia and the United States cooperated on steps to prevent the development of a nuclear program in Iran. They have been able to coordinate some of their policies with respect to Syria and North Korea even during very tense periods in their relations.

Globally speaking, Russia remains a defensive power aware of its responsibility for maintaining international stability. The politics of great power recognition remains the key to understanding Russia's relations with the United States. Russia's constant attempts to engage the United States in cooperation, including those following 9/11, regarding Iran, and over Syria, demonstrate the principal importance to the Kremlin of being recognized as a major power in relations with the outside world. Despite its internal institutional differences from Western nations, Russia sees itself as an indispensable part of the global world and will continue to reach out to Western leaders in order to demonstrate Russia's great power relevance and defense of the foundations of the international order, such as sovereignty, multilateralism, and arms control. If the United States continues to challenge Russia's great power status by favoring containment and political confrontation over engagement, Putin is likely to employ Russia's capabilities to fight back and protect the country's perceived interests and status. Even with a stagnating economy, the Kremlin commands strong domestic support, powerful conventional and nuclear capabilities, and an ample range of asymmetric tools for action.

DISCUSSION QUESTIONS

1. How have global and US internal changes affected Russia's international thinking?
2. Why was Putin hopeful that relations with the United States would improve?
3. What are some of the criticisms of Russian behavior by the United States?
4. What, in your opinion, is the US-Russia relationship going to look like during the next several years? Please provide specific examples to support your answer.

SUGGESTED READINGS

Official Statements

Putin, Vladimir. "Address to the United Nations' General Assembly." September 29, 2015. https://www.washingtonpost.com/news/worldviews/wp/2015/09/28/read-putins-u-n-general-assembly-speech.
———. "Address to the Valdai International Discussion Club." October 19, 2017. http://en.kremlin.ru/events/president/transcripts/55882.
———. "Address by the President of the Russian Federation." March 9, 2018. http://en.kremlin.ru/events/president/news/57077.

Scholarly Sources

Abdelal, Rawi, and Igor Makarov. *The Fragmentation of the Global Economy and U.S.-Russia Relations*. Working Group Paper 8. Cambridge: Working Group on the Future of U.S.-Russia Relations, 2017.
Adamsky, Dmitry. "From Moscow with Coercion: Russian Deterrence Theory and Strategic Culture." *Journal of Strategic Studies* 41, nos. 1–2 (2018): 33–60.
Legvold, Robert. *Return to Cold War*. London: Polity, 2016.
Stent, Angela. *Limits of Partnership: U.S.-Russian Relations in the Twenty-First Century*. Princeton, NJ: Princeton University Press, 2015.
Sakwa, Richard. *Russia against the Rest: The Post–Cold War Crisis of World Order*. Cambridge: Cambridge University Press, 2017.
Trenin, Dmitry. *Should We Fear Russia?* London: Polity, 2016.
Tsygankov, Andrei, ed. *The Routledge Handbook of Russian Foreign Policy*. London: Routledge, 2018.
Ziegler, Charles. 2017. "International Dimensions of Electoral Processes: Russia, the USA, and the 2016 Elections." *International Politics*, http://doi.org/10.1057/s41311-017-0113-1.

NOTES

1. Office of the Director of National Intelligence, "Background to 'Assessing Russian Activities and Intentions in Recent US Elections': The Analytical Process and Cyber Incident Attribution," January 6, 2017, https://www.dni.gov/files/documents/ICA_2017_01.pdf.
2. Natalie Nourayrede, "Refugees Aren't the Problem: Europe's Identity Crisis Is," *The Guardian*, October 31, 2016, https://www.theguardian.com/commentisfree/2016/oct/31/refugees-problem-europe-identity-crisis-migration.
3. Kenan Malik, "The Failure of Multiculturalism: Community versus Society in Europe," *Foreign Affairs* 94, no. 2 (2015): 21–32.
4. Rawi Abdelal and Igor Makarov, *The Fragmentation of the Global Economy and U.S.-Russia Relations*, Working Group on the Future of U.S.-Russia Relations, Working Group Paper 8, 2017, https://us-russiafuture.org/publications/working-group-papers/the-fragmentation-of-the-global-economy-and-u-s-russia-relations.
5. Richard Sakwa, *Russia against the Rest: The Post–Cold War Crisis of World Order* (Cambridge: Cambridge University Press, 2017).
6. Donald Trump, Inaugural Address, January 20, 2017, https://www.whitehouse.gov/inaugural-address.
7. Trump, Inaugural Address.
8. Jon Wolfsthal and Richard Burt, "America and Russia May Find Themselves in a Nuclear Arms Race Once Again," *National Interest*, January 17, 2018.
9. Wolfsthal and Burt, "America and Russia."

10. "[Putin] is really very much of a leader. I mean, you can say, oh, isn't that a terrible thing—the man has very strong control over a country. Now, it's a very different system, and I don't happen to like the system. But certainly, in that system, he's been a leader, far more than our president has been a leader." Ryan Teague Beckwith, "Read Hillary Clinton and Donald Trump's Remarks at a Military Forum," September 7, 2016, http://time.com/4483355/commander-chief-forum-clinton-trump-intrepid.

11. Putin's PhD thesis, "Mineral Raw Materials in the Strategy for Development of the Russian Economy," as cited in Robert L. Larsson, *Russia's Energy Policy: Security Dimensions and Russia's Reliability as an Energy Supplier* (Stockholm: Swedish Defence Research Agency, 2006), 58. The thesis was defended in 1999.

12. Vladimir Putin, "Poslaniye Prezidenta Federal'nomu Sobraniiu Rossiiskoi Federatsii," April 25, 2005, http://kremlin.ru/events/president/news/33219.

13. Vladimir Putin, "Poslaniye Prezidenta Federal'nomu Sobraniiu Rossiiskoi Federatsii," December 13, 2013, http://president.kremlin.ru.

14. Putin, "Samoopredeleniye russkogo naroda," *Kommersant*, December 19, 2012. Along these lines, the new official nationalities strategy until 2025 signed by Putin in December 2012 reintroduced Russia as a "unique socio-cultural civilization entity formed of the multi-people Russian nation" and, under pressures of Muslim constituencies, removed the reference to ethnic Russians as the core of the state.

15. Address by president of the Russian Federation, Moscow, Kremlin, March 18, 2014, http://president.kremlin.ru.

16. Andrew Roth, "Trump 'Is Not My Bride': Putin Wades into Diplomatic Row with U.S.," *Washington Post*, September 5, 2017, https://www.washingtonpost.com/world/putin-lashes-out-atunited-states-over-consulate-seizure-as-diplomatic-row-widens/2017/09/05/1e299aee-9227-11e7-8754-d478688d23b4_story.html?utm_term=.2b9b64d864e2.

17. Roth, "Trump 'Is Not My Bride.'"

18. *Strategiia dlia Rossii: Tezisy Soveta po vneshnei i oboronnoi politike* (Moscow: Sovet po vneshnei i oboronnoi politike, 2016), thesis 2.3.1, http://svop.ru/wp-content/uploads/2016/05/%D1%82%D0%B5%D0%B7%D0%B8%D1%81%D1%8B_23%D0%BC%D0%B0%D1%8F_sm.pdf.

19. Timofei Bordachev, "Pushki aprelya," *Russia in Global Affairs*, July 3, 2017, http://www.globalaffairs.ru/number/Pushki-aprelya-ili-Vozvraschenie-strategicheskoi-frivolnosti-19210.

20. Aleksei Miller and Fyodor Lukyanov, "Otstranennost' vmesto konfrontatsiyi," *Russia in Global Affairs*, November 27, 2016, http://www.globalaffairs.ru/number/Otstranennost-vmesto-konfrontatcii--18477; Boris Mezhuyev, "Ostrov Rossiya i rossiyskaya politika identichnosti," *Russia in Global Affairs*, April 5, 2017, http://www.globalaffairs.ru/number/Ostrov-Rossiya-i-rossiiskaya-politika-identichnosti-18657.

21. Andrei Kortunov, "Neizbezhnost' strannogo mira," July 15, 2016, http://old.russiancouncil.ru/inner/?id_4=7930#top-content.

22. See, for example, Dmitry Drobnitsky, "Zapad—eto dve tsivilizatsiyi, a ne odna," July 12, 2017, https://www.politanalitika.ru/v-polose-mnenij/zapad-eto-dve-tsivilizatsii-a-ne-odna; Ruslan Ostashko, "Zakat epokhi globalizatsiyi," *Natsional'naya oborona*, no. 10 (2017), http://oborona.ru/includes/periodics/geopolitics/2017/0126/140120429/detail.shtml. For a complimentary biography of Trump, see Kirill Bendiktov, *Chernyi lebed'* (Moscow: Knizhnyi mir, 2016).

23. Andrei Kortunov, "Rossiya proshchayetsya s Obamoi," October 5, 2016, http://ru.valdaiclub.com/a/highlights/rossiya-proshchaetsya-s-obamoy-poslanie.

24. Fyodor Lukyanov, "Opasnost' 'bolshoi sdelki,'" February 9, 2017, https://www.gazeta.ru/comments/column/lukyanov/10516553.shtml.

25. Tatyana Shakleyina, ed., *Vneshnyaya politika i bezopasnost' sovremennoi Rossiyi*, vol. 4 (Moscow: ROSSPEN, 2002), 110–11.

26. "Speech at the Munich Conference on Security Policy," Munich, February 10, 2007, http://www.kremlin.ru.

27. Vladimir Putin, speech at the Valdai International Discussion Club, September 19, 2013, http://www.kremlin.ru.

28. Vladimir Putin, speech at the plenary meeting of the 70th session of the UN General Assembly, New York, September 19, 2015, http://en.kremlin.ru/events/president/news/50385.

29. Barak Obama, "Transcript: Obama's Remarks on Russia," NSA at the Hague on March 25, 2014, https://www.washingtonpost.com/world/national-security/transcript-obamas-rema rks-on-russia-nsa-at-the-hague-on-march-25/2014/03/25/412950ca-b445-11e3-8cb6-28405255 4d74_story.html?utm_term=.d4dd43fd2abf.

30. Paul Sunders, "Donald Trump's Foreign Policy: Working with Russia from a Position of Strength," Valdai Club, March 2017, http://valdaiclub.com/a/highlights/donald-trump-s-foreign-policy-working-with-russia.

31. The defense budget was 5.3 percent of GDP. *Nezavisimaya gazeta*, November 15, 2017.

32. For analyses of Russian military thinking, see Samuel Charap, "The Ghost of Hybrid Warfare," *Survival* 57, no. 6 (2015): 51–58; Kristin Ven Bruusgaard, "Russian Strategic Deterrence," *Survival* 58, no. 4 (2016): 7–26; Andrew Monaghan, *Power in Modern Russia: Strategy and Mobilization* (Manchester: Manchester University Press, 2017); Dmitry (Dima) Adamsky, "From Moscow with Coercion: Russian Deterrence Theory and Strategic Culture," *Journal of Strategic Studies* 41, nos. 1–2 (2018): 33–60.

33. In June 2016, the alliance held a simulated defense against Russia known as Anakonda, which was the largest military exercise since the end of the Cold War involving some thirty-one thousand troops and thousands of combat vehicles from twenty-four countries. Michael T. Klare, "The United States and NATO Are Preparing for a Major War with Russia," *Nation*, July 7, 2016.

34. "Ukaz Prezidenta Rossiiskoi Federatsii ot 31 Dekabria 2015 goda N 683 'O Strategii natsional'noi bezopasnosti Rossiiskoi Federatsii,'" *Rossiiakaia gazeta*, December 31, 2015, http://m.rg.ru/2015/12/31/nac-bezopasnost-site-dok.html.

35. Andrew Osborn, "Russia Seen Putting New Nuclear-Capable Missiles along NATO Border by 2019," Reuters, June 23, 2016, https://www.reuters.com/article/us-russia-europe-shield-idUSKCN0Z90WT.

36. Leonid Bershidsky, "NATO Can Reduce the Threat of Escalation with Russia," Bloomberg, July 7, 2016, https://www.bloomberg.com/view/articles/2016-07-07/nato-can-reduce-the-threat-of-escalation-with-russia.

37. Sergei Starchak, "Severoatlanticheski razlad," *Kommersant-Vlast'*, May 30, 2016, https://www.kommersant.ru/doc/2996168.

38. Sergei Karaganov, "Russian Foreign Policy:'We Are Smarter, Stronger and More Determined,'" *Spiegel*, July 16, 2016, http://www.spiegel.de/international/world/interview-with-putin-foreign-policy-advisor-sergey-karaganov-a-1102629.html.

39. Sergei Lavrov, "Istoricheskaya perspektiva vneshnei politiki Rossiyi," *Russia in Global Affairs*, March 3, 2016, http://www.globalaffairs.ru/print/global-processes/Istoricheskaya-perspektiva-vneshnei-politiki-Rossii-18017.

40. Vladimir Putin, speech at the victory parade, May 9, 2016, http://en.kremlin.ru/events/president/news/51888.

41. "Putin Says Accepts U.S. Is Sole Superpower, Dilutes Trump Praise," Reuters, June 17, 2016, https://www.reuters.com/article/us-russia-forum-putin-usa-idUSKCN0Z31G4?mod= related&channelName=worldNews.

42. In particular, Putin stated, "We are ready for cooperation with the new U.S. administration . . . on the basis of mutual benefit and equality. We have a common responsibility for international security." "Russian President Putin's State of the Nation Address," Reuters, December 1, 2016, https://www.reuters.com/article/russia-putin/highlights-russian-president-putins-state-of-the-nation-address-idUSL8N1DV5HD.

43. Vladimir Putin, "Meeting with the Russian Federation Ambassadors," Moscow, Foreign Ministry, July 9, 2012, http://en.kremlin.ru/events/president/news/15902.

44. Background to "Assessing Russian Activities and Intentions."

45. Paul Krugman, "Donald Trump, the Siberian Candidate," *New York Times*, July 22, 2016, https://www.nytimes.com/2016/07/22/opinion/donald-trump-the-siberian-candidate. html; Nicholas Kristof, "There's a Smell of Treason in the Air," *New York Times*, March 23, 2017, https://www.nytimes.com/2017/03/23/opinion/theres-a-smell-of-treason-in-the-air.html.

46. Andrei Tsygankov, "Russia's (Limited) Information War on the West," *Public Diplomacy*, June 5, 2017, http://www.publicdiplomacymagazine.com/russias-limited-information-war-on-the-west; Charles Ziegler, "International Dimensions of Electoral Processes: Russia, the USA, and the 2016 Elections," *International Politics*, October 2017.

47. John Hudson, "Russia Sought a Broad Reset with Trump, Secret Document Shows," Buzzfeed.com, September 12, 2017, https://www.buzzfeed.com/johnhudson/russia-sought-a-broad-reset-with-trump-secret-document-shows.

48. Hudson, "Russia Sought a Broad Reset."

49. David Filipov and Anne Gearan, "Russia Condemns U.S. Missile Strike on Syria, Suspends Key Air Agreement," *Washington Post*, April 7, 2017, https://www.washingtonpost.com/world/europe/russia-condemns-us-missile-strike-on-syria/2017/04/07/c81ea12a-1b4e-11e7-8003-f55b4c1cfae2_story.html.

50. Fred Weir, "Does Trump Have a Foreign Policy? Mixed US Messages Leave Russia Wondering," *Christian Science Monitor*, April 12, 2017.

51. Vladimir Frolov, "Why Russia Won't Cave to Western Demands," *Moscow Times*, May 3, 2017, https://themoscowtimes.com/articles/why-russia-wont-cave-to-the-western-demands-op-ed-57892.

52. "Full Transcript of Trump's Remarks on Russia," *New York Times*, November 11, 2017, https://www.nytimes.com/2017/11/11/us/politics/full-transcript-of-trumps-remarks-on-russia.html.

53. David E. Sanger and William J. Broad, "To Counter Russia, U.S. Signals Nuclear Arms Are Back in a Big Way," *New York Times*, February 5, 2018, https://www.nytimes.com/2018/02/04/us/politics/trump-nuclear-russia.html.

54. Andrew Desiderio, "Trump's Russia Ambassador: U.S.-Russia Relations 'Done' if Kremlin Meddles in 2018 Elections," January 9, 2018, http://www.thedailybeast.com/trumps-russia-ambassador-us-russia-relations-done-if-kremlin-meddles-in-2018-elections.

55. Vladimir Putin, presidential address to the Federal Assembly, March 1, 2018, http://en.kremlin.ru/events/president/news/56957.

56. Angela Stent, *Limits of Partnership: U.S.-Russian Relations in the Twenty-First Century* (Princeton, NJ: Princeton University Press, 2015).

57. Hal Brands, "The Five Lessons That Must Guide U.S. Interactions with Vladimir Putin," *Washington Post*, September 22, 2017, http://www.washingtonpost.com/news/made-by-history/wp/2017/09/22/the-five-lessons-that-must-guide-u-s-interactions-with-vladimir-putin.

Chapter Eleven

Relations with the European Union

Jeffrey Mankoff

Russia's relationship with the European Union (EU) is deeply paradoxical. The European Union is simultaneously Russia's most important economic partner and a multilateral, sovereignty-questioning, value-based organization that fits uncomfortably with Moscow's state-centric view of international relations. Though Russia is deeply tied by history and culture to Europe, and all three of its post-Soviet presidents (Boris Yeltsin, Vladimir Putin, and Dmitry Medvedev) have at times described Russia as part of Europe, the organizing principles of Russian politics and foreign policy are far removed from those at the heart of the EU. The resulting challenges have become more acute in recent years with the outbreak of the conflict in Ukraine and mounting concern about Russian attempts to sow disinformation, manipulate democratic politics, and undermine intra-European (as well as trans-Atlantic) solidarity.

Even though the estrangement between Russia and the institutional Europe of the EU is in many ways structural, for much of the post-Soviet and post-Maastricht era, efforts to manage disagreements functioned reasonably well. To a significant extent, however, these efforts were based on an integrationist, transformationalist model of relations that has more recently proven unviable. This model failed for numerous reasons. Europe never developed a viable framework for Russian integration into the existing economic and security architecture, while Russia's expected democratic transition failed to take root. More recently, Europe's attractiveness as a model suffered in the aftermath of the 2008–2009 financial crisis and subsequent years of recession and slow growth. Vladimir Putin's return to the presidency in 2012, accompanied by large-scale protests on the part of urban, middle-class Russians (many of whom had spent time in Europe or the United States) set Russia on a more confrontational path. In addition to crackdowns at home, the Kremlin

began asserting the fundamental incompatibility between an allegedly decadent Euro-Atlantic West and a Russia that remained a bulwark of supposedly
"traditional" values.

Russian efforts to promote these values through its support of antiestablishment political parties in Europe, notably the UK Independence Party,
France's Front National, Hungary's Fidesz, and Germany's Alternative für
Deutschland, helped export this clash of values into the domestic politics of
several EU countries. What these parties share is less an ideology (while
most are right-wing populists, Russian support has also found its way to left-
wing parties and candidates such as Greece's Syriza and Germany's Die
Linke) than hostility to the EU and its promotion of pooled sovereignty and
values-based politics. Similarly, Moscow promotes this antiestablishment,
anti-EU narrative through its growing presence in European media, including
broadcast stations such as RT and Sputnik, as well as through manipulation
of social media to amplify anti-EU, nativist, and anti-American voices.
Underpinning this support is Russia's growing financial role in much of
Europe, particularly its investment in real estate, energy, infrastructure, and
other assets, often with local partners who provide political cover for Russian
money. This financial penetration has dissuaded many governments from
taking serious steps to push back against Russian influence at the state level
or from reaching consensus at the EU level about an appropriate response.

Similar tactics have, of course, been a staple in Russian relations with its
post-Soviet neighbors, which Moscow regards as part of its own sphere of
influence and where it has sought to check the expansion of European values
and institutions. Ahead of his reelection, Putin also called for the establishment of a Eurasian Union allegedly modeled on the EU, but espousing an
illiberal creed sharply at odds with European values. This Eurasian Union
(now officially the Eurasian Economic Union, or EEU) is designed to represent an alternative to Euro-Atlantic integration for Russia's post-Soviet
neighbors, several of whom have found themselves caught between a desire
to further integrate themselves with Europe and pressure from Moscow to
look to "Eurasia" instead.

Ukraine has been affected the most, with Russia's annexation of Crimea
and military intervention in Donbas a direct consequence of Kiev's attempt
to sign an association agreement with Brussels that would effectively preclude membership in the EEU for good. Similar, if less dramatic, dynamics
are at play in Armenia, Moldova, and Georgia, which are also being asked to
choose, perhaps irrevocably, between moving toward Europe or a Russian-
dominated Eurasia. Underlying what has become a geopolitical competition
over the post-Soviet periphery is Russia's own failure to find a secure path to
Europe and the resulting effort to build up the EEU as an alternative geopolitical pole based on values incompatible with those of the Euro-Atlantic
West.

The relationship has also been profoundly shaped by the deep economic and institutional crisis affecting all of Europe, including Russia itself. Russia's comparatively strong recovery, coupled with the continued dynamism of developing economies in Asia, helped strengthen a perception that the global center of gravity is shifting away from Europe, even though Russia's economy remains closely tied to Europe.[1] Meanwhile, European and American sanctions, applied initially in response to Russia's aggression against Ukraine, have accelerated Moscow's attempt to seek alternatives to integration with the West. Russia's belief in Europe's diminishing global importance underpins Russian efforts to promote a Eurasian alternative, to seek closer economic and political cooperation with China and other Asian powers, as well as its calls to reconfigure the framework of global governance to give non-Western powers a larger say through the promotion of alternative institutions such as the BRICS and the Shanghai Cooperation Organization (SCO).

Within the EU, the post-2008 crisis has precipitated a fundamental debate about the nature of European integration, while forcing governments and EU institutions to focus relentlessly on limiting the consequences of the worst economic downturn since the 1930s. The crisis made Europe less attractive as a model for Russia to emulate even as it contributed to rising skepticism within Europe about the EU, manifested in the June 2016 Brexit referendum and the rise of illiberal, Euroskeptic, and often pro-Kremlin parties. At the same time, difficult economic circumstances have left European leaders facing a difficult choice, between aggressively sanctioning Russia in ways that might harm their own economies, on the one hand, and failing to aggressively defend the values and principles at the core of the European political model, on the other.

The crisis has also reinforced the disparity between Europe's core and periphery, as it is the large Western European states that have the most developed economic relationships with Russia and whose security is least affected by Russian revisionism. The postcommunist states of Eastern Europe, especially Poland and the Baltic states, have been most alarmed at the emergence of a more aggressive Russia, one that is not only deploying troops in Ukraine but also carrying out provocations in many other European states. Meanwhile, states like Hungary, the Czech Republic, and some of the Balkan countries that aspire to EU membership have elected governments that are more tolerant of, if not openly supportive of, Russia's civilizational narrative and financial inducements and have focused on ameliorating EU pressure on Moscow in response to the invasion of Ukraine and other provocative steps.

This chapter focuses on the dilemma facing Europe, between a carefully cultivated interdependence with Russia and the challenge of an aggressively revisionist Russia that increasingly sees the EU—in addition to NATO—as a rival.

RUSSIA'S PLACE IN EUROPE

The EU's very existence challenges some of the fundamental assumptions underpinning official Russia's view of the world—namely, that states reign supreme and that cold calculations of national interest trump the abstract values driving European integration. The EU's emphasis on liberal values has often put it at odds with Russia, whose foreign policy has always been driven much more explicitly by the pursuit of narrowly defined interests and the personal profit of its elites.[2] The EU has pursued varying degrees of integration toward both Russia and its neighbors to promote democratic transition in Russia itself, even as many EU member states maintain a more realpolitik approach to Moscow.

Even if Russia would never join the EU itself, Brussels in the 1990s pursued a course whose outlines conformed with Willy Brandt's concept of *Wandel durch Annäherung*, or "change through engagement." The basic aim was to use the prospect of improved access to European markets as an inducement for the post-Soviet countries to assimilate European values relating to human rights, democracy, and respect for international law—principles that Russia appeared to be blatantly violating with its war in Chechnya.[3] Similar agreements were signed with a range of post-Soviet countries on the assumption that with the proper mix of incentives, the EU could bring about their gradual adoption of European values.

In practice, Russia's postcommunist transition did not follow the smooth path many Europeans foresaw during the institution-building boom of the early 1990s. The spat over Chechnya provided one of the first indications that, even in its post-Soviet guise, Russia did not share many of the fundamental values driving the process of European integration. This gap would be a recurring theme, one that was in many ways more problematic in the context of EU-Russia relations than in Moscow's relationship with the United States, which like Russia remains jealous of its sovereignty and more comfortable with the use of large-scale military force. Since the EU is as much a moral community as a geopolitical entity, Russia's rejection of the liberal principles underlying European integration remains a barrier.

Even if Russia would never find its way into the EU, Brussels did gradually expand eastward, taking in most of the postcommunist states of Central and Eastern Europe. The EU's new members helped push Brussels into taking a more assertive stance toward Russia on the basis of their own difficult history and continued fear about Russian revanchism. And if Russia did not initially raise much objection to the "widening" of the EU, it was generally more concerned by the parallel process of "deepening," particularly insofar as it entailed the development of the EU into an autonomous security player. Attempts to create an integrated European Defense and Security Policy (EDSP) and Common Foreign Policy (CFP) forced Moscow to confront the possible emergence of a united, powerful Europe with close links to Washington on its borders.[4]

With Russia's turn toward authoritarianism following Vladimir Putin's ascension to the presidency in 2000, the gap between Russian and EU political practice continued to widen. European officials and multilateral institutions frequently condemned Russia's seeming retreat from democratic liberalism and its still spotty record on human rights. The Council of Europe has been especially outspoken on these issues, criticizing Moscow for the long-running detention of former Yukos oil company chairman Mikhail Khodorkovsky, who was finally released from prison in December 2013; the killing of Russian journalists such as Anna Politkovskaia in 2006; and ongoing human rights abuses in the North Caucasus.[5] In 2011–2012, the European Commission, the Council of Europe, and several national governments condemned Russia's failure to hold free and fair elections for the Duma and the presidency, along with the Kremlin's occasionally heavy-handed response to the protests that broke out after the results were announced.[6] These criticisms only mounted as Putin steered Russia in a more authoritarian direction following his 2012 return to the Kremlin.

Russia strongly defends its own sovereignty and argues that European values are not universal and that consequently its own history and traditions steer it in a different direction. Moscow thus rejects the premise that Europe has a right to pass judgment on Russian behavior. This gap between the EU's promotion of what it views as universal rights and Russia's invocation of sovereignty as an absolute principle remain among the most significant barriers to integration as a model for structuring relations between Russia and the EU.

A deep chasm in values and institutions overlays increasingly extensive economic ties between Russia and Europe. In recent years, this chasm has widened dramatically as Putin has emphasized Russia's Eurasian (as opposed to European) identity, while openly challenging such pillars of European security as the now-suspended Conventional Armed Forces in Europe (CFE) Treaty, the 1975 Helsinki Final Act, the 1987 Intermediate-Range Nuclear Forces (INF) Treaty, and the 1990 Charter of Paris. Yet Russia and the EU are nevertheless bound together in a number of ways, notably through an interdependent economic relationship.

THE RUSSO-EUROPE ECONOMIC PARTNERSHIP

Taken as a whole, the EU is by far Russia's most important economic partner, both as a source of investment capital and as a trade partner. The EU is Russia's largest trading partner, accounting for 38.1 percent of Russian foreign trade in goods in 2017, although the total value of EU-Russia trade fell by 44 percent between 2012 and 2016, largely as a result of sanctions and Russia's adoption of import substitution policies in response.[7] Individual EU countries, including Germany and the Netherlands, are themselves among Russia's leading trade partners and sources of foreign investment as well.

A broader objective of policy in both Brussels and Moscow for much of the post–Cold War era has been to deepen mutual economic dependence, creating a community of interests within both the political elite and the business community, an effort symbolized by the successful campaign to bring Russia into the World Trade Organization (WTO).[8] These economic ties have traditionally provided ballast in relations with countries such as Germany and Italy that have the most extensive economic relationships with Russia. Economic ties are at the same time a source of Russian geopolitical leverage (while Russia is dependent on this trade to a significant degree as well, its authoritarian political system makes it less susceptible to economic pressure, as the inability of sanctions to end the conflict in Ukraine appears to demonstrate). One consequence of the struggle over Ukraine has been a more concerted effort on the part of Europeans as well as Russia to disentangle the two sides' economies, effectively reversing the push for Russian economic globalization and integration.

Of course, interdependence can be a double-edged sword. European industry remains wary of the impact of sanctions on its bottom line and has at times constrained the ability of individual European governments to respond aggressively to Russian actions in Ukraine and elsewhere. Perhaps the starkest example is the debate over the Nord Stream II gas pipeline being built from Russia to Germany that would allow Russia to sell gas to Europe while bypassing current transit states, notably Ukraine. Despite concerns about the impact of Nord Stream II on Ukraine, Angela Merkel's government has green-lighted the project, in large part because of the influence of German energy companies (some of them involved in the project), even while seeking to minimize its strategic implications.[9]

Regardless of efforts to disentangle their economies, Russia and Europe remain interdependent, above all in energy. Postcommunist states in Central and Eastern Europe in particular rely heavily on Russia as a supplier of oil and gas. This dependence has been the source of repeated problems, as deliveries from Russia have been curtailed on multiple occasions because of tensions between Russia and transit states Ukraine and Belarus. As Ukraine was long the site of major energy disputes (related to unpaid bills for Russian gas, but underpinned by Kiev's efforts to break out of the Russian geopolitical orbit), for over a decade now, Russia has sought to minimize Ukraine's importance to its lucrative energy relations with Europe. To cut Ukraine (and Belarus) out of the picture, Moscow has built some offshore bypass pipelines (the original Nord Stream, Blue Stream) and proposed others (South Stream, Turkish Stream), regardless of whether such pipelines make any economic sense. Nord Stream II, which would allow Russia to sell gas to Europe while completely bypassing Ukraine, would represent the culmination of these efforts.

Meanwhile, in the face of Russian opposition, the EU has sought to build its own new pipelines carrying non-Russian gas and bypassing Russian territory. This planned Southern Corridor aims to bring Caspian gas to Europe through pipelines across the South Caucasus and Turkey. The EU is also working to liberalize its own energy markets to weaken Gazprom's market power, and to develop alternative sources of energy. At the same time, the European Commission has pushed for additional steps to limit Gazprom's monopoly power. These include an antitrust enforcement action brought against Gazprom in 2011 accusing the Russian monopoly of abusing its market power to limit cross-border gas sales and drive up prices. The eventual resolution of the case, which saw Gazprom agree to accept EU jurisdiction and penalties for future (but not past) violations, indicated the extent to which the ability of the commission and EU members to push back remains limited by the importance of Russian gas in Europe.[10]

Questions about access to Russian energy have also exacerbated tensions within the EU, especially between countries that would directly benefit from the new pipelines, such as Germany and Italy, and those that fear being further marginalized, such as Poland and the Baltic states. At least until the outbreak of conflict in Ukraine, Germany, Italy, and France in particular sought to promote mutually beneficial economic cooperation with Russia, downplaying the idea that Russia continued to represent a real threat to European security, to the frequent consternation of their postcommunist neighbors in Eastern Europe. In the long run, though, the expansion of Europe's liquefied natural gas (LNG) import capacity and the discovery of new energy supplies, including shale gas in the United States, holds the long-term potential to lessen the importance of energy as a source of EU-Russia discord. The economic crisis accelerated this process by reducing European gas demand, even as new sources of supply continued coming on line. These developments all have the potential of further undermining Gazprom's hold on the European market and fundamentally altering the current interdependent economic relationship in Europe's favor.

SPECIAL RELATIONSHIPS

Given its own state-centric worldview and the fact that the EU itself has been in continuous flux since its creation in 1993, Russia has frequently preferred dealing directly with individual European states to working through Brussels. Russia's special relationships with many of the larger EU states, as well as the deep economic ties that resulted, have long been a source of tension within Europe. More recently, the success of populist, pro-Kremlin parties and political figures in several Central and Eastern European countries have turned this pattern on its head, as with figures like Hungary's Viktor Orbán and the Czech Republic's Miloš Zeman bringing the Kremlin's anti-EU narrative to the center of European politics and fueling concern about illicit Russian influence.

Germany has always been the key player among the European states. Not only is Germany the largest economy in the EU and one of Russia's top trade and investment partners, but its economic success relative to the rest of Europe during the crisis, along with its long tradition of *Ostpolitik*, have in many ways allowed Berlin to eclipse Brussels as the main driver of European policy toward Russia. Of course, Germany has possessed another asset during the most recent period of confrontation with Moscow: Chancellor Angela Merkel, whose upbringing in the German Democratic Republic, coupled with her political dominance inside Germany and unmatched standing among European leaders, has left her singularly equipped to understand and address the challenge posed by a more revisionist Russia on Europe's doorstep.[11]

As Russia has emerged as an increasingly revisionist power in Europe, it has been Merkel who has played the largest role in building consensus for a more assertive response, both within Germany and in Europe as a whole. Merkel's Germany remains the central player in the so-called Normandy process, the diplomatic framework established in the wake of the Minsk II cease-fire agreement that brought a halt to the major fighting in Donbas in the summer of 2015, and remains the key voice on Europe's approach to sanctions.

While Germany has been Russia's most important partner within the EU, other Western European states have also forged strong bilateral relationships with Moscow that have at times been the source of tension with their post-communist neighbors in Eastern Europe, and with the European Commission in Brussels. Like Germany, Italy, under Silvio Berlusconi, sought to position itself as something of a mediator between Russia and Europe, while in the process developing mutually beneficial economic ties. France, too, has often pursued an independent policy toward Russia that frustrated many of its European allies, most prominently with its agreement to build up to four Mistral-class amphibious assault ships for the Russian navy—an agreement that became a political lightning rod during the crisis in Ukraine. The election of Emmanuel Macron as French president in May 2017, despite apparent Russian assistance for the rival Front National candidate Marine Le Pen, led to a more assertive approach on the part of Paris, one that emphasized intra-European solidarity (especially with Germany) and forging a "tough" but pragmatic relationship with Russia.[12]

The UK was long something of an outlier among large Western European states in generally favoring a harder line against Russia (especially in the aftermath of the poisoning of the Russian defector Alexander Litvinenko in London in 2006). Yet the UK too was constrained by economic ties, in its case by the outsized role Russian money played in the city of London and in the British real estate market.

If Germany (and France and Italy to a lesser degree) traditionally served as Russia's bridge to the EU, Poland and the Baltic states have been the wariest of European attempts to engage and integrate Russia. A long history of Soviet (and in many cases, tsarist) occupation inclined the newly sovereign states of Eastern Europe to seek rapid integration with Euro-Atlantic structures following the 1989 revolutions to guard against any renewed danger from the East. Many of them continued to regard Russia as an ongoing threat to their independence and urged the EU and NATO to play a more active role in defending them from this perceived threat. They were instrumental in the development of new policy instruments to engage postcommunist states that remained outside the EU and NATO, including the Yugoslav successor states in the Western Balkans and Russia's European post-Soviet neighbors (Belarus, Ukraine, and Moldova). They also frequently pushed Brussels into taking a harder line with Moscow, for instance, over the 2008 war between Russia and Georgia.

The rise of populism and the victory of populist figures in a number of Central and Eastern European countries have scrambled this traditional geographic divide. While Poland's relationship with Russia has remained frosty despite the election of a populist government under the Law and Justice (PiS) party, populist leaders in the Czech Republic, Hungary, Slovakia, and elsewhere have openly courted Moscow. In part, the affinity appears ideological, as the Kremlin narrative of European decadence at odds with "traditional" values resonates with many supporters of the Czech, Slovak, and Hungarian leaders. At the same time, analysts point to financial and other forms of assistance from Moscow that potentially aided the populists' cause.

In Hungary, Orbán's shift to a more pro-Russia orientation coincided with the award of a contract to Russia's state-owned nuclear monopoly Rosatom to build two new reactors in Hungary and the concomitant weakening of anticorruption laws shortly before Hungary's 2014 elections, fueling concern about illicit Russian funding of Orbán's campaign.[13] Since his reelection, Orbán has been a leading pro-Kremlin voice in Europe, speaking out against the extension of sanctions, calling for Hungary to become an "illiberal democracy," and challenging Brussels' authority to enforce regulations that Hungary adopted upon becoming an EU member.

Russian attempts to cultivate individual partners in Europe aims at weakening EU solidarity and undercutting the legitimacy of the EU's model of pooled sovereignty and normative politics. Russia's energy policy has long aimed at provoking divisions within Europe, using differential pricing and destination clauses to pit consumer states against one another. Moscow's hand also appears behind various environmental NGOs that have spoken out against hydraulic fracking (which would reduce Europe's need to import Russian gas).[14] Support for pro-Russia and anti-EU populist parties plays a similar role.[15] To the extent that these parties entrench themselves in national or European politics, the more "Europe" itself becomes the topic of debate, rather than Russia itself.

Financial ties have also served to limit the ability or willingness of individual European governments to speak out or push back against malign Russian activities. The UK, with a vast pool of Russian capital swirling through its real estate market is perhaps the starkest example, but other European states have been less than enthusiastic in pursuing sanctions or other punitive measures, in part as a result of the role of Russian money in their economies and financial ties between members of their political elite and Russian oligarchs.[16]

RUSSIA, THE EU, AND THE SHARED NEIGHBORHOOD

The ability of the EU to confer prosperity and security on its members has made integration an appealing prospect for nonmembers, including many of Russia's post-Soviet neighbors. Russia's turn to a more revisionist foreign policy and elaboration of a Eurasian alternative are intimately connected to the challenge of preventing these states' drift into the EU's orbit. For many years, Russia argued strenuously against NATO's eastward expansion. Yet it remained sanguine about the prospect of a wider European Union that would both enhance the economic prospects of Russian trading partners and also, thanks to the EU's free trade rules, improve Russian companies' access to the wider European market. Hostility to the EU, encompassing both a geopolitical struggle over states like Ukraine and Moldova, as well as efforts to undermine EU institutions from within have emerged more starkly since Putin returned to power in 2012. The crisis in Ukraine grows directly out of this confrontation.

At the heart of this confrontation are competing narratives about the post-Soviet states and about Russia's own position vis-à-vis Europe. While Brussels argues that it is in Russia's interests to have secure and prosperous neighbors and that the smaller states of the former Soviet Union have the sovereign right to choose for themselves whether and how to integrate with Europe, Moscow fears that Brussels' gravitational pull represents a threat to Russian influence in countries like Ukraine and Belarus (of course, this fear sits awkwardly with Russia's portrayal of a decadent, declining Europe).[17] The ten eastern EU members (the original eight would be joined by Bulgaria and Romania in 2007) have in particular pushed Brussels to pay more attention to the still unstable area between the EU's new eastern borders and Russia.

Europe's "neighborhood" policies have focused on reforms that would erode the institutional links between Russia and its former dependencies, while Moscow's idea of Eurasia is portrayed as an alternative to direct integration with Europe. For Brussels, part of the problem has been a lack of strategic vision driving the process of outreach to the post-Soviet East. Bureaucratic inertia is one challenge; so too, though, are the divisions between European states about the importance of this region relative to other security and economic challenges facing the EU. To Poland and other Eastern European EU members, this lack of attention to the "neighborhood" has both weakened Brussels' hand in dealing with Moscow and undermined European security by allowing corruption and poor governance to flourish just beyond EU borders, while many Western European powers see the main threats to their interests emanating from elsewhere, particularly since the outbreak of the Arab Spring and the subsequent migration crisis.

Brussels has often struggled, however, to engage the region in a coherent way, given the competing interests of member states and a lack of clarity regarding ultimate goals. For much of the post–Maastricht Treaty era, Brussels crafted agreements with neighboring states on a bilateral basis. These accords were designed as an à la carte menu of steps to promote cooperation between the EU and former Eastern Bloc states. For some, these agreements were portrayed as a stepping-stone to full EU membership, whereas for others they were more limited agreements designed to address specific problems but lacking the force of law.

The European Neighborhood Policy (ENP), which Brussels elaborated in 2003, was the first attempt at developing a unified strategy for the countries east (and south) of the EU. While the association agreements signed under the auspices of the ENP would be tailored to the interests of each partner state, they were all governed by the principle of encouraging convergence on the basis of the EU's *acquis communautaire* (that is, the basic statutes defining the obligations of EU membership). [18] Brussels extended the offer of ENP membership to Moscow as well. The Russians categorically refused, however, believing that Russia's large size and special role in Europe would not allow it to accept a partnership that would put it on par with its smaller neighbors.

Moreover, the ENP was explicitly designed to bring partner states' legislation—and values—into harmony with the EU. Since Russia was not an aspiring EU member, it rejected the argument that it should adjust its legislation to be in line with the *acquis*, particularly given that Moscow had no role in writing them. Instead of being rolled into the ENP, Russia instead agreed with the EU on the creation of the so-called four Common Spaces, covering economics, freedom/security/justice, external security, and education/culture. The Common Spaces laid the foundation for convergence of Russian and EU practices in the four covered fields, but without the implication that Russia was being forced to adopt EU standards as the price of cooperation.[19]

Meanwhile, Brussels came to the conclusion that the ENP was insufficient as a mechanism for integrating its Eastern neighbors into a Europe that was increasingly viewed as coterminous with a zone of peace and prosperity. Largely to balance a perceived tilt toward the south during France's 2008 European Council presidency, Poland and others proposed the Eastern Partnership (EaP) in May 2008 to focus on the six post-Soviet states around Russia's borders: Belarus, Ukraine, Moldova, Azerbaijan, Armenia, and Georgia. The EaP sought to channel EU funds into these six countries to promote economic and institutional development, improve border management, and enhance EU energy security. Among the proposed steps on energy security was the formation of the Southern Corridor to bring gas from the Caspian region to Europe through new pipelines bypassing Russia, thereby reducing Gazprom's hold over European economies.[20]

The EaP also held out to partner countries the opportunity to sign association agreements with the EU that would create a platform for deeper convergence with EU norms and standards. The association agreements would also contain language on the creation of a so-called Deep and Comprehensive Free Trade Area (DCFTA) agreement between the partner states and the EU. The six EaP countries all had extensive economic ties to Russia; one consequence of a DCFTA would be to reorient their trade toward Europe. While the direct effects of this reorientation on Russia's economy would be small, the political consequences could be significant. Reforms demanded as part of the association agreement process would help sever the institutional ties between Russia and the EaP states, while the reorientation of trade would weaken one of the principal levers of influence Moscow has retained over these states.

The Kremlin was somewhat slow to perceive a danger in this process, but once it did, Moscow exerted enormous pressure on its neighbors to reject the promised association agreements in favor of affiliation with the Russian-sponsored Customs Union and Eurasian Union. Russia used a variety of inducements to make its case, including offers of discounted energy and financial assistance, as well as various types of threats. In the run-up to the EU's November 2013 Vilnius Summit, Russian pressure succeeded in convincing Armenia to backtrack from its association agreement and instead opt for the EEU. Similar pressure was applied to Ukraine, leading President Viktor Yanukovych to also announce a last minute change of plans just weeks before Vilnius. It was Yanukovych's change of heart that sparked the first protests on Kiev's Maidan Nezalezhnosti (Independence Square) in late 2013, ultimately leading to Yanukovych's fall from power, followed by Russia's annexation of Crimea and military intervention in eastern Ukraine in early 2014. Significantly, the new Ukrainian government, headed by President Petro Poroshenko, made signing the EU association agreement one of its first tasks. Georgia and Moldova also signed their association agreements in the face of Russian opposition.

Russia viewed the EaP as an attempt by the EU to carve out a new sphere of influence and weaken Russian access to European energy markets.[21] This skepticism was not entirely off the mark. The Russo-Georgian war had increasingly led EU members to overlook their concerns about the poor state of political freedom and human rights in several of the EaP states out of a growing belief that Moscow had rejected the post-1991 territorial status quo and that consequently Moscow and the West were again engaged in a contest for influence across the whole post-Soviet region.[22]

From the beginning, European leaders argued that Moscow was overreacting and that the EaP would actually benefit Russia by stabilizing conditions along its own borders—an argument that overlooked Russia's view that its primary interest in the region was as a zone of political influence and a strategic glacis against the West. The EaP (or any successful EU attempt to bring about political change in Russia's post-Soviet neighbors) would, moreover, break the link between corrupt elites in Russia and other post-Soviet states, undermining the very notion of the "post-Soviet space" as a coherent geographical and political expression. It was this geopolitical significance of the EU's outreach that alarmed Moscow, though Brussels continued asserting that the EaP and its association agreements were simple bureaucratic arrangements to facilitate trade.

UKRAINE AND THE FUTURE OF EUROPE

Ukraine, by far the largest and most consequential of the eastern neighborhood states, was always a source of particular tension. Sharply divided between a Ukrainian-speaking west, much of which was under Austro-Hungarian or Polish rule until World War II, and a Russian-speaking east and south that was long part of the Russian Empire, Ukraine continues to live up to its name (the word *Ukraina* means "borderland"). Within the Ukrainian elite, relations with Russia and the EU served as a proxy in power struggles between competing regional factions, at least until the Maidan protests, the fall of Yanukovych, and Russia's military intervention consolidated support for deeper integration with Europe across the population. Until his sudden reversal in September 2013, even Yanukovych and his Party of Regions supported deeper economic integration with the EU as the key to the country's future development and prosperity (not to mention the preservation of their own assets), as well as a hedge against overweening Russian influence.

Discussions over an EU-Ukraine association agreement commenced following Ukraine's 2008 accession to the WTO and continued even after Yanukovych took over the presidency in 2010. The proposed association agreement and the DCFTA were aimed not just at eliminating tariffs but at harmonizing Ukraine's domestic regulations with EU standards in areas such as intellectual property protection, customs regulations, and government procurement. [23]

Though Russian sensitivities were heightened by the presence of a strongly pro-European leadership in Kiev before 2010, the election of Yanukovych (whom Russia had assisted in his earlier, botched attempt to seize the presidency in 2004) did little to ameliorate tensions. Yanukovych continued talks on the association agreement while refusing to transfer control of the Ukrainian pipeline system to Moscow. Yanukovych even called for Ukraine's eventual membership in the EU itself. [24] Though negotiations on the association agreement were completed in October 2011, the deal was soon put on hold following the conviction and jailing of former prime minister Yulia Tymoshenko after what the Europeans argued was a politically motivated trial.

In any event, it was not the jailed former prime minister who created the principal stumbling block to implementation of the association agreement but the objections of Putin's Kremlin. After offers of discounted gas and direct financial assistance failed to change Yanukovych's mind, a single meeting with Putin in Moscow in November 2013 sufficed, with Yanukovych announcing on his return to Kiev that the agreement would be postponed. The Maidan protests began that same night. For perhaps the first time ever, tens of thousands of protesters took to the streets waving the blue and yellow EU flag, calling on Yanukovych to embrace the European future he had long promised.

Over the course of subsequent months, Ukraine plunged into a state of near collapse due to a combination of its leaders' own mismanagement and deliberate Russian provocations. At the same time, relations between the EU and Russia deteriorated to levels not seen since the Cold War. After Russia's February 2014 seizure of Crimea, Brussels followed Washington in imposing sanctions, even though the interdependence of the Russian and EU economies made sanctions more difficult for the Europeans. EU measures were initially limited to suspending talks on the new Partnership and Cooperation Agreement and a planned visa agreement, while halting preparations for a G8 meeting scheduled for June in Sochi. [25]

The escalation of Russia's involvement in the crisis led to further sanctions, including individual travel bans and asset freezes imposed in response to the annexation of Crimea, which were extended to cover Putin's "inner circle" following the start of Russian operations in the Donbas. [26] As the crisis in Donbas worsened, Brussels imposed "sectoral" sanctions on the

Russian economy in July, expanding them in September. Targeting whole sectors of the Russian economy was designed to raise the pressure on Moscow, but doing so also affected European economies accustomed to doing substantial business with Russia and stretched the ability of Merkel and other leaders to maintain consensus within Europe. Notably, Gazprom was exempted from all sanctions, despite its importance as a source of political leverage over both Ukraine and Europe.

Europe also played a central role in trying to bolster Ukraine against the mix of internal and external risks it faced, though many Europeans questioned whether their interests were sufficient for the level of commitment their leaders, and Washington, were asking them to make (notably, Europeans were strongly against the idea of providing lethal military assistance to the Ukrainians). Ambivalence expressed in opinion polls diminished as the confrontation deepened, but Europeans remained concerned about the economic consequences of the crisis, especially as many EU states face the possibility of renewed recessions.[27] Despite its own vulnerabilities, the EU had pumped more than €3 billion in financial aid into Ukraine's economy, along with another €8 billion in development assistance in 2014.[28] European states and the EU also worked to shore up Ukraine's energy security by reversing the flow of Russian gas from EU member states (especially Slovakia) and pressing for energy pricing reforms that would chip away at the mountain of debts Kiev owes to Gazprom. Through the Normandy format, European leaders also took the lead in negotiating and seeking to uphold the cease-fire that brought an uneasy halt to the most serious fighting in the fall of 2015.

While the EU does not want this region to turn into a geopolitical and legal gray zone, its attempts to use the tools of integration to stabilize the region and draw it closer to Europe continue meeting resistance from Moscow, which sees its influence in the region as the foundation for Russia's existence as a major global power. At the same time, states like Ukraine suffer from many of the same political and institutional shortcomings as Russia itself. The EU consequently faces a chicken-and-egg dilemma: integration is designed as a tool to promote reform, but (as with Russia itself) the EU is wary of pursuing even limited integration with countries that have not fully embraced European values and practices. The result is that Ukraine and its neighbors remain on the periphery, subject to the competing ambitions of Brussels and Moscow.

The conflict in Ukraine also set the stage for the rapid deterioration of EU-Russia ties across the board. Russia accelerated efforts to deintegrate its economy from Europe, including through the cultivation of China and other non-Western partners, as well as to destabilize European politics. In addition to support for populist, anti-EU candidates, Russia has employed a range of asymmetric tools to exacerbate social tensions and undermine the efficacy of liberal institutions throughout Europe (not to mention in the United States). Dissemination of propaganda through both traditional and social media has amplified concerns about, for instance, the impact of refugee flows, which in turn contributes to support for pro-Kremlin populists. In one notable case, in early 2016, Russian media outlets spread a false rumor that Syrian refugees in Germany had raped a thirteen-year-old German-Russian girl. The story, which was amplified by Russian foreign minister Sergei Lavrov, was picked up by mainstream news outlets in Germany and abroad, fed into a mounting backlash against Merkel's policy of welcoming refugees, and boosted support for populist and Far Right groups ahead of German elections.[29] Russia also appears to have used its disinformation capabilities to influence the outcome of the Brexit referendum and (unsuccessfully) the referendum on Catalonian independence.[30]

CONCLUSION

Moscow's ambivalent position with respect to Europe reflects in some ways a centuries-old dilemma of Russian identity. Russia is in Europe, but not of it. The EU's challenge lies in learning to reconcile values and interests in its dealings with Russia—a task for which the strategy of integration it has pursued for much of the past two decades appears inadequate. Since the outbreak of the crisis in Ukraine, relations between Russia and the EU have deteriorated dramatically. The leaders of even traditionally sympathetic states such as France and Germany have come around to seeing Putin's Russia as a menace and a threat to European stability. Meanwhile, Russia itself continues to see in the European project a threat not only to its influence in the post-Soviet region but to the very legitimacy of Russia's authoritarian government. Even with Russia-friendly governments in power in places like Budapest and with the UK on its way out after the Brexit referendum, intra-EU dynamics appear to have shifted substantially against Moscow in the course of less than a decade. The old paradigm of *Wandel durch Annäherung* has largely given way to one based on bolstering Europe's defenses against Russian interference and cutting off connections that appear to either reward Russia or act as a source of Russian leverage.

At the same time, Europe's own crises continue unabated. Brexit highlighted the dangerous lack of legitimacy from which the EU suffers among many Europeans. The rise of anti-EU populists in Central and Eastern Europe—including in countries like Poland that have benefited enormously from EU membership—testifies to the same challenge, even if such states are unlikely to follow Britain out the door (if only because of the financial benefits they receive as members). Relations with the United States have grown increasingly complicated since the election of Donald Trump, America's first Euroskeptic president, who also maintains a puzzling affinity for Putin's Russia that has been the subject of a long-running investigation by a special counsel in the United States. Even if the worst predictions about the fragility of Europe's peripheral economies have not yet come true, much of the continent remains economically fragile a decade after the onset of the crisis.

The crisis in Ukraine will ultimately determine much not only about the nature of EU-Russia relations, but about the EU itself. As the EU has suffered from a democratic deficit and rising populism at home, the Maidan protesters' willingness to face down Yanukovych's goons as well as the Russian military speak to the continued attractiveness of European ideals in at least part of the continent. Ensuring that Ukraine's transition succeeds and that Kiev remains on a glide path to Europe is in the EU's vital interests. Not only will instability (never mind active conflict) on Europe's borders eviscerate Europe's security, but failure to make good on its promises to Kiev will damage the soft power that Europe continues to enjoy in its wider neighborhood, including in the Western Balkan states, which remain prospective EU members but have seen a rising tide of Russian efforts at destabilization in recent years, not to mention states like Georgia and Moldova. Failure would also reinforce Russia's narrative about European decadence and raise the likelihood of additional challenges from Moscow in the years to come.

Despite the challenge posed by Ukraine, the EU and Russia will continue to have a complex, interdependent relationship. Russian leaders may talk about Asia's growing importance, especially as Moscow seeks to reduce its vulnerability to Western sanctions, but Europe will remain Moscow's indispensable economic partner for the foreseeable future, including in energy. Similarly, Europe's quest for diversification is beginning to bear fruit, but given existing infrastructure and future uncertainty, Europe for now has little choice but to continue buying large quantities of Russian gas.

Nor can Europe's major security challenges be solved without Russia playing a constructive role. In addition to Ukraine, these include the protracted conflicts in Moldova and the South Caucasus, the war in Syria and the resulting refugee crisis, the status of conventional forces in Europe, the ongoing dispute over European missile defense, and the potential breakdown of the INF treaty. For Russia, mounting uncertainty along its southern and eastern borders provides a powerful argument for limiting tensions in Europe. Yet the existing conflicts and Russia's perception of European decline mean that, at least for the foreseeable future, these tensions are likely to remain. Only if Europe can get its own house in order and present a united front to Moscow will it have any hope of being able to restore a modicum of stability.

DISCUSSION QUESTIONS

1. Why has Russia's attitude toward the EU, and especially the expansion of the EU's influence in the post-Soviet region, become more hostile over time? Was this development inevitable?
2. What were the goals of the EU's Eastern Partnership (EaP)? Are these goals incompatible with Russian interests?
3. Given the failure of Europe's strategy of change through engagement, what other approaches could the EU take today?
4. How much of a role has Russia played in causing or exacerbating Europe's internal crises?

SUGGESTED READINGS

Conley, Heather, James Mina, Ruslan Stefanov, and Martin Vladimirov. "The Kremlin Playbook: Understanding Russian Influence in Central and Eastern Europe." Center for Strategic and International Studies, October 2016. https://csis-prod.s3.amazonaws.com/s3fs-public/publication/1601017_Conley_KremlinPlaybook_Web.pdf.
Gower, Jackie, and Graham Timmins, eds. *The European Union, Russia, and the Shared Neighbourhood*. London: Routledge, 2013.
Janning, Josef. "Russia, Europe, and the New International Order." European Council on Foreign Relations, April 9, 2014. http://www.ecfr.eu/article/commentary_russia_europe_and_the_new_international_order245.
Klinke, Ian. "Postmodern Geopolitics? The European Union Eyes Russia." *Europe-Asia Studies* 64, no. 5 (2012): 929–47.
Snyder, Timothy. "Fascism, Russia, and Ukraine." *New York Review of Books*, March 20, 2014. http://www.nybooks.com/articles/archives/2014/mar/20/fascism-russia-and-ukraine.

NOTES

1. Thomas Gomart, "Europe in Russian Foreign Policy: Important but No Longer Pivotal," *Russie.Nei.Visisions*, no. 50, https://www.ifri.org/sites/default/files/atoms/files/ifrigomartrussiaeuengavril2010.pdf.

2. Jeffrey Mankoff, *Russian Foreign Policy: The Return of Great Power Politics*, 2nd ed. (Lanham, MD: Rowman & Littlefield, 2011), 1–21, 77–79. Also see Philip Hanson and Elizabeth Teague, "Big Business and the State in Russia," *Europe-Asia Studies* 57, no. 5 (2005): 657–80.

3. "Partnership and Cooperation Agreements (PCAs): Russia, Eastern Europe, the Southern Caucasus, and Central Asia," http://europa.eu/legislation_summaries/external_relations/relations_with_third_countries/eastern_europe_and_central_asia/r17002_en.htm.

4. Dov Lynch, "Russia's Strategic Partnership with Europe," *Washington Quarterly* 27, no. 2 (2004): 100.

5. Council of Europe, "PACE Rapporteur on Media Freedom Expresses His Deep Frustration at the Lack of Progress in Investigating the Murder of Anna Politkovskaia in Russia" (press release, February 2, 2009), http://wcd.coe.int/ViewDoc.jsp?id=1410219&Site=COE; Council of Europe, "Chechnya: PACE Committee Demands Full Elucidation of the Recent Spate of Murders" (press release, January 27, 2009), http://wcd.coe.int/ViewDoc.jsp?id=1398813&Site=DC.

6. European Union, "Statement by Catherine Ashton, High Representative of the European Union, on the Presidential Elections in Russia on 4 March 2012," http://www.consilium. europa.eu/uedocs/cms_Data/docs/pressdata/EN/foraff/128733.pdf.

7. European Union, "Trade in Goods with Russia," 2017, http://trade.ec.europa.eu/doclib/ docs/2006/september/tradoc_113440.pdf. European Commission, "Countries and Regions: Russia," n.d., http://ec.europa.eu/trade/policy/countries-and-regions/countries/russia.

8. Russian Ministry of Foreign Affairs, "Programma effektivnogo ispol'zovaniia na sistemnoi osnove vneshnepoliticheskikh faktorov v tseliakh dolgosrochnogo razvitiia Rossiiskoi Federatsii," May 11, 2010, http://www.runewsweek.ru/country/34184.doc. Also see Angela Stent and Eugene Rumer, "Russia and the West," *Survival* 51, no. 2 (2009): 95.

9. Tobias Buck and Roman Olearchyk, "Merkel Warns Nord Stream 2 Must Protect Ukraine Role," *Financial Times*, April 10, 2018, https://www.ft.com/content/42e31c82-3cc4-11e8-b9f9-de94fa33a81e.

10. Rochelle Toplensky and Henry Foy, "Brussels Set for Compromise Deal in Gazprom Antitrust Case," *Financial Times*, May 16, 2018.

11. For a good profile of Merkel, see George Packer, "The Quiet German," *New Yorker*, December 1, 2014. Also see Klaus Larres and Peter Eltsov, "Merkel in the Middle," Politico, July 17, 2014, http://www.politico.com/magazine/story/2014/07/merkel-in-the-middle-109071. html.

12. "Ahead of U.S. Visit, Macron Warns against Being 'Weak' with Putin," Radio Free Europe/Radio Liberty, April 22, 2018, https://www.rferl.org/a/russia-ahead-of-us-visit-macron-warns-against-being-weak-with-putin/29185589.html.

13. See Heather Conley et al., "The Kremlin Playbook: Understanding Russian Influence in Central and Eastern Europe," Center for Strategic and International Studies, October 2016, https://csis-prod.s3.amazonaws.com/s3fs-public/publication/1601017_Conley_KremlinPlay book_Web.pdf.

14. Andrew Higgins, "Russian Money Suspected behind Fracking Protests," *New York Times*, November 30, 2014, http://www.nytimes.com/2014/12/01/world/russian-money-suspected-behind-fracking-protests.html.

15. These parties and affiliated groups have all supported Russian actions in Ukraine (including sending observers to the Russian-organized referendum on Crimean independence) and may also receive direct backing from the Kremlin. Uniting these groups is an illiberal ideology at odds with the values of the Euro-Atlantic West, as well as hostility to the European Union and a desire to reassert national sovereignty against Brussels. See Mitchell Orenstein, "Putin's Western Allies," *Foreign Affairs*, March 25, 2014, http://www.foreignaffairs.com/articles/ 141067/mitchell-a-orenstein/putins-western-allies. For a more detailed analysis, see "The Russian Connection: The Spread of Pro-Russian Policies on the European Far Right," Political Capital Institute (Budapest), March 14, 2014, http://www.riskforecast.com/useruploads/files/ pc_flash_report_russian_connection.pdf; "Russia's Far Right Friends," Political Capital Institute (Budapest), December 3, 2009, http://www.riskforecast.com/post/in-depth-analysis/russia-s-far-right-friends_349.html; and Timothy Snyder, "Fascism, Russia, and Ukraine," *New York Review of Books*, March 20, 2014.

16. Ellen Barry, "British Banks Will Have to Cut Ties to Sanctioned Oligarchs, U.S. Says," *New York Times*, April 10, 2018, https://www.nytimes.com/2018/04/10/world/europe/britain-banks-sanctions-oligarchs.html. More generally, see Ben Judah, *This Is London: Life and Death in the World City* (London: Pan Macmillan, 2017).

17. F. Stephen Larrabee, "Russia, Ukraine, and Central Europe: The Return of Geopolitics," *Journal of International Affairs* 63, no. 2 (2010): 33–52; Filippos Proedrou, "Ukraine's Foreign Policy: Accounting for Ukraine's Indeterminate Stance between Russia and the West," *Southeast European and Black Sea Studies* 10, no. 4 (2010): 443–56.

18. European Commission, "The Policy: What Is the European Neighborhood Policy?," October 30, 2010, http://ec.europa.eu/world/enp/policy_en.htm.

19. See Thomas Gomart, "Predstavlenie pri polupustovom zale," *Nezavisimaia Gazeta*, May 11, 2005, http://www.ng.ru/politics/2005-05-11/2_kartblansh.html.

20. "Eastern Partnership" (Europa press release, March 12, 2008), http://europa.eu/rapid/pressReleasesAction.do?reference=MEMO/08/762. Russia's proposed South Stream pipeline is generally viewed as an attempt to preempt the construction of Nabucco.

21. Valentina Pop, "EU Expanding Its 'Sphere of Influence' Russia Says," *EU Observer*, March 21, 2009, http://euobserver.com/9/27827.

22. Ahto Lobjakas, "EU's Eastern Partnership Strains to Juggle Interests, Values," Radio Free Europe/Radio Liberty, April 29, 2009, http://www.rferl.org/content/EU_Eastern_Partnership_Summit_Strains_To_Juggle_Interests_And_Values/1618551.html.

23. Karel de Gucht, "EU-Ukraine Trade Negotiations: A Pathway to Prosperity" (address to INTA Committee Workshop, October 21, 2011), http://trade.ec.europa.eu/doclib/docs/2011/october/tradoc_148296.pdf.

24. Viktor Yanukovych, "Ukraine's Future Is with the European Union," *Wall Street Journal*, August 25, 2011, http://online.wsj.com/article/SB10001424053111903461304576524672209158138.html.

25. "Western Powers Move to Punish Russia," Al Jazeera, March 6, 2014, http://www.aljazeera.com/news/europe/2014/03/western-powers-move-punish-russia-201436154643709328.html.

26. "U.S., Russia Fail to Reach Breakthrough in Ukraine Talks," *Chicago Tribune*, March 14, 2014, http://articles.chicagotribune.com/2014-03-14/news/chi-russia-ukraine-crisis-20140314_1_crimea-rosneft-ukraine-talks; David Lerman et al., "U.S. Plans to Hit Putin Inner Circle with New Sanctions," Bloomberg, April 28, 2014, http://www.bloomberg.com/news/2014-04-26/russia-faces-more-sanctions-as-monitors-held-in-ukraine.html.

27. Adrian Croft, "Most Europeans in Poll Think EU Should Offer Ukraine Membership," Reuters, September 10, 2014, http://www.reuters.com/article/2014/09/10/us-ukraine-crisis-poll-idUSKBN0H524620140910.

28. European Commission, "Support Package for Ukraine," n.d., http://europa.eu/newsroom/files/pdf/ukraine_en.pdf.

29. Stefan Meister, "The 'Lisa Case': Germany as a Target of Russian Disinformation," *NATO Review*, 2016, https://www.nato.int/docu/review/2016/also-in-2016/lisa-case-germany-target-russian-disinformation/EN/index.htm.

30. Robin Emmott, "Spain Sees Russian Interference in Catalonia Separatist Vote," November 13, 2017, https://www.reuters.com/article/us-spain-politics-catalonia-russia/spain-sees-russian-interference-in-catalonia-separatist-vote-idUSKBN1DD20Y.

Chapter Twelve

Russia-China Relations

Jeanne L. Wilson

In the last few years, the Russian-Chinese relationship, formerly designated as the "comprehensive strategic partnership of coordination," has become steadily closer, indicating, as Chinese president Xi Jinping has stated, that the relations between the two states are "the best in history."[1] This development is all the more notable given the often fractious and discordant nature of the interactions between the two states. Ties attained a newfound stability with the coming to power of Vladimir Putin as the Russian president in 2000 and the signing of the "Treaty of Good-Neighborliness and Friendly Cooperation between the People's Republic of China and the Russian Federation" in July 2001. Even so, skepticism about the primary basis of the relationship and the extent of trust between the two states has been widespread. Bobo Lo famously characterized the relationship between the two states as an "axis of convenience" in his 2008 book, a judgment that he has partially revised.[2] There seems little doubt that the Russian-Chinese relationship has become more substantive, resting on an increasing convergence of views and identified mutual interests. At the same time, latent (and not so latent) tensions underlie a key number of issues central to the relationship. The most problematic feature of the interactions between these two states lies in their increasingly asymmetrical power relations. China is virtually universally considered to be a rising power, whereas Russia is, at least in a relative sense, a power in decline.[3]

This chapter provides an overview of the Russian-Chinese relationship with a focus on its evolution since the start of Putin's presidency in 2012. First, I address the most convergent aspects of Russian-Chinese relations. The two states share a largely consensual view of the dynamics of political interactions in the international system as well as a shared sense of political values that form one component of each state's evolving national identity. I

Jeanne L. Wilson

then turn to other aspects of the relationship that are more complex, indicating underlying tensions that are typically rooted in economic disparities. This includes a brief discussion of the key economic factors that serve to frame the relationship, Russian and Chinese efforts to link the Eurasian Economic Union (EEU) with the Silk Road initiatives, defense cooperation, and Russian demographic concerns and the status of the Russian Far East. The final section examines the implications of these developments for the future evolution of the Russian-Chinese relationship.

RUSSIA AND CHINA: THE GEOPOLITICAL DIMENSION

A considerable body of scholarly, journalistic, and policy-oriented work assumes a realist perspective as explanatory to the Russian-Chinese relationship. In this view, Russia and China act as self-interested states seeking to counterbalance the hegemonic dominance of the West, notably the United States. Russia, to a greater extent than China, has actively promoted the thesis that US hegemony is giving way to the rise of a multipolar world. Russia and China correspondingly occupy separate poles in a multivectored system that also includes regional organizations such as the Shanghai Cooperation Organization (SCO), the EEU, and the BRICS (Brazil, Russia, India, China, and South Africa) that present an alternative voice to that of the Western-dominated security and financial institutions. A plethora of joint statements on international affairs, as well as the comments of Russian and Chinese political elites, typically stress the similarity of their views on the international system. It is not the case that Russian and Chinese views are wholly coincident. China has managed to maintain a position of polite neutrality on the Ukrainian crisis, while Russia has typically sought to distance itself from unqualified support for Chinese actions in the South China Sea. Geography also plays a role. Russia is more invested, for example, in the topic of NATO enlargement than China, but considerably less concerned than China about the status of Taiwan. Nonetheless, it is largely the case, as the Russian and Chinese leaderships constantly reaffirm, that these two players do share a coincidence of views that can be distinguished from that of the Western states on major international issues. These include the topics of missile defense, the Syrian civil war, and the situation with North Korea.

The topic of missile defense has a long and complicated history. The US withdrawal from the Anti-Ballistic Missile (ABM) Treaty between the United States and Russia (originally between the United States and the Soviet Union) in 1991 set the stage for the proliferation of various proposals for the deployment of ABM systems. The original rationale adopted by the United States and its allies for the deployment of missile defense was twofold: deterrence was considered obsolete, and rogue regimes—notably Iraq, Iran, and North Korea—constituted a so-called axis of evil that posed a threat, if not directly to the United States, at least to its NATO allies in Europe and its defense treaty partners, specifically South Korea and Japan, in East Asia. Not only were Russia and China unpersuaded by this argument; they considered that they were the designated targets of a system that could at least theoretically render second-strike capability inoperable. At present, Russia and China are primarily concerned about the deployment of the Aegis Ashore ballistic missile defense system in Europe and the possible deployment of the Terminal High Altitude Area Defense (THAAD) missile defense system in Northeast Asia. The July 2017 Russian-Chinese joint statement on the "Current Situation in the World and Important International Issues" was highly succinct in specifying that the deployment of ABM systems in Europe and the Asia-Pacific Region would "negatively affect the international and regional strategic balance, stability and security" and that Russia and China were "strongly opposed to such a policy."[4]

Russia has long had a cordial relationship with Syria dating back to the Soviet era. Nonetheless, the Russian intervention in the Syrian civil war in September 2015 through the carrying out of air strikes was largely unanticipated and was likely the result of a number of external calculations—for example, Russia wanting to project itself as a great power, outright defiance of the West in the wake of the annexation of Crimea—not directly related to Syria. China's role in the Syrian conflict has been largely passive, providing support to Russia, especially within the United Nation's Security Council. Nonetheless, Russia and China are united in their fundamental assessment of the Syrian conflict and its international repercussions. In the first instance, they support the inviolable sovereignty of the Syrian state under the leadership of Bashar al-Assad. This commitment has likely been accentuated since a 2011 Russian and Chinese abstention on the Security Council led to a UN-mandated intervention in Libya (through the use of NATO forces) that resulted in the overthrow of Muammar Qaddafi and regime change in Libya. Secondly, Russia and China call for the resolution of the Syrian crisis through political and diplomatic means, under the auspices of the United Nations, while at the same time fighting international terrorism.[5] This leaves open the question as to which oppositional groups would be represented at the bargaining table, but there is no doubt that both Russia and China perceive militant Islam as a threat.

North Korea lacks any real allies, but China and secondly Russia can lay claim to having the closest ties globally with this isolated and reclusive state. In certain respects, Chinese and Russian policy conforms to the position laid out by the Western powers. They support the application of sanctions and call for the denuclearization of North Korea. Nonetheless, both states, although China more so than Russia, bear the brunt of criticism from the West as well as from the United Nations for tolerating North Korean efforts to evade sanctions as well as for providing the economic support necessary (as in the sale of Chinese coal) that helps to ensure the survival of the regime. Neither China nor Russia (nor South Korea for that matter) has an interest in the collapse of the Kim Jong-un leadership and its likely destabilizing and chaotic consequences. Russian-Chinese joint statements, including a July 2017 statement signed by the Russian and Chinese Foreign Ministries on the problems of the Korean Peninsula, express concerns over North Korean missile launches but are unequivocal in rejecting attempts to resolve the situation through military means. Rather, they propose a step-by-step process by which North Korea desists from any nuclear testing and the United States and South Korea refrain from large-scale joint exercises as well as the deployment of THAAD antimissile systems. Ultimately, in their view, any resolution of the situation mandates a diplomatic path of negotiations and consultation.[6]

In the last several years, Russia and China have not only become bolder in their critique of the international political situation but more assertive in setting themselves up as examples for global emulation. The 2016 Russian-Chinese joint statement indicated their mutual desire "to strengthen global strategic stability," which implicitly targeted the United States as the greatest source of global strategic risk.[7] Their 2017 joint statement took this assessment a step further, asserting that Russian-Chinese relations had gone beyond a bilateral framework to emerge as an "important factor in preserving the international strategic balance, peace, and stability throughout the world."[8] At least in terms of rhetoric, Russia and China are issuing a challenge to the hierarchy of power relationships in the international system and US primacy. This turn has more or less coincided with the exacerbation of relations with the United States and Europe, seen first with the West's imposition of sanctions on Russia after the annexation of Crimea and in the more militant stance adopted toward China by the presidential administration of Donald Trump.

TOWARD A CONVERGENT POLITICAL IDENTITY

Strictly speaking, realist approaches subordinate the role of political norms and values to strategic calculations of power as a motivating factor in state behavior.

In fact, as constructivists posit, national interests (long a difficult concept in the realist lexicon) often reflect the influence of issues of national identity. Although Russia and China possess distinctly different civilizational identities, they have increasingly come to share convergent political identities. In this sense, realist analysis alone is not adequate to explain the strengthening of ties between the two states. Gilbert Rozman, in particular, has stressed the importance of identity as a factor that brings these two political outliers in the international system closer together. He argues that this development is a reflection of their shared Marxist-Leninist heritage (which is, however, not immutable to change).[9] Although consensual norms and values partly indicate the commonalities of a similar political tradition—for example, a preference for strong leadership, centralized control, and political stability—Russia and China are also linked together by a shared view of the world that rejects the validity of values such as human rights and liberal democracy upheld by the West as universal. Rather Russia and China continuously reaffirm their commitment to themes of a Westphalian order. The 2016 Russia-China Joint Declaration on the Promotion of Principles of International Law stresses, moreover, the authority of the United Nations as a source of international law and the sanctity of state sovereignty, sovereign equality, a respect for the right of all states to choose their own political system, and noninterference in the internal affairs of other states.[10]

The extent to which Russia and China share normative values is also evident in their view of the international system. Both consider the hegemonic position of the West, along with its professed values and interventionist activities, nothing less than an existential threat. The threat is no less dangerous because it is perceived as primarily employed by Western actors—chief of all, the United States—through the use of soft power measures that seek to infiltrate and subvert the regime from within. Tactics include democracy promotion, efforts to create a civil society, the establishment of NGOs (often with foreign funding), use of the Western media, and the mobilization of youth. For the Kremlin and Beijing, these were the tactics employed in the color revolutions in Georgia (2003) and Ukraine (2004), during the political protests that occurred in 2013–2014 in Ukraine that led to the replacement of President Viktor Yanukovych, and in demonstrations in Hong Kong in 2014 during the so-called Umbrella Revolution. In the eyes of both the Russian and Chinese leadership, regime survival necessitates a strategy of resistance to Western norms and values as well as the development of an alternative legitimating ideology. Neither state has yet managed to construct a fully cohesive national identity, but they both stress their divergence from neoliberal precepts embraced by the West.

RUSSIAN-CHINESE RELATIONS: THE ECONOMIC DIMENSION

Economic ties have historically been considered a weak link—in fact the weakest link—in the Russian-Chinese relationship. This is in part a reflection of the economic disparity between the two states. China's GDP, according to the purchasing power (PPP) measures used by the CIA *World Factbook*, has surpassed that of the United States and, at an estimated $23.12 trillion, exceeds that of Russia ($4 trillion) by a factor of almost six.[11] In the post-Soviet era, moreover, Russia has struggled to regain its reputation as an industrial powerhouse, but without a great deal of success. Russia's economic profile, rather, is closer to that of an underdeveloped country dependent on raw materials as a source of exports. The loosening of previous prohibitions on Chinese involvement in foreign investment and the purchase of high-technology items, notably in the military sector, has intensified the Kremlin's fear that it could turn into a raw materials appendage of China. In the wake of the imposition of foreign sanctions by the West, the Kremlin felt compelled, as a matter of necessity, to turn to China as an alternative economic partner.

Estimates of the extent of Chinese foreign direct investment (FDI) in Russia are highly imprecise and vary widely. According to statistics from the Russian Central Bank, Chinese FDI in Russia comprised $645 million in 2015 and $350 million in 2016. These figures pale in comparison to estimates that total Chinese FDI was over $170 billion in 2016. Russian Central Bank statistics present an even lower level of Russian FDI in China: $11 million for 2015 and $6 million for 2016.[12] China is Russia's number-one trade partner, although Russia ranked fifteenth as China's trade partner in 2016.[13] Russia's economic ties with China are also indicated in the trade data outlined in table 12.1.

The lack of diversification in Russia's commodity trade profile is evident. Over half (52 percent) of Russia's exports to China consist of crude petroleum. With the exception of frozen fish (3.9 percent), all of the other products in the top-ten list of commodities exported to China are raw materials, comprising 80.7 percent of total exports. In contrast, the top commodities that Russia imported from China consist of manufactured goods, including those

Table 12.1. Russian-Chinese Trade in 2016 (in percentages)

Top Ten China Imports from Russia (total $32.3 billion)		Top Ten Russian Imports from China (total $38.1 billion)	
1. Crude petroleum	52.0	1. Machinery	10.0
2. Sawn wood	7.2	2. Broadcasting equipment	8.2
3. Raw nickel	6.6	3. Computers	6.7
4. Frozen fish	3.9	4. Telephones	3.1
5. Rough wood	3.9	5. Vehicles	2.2
6. Coal briquettes	3.3	6. Models & stuffed animals	1.9
7. Sulfate chemical wood pulp	2.4	7. Broadcasting accessories	1.8
8. Refined petroleum	2.3	8. Electric heaters	1.2
9. Potassium fertilizers	1.9	9. Rubber footwear	1.2
10. Iron ore	1.1	10. Spark ignition vehicles	1.1

Source: OEC, https://atlas.media.mit.edu/en/visualize/tree_map/hs92/import/chn/rus /show/2016 (accessed April 6, 2018) and https://atlas.media.mit.edu/en/visualize/tree _map/hs92/import/rus/chn/show/2016 (accessed April 6, 2018).

drawn from the higher-technology end of the spectrum, such as computers and broadcasting equipment. It is a testimony to Russia's lack of global competitiveness that the number-one import from China is machinery, comprising 10 percent of total imports.

As the data for Russian-Chinese trade implies, the Chinese leadership is primarily interested in developing economic ties with Russia in the energy sector. Negotiations between Russia and China have been protracted and often contentious as to pricing. Nonetheless, the Eastern Siberia Pacific Oil (EPSO) oil pipeline began operations with a spur to China in 2011, followed by a second link that began commercial operations in January 2018. The two states signed a deal in 2014 to construct a gas pipeline, the Power of Siberia, that is scheduled for completion in December 2019. A memo of understanding signed in 2017 provides for a Power of Siberia 2, though negotiations are ongoing. The Power of Siberia is the largest project initiated by Gazprom, the state-owned gas company, in the post-Soviet era. Considerable doubts have been expressed about its economic viability, but the oil fields that it draws upon are too far West to profitably send gas to Europe, making China the most likely alternative customer.[14]

To date, the hope that China could become an economic substitute for the loss of Western investments as a result of sanctions has not been realized. Nonetheless, it is notable that Chinese investment has been critical in maintaining the operations of certain key Kremlin-supported projects that have been targeted for sanctions: this includes the purchase of 9.9 percent of shares in the Yamal liquefied natural gas (LNG) project and the extension of a $12 billion loan and the purchase of 10 percent of the shares of Sibur, a petrochemical complex. The Chinese targeting of large-scale energy projects for investment also indicates the co-mingling of political and economic motivations. The Chinese have been seemingly especially concerned to provide special deals to a select group of individuals with close ties to President Putin. Perhaps the most controversial deal that involved Chinese financing, however, was the advance payment that Igor Sechin, the head of the Russian oil firm Rosneft, received in 2013 from the Chinese oil companies CNPC and Sinopec, which Sechin then used to repay debt that the company generated in absorbing rival TNK-BP. Sechin, who shares a *siloviki* background with Putin, is widely considered his most trusted associate. Similarly, both the Yamal LNG project and the Sibur petrochemical complex are co-owned by Gennady Timchenko, a close friend of Putin, who was one of the first people to be placed on the US sanctions list. Chinese financing of Russian projects has typically been extended by state-owned policy banks rather than commercial banks, which are reluctant to bear the economic consequences of violating the West's sanctions regime.

The doling out of special deals to Putin's cronies aside, the Chinese have not been inclined to promote friendship over profitability. Simultaneously

the agreements concluded by Russian oligarchs and *siloviki* reflect their individual self-interest, which does not necessarily correspond to that of the
Russian state. As oligarchs and members of the *siloviki* have come to rely on
Chinese loans to finance projects, the Kremlin risks the loss of decision-
making authority over the final destination of pipeline routes or energy supplies. In this sense, Russia's long-standing policy of diversification is challenged by the potential emergence of China as the dominant decision maker
in an increasingly unbalanced partnership.

China's Silk Road Initiative: A Challenge to Russia

In the fall of 2013, Xi Jinping proposed in a speech at Nazarbayev University
in Kazakhstan that China and the states of Central Asia cooperate to establish
trade and economic linkages through a modern version of the Silk Road to
promote regional cooperation. Eventually, this initiative morphed into a
megaproject that includes a maritime component and a near global scope.
Variously known as the Silk Road, One Belt One Road (OBOR), or the Belt
and Road Initiative (BRI), the endeavor in its land variant is primarily focused on the construction of large-scale infrastructure projects to be financed
through China's Silk Road Fund and the Chinese-sponsored Asian Infrastructure Investment Bank (AIIB). Chinese plans for this initiative met with
considerable consternation and unease in Moscow, where it was perceived as
a threat to Russia's goal of maintaining a sphere of influence in Central Asia.
The Kremlin initially chose to ignore OBOR and also turned down the invita-
tion to join the AIIB. Eventually, however, the Russian leadership realized
that they had little choice but to endorse it and sought instead to recoup the
best deal possible under the circumstances. At the 2015 meeting of Putin and
Xi, the two states agreed to link OBOR with the EEU, the regional economic
integration project promoted by Russia.[15] The Sino-Russian Joint Declaration on Cooperation between the EEU and the Silk Road Economic Belt,
signed during Xi's visit to Moscow, pledged to make efforts to coordinate the
two initiatives, as well as envisioning OBOR participation in ventures located in Russia.[16]

    To date, there is not much evidence of Russian-Chinese coordination of
the EEU and Silk Road policies, nor for the initiation of Silk
Road–sponsored projects within Russia. As many have noted, China's conceptualization of the Silk Road is highly amorphous, elastic in its scope, with
limited institutionalization and a lack of clearly defined goals.[17] The 2015
agreement mandated that the EEU and China begin negotiations on a trade
and investment agreement. The prospect that China and the EEU constitute a
free trade zone is a particularly contentious issue given high levels of protectionism within the organization, and the topic has been effectively tabled or
at least relegated to the status of a distant goal. Russia has also voiced

considerable concern over the location of OBOR transportation corridors, which have been plotted through Central Asia or contemplate shipment by sea, thus bypassing Russia. The Russian aim, in contrast, has been to have the Chinese tie the Trans-Siberian and Baikal–Amur railroads to Silk Road endeavors. More recently, however, the Chinese have begun to link the Silk Road to their Arctic ambitions. During Russian prime minister Dmitry Medvedev's November 2017 visit to Beijing, Xi called on Russia and China jointly to develop and cooperate on the utilization of the North Polar sea route and build a Silk Road on ice.[18] It is notable, furthermore, that the "white paper on China's Arctic policy" released in January 2018 explicitly refers to a "Polar Silk Road" as a component of OBOR.[19]

Although the package of agreements signed at the 2015 meeting designated the construction of a high-speed railway between Kazan and Moscow as a signature Silk Road undertaking, the initiative has been mired in dissention over construction and cost issues and seems unlikely to be realized. In fact, despite the massive attention given to the Silk Road, both within China domestically and abroad, the number of new projects adopted by the AIIB and the Silk Road Fund has declined on a yearly basis since reaching a peak in 2015.[20] China has failed to fund any of the more than forty potential transportation projects prepared by the Russian government and the Eurasian Economic Commission within the EEU.[21] Although Beijing is now also displaying an attentiveness toward prospective profit and financial viability, the Silk Road Fund has routinely been used to underwrite politically motivated projects. Chinese purchase of shares and a loan to the previously noted Yamal LNG project and the Sibur gas-processing and petrochemical complex constitute the two Silk Road projects in Russia, both of which are financed through the Silk Road fund.

The Kremlin has opted to portray the Silk Road initiatives as a mutually beneficial endeavor and the linking of OBOR with the EEU as a relationship between equals. However, the reality is that Russia cannot compete with China economically in the post-Soviet space. Table 12.2 provides comparative data on the extent of Russian and Chinese trade with the former Soviet republics (with the exception of the Baltic states). Chinese imports from Kazakhstan, Tajikistan, Turkmenistan, and Uzbekistan exceeded Russian imports in 2016, while Chinese exports surpassed those of Russia in Kyrgyzstan, Tajikistan, and Uzbekistan. Chinese total trade volumes were greater than those of Russia in Kazakhstan, Kyrgyzstan, Tajikistan, Turkmenistan, and Uzbekistan, which is to say all of the Central Asian Republics. It is also the case that Chinese economic activity in the entire post-Soviet region has increased significantly in the post-Soviet era. Chinese exports to Georgia are close to those of Russia, as is the case with Azerbaijani imports to China. China, moreover, has a sizable trade in both imports from and exports to

Ukraine. These numbers, moreover, forecast the increasing economic penetration of China into the Eurasian region over the longer term.

The Kremlin, moreover, has to deal with the enthusiasm voiced by leaders in the post-Soviet space for OBOR. This is tempered in Central Asia by the fear of Chinese domination of the domestic economy, but there still exists a widespread support for Chinese loans and investment opportunities. In particular, Kazakh leader Nursultan Nazarbayev has emerged as a supporter of OBOR. Kazakhstan is the largest recipient of Chinese FDI in the former Soviet Union, and Nazarbayev hopes to connect his Bright Road Economic Policy, which also focuses on infrastructure development, to OBOR. At present, the AIIB has funded two projects in Tajikistan and one in Azerbaijan and Georgia. Prospective projects include two sites in Uzbekistan and one in Georgia.[22]

There is no doubt that OBOR has the goal of expanding China's economic reach in Central Asia. It was similarly no coincidence that Xi Jinping selected Kazakhstan as the locale to announce the land-based component of OBOR. For a number of years previously, China had sought to work within the mechanism of the SCO to promote its economic proposals, including the establishment of an SCO bank and a free trade zone in the region. Russia's opposition to these measures was presumably a factor in the Chinese leadership's decision to jettison its ambitions for the SCO and move toward OBOR as an alternative.[23] Although the SCO is mentioned in the 2015 agreement as a multilateral mechanism for linking the EEU and OBOR, the dynamics and processes of this are unclear, as only two members of the SCO (Kazakhstan and Kyrgyzstan) are concurrently members of the EEU.

The Kremlin is well aware of China's burgeoning presence in Central Asia and equally aware that there is little it can do about it. Realizing that Russia simply cannot compete with China in the economic sphere, Moscow has constructed a narrative that instead posits a division of labor. Russia rather portrays itself as the dominant security provider in the region, largely through the mechanism of the Collective Security Treaty Organization (which includes Kazakhstan, Kyrgyzstan, and Tajikistan, but not Uzbekistan or Turkmenistan, as members). Russia's activities thus fall into the realm of the projection of hard power while China pursues its economic interests. These activities are depicted as complementary rather than competitive. Both states through their mutually reinforcing activities are thus portrayed as contributing to the maintenance of stability in the region.

RUSSIAN-CHINESE DEFENSE COOPERATION

In the last several years, forms of defense cooperation have deepened between Russia and China. This is seen in all three areas of the bilateral defense

Table 12.2. Chinese and Russian Imports, Exports, and Total Trade from the Post-Soviet States, 2016 (US$ thousands)

	Imports		Exports		Total Trade	
	China	Russia	China	Russia	China	Russia
Armenia	280,618	378,281	111,083	957,253	391,701	1,335,534
Azerbaijan	412,081	446,282	345,883	1,508,064	757,965	1,954,346
Belarus	435,188	9,406,284	1,090,019	14,050,696	1,525,207	23,456,980
China	—	38,088,969	—	28,021,260	—	66,108,229
Georgia	53,564	256,686	745,243	840,003	798,807	1,096,689
Kazakhstan	4,805,078	3,612,214	8,292,320	9,426,891	13,097,398	13,039,105
Kyrgyzstan	71,234	170,543	5,605,425	1,025,746	5,676,659	1,196,289
Moldova	24,371	248,695	76,626	912,016	100,997	1,160,711
Russia	32,360,147	—	37,339,600	—	69,599,747	—
Tajikistan	31,255	26,405	1,725,083	661,481	1,756,328	687,887
Turkmenistan	5,563,294	331,174	388,478	570,574	5,951,772	901,748
Ukraine	2,490,794	3,950,745	4,216,952	6,280,283	6,707,746	10,231,028
Uzbekistan	1,607,057	761,041	2,007,463	1,964,967	3,614,520	2,726,008

Sources: World Bank, https://wits.worldbank.org/CountryProfile/en/Country/CHN/Year/2016/TradeFlow/Export/Partner/by-country;
https://wits.worldbank.org/CountryProfile/en/Country/RUS/Year/2016/TradeFlow/Export.
Note: World Bank data for Russian and Chinese imports and exports are not equivalent.

relationship: military exercises, high-level military-to-military contacts, and forms of military technical cooperation.[24] China and Russia first participated in combined military exercises in 2003, and over time the exercises have displayed an increasing complexity, especially since 2014. This includes peace mission exercises conducted under the auspices of the SCO. Bilateral exercises have come to focus on naval operations, extending over a broad geographic range with consequent strategic implications. Joint naval exercises were conducted in the Mediterranean in 2015, the South China Sea in 2016, and the Baltic Sea in 2017. Although Russia has sought to remain neutral with respect to Chinese territorial claims in the South China Sea, its participation in the 2016 bilateral exercises could be interpreted as an implicit approval of the Chinese position. The same logic applies to suggest Chinese acquiescence to Russia's interpretation of the Mediterranean and Baltic Seas as legitimate spheres of Russian influence.

Russia and China engage in defense contacts through a multitude of ongoing bilateral and multilateral meetings, which have also increased over time. These include the China-Russia Intergovernmental Joint Commission of Military-Technical Cooperation, exchanges between services, and China-Russia Staff Headquarters Strategic Consultations. Since 1990, Russia and China have held over one hundred high-level meetings, the most prominent of which involved meetings between the Russian and Chinese ministers of defense and the vice chairman of the Central Military Commission of the Chinese Communist Party (CCP), deputy defense ministers, and deputy chiefs of the Russian and Chinese armed forces.[25] Although the leaders of both states support closer defense ties, the intensification of military contacts appears to be a special priority of the Chinese, who perceive the benefits to be gained from learning from Russia's deeper experience in the realm of planning, communication, and coordination.

Military-technical cooperation constitutes a key component of the Russian-Chinese relationship that extends beyond arms sales to encompass a broader range of activities that includes forms of joint research and development, weapon licensing agreements, and technology transfer. After the collapse of the Soviet Union, arms sales to China kept key sectors of the Russian military-industrial complex afloat in a period when domestic purchases were almost nonexistent. Chinese arms sales reached their peak in 2005–2006 and have subsequently declined. China is no longer Russia's biggest customer (a distinction that belongs to India), but arms sales to China remain an important segment of foreign exports. A chronic area of dissention in the Russian-Chinese military-technical relationship has been Russian irritation with the Chinese tendency to reverse engineer arms purchases. For example, the Russians complained that the Chinese repackaged the Su-27 fighter aircraft as the J-11 fighter aircraft, which in the Russian view violated the original licensing agreement for production.[26] Since 2014, however, the Russians have loosened the informal prohibitions that existed on the transfer of high-technology armaments to China. In 2015, the two states signed two high-profile deals on the sale of advanced weapons systems. The agreements arrange for the supply of six battalions of Russian S400 antiaircraft missile systems and twenty-four Sukhoi Su-35 fighter aircraft. Russia and China have also increased the range of joint production agreements and forms of technological transfer (including the Chinese provision of electronic components to Russia).[27] The most prominent joint production deal has been a 2015 agreement to produce heavy-lift helicopters, but other projects exist in the area of space hardware and aeroengineering.

The Russian motivation to remove many (but not all) of the technological restrictions on arms sales appears to be twofold. On the one hand, it appears to be a product of Russia's economic isolation, the loss of Western investors due to sanctions, and the problematic state of the Russian economy. There is also the sense that Russia needs China's political support, despite the risks that China could become a competitor through reverse engineering on Russia's export market, or worse, a military threat in the event of worsening relations.[28] On the other hand, Alexander Gabuev argues that Chinese armaments were more advanced than previously believed, thus paradoxically rendering the sale of advanced technology more palatable. Moreover, Russian analysts have concluded that many weapons systems previously considered to have been stolen had been acquired more or less legally, a consequence of the lack of regulation and oversight in Russian military industries in the chaotic years of the 1990s.[29]

RUSSIAN-CHINESE RELATIONS AND THE RUSSIAN FAR EAST

The Russian Far East was severely affected by the collapse of the Soviet Union and the subsequent loss of government subsidies. Over a million inhabitants left the region, leaving a population of approximately 6.3 million in an area that constitutes 36 percent of Russia's territory.[30] During the Soviet era, moreover, the border was highly militarized, leaving its residents isolated from contact with their Asian neighbors. The signing of the 2004 border agreement between Russia and China put the long-standing territorial dispute to rest and eased security concerns considerably along the 2,400-kilometer border.

In the last few years, the Kremlin has shown a greater commitment to the economic development of the Russian Far East. The Ministry for Development of the Russian Far East was established in 2012. This has been accompanied by the acknowledgment that China is a necessary partner in the revitalization of the area.[31] This is not to say, however, that the population has completely eradicated its suspicions and outright hostility toward the foreigners—and in particular the Chinese. Although not condoned by the Kremlin, the media as well as some members of the political class continue to propagate highly exaggerated and xenophobic accounts asserting that millions of Chinese migrants are overrunning the Russian Far East. Precise figures of the Chinese presence in Russia are not available, but regional official and academic data estimate the number of Chinese migrants as between four and five hundred thousand, more than half of whom reside in European Russia, with the largest population in Moscow.[32] It is by no means clear, moreover, that the average wage of migrants is higher in Russia than in China, and in recent years worsening economic conditions in Russia have led to the reversed flow of migrant workers back to China.

Previously, Russia sought to restrict Chinese economic activity in the Russian Far East, notably in the extractive industries, an exclusion that did not apply to the Japanese and Koreans. As late as 2012, Prime Minister Dmitry Medvedev warned that the Russian Far East could become a raw materials appendage to China as a result of China's "excessive expansion."[33] Since 2014, these constraints have been reduced, along with the initiation of additional programs to encourage Chinese investors. Recognizing the infrastructural problems facing Russian-Chinese trade, government officials have also placed more energy toward completing the Tongjiang–Nizneleninskoye railway bridge and the Heihe–Blagoveshchensk cross-border road bridge. Since 2014, Russia and China have established various formats to encourage the Chinese presence in the local economy, with an eye not only toward large-scale extractive industries—such as the Chinese purchase of shares in the Yamal LNG plant—that are favored by Beijing but smaller-scale ventures. A Memorandum on Cooperation in the Far East signed during Medvedev's December 2015 trip to China called for the relocation of Chinese production facilities in the Far East in sectors that included metallurgy, shipbuilding, textiles, cement, and telecommunications and agriculture as a means to stimulate export-oriented production.[34] At present, the Chinese have a notable presence in various agricultural endeavors in the region ranging from large-scale ventures leased by local officials to Chinese agribusiness to individual peasants renting land from owners. Statistics estimate that somewhere between 600,000 to 850,000 hectares of land are farmed by Chinese.[35] In the Jewish Autonomous Region, moreover, Chinese farmers are estimated to be tenants on up to 80 percent of the land.[36]

China does not rank among the major foreign investors in the Russian Far East. The positive spin put on economic cooperation in the Russian and Chinese media typically focuses on deals signed rather than realized results. Here, too, the situation in the Russian Far East exemplifies the tensions in the Russian-Chinese relationship born out of economic asymmetry. The inhabitants of the region fear the potential consequences of opening up to the Chinese economic juggernaut. The 2015 Memorandum on Cooperation, for example, was modest in its scope but nonetheless unleashed an intense backlash from those who opposed the construction of Chinese enterprises in the region. Similarly, Chinese agricultural workers are grudgingly admired for their work ethic but resented for their very presence on Russian soil. For their part, moreover, Chinese investors are not necessarily eager to invest in the Russian Far East, where they encounter a maze of bureaucratic obstacles, a lack of infrastructure, uncertain profits, and an often hostile reception. Other locales, in contrast, are more attractive and present fewer challenges. Despite evidence of enhanced goodwill on the part of the Kremlin and greater attention to structural reforms within the region, it is not clear that current efforts to stimulate economic activity between Russia and China will lead to a better outcome than previous attempts.

CHALLENGES IN THE RUSSIA-CHINA RELATIONSHIP

Both Russian and Chinese political elites are emphatic that their relationship is rooted in a near coincidence of views regarding the structure of the international system. As Elizabeth Wishnick has noted, the shared norms that underlie this relationship have been largely—and incorrectly—ignored by many Western analysts who dismiss the relationship as a marriage of convenience.[37] In fact the normative values that Russia and China share serve to structure the geopolitical dimension of their interactions. They are, moreover, the two most prominent states in the international system that reject the universality of Western liberal values. Their rhetoric (if not necessarily their actions) is a paean to Westphalian notions of statehood rooted in the premises of the inviolable nature of sovereignty and noninterference in the internal affairs of other states. China is far more diplomatic than Russia in the image that it presents externally, but it is far less restrained in its critiques of the West as presented in Communist Party publications for domestic consumption. Both states experience a sense of persecution and victimization rooted in the conviction that the Western actors ideally seek regime change in their polities, most likely through the instigation of some sort of color revolution scenario.

The Kremlin is highly cognizant of the respect that China pays to Russia. This has been a long-standing practice on the part of the Chinese dating back to the Yeltsin era when they tolerated a series of Russian diplomatic gaffes that would have aroused protest if they had come from another state. Some of the warmth of Russian-Chinese ties can be attributed to the personal friendship that has developed between Xi and Putin. China, for example, paid Russia the honor of placing Putin's speech second on the agenda after Xi's at the May 2017 Silk Road forum in Beijing. The deference that China extends to Russia by extension bolsters Russia's own claim to great power status, which has not only external but also domestic ramifications inasmuch as the Kremlin positions itself as a great power to the Russian population as a legitimating device.

Russia and China occupy divergent positions in the international hierarchy, which informs their perspective and goals. The Kremlin projects Russia as a great power, but it locates Russia as a regional hegemon in a world system increasingly defined by a multipolarity that is distinguished not only by states but by multilateral institutions that challenge US hegemony. Russia is correspondingly more interested in promoting the SCO and the BRICS as influential actors on the global stage than is China. To a considerable extent, Russia's claim to regional hegemony has been tied to the emergence of the EEU as a dominant player. The Kremlin's prospects for achieving this were dealt a seemingly fatal blow by Ukraine's rejection of membership in the organization. But the Russian presence in Central Asia is also undercut by China's increasing economic integration with the region, and indeed with the entire post-Soviet space.

Russia's economic asymmetry with China is a pervasive factor that insinuates itself into any number of aspects of the Russian-Chinese relationship. Russia cannot begin to compete with China in Central Asia and, apart from the raw materials and defense sectors of the economy, it for the most part offers a less than attractive venue for Chinese investment or trade. The loss of Western markets to sanctions has necessitated a turn to China as an alternative, but it has also meant the relaxation of previous constraints on Chinese investment and high-technology purchases. China is a self-interested player, but domestic considerations—notably the provision of special deals to oligarchs and close associates of Putin—obscure Russia's status as a rational actor in its decision making with respect to China. The threat, always lurking beneath the surface of Russian-Chinese interactions, is that Russia is failing in its goal of economic diversification and is in danger of becoming a raw materials appendage of China.

The Kremlin, dating back to the Soviet era, has long acknowledged the need to position Russia as both a European and an Asian state. The Russian pivot to the East has been accentuated not only by the West's sanctions regime but also because the Kremlin realizes that East Asia is the most vital and dynamic locus of the global economy. Nonetheless, the Russian political class has been oriented to Europe as a primary focus and has historically defined its identity one way or the other with reference to Europe.

For much of the 2000s, Moscow attempted to integrate Russia into the European space. This is seen in the call by Medvedev to construct a Euro-Atlantic security community stretching from Vancouver to Vladivostok and in Putin's call for a parallel harmonious economic community extending from Lisbon to Vladivostok.[38] In this sense, the pivot to the East requires a reorientation in the consciousness of the Russian political elite to acknowledge the importance of developing political and economic ties with Asia.

Alexander Gabuev has written about the lack of understanding and interest in China among Russian political elites, referring to their "near complete ignorance."[39] Sergei Karaganov, a prominent public intellectual, who has been a spokesperson for the Russian orientation to Asia, has also acknowledged that Russian elites have had a difficult time finding the "intellectual substantiation for the need to make an economic turn to the East."[40] It is notable that Karaganov is not referring to a borrowing of Asian civilizational attributes, but simply recognizes that even the task of developing economic ties with Asian states is met with some reluctance.

Whereas Russia primarily seeks to project itself as a regional power, China has largely embraced the role as a global power. China, for many years, downplayed its global position, adhering to the aphorism, supposedly mandated by Deng Xiaoping, to "keep a low profile and bide one's time" (*tao guang yang hui*). Xi has quite conclusively moved China away from this stance. He signaled China's rise in a 2013 meeting with US president Barack Obama when he heralded a "new type of great power relations" (*xinxing daguo guanxi*) between the United States and China. Subsequently, Xi has expanded the parameters of China's stake in great power status. He identified China as a great power or a strong power twenty-six times in his May 2017 speech at the Silk Road forum, which also identified the OBOR initiative as the project of the century.[41]

The election of Donald Trump to the US presidency in 2016 has seen a partial retreat of the United States from a position of global leadership, which has left China in a position to seek to fill the vacuum. In his January 2017 speech at Davos, Xi implicitly claimed the mantle of global leadership in asserting the benefits of economic globalization.[42] Trump's decision in June 2017 to pull the United States out of the Paris Climate Accords provided China—somewhat ironically, since it is by far the largest carbon emitter—another opportunity to assume a position of global leadership. To be sure, Xi's successful endeavor to change the Chinese constitution to allow him a seemingly unlimited tenure as president has reduced his luster in the West. But China's sheer economic presence ensures that China's claim to international leadership will be treated with respect. China's seemingly inexorable rise leaves open the question of not only its implications for the West, especially the United States, but also its significance for Russia.

CONCLUSION

There is a paradoxical aspect to the Russian-Chinese relationship. On the one hand, there exists a strong legacy of distrust, fueled by the decades-long dispute of the Soviet era. Nonetheless, trust between the two states is growing. The Russian decision to relax previous restrictions on Chinese trade and investment is no doubt a product of perceived economic necessity, but it still involves a choice reflecting the agency of the Kremlin leadership. Russia and China do share convergent norms and values that are reflected in their coordinated responses in the international sphere. Normative issues of identity in this sense overlap with geopolitical considerations. To date, China has been scrupulous in treating Russia as an equal partner, but the reality is that the economic asymmetry between the two—which permeates into many spheres of their activities—is forecast to continue to diverge in the future. It is China, not Russia, that has the upper hand, and it is China's behavior that by and large will determine how this relationship will play out in the future.

DISCUSSION QUESTIONS

1. To what extent do you believe that the Russian-Chinese relationship rests on geopolitical factors? Justify your answer.
2. What is the weakest link in the Russian-Chinese relationship? How might the Russian state overcome this problem?
3. To what extent do you feel that Russian policy toward China threatens to turn Russia into a resource appendage of China.
4. To what extent do you see the cordial relationship between Russia and China continuing in the future?

SUGGESTED READINGS

Kaczmarski, Marcin. *Russia-China Relations in the Post-Crisis International Order*. London: Routledge, 2015.
Lo, Bobo. *A Wary Embrace? What the China-Russia Relationship Means for the World*. Lowy Institute. Docklands, Australia: Penguin Random House, 2017.
Lukin, Alexander. *China and Russia: The New Rapprochement*. New York: Polity, 2018.
Rozman, Gilbert. *The Sino-Russian Challenge to the World Order*. Stanford, CA: Stanford University Press, 2014.
Trenin, Dmitri. *From Greater Europe to Greater Asia? The Sino-Russian Entente*. Moscow: Carnegie Moscow Center, 2015.
Wishnick, Elizabeth. "In Search of the 'Other' in Asia: Russia-China Relations Revisited." *Pacific Review* 30, no. 1 (2017): 114–32.

NOTES

1. Shan Jie, "Russian Ties 'Best in History,'" *Global Times*, July 4, 2017, http://www.globaltimes.cn/content/1054757.shtml (accessed January 2, 2018).
2. See Bobo Lo, *Axis of Convenience* (London: Chatham House, 2008); and *Russia and the New World Disorder* (London: Chatham House, 2015).
3. See Simon Saradzhyan, "Is Russia Declining?," *Demokratizatsiya* 24, no. 3 (2016): 339–418.

4. "Sovmestnoe zaiavlenie Rossiiskoi Federatsii i Kitaiskoi Narodnoi Respubliki o tekyshchei situatsii v mire i vazhnykh mezhnunarodnykh problemakh," The Kremlin, July 4, 2017, http://kremlin.ru/supplement/5219 (accessed April 17, 2018).

5. See ibid. and "Sovmestnoe zaiavlenie Rossiiskoi Federatsii i Kitaiskoi Narodnoi Respubliki," The Kremlin, June 25, 2016, http://www.kremlin.ru/supplement/5100 (accessed March 23, 2018).

6. "Joint Statement by the Russian and Chinese Foreign Ministries on the Korean Peninsula's Problems," Ministry of Foreign Affairs of the Russian Federation, July 4, 2017, http://www.mid.ru/en/foreign_policy/news/asset_publisher/cKNonkJE02Bw/content/id/2807662 (accessed April 17, 2018).

7. "Sovmestnoe zaiavlenie Rossiiskoi Federatsii i Kitaiskoi Narodnoi Respubliki."

8. "Sovmestnoe zaiavlenie Rossiiskoi Federatsii i Kitaiskoi Narodnoi Respubliki o dal'neishem uglublenii otnoshenii vseob'emliushchego partnerstva i strategicheskogo vzaimodeistviia," The Kremlin, July 4, 2017, http://kremlin.ru/supplement/5218 (accessed January 29, 2018).

9. Gilbert Rozman, *The Sino-Russian Challenge to the World Order: National Identities, Bilateral Relations, and East versus West in the 2010s* (Stanford, CA: Stanford University Press, 2014). Also see Elizabeth Wishnick, "In Search of the 'Other' in Asia: Russia-China Relations Revisited," *Pacific Review* 30 (2016): 114–32.

10. Kenneth Anderson, "Text of Russia-China Joint Declaration on Promotion and Principles of International Law," Lawfare, July 7, 2016, https://www.lawfareblog.com/text-russia-china-joint-declaration-promotion-and-principles-international-law (accessed January 28, 2018).

11. Central Intelligence Agency, *The World Factbook*, https://www.cia.gov/library/publications/the-world-factbook/geos/rs.html; https://www.cia.gov/library/publications/the-world-factbook/geos/ch.html (accessed March 25, 2018).

12. The Central Bank of the Russian Federation, http://www.cbr.ru/eng/statistics/?ch=Par_47562&prtid=svs#CheckedItem (accessed March 24, 2018); also see Vasily Kashin, "Is China Investing Much in Russia?," Valdai Club, September 6, 2017, http://valdaiclub.com/a/highlights/chinese-investments-in-russia (accessed March 24, 2018).

13. Daniel Workman, "China's Top Trading Partners," March 24, 2018, http://www.worldstopexports.com/chinas-top-import-partners (accessed 24 March 24, 2018).

14. See Richard Weitz, "The Russia-China Gas Deal," *World Affairs* 177, no. 3 (September/October 2014): 80–86; and Henry Foy, "Russia's $55b Pipeline Gamble on China's Demand for Gas," *Financial Times*, April 3, 2018, https://ig.ft.com/gazprom-pipeline-power-of-siberia (accessed April 10, 2018).

15. The members of the EEU are Russia, Kazakhstan, Belarus, Armenia, and Kyrgyzstan.

16. "Zhonghua renmin gongheguo yu eluosi lianbang guanyu sichou zhi lu jingji dai jianshe he jianshe duijie hezuo de lianhe shengmin (quanwen)," May 9, 2015, http://www.qstheory.cn/zhunqu/zywz/2015-05/09/c_1115229503.htm (accessed September 16, 2015).

17. See, for example, Alexander Gabuev, "Belt and Road to Where?," Carnegie Moscow Center, December 8, 2017; and Marcin Kaczmarski, "Two Ways of Influence-Building: The Eurasian Economic Union and the One Belt, One Road Initiative," *Europe-Asia Studies* 69, no. 7 (2017): 1027–46.

18. Zhang Yunbi and Zhang Yue, "Xi Backs Building of Polar Silk Road," *China Daily*, November 2, 2017, http://www.chinadaily.com.cn/world/cn_eu/2017-11/02/content_34007511.htm (accessed April 10, 2018).

19. "China's Arctic Policy," State Council Information Office, January 2018, http://english.gov.cn/archive/white_paper/2018/01/26/content_281476026660336.htm (accessed April 11, 2018).

20. Johan van de Ven, "The Belt and Road Initiative: Is China Putting Its Money Where Its Mouth Is?," Jamestown Foundation, *China Brief* 18, no. 5 (March 26, 2018). As of May 2017, the Silk Road Fund had contracts for 15 projects, while the AIIB had approved 24 projects as of February 2018. See Silk Road Fund, http://www.silkroadfund.com.cn/enweb/23798/index.html (accessed April 10, 2018); and AIIB, "Approved and Proposed Projects," https://www.aiib.org/en/projects/approved/index.html (accessed April 10, 2018).

21. Alexander Gabuev, "Belt and Road to Where?"

22. AIIB, "Approved and Proposed Projects."

23. See Alexander Lukin, "Consolidation of the Non-Western World during the Ukrainian Crisis: Russia and China, SCO, and BRICS," *International Affairs* 61, no. 2 (2015): 30–46; and Alexander Gabuev, "Russia's Policy towards China: Key Players and the Decision-Making Process," The Asan Forum, March 5, 2015, http://www.theasanforum.org/russias-policy-towards-china-key-players-and-the-decision-making-process (accessed November 7, 2015).

24. See Ethan Meick, "China-Russia Military-to-Military Relations: Moving Toward a Higher Level of Cooperation," US-China Economic and Security Review Commission, Staff Research Report, March 20, 2017; and Paul Schwartz, "Russia-China Defense Cooperation: New Developments," The Asan Forum, February 9, 2017, http://www.theasanforum.org/russia-china-defense-cooperation-new-developments (accessed April 10, 2018).

25. Meick, "China-Russia Military-to-Military Relations," 18.

26. See Sebastien Roblin, "China Stole This Fighter from Russia—and It's Coming to the South China Sea," *National Interest*, July 24, 2016.

27. Schwartz, "Russia-China Defense Cooperation," 6–7.

28. Denis Abramov, "In Arms Trade, China Is Taking Advantage of Russia's Desperation," *Moscow Times*, November 1, 2016.

29. Alexander Gabuev, "Friends with Benefits? Russian-Chinese Relations after the Ukraine Crisis," Carnegie Moscow Center, June 29, 2016, https://themoscowtimes.com/articles/in-arms-trade-china-is-taking-advantage-of-russian-desperation-55965 (accessed July 15, 2016).

30. Paul Stronski and Nicole Ng, "Cooperation and Competition: Russia and China in Central Asia, the Russian Far East, and the Arctic," Carnegie Endowment for International Peace, February 2018, https://carnegieendowment.org/2018/02/28/cooperation-and-competition-russia-and-china-in-central-asia-russian-far-east-and-arctic-pub-75673 (accessed February 7, 2018).

31. See Stephen K. Wegren, Alexander M. Nikulin, and Irina Trotsuk, "Russia's Tilt to Asia and Implications for Agriculture," *Eurasian Geography and Economics* 56, no. 2 (2015): 127–49.

32. Alexander Gabuev and Maria Repnikova, "Why Forecasts of a Chinese Takeover of the Russian Far East Are Just Dramatic Myth," Carnegie Moscow Center, July 14, 2017, https://carnegie.ru/2017/07/14/why-forecasts-of-chinese-takeover-of-russian-far-east-are-just-dramatic-myth-pub-71550 (accessed August 2, 2017).

33. Stronski and Ng, "Cooperation and Competition," 18.

34. Silvana Malle, "Russia and China in the 21st Century: Moving toward Cooperative Behaviour," *Journal of Eurasian Studies* 8 (2017): 142.

35. Malle, "Russia and China in the 21st Century," 143; and Rensselaer Lee, "The Russian Far East and China: Thoughts on Cross-Border Integration," Foreign Policy Research Institute, November 2013, https://www.fpri.org/docs/Lee_-_Russia_and_China.pdf (accessed December 2, 2013).

36. Alexander Gabuev and Gary Shtraks, "China's One Belt, One Road Initiative and the Sino-Russian Entente" (policy Q & A, National Bureau of Asian Research, August 9, 2016), https://carnegie.ru/2016/08/09/china-s-one-belt-one-road-initiative-and-sino-russian-entente-pub-64297 (accessed August 15, 2016).

37. Elizabeth Wishnick, "In Search of the 'Other' in Asia."

38. Dmitry Medvedev, "The Draft of the European Security Treaty," The Kremlin, Moscow, November 20, 2009, http://en.kremlin.ru/events/president/news/6152 (accessed December 30, 2015); Vladimir Putin, "Putin Envisions a Russia-EU Free Trade Zone," Spiegel Online, November 25, 2010, http://www.spiegel.de/international/europe/from-lisbon-to-vladivostok-putin-envisions-a-russia-eu-free-trade-zone-a-731109.html (accessed December 30, 2015).

39. Alexander Gabuev, "Russia's Policy towards China."

40. Sergei Karaganov, "A Turn to Asia: The History of the Political Idea," *Russia in Global Affairs*, January 13, 2016, http://eng.globalaffairs.ru/pubcol/A-turn-to-Asia-the-history-of-the-political-idea-17926 (accessed February 24, 2016).

41. Chris Buckley and Keith Bradsher, "Xi Jinping's Marathon Speech: Five Takeaways," *New York Times*, October 18, 2017, https://www.nytimes.com/2017/10/18/world/asia/china-xi-jinping-party-congress.html (accessed October 22, 2018); also see "Full Text of President Xi's Speech at Belt and Road Forum," *Xinhua*, May 14, 2017, http://www.xinhuanet.com/english/2017-05/14/c_136282982.html (accessed May 25, 2017).

42. "President Xi's Speech to Davis in Full," January 17, 2017, https://america.cgtn.com/2017/01/17/full-text-of-xi-jinping-keynote-at-the-world-economic-forum (accessed February 28, 2017).

Chapter Thirteen

Food and Foreign Policy

Stephen K. Wegren and Alexander M. Nikulin

There are many foundations of international power—trade, military might, economic production, financial resources, size of population, and soft power (cultural influence) are several well-known sources. Often overlooked is the fact that food reflects and creates power. Throughout history food has been a powerful instrument that drives development within civilizations and interactions between them.[1] To the present, food trade is used as a lever of foreign policy. Food assistance is a type of soft power. The idea that food is linked to foreign policy is not unique to Russia or to the contemporary age. Historically, food trade was used to curry favor or as a behavioral reward; conversely, withholding food trade could act as punishment.

Both political and economic variables influence food trade. One economic variable is surplus supply, without which trade could not occur. A political variable is the openness of the other side to import food, which is to say that states may erect protectionist barriers to prevent imports.[2] A third political variable concerns the relationship between two nations. This chapter uses these three variables to explore the linkages between Russia's food trade and foreign policy. Our basic question is, to what extent is food trade used as a lever of Russian foreign policy? The context of our analysis is the emergence of a protectionist, nationalist Russia combined with great power ambitions and growing food export potential.

FOOD AND FOREIGN POLICY

The idea that food is used as an instrument of foreign policy to punish or reward has a long history for countries in every region of the world. As a global power and major agricultural producer, the United States has been especially active in using food as an instrument of foreign policy. US food aid has been inherently politicized for decades, starting with the creation of the Food for Peace program in 1954, under which food was sold on concessionary terms (Title 1) or donated as food aid (Title II). During the 1970s, for example, US food aid was strategically sent to allies in South Vietnam, Cambodia, and South Korea in an effort to combat the spread of communism in Asia. When the peace accord between Israel and Egypt was being negotiated in 1979 (signed in 1980), President Carter used grain as an inducement to get Egyptian leader Anwar Sadat to sign the Sinai agreement.[3]

It is reasonable to hypothesize that poor relations result in lower trade or even the withholding of food via trade. There certainly are examples of this happening with US food, for example, the denial of credit for Chile to buy wheat in mid-1973. Chilean president Salvador Allende was overthrown by the United States later in 1973. Two historical examples between the United States and Russia, however, show that even being political adversaries does not necessarily preclude agricultural trade. In a first example, to help combat famine in Soviet Russia during 1920–1921, under the direction of Herbert Hoover the United States created the American Relief Administration (ARA), funded with $20 million to set up food kitchens in hundreds of locations in the Volga valley. The program was run by three hundred Americans in Russia and staffed by 120,000 Russians. At its highpoint, the ARA was feeding eleven million people suffering from starvation per day, most of whom were children.[4] In 1921, the United States also sent seed for winter sowing so the famine would not extend another year. This program was remarkable not only for its scope and positive impact, but also because at that time the United States did not even have diplomatic relations with the Soviet government and in fact had just gone through its first "red scare" in 1919–1920 when the American Communist Party was formed.

In a second example, détente between the United States and the Soviet Union in the early 1970s opened up possibilities for food trade. The granting of most favored trade status to the USSR in 1972 seemed to be the start of what was expected to be a sharp increase in bilateral trade. The Soviet's "great grain robbery" of 1973–1974, however, embarrassed the Nixon administration and infuriated American consumers who ended up subsidizing wheat exports to the USSR.[5] While the Soviets were buying grain at low market prices, the price for a loaf of bread in the United States soared to unprecedented levels. The grain robbery soured Nixon's détente policy, so much so that the term proved to be a disadvantage to Republican presidential candidate Gerald Ford in the 1976 election, which he ultimately lost. In the 1980 presidential election, Republican candidate Ronald Reagan derisively referred to détente by arguing that the Soviet Union took advantage of the United States under the pretext of peaceful coexistence.

During President Ronald Reagan's first term, US-Soviet relations were very tense, and in 1980 the United States banned wheat exports to the USSR in retaliation for the Soviet invasion of Afghanistan in December 1979.[6] The wheat export ban continued to 1985 and became one of the pillars of Reagan's vehement anti-Soviet policy when he referred to the Soviet Union as the "axis of evil" and the "evil empire." In this way, the United States used food trade to punish the USSR for its actions.

RUSSIA'S EMERGENCE AS A FOOD POWER

In recent years, Russia has emerged as a grain powerhouse, similar to the pre–World War I period when Russian wheat fed Europe. We normally do not think of Russia as a food power. Our collective memories include food lines in cities and massive food imports from the West during the Soviet period. That situation has changed. Russia's return to agricultural prowess is evidenced by the fact that two of the past three agricultural years Russia has been the number-one wheat exporter in the world, and in the third year Russia finished a few hundred tons behind the United States but would have finished first if not for a late-season trade dispute with Turkey.[7]

Russia's agricultural rebound is based on grain production, specifically wheat. As total grain harvests increased, wheat output rose from 56.2 million tons in 2011 to about 86 million tons in 2017. During the 2000–2005 period, Russia's total average grain harvest was under 79 million tons. In the 2008/09 agricultural year, the harvest broke the 100-million-ton barrier for the first time in the post-Soviet period. Since 2014, grain harvests have stayed above 100 million tons. In the 2016/17 agricultural year the harvest hit a record high of 120 million tons. In the 2017/18 agricultural year that record was shattered as Russia's harvest reached 140 million tons (net 135 million tons after cleaning), with total grain exports exceeding 50 million tons and wheat exports above 35 million tons.[8]

The 2017 record harvest revealed problems that previously were concealed. Successively large harvests in 2015 and 2016, combined with the record harvest in 2017, created surpluses that Russia's agricultural infrastructure was not designed to handle. When it became clear that the 2017 harvest would exceed previous forecasts, former minister of agriculture Alexander Tkachev indicated that the usual method to deal with grain surplus, state purchases, was not useful because the supply was large and storage facilities were already full, so new methods would be needed to deal with unanticipated volumes of grain.[9] Tkachev argued that grain exports should become a priority to alleviate the surplus, but the 2017 harvest revealed a significant shortage of train cars to transport grain to ports.[10] The inability to transport grain to ports, thereby endangering the financial condition of hundreds of farms, led to calls for fundamental reform of the grain sector.[11] Nonetheless, with too much surplus, the federal government subsidized the transport of grain to ports for export. In late December 2017, the government allocated R3 billion to subsidize the transport of more than three million tons of grain by rail for export from thirteen regions in central and eastern Russia, and this subsidy extended through June 2018.[12] For the 2018/19 agricultural year, the rail subsidy was retained but lowered, and the number of regions eligible for the subsidy was reduced to five. Overall, in 2017 Russia's agricultural exports totaled more than $20 billion, making it three consecutive years that food exports exceeded the value of arms sales. To deal with anticipated high harvests in future years, the Ministry of Agriculture indicated plans to build new terminals in the Far East, Black Sea, and Baltic Sea to allow export of forty-five million tons of grain or more per year.[13]

Several factors explain Russia's emergence as a major grain producer. One factor is weather. Russia's last major drought was in 2012, and before that a severe drought occurred in 2010, but in recent years the weather has cooperated. In 2018, drought in the south and cold in the Urals district led to a smaller harvest than originally anticipated, but the decrease was not catastrophic. The weather factor is a wild card, however, and can change in any given agricultural year, as is true throughout the world. A second factor is reduced domestic demand for grain that helps to generate surplus for export. Total domestic grain usage ranged between sixty-eight and seventy-eight million tons during 2014–2016 for human consumption, seed, and animal feed.[14] Reduced usage results from a change in consumers' diet from bread and other starches to proteins as their income rises. In addition, the significant contraction in the size of livestock herds has reduced demand for feed grain. Russian farms had about 66 percent of cows at the end of 2016 that they had in 2000.[15]

A third factor has been the increase in the amount of arable land. At the beginning of 2016, Russia had 116 million hectares of arable land, which ranked third after the United States and India. Because of Russia's large size, the percentage of arable land to total land is relatively low at about 7.5 percent. Russia is trying to increase the amount of arable and cultivated land through reclamation (repairing and building dams to prevent flooding), expanding irrigation, and preventing soil erosion. In 2017, the federal government spent just over R11 billion on land reclamation and plans the same level for 2018.[16] The government has also attempted to bring abandoned and unused agricultural land into production. In 2017, 650,000 hectares of previously unused land were brought into production.[17]

A fourth factor has been government grain intervention and a price floor that the government offers in good harvest years. The intent is to prevent a price crash by offering price supports and a secure market for surplus grain. The government does not want to see grain producers become unprofitable or go out of business. The effectiveness of grain intervention has been contested in policy circles. During the record-shattering 2017 harvest, grain supply was so high that grain intervention was deemed inexpedient, and sales from reserve stocks began in 2018 to make more storage available.[18] The importance of government grain intervention is not so much the size of the reserve fund (generally ranging between three to five million tons), but rather the psychological effect that producers feel when the government is willing to help them by offering price supports and a reliable market to sell surplus grain.

A final set of factors includes an increase in yield per hectare, facilitated by an increase in the application of fertilizer and higher productivity per tractor and combine. In support of higher levels of grain exports, the government has undertaken the expansion and modernization of existing seaports on the Black Sea and in the Far East, the construction of new grain storage inland and terminals at ports, the subsidization of grain transport by railway, and a lowering of the export tariff on grain to 0 percent to July 2019.

FOOD TRADE WITH THE WEST

Russia has alternated periods of integration and distancing from the West throughout its history. Stephen Kotkin argues, "Russian governments have generally oscillated between seeking closer ties with the West and recoiling in fury at perceived slights, with neither tendency able to prevail permanently."[19] In 2014 the historical cycle may have been broken and Russia may pursue a long-term strategy of nonintegration with the West. Although analysts point to disputes and troubles in the relationship between the West and Russia since at least 2007, marked by Putin's February 2007 speech at the Munich Conference on Security, the Ukraine crisis of 2014 represented a watershed in relations between the West and Russia. After Russia annexed Crimea in March 2014, the West introduced several rounds of sanctions against Russia, and Russia responded with a food embargo in August 2014.[20] That food embargo against Western nations (called countersanctions by Russian leaders) was subsequently extended several times and is now scheduled to run to the end of 2019. After the fact, President Vladimir Putin claimed that countersanctions will benefit domestic food producers, a sentiment repeatedly backed by former minister of agriculture Alexander Tkachev, who asked that countersanctions remain in place for several years even after Western sanctions end. But in 2014, the introduction of the food embargo was not explained in terms of helping or protecting domestic producers. In fact, it is difficult to understand, even in retrospect, what the goals were or the purpose of the food embargo other than to express anger at the West and to punish those who were trying to punish Russia. The embargo was not linked to any specific policy outcome other than "we will stop punishing you when you stop punishing us." But how the two sides were to get to that point was not clear.

The two sides thus painted themselves into a corner. The West's position is that sanctions will remain until Crimea is returned to Ukraine. Russia's position is that Crimea is now part of the Russian Federation and the food embargo will not be repealed until the West drops its sanctions. The dispute over Ukraine set in motion a slowing, even cessation, of integrative process-es with the West. Russia set out to create or join institutional structures that are non-Western: the BRICS-backed development bank to rival the World Bank in 2014; the creation of the Eurasian Economic Union in 2015 to rival the European Union; joining the Asian Infrastructure Investment Bank (AIIB) in 2015, becoming the third-largest shareholder after China and India to rival the World Bank; and enhanced cooperation with other members of the Shanghai Cooperation Organization (SCO), including military coopera-tion to rival NATO. The period since 2014, therefore, represents Russia's decoupling from the West and the West's attempt to exclude Russia from the global leadership club, evidenced by its removal from the G8.

When Donald Trump took office, optimism that US sanctions might end early were reciprocated on the Russian side by suggestions that the food embargo could be ended early or not renewed. Early optimism faded, howev-er, and by the end of January 2017 Prime Minister Medvedev characterized the chance of a repeal of sanctions as "an illusion." In April 2017 Medvedev boasted that the level of food security that exists today in Russia had never been attained in any period in the country's history, not during the Soviet period or even the post-Soviet period. He claimed, "In essence, we are feed-ing ourselves. It is a remarkable accomplishment."[21]

Going forward, the question becomes not simply how to reverse the dete-rioration in relations between the West and Russia, but how to get Russia to restart integrative processes. Given the deep mistrust between Russia and the West, a return to relations of the pre-2014 period is perhaps not even pos-sible. The Trump administration's decision in December 2017 to arm Ukraine with lethal weapons will lessen Russia's motivation to be coopera-tive and only add to the level of hostility. Further, Russia's decoupling from the West means that Russia is *less* vulnerable to sanctions or embargoes in the future, a scenario that presents Western leaders with few options to pun-ish Russia for errant behavior or to send a signal of displeasure.

The dramatic decline in relations between the West and Russia has been so deep, and has encompassed such a wide array of policy issues, that Robert Legvold characterizes it as a return to the Cold War.[22] The new Cold War, which incidentally had been argued by others such as Edward Lucas since 2008, concerns mainly the United States and Russia, but nations in the Euro-pean Union (EU) have been caught in the rapid deterioration of relations since 2014 as well.[23] Prior to 2014, the EU was Russia's largest export market, and Russia was the EU's fourth-largest export market. In 2013, the EU sold 32 percent of its fruit, 25 percent of its vegetables, 25 percent of its pork, and 20 percent of its beef to the Russian market. France, Lithuania, and Finland exported large volumes of milk and dairy products to Russia. Canada, Denmark, Germany, and the Netherlands exported pork. Poland sold fruits, especially apples.

Total trade was affected by the political relationship between the West and Russia. The souring of the relationship resulted in total trade dropping from €339 billion in 2012 to €191 billion in 2016. Food trade was similarly affected. Russia received about 10 percent of the EU's food and agricultural exports in 2013, which fell to 4 percent in 2016 as a result of Russia's food embargo. In monetary value, food and agricultural trade fell from almost €12 billion in 2013 to €5.6 billion in 2016. Since the start of Russia's food embargo to mid-2017, it is estimated that EU nations lost €20 billion in food and agricultural trade.[24] The impact of the embargo hit some countries harder. Italy, for example, has been severely affected, losing an estimated €11–12 billion in agricultural and food export revenue and as many as two hundred thousand jobs. In contrast, Germany was not nearly as impacted.[25] In 2015, the European Commission spent €30 million to help farmers diversify export markets away from Russia. In the early months, Russia's embargo seemed to be effective as struggling farmers in the EU protested the loss of trade and the erosion of their bottom line from the ending of milk quotas that had been in place for thirty years, leading to a decline in prices. In 2015, more than six thousand farmers from nine member states blocked streets in Brussels and demanded relief. The European Commission responded by allocating €500 million to help farmers with cash flow and market stabilization. The protests played into Russia's strategy of divide and conquer, but ultimately the EU remained united in its sanctions against Russia despite early economic pain.

FOOD TRADE DISPUTES WITH FORMER REPUBLICS

During the Soviet period, what are now independent states surrounding Russia were republics in the USSR. Although the USSR was not completely autarkic, a very high percentage of all trade, including food trade, occurred among the republics. This trade would have been considered domestic food trade in the Soviet period. Following the breakup of the USSR, former republics became independent nations. Into the 2000s, "Russia still perceived its former subjects as parts of itself," signified by the label of "near abroad" by Russian leaders.[26] Relations with the near abroad were not even in the purview of the Ministry of Foreign Relations but rather were handled by the presidential administration. Economic integration and established trading partners meant that food trade among former republics remained high. If

Russia was to have good political and trade relations, it was likely to be with nations in the near abroad. For the most part, bilateral trading relations with Russia remained cordial and cooperative during the 1990s as both sides needed the other.

Over time, however, political relations changed as some nations wanted to move out of the Russian orbit. As a consequence, food trade was impacted. One example is Georgia. Georgia had been in the Russian Empire with the exception of the 1917–1920 period of civil war and the post-Soviet period. In the 1990s, Georgia remained loyal to Russia even though the Kremlin was not thrilled with Georgian leader Eduard Shevardnadze. In 2003, during the so-called Rose Revolution, young pro-Western political activists overthrew Shevardnadze and installed a pro-Western government that had aspirations of joining the EU and eventually NATO. Despite Putin's observation and veiled warning that Russia and Georgia had "brotherly relations" for several centuries, the relationship cooled, eventually culminating in a major trade and travel war during 2006–2012 when Russia banned the import of Georgian wine, mineral water, and agricultural products, all of which were major revenue producers for the Georgian economy. Direct flights between the two countries were stopped. The ban against Georgia finally ended in 2013.

In recent years, a pattern of behavior has emerged in which Russia is engaged in numerous food trade disputes with former republics. This behavior is unique in its persistence and scope. While trade disputes between states are common, it is unusual for a state to have trade disputes with so many border nations simultaneously. Minor disagreements have occurred with China, resulting in food shipments being temporarily suspended or turned back. In addition, trade disputes have occurred with several former Soviet republics. Disputes are rooted in politics, but as is clear from the discussion below, Russia uses food trade as an instrument of foreign policy to indicate displeasure with the other nation. Selected political disputes-turned-food-trade-wars are surveyed below, presented in chronological order of when they began. This list is not exhaustive, and many other food trade disputes have occurred since 2014 that are part of Russia's quest for food security. The reader is referred to a longer analysis elsewhere.[27]

Moldova

Moldova is one of Europe's poorest nations and is deeply affected by disruptions in trade. For about the last decade, Russian influence has been decreasing as Moldova expands economic relations with the EU. In addition to differences over the Transnistrian conflict, one of the key issues in the Russian-Moldovan dispute revolves around Moldova's signing of an association agreement and the Deep and Comprehensive Free Trade Area (DCFTA) agreement with the EU in June 2014, which became provisionally effective in September 2014 and fully in force following ratification in July 2016. In the run-up to the June 2014 signing, Russia introduced a series of trade restrictions with Moldova, many of which affected food exports to Russia. The purpose was to send a signal and warning to Moldova not to follow through with its pivot to the EU. In September 2013 Russia banned imports of Moldovan wine. In April 2014 Russia banned imports of processed pork products from Moldova. In July 2014, Russia banned imports of Moldovan canned vegetables, as well as fruit exports such as apples, plums, peaches, cherries, and nectarines. In August 2014, Russia also scrapped duty-free exemptions for nineteen categories of Moldovan commodities that were included in the free trade agreement of October 2011 agreed to by members of the Commonwealth of Independent States. Products that lost their duty-free status included wine, meat, vegetables, fruit, and grains. Prior to the ban, Moldova had exported 90 percent of its apples to Russia, so Russia's import ban led to attempts to reexport Moldovan apples to Russia through Belarus. Only at the end of 2016 was trade resumed after the presidents from Russia and Moldova met. Russia permitted the import of twenty different brands of Moldovan wine. In 2017, exports of Moldovan fruits began to increase but did not reach the pre-2013 level.

Ukraine

Russia and Ukraine had historically shared strong trade ties, particularly in food and agriculture. That trading relationship was ruptured by political events in February 2014 when Ukrainian president Viktor Yanukovych was overthrown through a popular revolt and forced to flee the country following his decision to pivot away from the EU and toward Russia. Shortly after Yanukovych fled to Moscow, Russia annexed Crimea in March 2014, and this led to Western sanctions against Russia. Following the shooting down of a civilian airliner in July 2014, which was blamed on Russian-supported separatists in eastern Ukraine, more sanctions were placed on Russia. In retaliation, Russia placed a ban on all dairy products from Ukraine beginning August 4, 2014. Juice, including children's juice drinks, was subsequently added to the list of banned items from Ukraine. On August 19, 2014, Russia banned exports of milk, meat, eggs, and canned meat and milk from Ukraine into Crimea, effective January 1, 2015. Russia also banned the import of confectionaries from Ukraine effective September 5, 2015. In October 2015, all crops from Ukraine into Russia were banned. In January 2016, Russia announced a total ban on all food products from Ukraine following the signing of an EU-Ukraine Association Agreement and the establishment of a free trade zone between Ukraine and the EU (DCFTA), similar to what Moldova had signed. The Russian trade ban remains in effect to today. This ban severely hurts Ukrainian farmers as Russia had been the number-one market for Ukrainian exports, with 12 percent of market share. Ukrainian pork exports to Russia collapsed, with virtually no pork exports as Ukraine struggled to open new export markets. Economists estimate that it will take years for Ukraine to find new markets to replace Russia.

The Baltics

As members of the EU, the Baltic states are subject to Russia's food embargo. The Baltic states traditionally sent a large portion of their total exports to Russia. For example, in 2013 almost 20 percent of Lithuania's GDP was comprised of exports to Russia, 16 percent of GDP in Latvia, and more than 11 percent of GDP in Estonia. Likewise, the Baltic farmers were tied to the Russian market. In 2013, Estonia exported 24 percent of its dairy products to Russia, Lithuania exported 25 percent, and Latvia exported 16 percent of its fish products to Russia. For this reason, Baltic farmers were severely affected by Russia's embargo, although the 2014 embargo was not the first time Russia had restricted access to its market. The Baltic states had experienced previous bans on their exports to Russia before and had adapted. At the end of 2009 and during October–December 2013, Russia banned or heavily restricted food exports from Baltic states. Russia's current food embargo, however, suggests a shift in trading patterns that are likely to be permanent.

Dairy is a major agricultural sector for Baltic farmers, so they had to find new markets for their perishable products once Russia introduced its embargo. Certain difficulties were originally experienced; for example, milk producers had to reduce their prices to be competitive on the global market, the result being a decline in farm income. In addition to dairy products, starting in May 2015 Russia prohibited the import of canned fish from Latvia and Estonia. Since the early period of the embargo, Baltic dairy farmers have found replacements for food that previously was exported to the Russian market. In Estonia, 98 percent of dairy exports go to other EU nations. Other nations that import Estonian dairy include Japan, Malaysia, Vietnam, and South Africa. In Lithuania, about 77 percent of its dairy exports are made to EU members, chief among them are Italy, Poland, and Germany. Despite Russia's food embargo, raw milk sales have increased. The development of alternative markets, EU assistance funds to help cope with the embargo, and EU development funds have allowed Baltic farmers to show positive growth despite Russia's food ban.

Belarus

Russia and Belarus have had a hot and cold relationship for many years. Their dispute is fueled by political and economic disagreements. In the political realm, Belarussian president Alexander Lukashenko, whose country had been the odd man out among post-Soviet states integrating with the West, began to make mild overtures to the EU to thaw the relationship and bring trade and investment to his stagnant economy. Minsk mediated the Ukraine crisis and won praise from the EU for its positive role. The EU subsequently ended its own sanctions against Belarus in February 2016. Lukashenko criticized Russia's annexation of Ukraine in 2014, which upset Moscow. By early 2018 Lukashenko still had not recognized Russia's annexation.

In January 2017, Belarus introduced a five-day visa-free regime with eighty countries for foreign visitors arriving at the Minsk airport. The visa-free regime included the United States and the EU, but not flights from Moscow. Russia began to station troops on the shared border for the first time. Concerns were expressed in Washington and in Minsk that Belarus could be the next Crimea.

There are also economic disagreements. One dispute concerns energy. Russia had continued the Soviet practice of providing Belarus with cheap energy and preferential loans in return for close political ties and cooperation. At the beginning of 2016, Belarus unilaterally reduced the price it would pay for Russian gas, arguing that as a member of the Eurasian Economic Union (EEU), it should be able to purchase Russian gas at domestic Russian prices. In return, Russia began to reduce its oil shipments to Belarus.[28] Lukashenko showed his displeasure by skipping the meeting of the Supreme Council of the EEU in December 2016 in St. Petersburg, the only EEU leader not to attend.

A second dispute arises because of the milk and dairy deficit in Russia. Russia runs an annual deficit of about seven million tons of milk, which forces it to import. This gap is not expected to be filled by domestic production for at least five to seven years. With dairy exports from the Baltics precluded due to the food embargo, the top dairy exporter to Russia is Belarus. The dispute has revolved around the quality of Belarussian milk and dairy products. Russian officials allege that falsified milk products enter Russia because of deceptive labeling and counterfeit customs documents. Russia also alleges that added ingredients and antibiotics make milk and cheese less than pure. Impure milk enters Russia because of false labeling and counterfeit customs documents. Belarussian president Alexander Lukashenko has strongly defended the quality of his country's food exports, and Belarussian officials rejected the criticisms of Russia's Rossel'khoznadzor, citing hundreds of instances in which falsified food products were seized in transit to Russia during 2016 and continued to be seized in 2017.[29] The minister of agriculture for Belarus, Leonid Zaiats, sarcastically noted in March 2017 that not only does Belarus have veterinary and sanitary standards that are "harmonized" with those in Russia, but it exports milk and dairy to many countries including within the European Union, and Russia is the only country that complains about Belarussian quality.[30]

Russia's agency in charge of checking food transit and food safety, Rossel'khoznadzor, has issued numerous temporary bans on the importation of milk and dairy products from Belarus since 2014. Other products such as meat and poultry have also been targeted. The two sides are trying to resolve the dispute through negotiations to cover product labeling, quality control, and on-site inspections of facilities by Rossel'khoznadzor. Progress is slow. Processing facilities in Belarus are seemingly approved and then others banned on a monthly basis. Meanwhile, Belarus began to diversify its milk sales. During the first quarter of 2017 it increased its milk sales by 40 percent, equal to $600 million, by developing new markets in the Persian Gulf, Africa, China, and Vietnam.

In December 2016, the vice premier of Belarus, Mikhail Rusyi, suggested that the two countries work together to combat falsified food products, and at the end of the month the two countries announced the creation of a joint working group to discuss the problem of inaccurate labeling. Subsequently, in February 2017 Russia's Ministry of Agriculture renewed its appeal for strict labeling of dairy products with a full list of contents.[31] The ministry also suggested that any imported food product that does not clearly indicate the country of origin should be destroyed.[32] From January 2017, Belarus accepted Russia's suggestions and introduced new quality standards.

Nonetheless, in a dispute that apparently has no end, Russia continues to complain about falsified and contraband milk from Belarus, which is alleged to "disbalance" the Russian milk market by driving down prices. Former minister Tkachev, for example, argued that Belarussian milk prices in 2018 were 40 percent lower than in 2017, and he alleged that milk supplies were coming from Baltic states through Belarus. In February 2018, Vice Premier Arkady Dvorkovich stated, "We are working constructively with our Belarussian colleagues, explaining the regulation of the balance between demand and supply."[33] Russian officials allege that Belarus exports up to two times more milk than it produces.[34] Dvorkovich called on Belarus to "more actively combat with illegal transport [of milk] through Belarus into Russia," indicating that Russia was considering additional measures to strengthen their antismuggling efforts.[35]

In late February 2018, Rossel'khoznadzor announced plans to ban all milk and dairy imports from Belarus effective March 6, 2018, due to violations in sanitary norms established by the Eurasian Economic Union. The ban was subsequently moved back to March 15 and then canceled altogether, but it indicated the direction of Russian thinking. As a compromise, officials from Belarus suggested the creation of an independent laboratory to test for food quality.[36] Although the Russian ban was not enacted, President Lukashenko indicated that his country may find other markets for its milk. In early April 2018, Tkachev encouraged Belarus to sell its milk elsewhere, a serious escalation of the dispute.[37] Once the two sides finished posturing, they got down to serious negotiations in April–May 2018. One suggestion was to designate a single Belarussian company that would have responsibility for deliveries of milk and dairy to Russia.[38] Despite negotiations, on June 6 Russia introduced a temporary ban on milk and dairy products from Belarus; as of August 2018 the ban was still in effect, and it is not clear how long the "temporary" ban will last.

Another economic disagreement concerns Russia's allegation that Belarus is the primary source for transiting food from embargoed nations into Russia. Russia accuses Belarus of being a willful conduit for "contraband" food—products from embargoed countries. For example, Russia alleged that Belarus exports five times more apples than it produces, the implication being that embargoed Polish apples are being transited through Belarus. In 2017, Belarus was the seventh-largest exporter of apples to Russia at forty-seven thousand tons. In early February 2018, Russia's Rossel'khoznadzor inspected eighty-four companies in Belarus. As a result of this inspection, effective February 14 the export of apples to Russia was banned from thirty-one companies in Belarus who were accused of lacking storage facilities for apples prior to shipment.[39] The day after the prohibition was announced, Minsk dismissed the allegations as groundless and the ban unnecessary.[40]

President Lukashenko rejects Russian complaints and argues that it is "Russian bandits" who are reexporting contraband food to Russia. To combat this problem, Russia has empowered Rossel'khoznadzor to seize and destroy contraband food at border crossings and even inside the country. A stiff system of fines for transporting contraband food was adopted, while former minister Tkachev even suggested making it a criminal offense. In February 2017 Russia enacted a total ban on beef from Belarus alleging illegal transit and other violations. During the first quarter of 2017, more than 260 tons of beef from Belarus were prohibited from entering Russia. Russia has also pressured other states in the Eurasian Economic Union to combat the transit of contraband food into Russia. In May 2017 Russia began to spray beef that it considered to be contraband or in violation of health standards with green paint so it could not be sold.

FOOD TRADE DISPUTES WITH TURKEY

Russia and Turkey historically have been major trading partners, and similar to relations with Belarus the relationship has alternated between cooperative and confrontational. In the agricultural sphere, Russia imports Turkish fruits and vegetables, and Turkey buys Russian grain and poultry. In 2017, Turkey replaced Egypt as the largest purchaser of Russian grain, more than half of which was wheat.[41] The trade relationship has favored Russia. The value of Russian food exports to Turkey is annually worth two to three times the value of Turkish food exports to Russia. This inequality has caused consternation in Ankara and led to complaints, but the disparity was not in and of itself the cause of a rupture in food trade.

The trade dispute arose because the two nations are on opposite sides in the Syrian civil war, with Turkey favoring the removal of Syrian president Bashar al-Assad. In November 2015, Turkey shot down a Russian fighter that allegedly strayed into Turkish airspace. One Russian pilot was killed. The Russians denied that its plane was over Turkish territory. The dispute over responsibility led to restrictions on Turkish food exports for the rest of 2015 and then culminated in a total ban on Turkish food exports to Russia during most of 2016, including tomatoes, onions, cabbages, cucumbers, and citrus. The consequence was nearly a halving of trade between the two countries, from $32 billion in 2014 to $16.9 billion in 2016.[42]

In August 2016, Russia agreed in principle to end its import ban on Turkish food, but full trade was slow to resume because Russia had already begun to substitute domestic products, for example, its own greenhouse tomatoes for Turkish tomatoes. In November 2016, the two countries agreed to a gradual, product-by-product repeal of Russia's import ban. Russia subsequently approved a significant number of Turkish agricultural commodities for import. By March 2017, Turkey objected to the fact that access to the Russian market had not been fully restored. In fact, in early March 2017 Russia amended the list of banned products from Turkey, allowing imports of yellow onions, shallots, cauliflower, and broccoli. But other Turkish commodities remained banned, including frozen turkey and chicken, strawberries, pears, grapes, cucumbers, and tomatoes.

In a retaliatory move, in March 2017 Turkey excluded Russia from the list of countries whose food exports are duty free into Turkey. Effective March 15, 2017, Russian exports to Turkey faced tariffs on wheat (130 percent), corn (130 percent), beans (9.7 percent), rice (45 percent), and sunflower oil (36 percent). Up to that point, during the 2016/17 agricultural year, Turkey imported more than two million tons of Russian wheat and 431,000 tons of corn, making it the second-largest importer of Russian grain, trailing only Egypt. Up to the introduction of import duties, Turkey had accounted for 10 percent of Russian wheat exports and 45 percent of its corn exports during the 2016/17 agricultural year.

Russian grain exports to Turkey were immediately stopped after March 15, 2017. Turkey said that it would replace Russian grain from other suppliers. Russia indicated that it would redirect its grain sales to North Africa, the Middle East, and Asia Pacific nations. At the time, Russian experts estimated that Russia could lose up to one million tons in wheat and four to seven hundred thousand tons in corn sales to Turkey, with total monetary losses reaching $1.3 to $1.5 billion. In April 2017 Russia considered reintroducing limitations on Turkish food exports to Russia, including tomatoes, apples, grapes, cucumbers, and pears. At the end of April, Russia sent a delegation to Turkey to negotiate the dispute. In advance of the negotiations, Russian vice premier Arkady Dvorkovich said that removal of the ban on products other than tomatoes could be enacted quickly if Turkey cooperated on Russian grain deliveries, but imports of Turkish tomatoes were more complicated.

In May 2017, Presidents Putin and Erdogan agreed to end the import tariffs on Russian exports and the Russian ban on Turkish food exports except tomatoes. Prime Minister Medvedev officially signed an order that lifted most restrictions on Turkish food exports in June 2017.[43] But the dispute was not over, and other complications arose. Turkey indicated that it would impose a quota on wheat imported from Russia. Under this policy, Russian wheat imports could not exceed 25 percent of Turkey's total wheat imports.[44] Turkey also wanted to inspect the enterprises from which Russian meat exports would originate.

In September 2017, former minister Tkachev referred to Turkey as one of Russia's most important agricultural trading partners and called for compromise on both sides. Tkachev noted that from its low in 2016, bilateral agricultural trade grew 14 percent in 2017, totaling over $1.2 billion during the first seven months.[45] Agricultural trade resumed in stages. From September 1, 2017, Russia allowed the import of lettuce, peppers, zucchinis, and pumpkins from nine enterprises in Turkey. In late September 2017, Turkey indicated that it was prepared to allow Russian meat exports if they met Turkish sanitary standards, and discussions began over inspection of Russian processing facilities. Starting October 30, Russia allowed the import of Turkish eggplant and pomegranates from twenty-seven enterprises.[46] Moreover, starting November 1, 2017, Russia indicated that it would allow up to 50,000 tons of Turkish tomato exports. To put that volume into perspective, in 2016 Russia imported a total of 462,000 tons of fresh and chilled tomatoes from all sources.[47] Turkish tomato exports are permitted during December–April when they would not compete with Russia's domestic production. Tkachev promised Russian producers that Turkish tomatoes would have an "insignificant" impact on the Russian market. Over the longer term, Russia is striving to substitute all tomato imports with domestic production from greenhouses. Investment in greenhouses is increasing, the number of greenhouse complexes and the area they occupy is growing, and output is rising.[48]

Just when Russian-Turkish food trade appeared to be settled, differences over the Kurds fighting in Syria emerged. In February 2018, Syrian forces backed by Iran used Russian-made missiles to shell a Turkish convoy with Russia's reluctant consent. Turkey has turned its forces against Syrian Kurds. Putin has asked Erdogan to show restraint but has received the cold shoulder.[49] Shortly thereafter, citing irregularities in the transit of tomatoes and insufficient documentation, in mid-February 2018 Rossel'khoznadzor seized eighteen tons of imported Turkish tomatoes.[50] The Russia-Turkey food trade case demonstrates the fragility of trade and its vulnerability to politics.

CONCLUDING ASSESSMENT

This chapter has argued that Russia's agricultural rebound has allowed the Putin regime to use food trade as an instrument of foreign policy. The world is unaccustomed to a Russia that uses food trade so blatantly as an instrument of foreign policy, but this chapter also indicated that Russia is similar to other nations in its behavior, notably the United States. The United States has used food as an instrument of foreign policy repeatedly through its history and continues to do so. In a similar vein, this chapter has shown how Russia is using its food import policy to punish states with which it has political disputes. The Putin regime remains committed to a strong agricultural sector and sees it as an important component of Russia's international influence and prestige. Russia's emergence as the number-one wheat exporter in the world has not gone unnoticed by the Kremlin. The upshot is that the Kremlin's linkage between food trade and foreign policy is not likely to go away anytime soon.

The question we are left with concerns the efficacy of the strategy to use food trade to punish and show displeasure toward other states. The issue is whether the use of food as a political weapon achieved a foreign policy goal, or really any goal, or was simply an expression of negativity. We assess each of the outcomes for the trade disputes discussed above.

- *Food embargo toward Western states.* The food embargo was intended to punish states that participated in sanctions against Russia but otherwise had no goal. The food embargo did *not* end sanctions against Russia, which continued into 2018 as this book goes to press. The food embargo did *not* drive a wedge between EU states that led to defections from the sanctions regime. The food embargo did *not* drive the West to the bargaining table to work out an accommodation over Crimea and the conflict in eastern Ukraine. In retrospect, the food embargo was an expression of anger, wounded pride, and a feeling of being disrespected more than a strategy to end sanctions. The food embargo ended up benefiting Russia's domestic agricultural producers and exporters, but in 2014 this outcome was unknown to Russian leaders. There is no way that Russian leaders could have predicted that trade protectionism brought about by the embargo would lead to surprisingly positive results for the agricultural sector. In fact, the embargo was something of a leap of faith, and if the agricultural sector had experienced severe drought (as in 2010) or some other catastrophe, the leadership would have had to retreat quickly.

- *Moldova.* Russia's food bans against Moldovan products did *not* prevent Moldova from drawing closer to the EU and in fact may have facilitated closer relations. In the end, Russia acquiesced and dropped its trade restrictions, signaling a change in strategy.
- *Ukraine.* The product-specific bans leading up to 2016, and then the total ban against Ukrainian food exports since January 2016, have *not* changed the trajectory of Ukraine's political development. The food trade ban has *not* changed Ukraine's desire to develop closer relations with the EU. In fact, following the January 2016 EU-Ukraine Association Agreement, the EU has become the largest export market for Ukraine. The EU now accounts for more than 37 percent of all Ukrainian exports, replacing Russia as its main trading partner. While Ukrainian exports declined to the rest of the world by almost 9 percent in 2016, its exports to the EU grew by almost 4 percent. If Russia's intent for the trade ban was to force Ukraine back into the fold by intimidation and compulsion, the strategy failed.
- *The Baltics.* Russia's food ban, which encompasses dairy products, has *not* changed political or economic orientations toward Russia. If anything, Russia's behavior, including the food ban, has strengthened the Baltic states' commitment to the EU, to NATO, and to their membership in the Western community. Baltic states are finding alternative markets for dairy that was once exported to Russia. As a consequence, Russia remains dependent on Belarus, with whom relations are complicated.
- *Belarus.* Russia's food embargo has *not* altered the desire of Belarus president Lukashenko to draw closer to the EU for trade and economic assistance. Russia's food embargo has *not* stopped counterfeit custom documents or falsified dairy content. In fact, the embargo may have made that activity lucrative. The food embargo has *not* stopped the reexport of contraband food through Belarus, in all likelihood making it more profitable. The food embargo has created black markets for food that is banned and has made food smuggling a lucrative business.
- *Turkey.* The food trade ban during most of 2016 did *not* change Turkey's orientation toward Syrian president Assad.

The takeaway from this discussion is that Russia's use of food as an instrument of foreign policy has not been successful in terms of changing policy on the other side. Russia, perhaps, should have learned from the American example that sanctions and trade restrictions are often not effective in changing states' behavior.[51] In this case, Western sanctions have not forced Russia to change its stance regarding Crimea. Similarly, Russia's use of food as a political weapon has not forced other states to change their behavior.

In closing, food trade as an instrument of foreign policy is also used in a positive manner, to build better relations or to reward close relations. Space restraints preclude a discussion, but since 2014 Russia has forged new or strengthened existing trade relations with Saudi Arabia, Serbia, Syria, Iran, Egypt, India, Bangladesh, Vietnam, China, and several South American nations. We defer a longer analysis of Russia's positive uses of food trade to a different publication.

DISCUSSION QUESTIONS

1. Why did Russia introduce a food embargo in 2014? What were its goals?
2. In what ways is Russia unique in using food trade as an instrument of foreign policy?
3. What are the prospects for a continuation of food trade as an instrument of Russian foreign policy?
4. Has Russia's food embargo been successful? Define types of success and then answer why or why not.

SUGGESTED READINGS

Wegren, Stephen K., and Christel Elvestad. "Russia's Self-Sufficiency and Food Security: An Assessment." *Post-Communist Economies* 30, no. 5 (2018).

Wegren, Stephen K., Frode Nilssen, and Christel Elvestad. "The Impact of Russian Food Security Policy on the Performance of the Food System." *Eurasian Geography and Economics* 57, no. 6 (2016): 671–99.

Wegren, Stephen K., Alexander Nikulin, and Irina Trotsuk. "The Russian Variant of Food Security." *Problems of Post-Communism* 64, no. 1 (2017): 47–62.

———. *Food Policy and Food Security: Putting Food on the Russian Table.* Lanham, MD: Lexington Books, 2018.

NOTES

1. Reay Tannanhill, *Food in History* (New York: Crown Trade Paperbacks, 1988).

2. Kym Anderson, "Growth of Agricultural Protection in East Asia," *Food Policy* 8, no. 4 (1983): 327–36; and Kym Anderson and Yujiro Hayami, *The Political Economy of Agricultural Protection* (Sydney: Allen and Unwin, 1986).

3. Jack Shepard, "Ethiopia: The Use of Food as an Instrument of U.S. Foreign Policy," *Issue: A Journal of Opinion* 14 (1985): 4–9.

4. See H. H. Fisher, *The Famine in Soviet Russia, 1919–1923: The Operations of the American Relief Administration* (New York: Macmillan, 1927).

5. See James Trager, *The Great Grain Robbery* (New York: Ballantine, 1975).

6. Despite the export ban by the United States, the Soviet Union remained a large importer of grain, with imports rising from 27.8 million tons in 1980 to 44.2 million tons in 1985. Goskomstat SSSR, *Narodnoe khoziaistvo SSSR za 70 let* (Moscow: Finansy i statistika, 1987), 643. It should be remembered that a substantial percentage of imported grain was linked to the party's attempt to increase meat production, and thus corn imports were used as feed for cattle. The more successful the regime was in increasing meat consumption, the more grain it had to import. See D. Gale Johnson and Karen McConnell Brooks, *Prospects for Soviet Agriculture in the 1980s* (Bloomington: Indiana University Press, 1983), 106.

7. An agricultural year is July 1 of one year to June 30 of the next year. Russia finished as the number-one wheat exporter in the 2014/15 and 2016/17 agricultural years and finished number two in the 2015/16 agricultural year. It reclaimed the number-one status as the largest wheat exporter in the 2017/18 agricultural year.

8. Tat'iana Kulistikova, "Eksport sel'khozproduktsii uvelichilsia v 15 raz," January 2018, http://www.agroinvestor.ru/markets/news/29298-eksport-selkhozproduktsii-uvelichilsya-v-15-raz (accessed January 25, 2018).

9. "Minsel'khoz reshit problem eksporta zerna," November 24, 2017, http://kvedomosti.ru/news/minselxoz-reshit-problemu-eksporta-zerna.html (accessed November 24, 2017).

10. "Ekonomicheskie posledstviia bol'shogo urozhaia," *Sel'skaia zhizn'*, October 19–25, 2017, 8–10.

11. Ekspert, "Rynok zerna trebuet perestroiki," October 26, 2017, http://www.agromedia.ru (accessed October 26, 2017).

12. USDA Foreign Agricultural Service (Moscow), "Decree on Grain Transportation Subsidies," GAIN Report RS1801, January 10, 2018, http://gain.fas.usda.gov (accessed February 4, 2018).

13. "Minsel'khoz reshit problmeu eksporta zerna," November 24, 2017, http://kvedomosti.ru/news/minselxoz-reshit-problemu-eksporta-zerna.html (accessed November 24, 2017).

14. Rosstat, *Osnovye pokazateli sel'skogo khoziaistva v 2016* (Moscow: Rosstat, 2017), 20.

15. Compare data from Rosstat, *Sel'skoe khoziaistvo, okhota i okhotnich'e khoziaistvo, lesovodstvo v Rossii 2015* (Moscow: Rosstat, 2015), 91, and Rosstat, *Osnovye pokazateli sel'skogo khoziaistva v 2016*, 15.

16. "Minsel'khoz Rossii: v 2018 godu na razvitie melioratsii vydeleno 11.3 mlrd rublei," January 30, 2018, http://www.mcx.ru (accessed January 30, 2018).

17. For years, it had been estimated that Russia had about forty million hectares of unused agricultural land, but the 2016 agricultural census discovered that the true number was closer to ninety-seven million hectares, an amount that exceeds all cultivated land presently in production. Of the forty million hectares, however, Russian experts estimate that only about five million hectares could be used effectively and have a significant economic benefit. Ekaterina Diatlovskaia, "V 2017 godu v sel'khozoborot vozvrashcheno 650 tysiach gektarov zemel'," December 2017, http://www.agroinvestor.ru/analytics/news/29148-v-selkhozoborot-vozvrashcheno-650-tysyach-gektarov (accessed December 23, 2017).

18. Inna Ganenko, "V etom godu iz gosfonda budet realizovano 500 tysiach tonn zerna," February 2018, http://www.agroinvestor.ru/regions/news/29325-iz-gosfonda-budet-realizovano-500-tysyach-tonn-zerna (accessed February 2, 2018).

19. Stephen Kotkin, "Russia's Perpetual Geopolitics," *Foreign Affairs* 95, no. 3 (2016): 4.

20. The August 2014 food embargo was initially applied against most food imports from the EU, the United States, Norway, Australia, and Canada. It was subsequently expanded in August 2015 to include Albania, Iceland, Liechtenstein, and Montenegro. For an analysis of the food embargo, see Stephen K. Wegren, Frode Nilssen, and Christel Elvestad, "The Impact of Russian Food Security Policy on the Performance of the Food System," *Eurasian Geography and Economics* 57, no. 6 (2016): 671–99.

21. "Medvedev nazval uroven' dostignutoi prodovol'stvennoi bezopasnosti bespretsedentnym," April 20, 2017, http://kvedomosti.ru/news/medvedev-nazval-uroven-dostignutoj-prodovolstvennoj-bezopasnosti-besprecedentnym.html (accessed April 20, 2017).

22. Robert Legvold, *Return to Cold War* (Cambridge: Polity, 2016).

23. Edward Lucas, *The New Cold War: How the Kremlin Menaces Both Russia and the West* (London: Bloomsbury, 2007).

24. "Evropeiskie fermery poteriali 20 mlrd evro iz-za Rossiiskikho kontrsanktsii," November 13, 2017, http://kvedomosti.ru/news/evropejskie-fermery-poteryali-20-mlrd-evro-iz-za-rossijskix-kontrsankcij.html (accessed November 13, 2017).

25. "Ubytki podschitany," *Sel'skaia zhizn'*, September 14–20, 2017, 14.

26. Masha Gessen, *The Future Is History: How Totalitarianism Reclaimed Russia* (New York: Riverhead Books, 2017), 238.

27. Stephen K. Wegren, Alexander Nikulin, and Irina Trotsuk, *Food Policy and Food Security: Putting Food on the Russian Table* (Lanham, MD: Lexington Books, 2018).

28. Alla Leukavets, "Belarus-Russia Relations in 2017: Behind the Curtain of Long-Lasting Drama," *Russian Analytical Digest* 206 (2017): 3.

29. "Sergei Dankvert: 'Nasha systema kontrolia rabotaet,'" March 10, 2017, http://kvedomosti.ru/news/sergej-dankvert-nasha-sistema-kontrolya-rabotaet.html (accessed March 10, 2017).

30. "Tol'ko Rossiia zhalyetsia na kachestvo Belorusskikh produktov, zaiavili v Minske," March 7, 2017, http://kvedomosti.ru/news/tolko-rossiya-zhaluetsya-na-kachestvo-belorusskix-produktov-zayavili-v-minske.html (accessed March 7, 2017).

31. Press-sluzhba Minsel'khoza Rossii, "Minsel'khoz Rossii vystupaet za uzhestochenie markirovki molokosoderhashchikh produktov," February 27, 2017, http://www.mcx.ru/news/news/show/59195.355.htm (accessed February 27, 2017).

32. "Minsel'khoz predlozhil unichtozhat' vsiu produktsiiu s neiasnoi stranoi proiskhozhdeniia," March 6, 2017, http://kvedomosti.ru/news/minselxoz-predlozhil-unichtozhat-vsyu-produkciyu-s-neyasnoj-stranoj-proisxozhdeniya.html (accessed March 6, 2017).

33. Kvedomosti.ru, "RF prizvaet aktivno borot'sia s nezakonnymi postavkami moloka cherez Belorussiiu," February 7, 2018, http://kvedomosti.ru/news/rf-prizyvaet-aktivno-borotsya-s-nezakonnymi-postavkami-moloka-cherez-belorussiyu.html (accessed February 7, 2018).

34. Kvedomosti.ru, "Airat Khairullin: kontrabanda iz Belarusi sil'no razbalansiruet rynok," January 26, 2018, http://kvedomosti.ru/news/ajrat-xajrullin-kontrabanda-iz-belarusi-silno-razbalansiruet-rynok.html (accessed January 26, 2018).

35. Kvedomosti.ru, "RF prizvaet aktivno borot'sia s nezakonnymi postavkami moloka cherez Belorussiiu."

36. Kvedomosti.ru, "Minsk vystupaet za sozdanie nezavisimoi laboratorii po otsenke kachestva prodovol'stviia," March 5, 2018, http://kvedomosti.ru/news/minsk-vystupaet-za-sozdanie-nezavisimoj-laboratorii-po-ocenke-kachestva-prodovolstviya.html (accessed March 5, 2018).

37. "Aleksandr Tkachev predlozhil Belorussii uskat' novye rynki sbyta moloka," April 5, 2018, http://mcx.ru/press-service/news/aleksandr-tkachev-predlozhil-belorussii-iskat-novye-rynki-sbyta-moloka (accessed April 5, 2018).

38. RIA Novosti, "Sozdanie edinogo postavshchika moloka v RF mozhet stat' vygodnym Moskve i Minsku," May 4, 2018, http://www.agromedia.ru (accessed May 4 2018).

39. Ekaterina Diatlovskaia, "Rossiia zapretila vvoz iablok is Belorussii," February 2018, http://www.agroinvestor.ru/regions/news/29379-rossiya-zapretila-vvoz-yablok-s-30-belorusskikh-predpriyatiy (accessed February 14, 2018).

40. Kvedomosti.ru, "V Minske prokommentirovali ogranicheniia na postavku iablok v Rossiiu," February 15, 2018, http://kvedomosti.ru/news/v-minske-prokommentirovali-ogranichen iya-na-postavku-yablok-v-rossiyu.html, http://kvedomosti.ru/news/minsk-vystupaet-za-sozdanie-nezavisimoj-laboratorii-po-ocenke-kachestva-prodovolstviya.html (accessed February 15, 2018).

41. Tat'iana Kulistikova, "Turtsiia stala krupneishim importerom Rossiiskogo zerna," November 2017, http://www.agroinvestor.ru/markets/news/28866-turtsiya-stala-krupneyshim-importerom-zerna (accessed November 15, 2017).

42. Tat'iana Kulistikova, "Turtsiia izmenila pravila importa Rossiiskoi sel'khozproduktsii," October 10, 2017, http://www.agroinvestor.ru/analytics/news/28683-turtsiya-izmenila-pravila-importa-rossiyskoy-selkhozproduktsii (accessed October 10, 2017).

43. "Russia Eases Sanctions on Turkey," June 2, 2017, https://themoscowtimes.com/news/russia-lifts-most-sanctions-from-turkey-58145 (accessed June 15, 2017).

44. Ekaterina Diatlovskaia, "Turtsiia vvela kvoty na Rossiiskie pshenitsu i maslo," May 24, 2017, http://www.agroinvestor.ru/markets/news/27617-turtsiya-vvela-kvoty-na-rossiyskie-pshenitsu-i-maslo (accessed May 24, 2017).

45. Natal'ia Novopashina, "Rabotat' s maksimal'noi otdachei," *Sel'skaia zhizn'*, September 7–13, 2017, 3.

46. Viktor Cherepovets, "Ustupki i ogranicheniia," *Sel'skaia zhizn'*, November 16–22, 2017, 11.

47. This level represented a 45 percent decline since 2014. Ekaterina Diatlovskaia, "Rossiia razreshit vvoz do 50 tys. tonn Turetskikh tomatov," October 4, 2017, http://www.agroinvestor.

ru/markets/news/28662-rossiya-razreshit-vvoz-do-50-tys-tonn-turetskikh-tomatov   (accessed October 4, 2017).

48. Elena Maksimova and Inna Ganenko, "Eko-kul'tura za god vlozhila v teplichnye kompleksy pochti 20 mlrd rublei," January 2018, http://www.agroinvestor.ru/investments/news/29177-eko-kultura-za-god-vlozhila-v-teplichnye-kompleksy-20-mlrd   (accessed January 8, 2018).

49. "The Syrian Gambit," *The Economist*, February 17, 2018, 14.

50. IA Rambler, "Rossel'khoznadzor zaderzhal bolee 18 tonn Turetskikh tomatov," February 12, 2018, http://www.agromedia.ru (accessed February 12, 2018).

51. "The Punishment Continues," *The Economist*, August 5, 2017, 37.

Chapter Fourteen

Energy

Stefan Hedlund

In Russia, everything is about oil. This is the very essence of being a "petro-state." The importance of revenue from oil exports is such that pretty much any important change in socioeconomic indicators may be traced back to fluctuations in the price of oil. This holds true across the board, for GDP growth, manufacturing, budget performance, consumer expenditure, and more. Perhaps most importantly, the dollar/ruble exchange rate has tended to follow the dollar price of oil very closely.

This said, the Russian energy complex also includes a large gas industry. In terms of energy content, the two are just about equal, producing around five hundred million tons of oil equivalent each year. But their respective roles are miles apart. While Russia exports three-quarters of its oil output, it consumes nearly two-thirds of its gas at home, at low regulated prices. In the words of Thane Gustafson, "without much exaggeration, one could say there is a division of roles: oil pays the bills abroad, while gas subsidizes the economy at home."[1]

One of many implications of the dependence on oil revenue is that any ambition to forecast the performance of the Russian economy has boiled down to forecasting movements in the price of oil. Since analysts do not have a particularly impressive track record in forecasting the price of oil, it is not surprising that forecasts of Russian economic performance have also tended at times to be rather far removed from reality.

These observations not only underscore how hard it has been to get matters right in assessing developments in Russia. They also illustrate how hard it is to govern a petro-state, as well as how economic policy is made hostage to the vagaries of international markets for oil and to infighting between powerful vested interests vying for access to ground rents.

This chapter provides an account of the emergence and development of the Russian energy complex. Following a brief look at historical legacies, it focuses on events after the collapse of the USSR. It describes how the oil and gas sectors went through very different processes of privatization, with different implications for corporate governance and for foreign involvement. It also provides an account of Russian pipeline politics and of the ambition to transform Russia into an "energy superpower." The chapter concludes with an outlook of what the future may hold.

SOVIET ENERGY

The history of Russian oil antedates that of the Soviet Union. The first discovery was made in the region around Baku, in present-day Azerbaijan, in the mid-nineteenth century.[2] The takeoff was marked in 1873, when a real gusher was struck.[3] That year also saw the arrival of the Swedish Nobel family, founders of the Nobel Brothers Petroleum Company. Over the coming decades Baku would constitute the hub of an oil boom that entailed the introduction of the world's first oil tanker and the world's first oil pipeline.

In the post–World War II era, Soviet oil production was marked by a geographical shift. Damage done to oil installations in Azerbaijan during the war caused efforts to be aimed instead at fields in the Volga basin and the Ural Mountains, where output continued to increase until about 1970.

The real game changer would prove to be Western Siberia. With the discovery, in 1969, of the supergiant Samotlor field, the region was poised for a spectacular takeoff. Over the years from 1970 until 1977, annual output increased sevenfold. Stephen Kotkin may well be right in stating that "without the discovery of Siberian oil, the Soviet Union might have collapsed decades earlier."[4] It was a tremendous bonanza, producing a strong sense of complacency.

As fields in the Volga-Urals region went into decline, the Soviet oil industry became increasingly dependent on fields in the Tyumen region, especially Samotlor. Little was done to explore for new fields that might have broadened the basis. As oil is a "wasting resource," meaning that pumping will inevitably lead to exhaustion, this was a recipe for deep trouble down the road. In 1977, the CIA produced a set of three reports predicting that Soviet oil and gas output would peak in 1980 and decline sharply thereafter.[5]

In that same year, General Secretary Leonid Brezhnev ordered a massive increase in resource inputs. By 1982, investment in the oil sector had nearly doubled, leading to a boost in output that, temporarily, more than offset the decline in older fields.[6] But it was no more than a quick fix, failing to address the endemic problems of lack of exploration, escalating costs of drilling, and a complete neglect of energy conservation.

Another short-term reprieve was found in an all-out wager on natural gas. In 1980, it was announced that the output of gas would be increased by nearly half over the coming five years. As the bulk of the reserves again were in Western Siberia, exploitation was coupled with the construction of six huge trunk lines to the European parts of the USSR. One of these, named Druzhba, or "Friendship," would extend all the way to Western Europe, allowing gas to be sold for badly needed hard currency. It remains to date the longest pipeline in the world.

The combined stories of Soviet oil and gas provide important insights into one of the main shortcomings of the Soviet economic growth strategy, namely, the belief that falling efficiency in resource use may be offset by boosting the input of resources. In the short term, this generates an illusion of success.

During 1970–1988, the volume of Soviet net energy exports increased by 270 percent, and in the early 1980s, energy exports brought in 80 percent of desperately needed hard currency earnings.[7] The downside of these achievements was that the energy sector crowded out investment in other sectors. In 1981–1985, it absorbed 90 percent of total industrial investment growth.[8]

The forced production techniques that were used to meet exaggerated production targets also caused damage to reservoirs, which led to lower ultimate recovery rates. Most important, the depletion rate for oil, that is, the share of new oil that simply offsets decline in older fields, was rising. By 1985, it had reached 85 percent.[9]

It was at this inauspicious point in time that Mikhail Gorbachev succeeded to power, as the last leader of the Soviet Union. When he set out to implement reforms he hoped would revitalize the Soviet order, he was hostage to an energy complex that had been transformed from an engine of growth into a millstone around his neck; it has even been suggested that the sharp fall in energy prices that marked the 1980s played an important part in the collapse of the USSR.[10]

The core of the economic legacy that was left for Gorbachev's successors may be defined as an overwhelming dependence on revenues from an energy complex that was running dry. Entailed here was a geographic dilemma that still haunts Russian economic policy makers. As the once supergiant West Siberian oil fields are being depleted, new reservoirs must be found and developed. This means moving into Eastern Siberia and the Far East, under highly complex geological and offshore conditions.

Gustafson sums up the contrast between old and new oil rather elegantly, noting that while the conditions of geology in Western Siberia had represented "an oilman's dream," those in the eastern regions represent "an oilman's nightmare."[11] The bottom line is that success will require new infrastructure and modern technology, neither of which is readily available without foreign assistance.

The story of Russian energy during the first couple of decades after the collapse of the USSR would on this count be marked by an ambition to have the cake and eat it too, to invite foreign energy companies to join while making every effort to deny them true ownership in the process. It was simply bound to lead to conflict and to a failure to realize potential long-term gains from true cooperation.

RUSSIAN ENERGY

The collapse of the Soviet Union has often been portrayed as being both sudden and unexpected. This is not entirely true. Although the abrupt nature of the endgame may have come as a bit of a surprise, well-placed insiders had sensed well in advance what was about to happen. And they had made their moves accordingly, in some cases with striking success in amassing vast personal fortunes.

The core feature in post-Soviet reform was privatization. As various members of the Russian elites rushed to agree that former Soviet state property must be privatized, they also began maneuvering for positions to secure the best cuts for themselves.

Some of those who moved to pick up major stakes in newly created private enterprises were insiders, senior bureaucrats with ample experience, and networks in the relevant ministerial structures. Others were outsiders, former operators in the Soviet underground economy who had developed skills that would be helpful in working the emerging market economy. Across the board, the process would be marked by at times egregious rigging and bending of the rules.

Given the sorry state of Soviet manufacturing (outside the military industries), the biggest prize in the process of mass privatization was commodities, mainly in the mining and energy industries. The latter in particular would prove to be a battlefield for at times heated struggles between different sets of actors, to the detriment of the formulation of a much-needed long-term development strategy.

Privatizing Russian Gas

An outstanding example of skills in "insider privatization" was provided by the last Soviet minister of gas, Viktor Chernomyrdin. His first step, taken already in August 1989, was to transform his ministry into a joint stock company, the RAO Gazprom, which he placed under his own leadership. Rumors have it that a sizable part of the stocks ended up in his own pockets, via holding companies controlled by him and his family and friends.

When Chernomyrdin was appointed prime minister by President Boris Yeltsin in December 1992, he handed the reins of power over Gazprom to his close associate Rem Vyakhirev. Throughout the Yeltsin era, the two would run in such a tight tandem that many began to question if it was the Kremlin that controlled Gazprom or if it was perhaps the other way around. In the important December 1995 elections to the State Duma, Chernomyrdin even launched a political party. Formally named "Our Home Is Russia," it was quickly nicknamed "Our Home Is Gazprom."

His hold on power would last until September 1998, when he was replaced by Sergei Kiriyenko. By then, Gazprom would have provided ample illustration of the impact of predatory corporate governance on corporate performance. The company abused its monopoly control over gas export pipelines to variously punish and reward foreign countries, and it developed elaborate schemes to "tunnel" profits into the accounts of privately owned companies serving as middlemen.

A case in point was ITERA, an opaque trading company headquartered in Florida. Founded in 1992 to trade consumer goods with Turkmenistan, it soon began exploiting its powerful connections to tap into the trade in natural gas. This move brought the company into a relation with Gazprom that would prove to be strikingly successful.

ITERA would over the coming years evolve into a small business empire of its own, expanding from an intermediary in trade to a major independent gas producer. It would pocket substantial margins on reselling Gazprom gas and would even assume effective control over some of its gas fields. By 2001, it had become the largest supplier of gas to other CIS states (former Soviet republics).

The spectacular growth of ITERA was remarkable, given that it operated in a sector that was so economically important and so heavily politicized. Over the decade from 1991 until 2001, Gazprom sales of gas to other CIS states were more than halved. What remained, moreover, was chiefly deliveries as payment for the transit of gas via Ukraine, Belarus, and Moldova. By the end of the Yeltsin era, Gazprom had withdrawn almost fully from trade with other CIS states.

In the meantime, the company had achieved little to no increase in gas production. Its failure to exploit the substantial resources under its control was especially striking when compared to the performance of independent Russian gas producers like Novatek, Nortgaz, and indeed ITERA. Its lackluster performance would last well into the Putin era.

Privatizing Russian Oil

The fate of Russian oil would be very different. The last Soviet minister of oil did not have the clout to rival the achievement of Chernomyrdin in preserving his ministry as a monolith. In September 1991, the Ministry of Oil was transformed into a joint stock company, named Rosneftegaz. But its assets would not long remain under unified control.

The Russian oil industry was subjected to subdivision and privatization, resulting in a near dozen formally independent oil companies. The leading actors would come from a variety of directions, representing insiders as well as (initial) outsiders. Some would be skilled managers, meaning that despite shady operations and massive personal enrichment, some companies would perform quite well in their core business of oil production. Across the board, the oil industry would also be opened up to participation by foreign oil majors in a process that would be rife with serious controversy.

The first spinoff from Rosneftegaz was created in November 1991, when the acting minister of oil, Vagit Alekperov, set aside three oil fields—Langepaz, Urengoi, and Kogalym—that he packaged into a new entity named Lukoil. Placed under his own control as CEO, Lukoil remains to date one of the major Russian oil companies.

In 1993, two further companies of subsequent renown—Yukos and Surgutneftegaz—were spun off. While the former would end up controlled by Mikhail Khodorkovsky, destined to become the wealthiest of all the Russian oligarchs, the latter was taken over by another prominent insider, Vladimir Bogdanov, whose role at the Ministry of Oil had been to supervise precisely that entity.

Although greatly diminished, the parent company, now renamed Rosneft, still accounted for more than 60 percent of the country's oil output. This was soon to change. The real watershed in the transformation of the Russian oil industry arrived in 1995.

Being in dire need of funds to cover gaping holes in the budget, the government embarked on a process of "loans for shares," whereby a group of private bankers advanced credits against collateral in the form of government-held blocks of shares in strategic industries. As the government did not and perhaps never even intended to repay the loans, the banks were allowed to recover their money by auctioning off the collateral. This they did to themselves, in rigged proceedings where there was rarely more than one bidder.

The end result was that a small set of well-connected operators were allowed to acquire major stakes in the country's most valuable industries at rock-bottom prices. This was the origin of the creation of the Russian "oligarchy" that would dominate Russian politics for decades to come. Private financial fortunes amassed via short-term speculation on currency markets and in government securities could now be transformed into substantial holdings of real assets with serious worth.

Given the prominent role that would be played by Rosneft in Vladimir Putin's subsequent "authoritarian restoration," it is intriguing to note how close it too came to being thrown to the wolves, along with the rest of the assets of the former Ministry of Oil. In 1998, still desperate to cover gaping holes in the budget, the Kiriyenko government tried but failed to auction it off.

ACCEPTING FOREIGN PARTNERS

Proceeding to the parallel involvement of foreign energy companies, the first steps were taken on Sakhalin Island, located off the east coast of the Russian mainland. The presence in this region of substantial hydrocarbon reserves had been known since the late nineteenth century, but due to the severity of the climate and the need to engage in technologically challenging offshore drilling, no serious operation was undertaken in the Soviet era.

Following the Soviet breakup, the Russian government decided to allow the entry of foreign companies. This implied accepting production sharing agreements (PSAs), whereby the foreign partner would be allowed to recoup all costs before the sharing of proceeds could begin. Although the Kremlin would later express great regret over this decision, at the time it did not have much choice. With the price of oil at just over $20 per barrel, Russia was in a financially and politically weak position.

The first PSA was concluded in 1994, for Royal Dutch Shell to explore the giant Sakhalin II gas field. Having acquired 55 percent of the shares, it assumed control over operations with no Russian participation. Phase 1 involved a giant offshore production platform that began delivering Russia's first offshore oil in 1999. Phase 2 also involved a liquefied natural gas plant that reached full capacity by the end of 2010.

A second PSA was concluded with ExxonMobil in 1996 to develop the Sakhalin I oil and gas field. Compared to the Shell venture, ExxonMobil took longer to get on line, beginning production only in 2005. It was different also in having major Russian participation; although ExxonMobil assumed operating responsibility, it had no more than a 30 percent share. Again, in contrast to Sakhalin II, Sakhalin I passed cost recovery after only three years of operation.

The high-water mark of foreign involvement was reached in June 2003 with a joint venture between BP and the Russian Alfa Group. The merger called for the two sides to contribute their respective assets in Russian oil and gas, creating the country's third-largest oil company. It was not only the size of the deal—$14 billion—that caused banner headlines to appear. Even more important was the fact that BP would enter into the new venture—named TNK-BP—as an equal partner.

Markets hailed what was then generally viewed as the start of a new era of strategic energy cooperation between Russia and the West. The anticipated next step was a deal between ExxonMobil and Yukos, at the time Russia's flagship oil company. The stated vision of Mikhail Khodorkovsky, the CEO of Yukos, was to create a privately owned—and thus controlled—route for the export of Russian oil via Murmansk to the United States.

If successful, he would have provided himself with important outside protection in his increasingly confrontational relation to President Putin. But within the coming year, the Kremlin reversed course and proceeded to roll back the influence of foreign oil on all fronts.

Privatizing Exploration

During the Soviet era, responsibility for geological mapping and exploration rested with the Ministry of Geology. It enjoyed high political priority, being staffed by highly professional specialists educated at fine academic institutions. During the turbulent 1990s, that all changed. As government financing plummeted, massive reductions in staff led to cutbacks in exploration, which in turn increased the dependence of Russian oil and gas industries on a small number of supergiant fields that were entering terminal decline.

The government appears to have believed that the newly privatized energy companies would find it in their own interests to shoulder the burden of continued exploration. This might also have happened had they been provided with adequate incentives to make longer-term commitments. But that was not to be.

As the Putin era unfolded, it was becoming clear that the outlook for both oil and gas had become heavily contingent on new fields being brought on line and on cutting-edge technology to make that possible. At a July 2008 meeting in Severodvinsk, Putin frankly noted, "The potential for growth based on the former resource base and outdated technologies has in fact been exhausted."[12] Knowing what was broken, however, was not the same as knowing how to fix it.

In the case of gas, large new discoveries had been made, ranging from the giant Kovytka field in Eastern Siberia to several smaller but jointly important fields on the Yamal Peninsula and the giant Shtokman field in the Barents Sea. The core question here concerns when and if these fields will be brought on line. The track record of poor governance at Gazprom must in this respect be viewed as very serious.

The case of oil is again different. During the chaos of the Yeltsin era, the output of oil plummeted, from levels over ten million barrels per day (bpd) at the end of the 1980s to an average of six million bpd during the 1990s. In stark contrast to the continued stagnation of gas, the Putin era would witness substantial recovery, to over nine million bpd by 2008.

The latter was partly due to the skills of the new private owners, but the real key to the production upsurge in the early 2000s was that "the most profitable private companies are the ones that have squeezed the cream of their reserves the hardest." The inevitable consequence of this "predatory approach" was an enhanced need for more intensive exploration. [13]

PIPELINE POLITICS

When the Soviet Union built its first export pipelines to Europe, there was an obvious ambition to trade gas for much-needed hard currency. But there was also the added benefit of making the Europeans dependent on that gas. As this took place at the peak of the Cold War, it was not surprising that US president Ronald Reagan issued stark warnings to his NATO partners about willingly accepting such dependence. But the Europeans would not listen. Today, in consequence, the EU depends on Russia for about one-third of its gas, and the politics surrounding this dependence has become increasingly conflict ridden.

The key feature of a pipeline is that once it has been built, the parties are locked into mutual dependence. If the relation is purely commercial, this need not be much of a problem, but if it becomes politicized, then there will be no end to trouble. In the wake of the Soviet breakup, the Kremlin soon enough discovered that the dependence of states in its neighborhood on piped Russian gas could be exploited for political gain.

While governments that were deemed to be "friendly" would be offered discounted prices and secure deliveries, those that were not would be required to pay "market" prices and face threats of delivery disruptions. Those that found themselves in the "unfriendly" category would voice loud complaints about how Russia was wielding its "gas weapon" to make neighbors more pliant.

Although Ukraine was far from alone in getting the rough end of the stick, its size and strategic location between Russia and the EU would ensure that it was at the forefront of such confrontations. On two occasions, in January 2006 and again in January 2009, a standoff between Moscow and Kiev over the pricing of gas led Gazprom to shut down its deliveries. Since gas consumed by Ukraine is taken from pipelines that also transport gas to Europe, shutting down the flow to Ukraine also implied shutting down the flow to countries that had now become EU member states.

In its ambition to counter this type of behavior, the EU has been marred by the absence of consensus on how to manage the overall relation to Russia. While Germany has remained positive toward increasing its dependence on Russian gas via the Nord Stream pipelines that transport gas via the Baltic from Vyborg in Russia directly to Greifswald in Germany, Poland and the Baltic states have voiced strong opposition, to the point of even conjuring up the threat of a new Russo-German pact against Poland.

Although the tensions over Ukraine have created banner headlines, Russian pipeline politics have been about much more than merely Gazprom and Ukraine. Relations with the newly independent republics in Central Asia and in the South Caucasus have also figured prominently.

While Moscow was the center of Soviet power, emphasis was placed on developing energy resources within the Russian Federation. When the Soviet Union collapsed, the governments in newly independent republics to the south turned to foreign energy majors for help in developing their long-neglected energy resources. As a result, Kazakhstan, Turkmenistan, and Azerbaijan were found to possess substantial reserves, mainly but not exclusively offshore in the Caspian Sea. These finds would have important implications, commercial as well as geopolitical.

Frequent reference would be made to the Great Game over Central Asia that was played out in the nineteenth century between the Russian and British Empires. This time around, the players had multiplied to include not only Russia and Britain but also China, America, and the European Union. China in particular would enter the fray with a voracious appetite for energy to feed its booming economy.

The problem for the new actors was that absent means of transportation, energy in the ground has no value. Gas extraction in particular would simply not be possible without pipelines, and the existing pipeline grid was controlled by Russia. Further developments would in consequence be heavily focused on pipelines. In the early stages it looked like Moscow would be able to retain its control, but that would change.

The first challenge to Russian hegemony emerged from Kazakhstan, where exploitation of the giant Tengiz field would serve to redraw the map of global oil. Already discovered in 1979, it is the sixth-largest oil field in the world. Development began in 1993. In 2000, the role of Kazakhstan was enhanced even further with the discovery of the giant offshore Kashagan field, held at the time to be one of the most important discoveries in the world in the past thirty years. Following numerous delays, commercial production was finally begun in 2016.

When exploitation of the Tengiz field began, Moscow was successful in ensuring that the export pipeline was routed over Russian territory to the Russian Black Sea port of Novorossiisk. While Kazakhstan and its foreign partners thus remained firmly within the Russian orbit, the case of Azerbaijan would present a very different story.

In 1994, Azeri president Heydar Aliyev concluded a PSA with a BP-led consortium to begin exploiting the country's giant offshore oil and gas fields. Hailed as the "deal of the century," between 1997 and 2007 output from the Azeri-Chirag-Gunashli oil field would rise more than fourfold, triggering a boom that transformed both Azerbaijan and the way in which the regional game over oil is played. In 1999, BP added to its success with discovery of Shah Deniz, one of the largest gas condensate fields in the world.

The main reason that Azerbaijan would prove to be so important was that it dealt Russia the first real blows to its inherited transport hegemony. First was the Baku–Tbilisi–Ceyhan (BTC) pipeline, built to allow Azerbaijan to export oil via Georgia to the southern Turkish port of Ceyhan. Promoted by Washington for political reasons, it is the second-longest oil pipeline in the world after the previously mentioned Soviet-era Druzhba that links Western Siberia with Europe. First oil was pumped in 2005.

Then followed the Baku–Tbilisi–Erzurum (BTE) gas pipeline that became operational at the end of 2006. Also known as the South Caucasus Pipeline, it transports gas from the Shah Deniz field via Georgia to Turkey. The launch of the BTE was even more important than that of the BTC, in the sense that it could serve as a crucial link in a chain designed to transport substantial volumes of gas to Europe without crossing Russian territory. The reason this has remained hypothetical is that Azeri gas reserves are much too limited for this link to assume any strategic importance on its own.

A real game changer would be to construct a Trans-Caspian Pipeline (TCP) to link Azerbaijan with Turkmenistan. While total reserves in Azerbaijan are estimated at no more than 30 billion cubic meters (bcm), the combined long-term potential of gas from Kazakhstan, Uzbekistan, and above all Turkmenistan is in the range of 150–200 bcm, corresponding to about two-thirds of Russia's long-term potential.[14]

The possibility of actually building the TCP had been under periodic discussion since the mid-1990s but had been repeatedly delayed by disputes over the exploitation of oil and gas resources in the middle of the Caspian Sea. The speedy and successful construction of the BTE provided new impetus. By proposing to build its own pipeline, Nabucco, to transport gas into southeastern Europe, the EU threatened to deprive Moscow of its hegemony over energy flows from the Caspian basin to customers in Europe.

This challenge in turn placed in focus the need to secure long-term control over the sources of gas in Central Asia. Recalling the new Great Game, this is where Turkmenistan enters center stage. During the Soviet era, it had been an important provider of gas to other Soviet republics. Following independence, it embarked on a dual policy of exploiting this position, demanding higher prices and breaking its dependence on pipelines leading north to Russia.

The outcome on the former count was a long series of incidents involving pricing disputes and delivery disruptions. Given that the bulk of the gas it took from Turkmenistan was destined for Ukraine and onward to Europe, Gazprom agreed to substantial price hikes, firmly convinced it would be able to pass the burden on to its customers in the EU.

The threat of finding alternative routes for gas out of Central Asia was more serious. It was brought to a head in 2006 when China concluded a deal on a seven-thousand-kilometer pipeline that would allow it to purchase gas for thirty years starting in 2009. Although Russia would remain the major route for Turkmen export, the China deal indicated that the playing field was being widened. The Kremlin could no longer count on retaining its hegemony. The main cause for concern was that the pipeline to China would be followed by a pipeline route to Europe in the form of a TCP and Nabucco.

Estimates of total Turkmen gas reserves ran so high, to potentially twenty-two trillion cubic meters, that there was plenty of room to play a "multivectored" game of courting several partners. In 2006, the newly discovered Yolotan-Osman field was claimed to hold no less than seven trillion cubic meters of gas, representing more than double the reserves in Russia's giant Shtokman field. Yet, although Ashgabat embarked on gradually increasing foreign policy activism, Russia still appeared to have the upper hand.

The peak of the Kremlin's ambition to secure the Caspian basin was reached in the spring of 2007. Following lengthy negotiations, President Putin finally managed to secure a deal with Kazakhstan, Turkmenistan, and Uzbekistan to build a "Pre-Caspian," or Prikaspiiskoe, gas pipeline. Designed to hug the northern shore of the Caspian, it was to ensure that the bulk of Central Asian gas would continue flowing north into the Russian grid. The deal was generally viewed as a final Russian victory in the Great Game.

It was at this time, when it began to look as though a resurgent Russia was about to walk off with the spoils, that the notion of an emerging Russian "energy superpower" made its appearance. In the words of Fiona Hill, "Russia is back on the global strategic and economic map. It has transformed itself from a defunct military superpower into a new energy superpower."[15]

AN ENERGY SUPERPOWER

The first two terms of Vladimir Putin's presidency were marked by a truly seismic shift in Russian oil revenues. In market economies, price and quantity normally move in opposite directions. In the case of Russian oil, they began rising in tandem, and quite dramatically too. The price per barrel for benchmark Brent oil went from a low of $9.82 in December 1998 to $25.51 in January 2000 and to a peak of $144.5 in July 2008. Meanwhile, production volumes increased by more than 50 percent.

The sudden spike in petrodollar inflow had two rather unfortunate political consequences. One was that it generated a sense of complacency that put an effective end to the ambitions for radical economic reform that marked Putin's first years in power. By 2003, that game was for all intents and purposes over. Why engage in politically painful reforms when you can live high off the hog on oil revenues?

Even more sinister was that the overarching ambition to make Russia great again had found a tempting outlet. The deep economic depression during the 1990s had brought devastation to the country's erstwhile military superpower. Hopes in the early 2000s that rapid economic growth would build an economic superpower were also quickly frustrated. As the petrodollars began gushing in, the Kremlin was deluded into believing that by wielding its "energy weapon" it would succeed in reclaiming its coveted role as a major player in global affairs.

The envisioned creation of a Russian "energy superpower" would proceed along three tracks. First was the need to break the hold of the oligarchs and restore state control over the energy complex. Second was the associated need to roll back the influence of foreign oil companies, and third was the need to harness control over pipelines as a means of getting a stranglehold over the energy supply to other countries, including those inside the EU.

Breaking the Oligarchs

The task of restoring state control over the country's energy assets yet again brings home the difference between oil and gas. Viktor Chernomyrdin's success in preserving the assets of the former Ministry of Gas under unified control meant that restoring state control over Gazprom would mainly be a question of a changing of the guard. Once he had been elected president, Vladimir Putin proceeded to do precisely that.

In June 2000, Chernomyrdin was replaced by Dmitry Medvedev as chairman of the board, and in May the following year, Vyakhirev was in turn replaced by Aleksei Miller as CEO. Both of the new appointments were "friends of Putin," harking back to his days in St. Petersburg. While the new management team would prove quite successful in clawing back assets transferred to ITERA under Yeltsin, their skills as managers of a gas company would not be as impressive.

While independent gas producers like Novatek and Nortgaz scored a real takeoff and oil companies greatly increased their output of "associated gas," Gazprom registered a slight decline in output. Merely changing the guard had not led to improvement in the company's performance as a gas producer.

Restoring state control over the oil industry would be an altogether different matter. The process of insider privatization had created companies that in some cases provided their owners with ample resources to challenge the Kremlin. A case in point was Yukos, whose CEO, Mikhail Khodorkovsky, escalated his conflict with Putin to an open challenge for the presidency. The Kremlin retaliated by arresting and imprisoning him and by destroying Yukos.

The company was first presented with a claim for back taxes that would eventually reach $28 billion. It then had its assets frozen, meaning it could not settle the tax claim, and in conclusion its assets were sold at a series of rigged auctions. The prized asset was Yuganskneftegaz, representing about 60 percent of the Yukos total. On December 19, 2004, it was sold at an auction to recoup outstanding taxes.

Although Gazprom had been the originally intended buyer, the risk of international legal action to seize its assets abroad was deemed to be so large that a last-minute swap was made. The designated main beneficiary instead turned out to be Rosneft, at the time the only piece of the old Soviet oil industry that remained in state hands.

The single bidder at the auction was an obscure company named Baikal Finance Group, which had been created only two weeks before the event. The price it paid was $9.3 billion, representing just over half of the estimated market value. Only days later, it was in turn taken over by Rosneft, which also had been the source of financing for the deal.

The destruction of Yukos Oil stands out as one of the most controversial events of the Putin era. The degree of sheer vengefulness was such that Yukos, in Gustafson's words, "was not so much plundered as lynched."[16] Andrei Illarionov, at the time still Putin's senior economic adviser, also blasted the auction of Yuganskneftegaz as the "scam of the year."[17]

Following the absorption of Yuganskneftegaz, Rosneft emerged as Russia's second-largest oil company, producing 74.4 million tons. By 2010, with the giant Vankor field on line, the company reached 115.8 million tons. It was then also one of the leading independent gas producers in Russia, with an annual output of natural and associated gas of about 12 bcm. The CEO of Rosneft, Igor Sechin, emerged as one of the most powerful men in Russia, with very close links to President Putin.

Gazprom, however, would not be left without gain. The conclusion of the Yukos affair had sent a powerful message to other members of the oligarchy, who would prove more than willing to bow to the Kremlin's demands. In September 2005, oligarch Roman Abramovich accepted to surrender the Sibneft oil company to Gazprom for $13.1 billion. It was the biggest-ever takeover in Russia, and it brought the company a fair bit of the way toward becoming an energy supergiant.

Rolling Back Foreign Oil

The ambition to roll back the influence of the foreign oil majors began where the first steps toward foreign involvement had been taken, namely, at Sakhalin. The Kremlin was particularly angered by the PSAs, which most observers would subsequently agree had been inherently unfair to Russia. Speaking in

2007, Putin would describe the Sakhalin II PSA as a "colonial project" that had nothing to do with the interests of the Russian Federation.

There were grounds for resentment. The PSA with Shell was signed when Russia was on its knees, giving the company the right to recoup all costs plus a 17.5 percent rate of return before Russia would get a 10 percent share of the proceeds. The Kremlin felt vindicated in its anger by the fact that the cost of the project had ballooned from an original estimate of $10 billion in 1997 to $20 billion in 2005, postponing the time when Russia would begin to receive income. This said, the means that were used to redress the imbalance came close to sheer extortion.

Shell suddenly found itself the target of a campaign claiming that serious ecological damage was being done. Faced with threats of a $50 million lawsuit and the risk of having its concession revoked, by December 2006 the company agreed to reduce its stake from 55 to 27.5 percent, allowing Gazprom to pick up 50 percent plus one share. Following this transfer of control, nothing more would be said about ecological damage.

The next victim was the TNK-BP joint venture. At the time of the original deal, BP had nurtured grand ambitions to develop the giant Kovytka gas field in East Siberia. Those plans had entailed building a pipeline to China, which Gazprom refused to accept. Faced with an added blank refusal to have its gas pumped westward, the company was restricted to the local market. As this fell far short of volumes stipulated in the licensing agreement, TNK-BP was faced with the same threat that had confronted Shell, namely, losing its license. In June 2007, it agreed to sell its stake.

Then followed ExxonMobil. Its operation of the Sakhalin I oil and gas field had also been linked from the very outset with plans for exports to China. In October 2006, it signed a preliminary agreement with the China National Petroleum Corporation. But Gazprom instead insisted that the full output from Sakhalin I be sent via its own Sakhalin–Khabarovsk–Vladivostok pipeline. In May 2009, the consortium agreed to sell 20 percent of Sakhalin I gas to Gazprom.

Leaving Sakhalin Island and Eastern Siberia, Gazprom would also become embroiled in controversy at the other end of the country. Offshore in the Russian sector of the Barents Sea lies the Shtokman field, one of the world's largest natural gas fields. Discovered in 1988, its estimated final output is comparable to the annual gas output of Norway.

Due to the extreme Arctic conditions prevailing in the area and a sea depth that varies from 320 to 340 meters, it was realized early on that Gazprom would not be able to go it alone. But the Kremlin was no longer ready to accept genuine partnership with foreigner companies. In 2008, Gazprom agreed with Total and StatoilHydro that they would be involved in organizing the design, financing, construction, and operation of the Shtokman infrastructure. Upon completion, their shares would be transferred to Gazprom.

It was symptomatic of the changing times that where the early Sakhalin pioneers—Shell and ExxonMobil—had succeeded in getting the Kremlin to accept PSAs that were clearly biased against Russia, in the Shtokman case the foreigners ended up offering their technology for a mere fee rather than an ownership stake or even a share in output. Putin's Russia had morphed into a very different kind of partner than that presided over by Yeltsin. The times of bargain basement dealing had come and gone.

Rounding off the story of trouble faced by Big Oil in Russia, in the summer of 2008, TNK-BP was shaken by a bitter internal power struggle that caused its CEO, Robert Dudley, to flee the country and be replaced by the president of the Russian Alfa Group, Mikhail Fridman. Given that TNK-BP accounted for a quarter of BP's output and a fifth of its total reserves, this was no small matter. But the saga of BP involvement in Russia was set to continue, with surprising new twists and turns.

In January 2011, markets were stunned by the announcement of a major deal between BP and Rosneft, aimed at exploring the Kara Sea on Russia's Arctic continental shelf. The deal entailed a share swap whereby BP would become the biggest nonstate shareholder in Rosneft, which is 75 percent controlled by the Russian government, and Rosneft would become the second-largest shareholder in BP.

The deal seemed to ensure ironclad political protection from the very top. Yet when the Russian Alfa Group co-owners of TNK-BP brought legal action, Prime Minister Putin did not have any objection. Following a four-month legal battle, BP had to face the fact that its proposed alliance with Rosneft had collapsed. The prize of Arctic hydrocarbon exploitation was again back on the market.

The next round was a strategic exploration partnership between Rosneft and ExxonMobil. Having long and positive experience of working together on Sakhalin, in August 2011 the two announced the first in a series of agreements that would entail investing up to $500 billion in developing Russia's Arctic and Black Sea oil reserves. In October 2012, Rosneft added that it would itself take over TNK-BP. The Alfa Group was paid $28 billion in cash to get out, and BP was offered a package of cash and a close to 20 percent stake in Rosneft.

The stage appeared to be set for long-term cooperation between Rosneft and ExxonMobil, taking the exploration for oil to entirely new levels. But then followed the crisis in Ukraine and the imposition of Western sanctions that target both Rosneft and its CEO, Igor Sechin. Following a drawn-out conflict with the US Treasury Department, in March 2018 ExxonMobil announced it was walking away from its Russian ventures, excepting that on Sakhalin.

A Pipeline Stranglehold

The very mention of the notion of an "energy superpower" presumes that the possession of large reserves of energy may be somehow "weaponized," which is a highly dubious proposition. It can, to begin with, not include oil. Oil does mean revenue, which in turn may help boost military production and thus indirectly support ambitions to achieve power. But oil cannot be construed as a "weapon" in its own right.

To the extent that Russia does possess an "energy weapon," it must be in the form of pipelines for gas. Threats by suppliers of oil to cut off deliveries may be countered by turning to other suppliers, who may reroute their tankers. In the case of gas, that is not possible. Countries connected to the Russian grid of gas export pipelines would find that they were vulnerable to Russian pressure.

As discussed above, Gazprom would not be shy of using political pricing, coupled with threats of supply shutoffs, to reward countries held to be loyal and to punish those that were not. Ukraine would find itself over time on both sides of the fence. Following the gas wars in 2006 and 2009, the Kremlin turned around and began offering substantial discounts on gas in return for political concessions. If Kiev abstained from seeking deeper relations with the EU, it would get both credits and cheap gas. Following the collapse of the Yanukovych government in 2014, all such concessions were withdrawn.

On a parallel track, the Kremlin also launched a project to reduce its dependence on Ukraine as a transit country by constructing bypass pipelines. To the north was the Nord Stream project that would pump gas to Germany via the Baltic Sea. To the south was South Stream, designed to pump gas via the Black Sea into the Balkans and Central Europe.

While Nord Stream I came on line in 2011, South Stream would end up being blocked by EU regulators. But the outlook for Ukraine remains somber. When Nord Stream II and the replacement southern option Turk Stream come on line, Gazprom will no longer need Ukraine. Given the importance to its budget of transit fees, this will greatly exacerbate Kiev's vulnerability to Russian pressure.

An additional ambition from the Gazprom side was to increase its commercial presence inside the EU by purchasing downstream assets. In Germany and the Netherlands in particular, it was very successful in picking up stakes in gas distribution companies. The crunch came in 2006, when British regulators moved to block an anticipated bid by Gazprom for Centrica, Britain's largest gas distributor. Gazprom CEO Aleksei Miller responded with a thinly veiled threat that the EU should not block Gazprom's "international ambitions" or the company could redirect its gas instead to markets in China and Japan.

By the time Putin handed over power to Dmitry Medvedev, who was duly elected president in March 2008, the rhetoric from the Kremlin was assertive. With only months to go before the global financial crisis would strike, the Russian elites seemed confident that their country had been returned to its rightful place as a great power.

The Europeans did have cause to be concerned. A complete cessation of the Russian gas flow at the time would have been calamitous for municipal heating systems and for energy-intensive industries. But as subsequent events would show, the Kremlin's assertive foreign policy rested on a serious underestimation of the opposition. The outcome would be a classic case of "policy blowback."

Western democracies may be slow to respond to challenges, but once they do they are capable of harnessing considerable soft power. Propelled into action by the 2009 gas war, which left several EU member states freezing in the dead of a very cold winter, the EU took a series of highly effective measures aimed at diversification of the sources of supply, at the construction of connector pipelines to allow gas to be transported between EU member states, and at conservation measures.

The core of its Third Energy Package, adopted in the fall of 2009, was a call for "ownership unbundling," meaning that gas producers would not also be allowed to operate transmission systems. This clause was so clearly pointed at Russia that it came to be known as the "Gazprom clause." Yet, in a further illustration of the lack of internal EU cohesion, the call for unbundling would remain to be implemented, and Germany would remain supportive of Nord Stream.

This said, by the time Putin was elected to the presidency for a third term, in March 2012, the situation had been fundamentally transformed. A complete shutdown of the Russian gas flow to Europe would be problematic but no longer catastrophic. The edge of the "gas weapon" had been blunted.

OUTLOOK

The outlook for Russian energy is heavily marked by the fact that all the major fields in operation, oil as well as gas, have long since reached their peak and are now being depleted. In the case of Samotlor, so much water has been injected to maintain pressure that what comes to the surface is 90 percent water, causing it to be branded "the largest water company in the world."[18] Given how dependent the Russian economy has become on revenues from energy exports, this has serious long-term implications.

During the good years of abundant petrodollar inflow, the Russian government acted prudently to set aside a considerable part of that income into a precautionary Reserve Fund, to serve as a cushion against drops in the price of oil. In the aftermath of the global financial crisis, it served that purpose very well. By the end of 2017, when the fund had been exhausted, the Ministry of Finance had enjoyed sufficient time to ensure that the federal budget would break even at oil prices just over $50 per barrel, less than half of what had been the case when the price of oil peaked.

While this goes to prove that the consequences of being heavily dependent on oil revenue can be managed, skillful fiscal policy cannot remove the fact that Russia remains dependent on resource extraction, chiefly, albeit not exclusively, energy.

The outlook for energy production in the short term is that Russia will remain on a plateau of reasonably stable output levels. Although there is little to suggest that Gazprom will improve its performance anytime soon, it is likely going to be able to maintain current output levels for some years to come.

The oil companies have on their side succeeded in "creaming" their existing fields to allow a continued uptick in output. Even if these increases have only been marginal, they have allowed new records of production to be set. Such forced extraction is clearly not sustainable. New fields must be both discovered and brought on line, and this is not achievable without foreign cooperation, which in turn will not materialize while Western sanctions remain in place.

Russia does have abundant reserves in the ground. The Arctic offshore in particular has been estimated by the US Geological Survey to hold one-fifth of all still undiscovered global reserves of oil and gas. It was the lure of these riches that prompted ExxonMobil to conclude its massive deal with Rosneft.

Yet, even if the sanctions were to be lifted, this would not automatically translate into a renewed Russian energy boom. The Arctic offshore represents challenges that make it a very long-term undertaking, requiring high energy prices to be commercially viable. The sensitive ecosystem also makes it vulnerable to environmental protests. Similar caution pertains to new fields in Eastern Siberia and the Far East that are marked by severe cold and difficult geology. Successful exploration and exploitation will require cutting-edge technology that again makes the costs of extraction very high.

While the longer-term outlook for sustained Russian energy production must in consequence be viewed as gloomy, the more political shorter-term outlook for the construction of pipelines presents a more nuanced picture.

In its relations to the EU, Gazprom looks set to have continued success in building pipelines to bypass Ukraine. Nord Stream II is expected to come on line in 2019. Although South Stream has been abandoned, that project did help to fatally undermine the EU's own Nabucco, which may well have been the real purpose. The replacement Turk Stream is also due to come on line in 2019. While this ensures a continued grip over the European market for gas,

Gazprom has been forced to accept concessions on price that impact heavily on its bottom line.

Looking toward the east, the Kremlin is less likely to remain successful in building pipelines to China. While Russia was in a financially weak position, Beijing was keen to strike megadeals on Russian oil that created banner headlines. The Middle Kingdom is not equally keen to do the same in gas. An important reason is that it has built an extensive network of pipelines of its own into Central Asia that ensure it has an adequate supply of gas for its western provinces.

The combined outcome for Gazprom has been that its previously mentioned ambition to ensure continued hegemony over the flow of gas out of Central Asia via a "Pre-Caspian" pipeline has been scrapped, and long-discussed plans to build an Altai pipeline to pump gas from Western Siberia to China have been placed in serious doubt. This enhances the company's geographical dilemma of having its main reserves in the east and its main markets in the west.

What may still provide some relief is the "Power of Siberia" pipeline, which is destined to carry gas from fields in the Far East. It will provide gas for the northeast in China, where gas is in short supply, and is expected to come on line at the end of 2019. It will, however, still leave open the question of broader infrastructure development that will be needed to fully exploit the energy complex in Eastern Siberian and the Far East.

The bottom line of the story of Russian energy is that the country has locked itself into a long-term strategy of dependence on resource extraction, coupled with authoritarian, predatory governance that impairs the introduction of efficient markets and production techniques. This is a legacy that will be very hard to overcome, even if Western sanctions are lifted and cooperation is resumed.

DISCUSSION QUESTIONS

1. Why is it important to distinguish between oil and gas in the Russian energy complex?
2. What is the "geographic dilemma" of Russian energy?
3. Has the history of foreign involvement in Russian oil been a success?
4. How has Russia wielded its "gas weapon"?
5. Who are the players in the new "Great Game" over energy in Central Asia?

SUGGESTED READINGS

Fortescue, Stephen. *Russia's Oil Barons and Metals Magnates: Oligarchs and the State in Transition.* New York: Palgrave Macmillan, 2006.

Goldman, Marshall I. *Petrostate: Putin, Power, and the New Russia.* Oxford: Oxford University Press, 2008.

Gustafson, Thane. *Wheel of Fortune: The Battle for Oil and Power in Russia.* Cambridge, MA: Belknap, 2012.

Hedlund, Stefan. *Putin's Energy Agenda: The Contradictions of Russia's Resource Wealth.* Boulder, CO: Lynne Rienner, 2014.

Stulberg, Adam N. *Well-Oiled Diplomacy: Strategic Manipulation and Russia's Energy Statecraft in Eurasia.* Albany: State University of New York Press, 2007.

Yergin, Daniel. *The Prize: The Epic Quest for Oil, Money, and Power.* London: Simon & Schuster, 1991.

NOTES

1. Thane Gustafson, *Wheel of Fortune: The Battle for Oil and Power in Russia* (Cambridge, MA: Belknap, 2012), 3.

2. Steve Levine, *The Oil and the Glory: The Pursuit of Empire and Fortune on the Caspian Sea* (New York: Random House, 2007), chaps. 1–2 passim.

3. The story of early oil, and of early conflicts around oil, is told in Daniel Yergin, *The Prize: The Epic Quest for Oil, Money, and Power* (London: Simon & Schuster, 1991), part 1.

4. Stephen Kotkin, *Armageddon Averted: The Soviet Collapse, 1970–2000* (Washington, DC: Brookings Institution, 2001), 15.

5. Gustafson, *Wheel of Fortune*, 28–29.

6. Thane Gustafson, *The Politics of Soviet Energy under Brezhnev and Gorbachev* (Princeton, NJ: Princeton University Press, 1989), 64.

7. Gustafson, *The Politics of Soviet Energy*, 55–56.

8. Gustafson, *The Politics of Soviet Energy*, 39–40.

9. Gustafson, *The Politics of Soviet Energy*, 67.

10. Yegor Gaidar, *Collapse of an Empire: Lessons for Modern Russia* (Washington, DC: Brookings Institution, 2007).

11. Gustafson, *Wheel of Fortune*, 466.

12. Arild Moe and Valery Kryukov, "Oil Exploration in Russia: Prospects for Reforming a Crucial Sector," *Eurasian Geography and Economics* 51, no. 3 (2010): 313.

13. Leslie Dienes, "Observations on the Problematic Potential of Russian Oil and the Complexities of Siberia," *Eurasian Geography and Economics* 45, no. 5 (2004): 325 passim.

14. Roland Götz, "The Southern Gas Corridor and Europe's Gas Supply," *Caucasus Analytical Digest*, no. 3 (2009): 2.

15. Fiona Hill, *Energy Empire: Oil, Gas and Russia's Revival* (London: Foreign Policy Centre, 2004), i, http://fpc.org.uk/fsblob/307.pdf.

16. Gustafson, *Wheel of Fortune*, 314.

17. "Putin Aide Slams Yukos Selloff," BBC News, December 28, 2004, http://news.bbc.co.uk/2/hi/europe/4129875.stm.

18. Gustafson, *Wheel of Fortune*, 191.

Chapter Fifteen

The Military

Bettina Renz

The rapid annexation of Crimea and the surprise Russian involvement in the Syrian civil war led many commentators to conclude that the West had seriously underestimated Russian military capabilities. There may be some truth in that, but now overestimation is the greater danger.

—Tor Bukkvoll[1]

For more than two decades following the end of the Cold War, Western interest in the Russian military steadily decreased. Given the ongoing decay of the country's armed forces and the significant operational shortcomings their troops routinely displayed in the various conflicts they fought across the former Soviet region, it seemed that Russia's days as a global military power were over and that it was of relevance, at best, as an example of a "failed exercise in defense decision making."[2] Since the annexation of Crimea in spring 2014, developments in the Russian military have reemerged as a major concern not only for its neighbors, but also for the West. As noted by Tor Bukkvoll above, assessments today can tend to overstate the scale of the changes that have occurred, not least because the subject had been neglected for so long. This chapter aims to provide some important historical, political, and international context required for a nuanced analysis of recent events. Outlining military reforms, developments in Russian military thinking, and continuity and change in the Kremlin's views on the utility of military force as an instrument of foreign policy, it suggests that the transformation of Russian military capabilities and defense policy was neither as sudden nor as comprehensive as it appears.

THE RUSSIAN ARMED FORCES AND POST-SOVIET TRANSITION

The fairly sudden collapse of the Soviet Union did not take only the outside world by surprise. It presented the leaders of the fifteen newly independent states, including Boris Yeltsin as the president of the Russian Federation, with the unprecedented task of creating the political, societal, and economic structures and conditions required for their countries to function on an even basic level. Given the scale of the mission of state building, and the fact that Cold War tensions were much diminished, plans for systematic military reforms were not considered the highest priority. Various reform programs were instigated during Yeltsin's time in office, demonstrating that the awareness of the necessity of such reforms was certainly apparent; but none of them resulted in fundamental modernization.[3] The country's conventional military capabilities deteriorated, as did the image of its armed forces, both internationally and within Russia itself. Yeltsin's failure to push through reforms was often put down to his lack of political willingness to go against the wishes of the armed forces' conservative leadership.[4] It is important to consider, however, that other significant obstacles stood in the way of structured reforms during the 1990s.

The fate of the defunct Soviet armed forces, the personnel and assets of which were located across a vast region, including in Eastern Europe, was the most immediate concern. The process of relocating military personnel back to the Russian Federation in itself was costly and preoccupied the leadership for several years.[5] Negotiations with the other newly independent states over the ownership of Soviet military hardware and bases were another difficult and time-intensive endeavor. In the case of particularly sensitive and valuable installations, such as the Sevastopol naval base, disputes were not resolved until well into the 1990s.[6] Given the weakness of the Russian economy at the time, even a comparatively high proportion of the gross domestic product (GDP) spent on defense—around 4 percent throughout Yeltsin's time in office—amounted to very little, especially compared to the volume of funding the Soviet armed forces had grown accustomed to during the Cold War.[7] The necessity to relocate personnel and assets back to Russia, in addition to the costs attached to retiring tens of thousands of former soldiers in order to reduce the size of the military to a more realistic level, meant that little time and money were left for significant modernization in the early post-Soviet years.

The newly created Russian armed forces were also immediately drawn into various violent conflicts that had erupted across the former Soviet territory, for example, in Transnistria, Abkhazia, Tajikistan, and within Russia's own borders in Chechnya from 1994. These deployments were of significant scale, with estimates of around forty thousand Russian troops engaged in regional wars by the mid-1990s.[8] All of these conflicts continued for many years. Russian soldiers fought in some of these areas even before the country's Ministry of Defense was set up in May 1992, let alone before there had been a chance to reform or to prepare them for conflict scenarios other than conventional warfare in a European theater, which they had been trained for during the Cold War. The management of these ongoing conflicts preoccupied the political and military leaderships and made the pursuit of structured and well-thought-out reforms less likely, if not impossible.

Finally, while it is one thing to note that Russian military reforms during the 1990s were botched, it is quite another thing to assume that there was a clear pathway toward successful reforms that the leadership simply failed to follow. Yeltsin's government faced a task that went far beyond merely *reforming* or *modernizing* an already existing military. Instead, the Russian leadership had to *create* armed forces for a newly established state, operating in a domestic and global context that was fundamentally different from what went before. Military reforms in Russia were not a simple matter of downsizing, professionalization, or procuring up-to-date technology. Instead, all-encompassing structural, organizational, and doctrinal changes were required to make the armed forces suitable for the country's new system of governance and the post–Cold War security environment. When the Soviet Union had collapsed, it was far from clear what kind of military Russia needed or wanted, because its future, especially regarding its role as a global actor in a changing international security environment, was so uncertain.[9]

Russian military reforms were never going to be an easy undertaking and, for the reasons outlined above, very little systematic change was achieved during the 1990s. It is important to note, however, that Moscow's desire to reestablish and maintain a powerful military per se was never in question. Russia's self-perception as a great power has been a central feature in the country's identity dating back centuries.[10] This did not change when the Soviet Union collapsed in 1991. In the words of Margot Light, in the early post-Soviet years, "Russia was clearly not a superpower; indeed, it was questionable whether it was a Great power. Yet to ordinary people, as well as to politicians, it was unthinkable that Russia could be anything less than this."[11] Although military power is not the only characteristic on which a country's status in the international system is based, it has always been an indispensable symbol of strength for any great power, including for Russia.[12] As the Russian armed forces decayed during the 1990s, so did the country's standing as a global actor. It soon became apparent to the political leadership that a strong nuclear deterrent alone was not enough to uphold the country's great power status. The Russian Federation's first military doctrine, issued in 1993, already reflected the intention to maintain parity in conventional military strength with other great powers.[13] For the first decade of the post-Soviet era, however, this remained nothing but an unattainable ambition.

VLADIMIR PUTIN AND MILITARY MODERNIZATION

When Vladimir Putin rose to political prominence, first as prime minister in 1999 and then as president in March 2000, he made the restoration of Russia's international status as a great power, including a strong military, a priority from the outset.[14] The Second Chechen War, which commenced in autumn 1999 and was overseen by the new prime minister, revealed significant operational difficulties and reinforced the need for reforms. In a speech delivered in November 2000, Putin presented the conclusions reached from various meetings on military policy held by the Russian Security Council. Recognizing the work of service personnel operating in Chechnya, he explained that the conflict had also demonstrated the armed forces' lack of preparedness to "neutralize and rebuff any armed conflict and aggression" against Russia, which, in his words, could "come from all directions." He also noted that the operations there had come at too high a cost and that the loss of soldiers' lives was "unpardonable," making reforms a necessity. In particular, Putin emphasized the need to restore the prestige of the Russian military within the country itself, including the image of the military career as a profession, which had suffered significantly during the troubled 1990s: "The problem is directly linked with national security interests. The trust of the army in the state, and having the army 'feel good' about itself is the bedrock foundation of the state of the Armed Forces."[15]

Aided by a recovering economy, supported not least by rising oil and gas prices from 2000 onward, ambitions to rebuild Russia's conventional military power became yet again a realistic prospect, even without significantly raising the percentage of GDP spent on defense. Various areas of military reform that had already been identified during the Yeltsin years, such as increasing the number of professional soldiers, strengthening permanent readiness, procuring modern equipment, and rooting out corruption, returned to the agenda. The five-day war with Georgia in 2008, which resulted in a swift strategic victory for Russia but also demonstrated a number of ongoing operational difficulties, provided the impetus for accelerated reforms.[16] A wide-ranging military modernization program was announced the same year, supported in 2010 by an ambitious procurement plan, the State Armament Program to 2020.

Under the leadership of a civilian defense minister with a background in finance and accounting—Anatoly Serdiukov—the 2008 modernization program, which focused on making the Russian armed forces more usable by increasing their efficiency and cost-effectiveness, was implemented with unprecedented determination and financial backing. The program encompassed a wide spectrum of changes. A move from divisions to smaller brigades was intended to improve the mobility and combat readiness of the ground forces. Understaffed mobilization units—a remnant of the Soviet past—were disbanded to create room for more units with permanent readiness. Central command bodies were streamlined, and the size of the officer corps, which had made the Russian military too top-heavy, was slashed. Efforts were made to enhance the recruitment of professional soldiers and to lessen the reliance on conscription, including measures aimed at improving the image of military careers, such as higher salaries and better welfare provisions. The education of soldiers was adjusted to make it relevant for the twenty-first-century security environment.[17] Large-scale interservice exercises, which had not been held during the 1990s for financial reasons, were reintroduced.[18] Finally, Serdiukov's reforms were accompanied by an ambitious procurement plan, seeking to modernize 70 percent of the military hardware by 2020.

It is beyond doubt that these reforms have been an unambiguous success in making the Russian military incomparably better than it was during the 1990s. Although very little physical force was used for the annexation of Crimea, the operation there demonstrated vast improvements in command and control and showed that Russian military planners were now able to fine-tune tactics to the requirements of a specific situation, rather than relying on overwhelming force as they had done in the past. The air campaign over Syria commencing in 2015 showed that Moscow's conventional military reach was no longer restricted to its immediate neighborhood. It also exhibited a range of new technologies that Russia had not used in armed conflicts before. The operations in Crimea and Syria heightened Russia's international image as a serious military actor and also vastly improved the prestige of the military as an organization and employer domestically.[19] Improvements in capabilities, performance, and image compared to the 1990s do not mean, however, that all obstacles in the way of reforming the military have been decisively overcome, or indeed that Russia has achieved the parity in conventional military power with the West that it desires.

Russia's outdated defense industry precluded the modernization of military hardware during the 1990s, and problems in this area are still a restraint on Moscow's ambitions. Although the need to overcome the technology gap between Russian and Western producers was addressed in the reform plans of 2008, systemic deficiencies, like outdated management practices, an obsolete manufacturing base, a lack of innovation culture, and corruption, could not be rooted out in a few years. On the one hand, the State Armament Program to 2020 resulted in impressive technological modernization of the armed forces. The interim target of updating 30 percent of equipment by 2015 was even exceeded in certain areas, with particularly notable upgrades of the strategic nuclear arsenal, air defense systems, and a large number of new aircraft made available to the air force.[20] On the other hand, the State Armament Program failed to deliver equipment that would make Russian technology truly modern, especially compared to the most advanced armed forces of the West. Plans for the serial production and delivery of next-generation platforms, such as the Armata main battle tank and the fifth-generation PAK FA fighter, which have been in development for many years, have not been realized.[21] A relatively low level of investment in research and development, in addition to the general lack of innovation culture in Russian industry, means that plans for the extensive robotization and automatization of warfare remain little more than an aspiration. Most significantly for global power projection, the restoration of the Russian navy turned out to be a difficult undertaking. Although a large proportion of funding from the State Armament Program to 2020 was allocated to naval modernization, the defense industry has been unable to deliver the quantity and quality of large surface vessels required for a blue-water navy. Western sanctions on the export of military and dual-use equipment into Russia have been particularly painful in this respect because many electronic components on Russian ships are foreign made.[22]

In spring 2018 a new State Armament Program to 2027 was introduced.[23] Although little detail about the program is known at this point, it has been noted that its outlook was "more cautious and conservative in terms of ambition" than its predecessor, prioritizing further modernization of the nuclear triad and upgrading existing systems at the expense of new and innovative products. Most notably, in view of the production problems experienced since 2011, naval ambitions were apparently lowered significantly, with a shift in focus from the creation of a blue-water navy to strengthening existing capabilities in coastal protection.[24]

Russian defense spending today is significantly higher than it was during the 1990s, but economic and financial factors are still a restraint on the Kremlin's military ambitions. As is well known, the country's defense budget in comparative perspective remains limited and is much closer in scale to countries such as Saudi Arabia, France, and the United Kingdom than to other great powers like the United States and China. According to SIPRI's latest figures, Russian spending on defense in 2017 amounted to just over 10 percent of the US defense budget and just under one-third of the Chinese budget, in spite of the fact that Moscow's expenditure is comparatively high in terms of percentage of GDP (4.1 percent compared to 3.1 in the United States and China's estimated 1.9 percent). Given the size of the Russian armed forces, which according to a decree signed by the resident is set at a maximum of just over one million soldiers, and the array of roles they are expected to fulfill, the amount of money allocated to defense has not matched the country's aspirations.

It is also clear that a million-man military remains only an ambition and has been impossible to maintain, even with the continuing practice of filling the ranks with conscripts. Although exact numbers are not known, and even official Russian estimates are often contradictory, it is widely assumed that the numerical strength of the armed forces by the end of 2017 stood at approximately 850,000 soldiers, of which around 350,000 were conscripts, 354,000 contract soldiers, and the rest officers.[25] A reduction in the terms of conscription from two years to one year in 2008 reportedly helped diminish problems with draft evasion and *dedovshchina*—a brutal practice of hazing that had made military service particularly unpopular.[26] On the flip side, shorter service also had a negative impact on the levels of training and experience gained by conscripts before they enter into the reserves, and thus on their preparedness to engage in any potential combat operation. Russia's ongoing demographic problems mean that the number of conscripts cannot be ramped up to make up for shortcomings in manpower. Substantially increasing the number of contract soldiers is unaffordable, and there are questions whether, even with adequate funding, this would be achievable. As a Russian journalist noted in 2016, although the popular image of the military in the country had massively improved in recent years, "the popularity of the army is growing quicker than the actual willingness to serve."[27] There is also evidence to suggest that many professional soldiers do not renew their contract after an initial three-year term, indicating, as Aleksandr Golts claimed, "that the conditions of service must not be as attractive as described by the military propagandists."[28]

Russian military modernization since 2008 has successfully overcome many of the problems the country's armed forces experienced as a result of a long period of neglect following the collapse of the Soviet Union. Wide-ranging reforms, supported by significant financial backing, have driven up their capabilities and combat readiness and restored their image as a formidable military both at home and abroad. At the same time, modernization is far from complete, and the prowess of Russia as a global military power, especially when it comes to its conventional capabilities, should not be overstated. Although the operations in both Crimea and Syria were a far cry from the often shambolic efforts in the past, both were limited in scope and scale, and neither gave an insight into Russia's capabilities to conduct a large, combined combat operation against a comparable or superior enemy. Within its immediate neighborhood and the former Soviet region, Russia always had by far the most powerful military, even during the troubled 1990s. Compared to the world's most advanced militaries—and the US armed forces in particular—Russia still has a long way to go. As was the case in the past, Russia's position as a military great power today is based, above all, on its massive nuclear arsenal.

HYBRID WARFARE IN RUSSIAN STRATEGIC THOUGHT

As noted above, military modernization cannot be achieved with structural changes and the procurement of advanced technology alone. It also requires adjustments to doctrine and strategic thinking in order to prepare the armed forces for dealing with a variety of possible conflict scenarios and threat perceptions, which will vary from country to country and change over time.[29] Before the annexation of Crimea, analysts believed that the Russian military leadership's inability to move on from Cold War thinking on conventional war fighting had been a major obstacle in the way of reforms, while the West had made the transition to small wars and insurgencies.[30] This perception fundamentally changed in 2014, when the seemingly effortless annexation of Crimea, achieved with a minimum level of violent force, led some observers to conclude that Russia had developed "new and less conventional military techniques."[31] These techniques quickly became known as "hybrid warfare," a concept that has become a focal point in discussions of Russian military capabilities in recent years. The salience of the hybrid warfare concept cannot be evaluated from the operations in Crimea and events since 2014 alone. In other words, the view of hybrid warfare as a new war-winning approach is too simplistic. The concept can only be understood within the context of wider developments in Russian military thinking. An awareness of why the concept has become so popular offers further context for a nuanced assessment.

It is by now a widely acknowledged fact that the term "hybrid warfare" (*gibridnaia voina*) did not originate in Russian military thinking. Although Russian strategists and commentators today often refer to it, they have done so only since 2014, once it had become popularized by Western authors.[32] The term itself is often traced back to a US author, Frank Hoffman, who had written a piece on the rise of hybrid wars in 2007.[33] Broadly speaking, Hoffman characterized hybrid warfare as a mix of traditional military tactics with unconventional and nonphysical approaches, including information and psychological tools. The use of hybrid warfare, in his eyes, could explain how, in some cases, weaker opponents could gain an advantage over technologically and numerically superior adversaries. Hybrid warfare seemed an apt description of Russia's approach in Crimea, because it was mostly unconventional and nonphysical tools, such as subversion and the use of "little green men,"[34] disinformation and propaganda, rather than reliance on traditional military approaches that led to the success in this case. The concept was useful insofar as it drew attention to the success of Russian military modernization in certain areas and highlighted potential new challenges for its neighbors and the West. As various scholars quickly noted, however, the success of the hybrid warfare approach in Crimea was due to a particularly favorable operational environment for Moscow, including the availability of troops already stationed on the peninsula, the lack of a coordinated response from the Ukrainian authorities and the international community, and a large pro-Russia civilian contingent that welcomed, rather than resisted, the annexation. The absence of these conditions would make a successful repetition of such an approach unlikely in other circumstances, for example, in the Baltic states.[35] Although the use of nonmilitary tools in warfare, such as disinformation and psychological operations, merits detailed study, it is important not to overstate the extent to which such approaches have become a central concern in Russian military thinking. As Charles Bartles points out, "Russia is experimenting with some rather unconventional means to counter hostile indirect and asymmetric methods, but Russia also sees conventional military forces as being of the utmost importance."[36]

Russian approaches to war fighting are grounded in a long history of strategic thought that is much more complex than a simple "Cold War tradition" and new "hybrid warfare" divide suggests. Even during the Cold War, conventional theater warfare with intensive firepower and mass militaries was only one strand in the debate.[37] Thinking about the utility of indirect and unconventional approaches, including information and psychological operations, also has always been part of the Russian military tradition.[38] During Soviet times in particular, a number of thinkers became known internationally for innovative, forward thinking regarding the role of advanced technology in future wars. During the 1970s they devised the concept of the "Military-Technical Revolution," the intellectual origin of the "Revolution in Military Affairs," which came to dominate US strategic thought during the 1990s.[39] The modern version of this forward-thinking and technology-focused view on warfare is the work by Russian authors writing about "sixth-generation war," where information, communication, and command and control are increasingly seen as the keys to success. As Timothy Thomas has noted, it is this tradition in strategic thought, rather than something completely new, that best characterizes the writings of those contemporary Russian authors that are often identified in the West as the originators of hybrid warfare.[40]

As the outline of Russia's military modernization in the previous section shows, the development of hybrid warfare approaches has not been a major focus. The aspiration of achieving an army of one million soldiers and developing its potential for global conventional power projection, in addition to maintaining and upgrading a strong nuclear deterrent, clearly demonstrates that Russia is seeking to modernize across the full spectrum of military capabilities. "Hybrid" methods that led to success in Crimea are likely to figure in low-intensity conflict scenarios in Russia's neighborhood in the future. However, it is also clear that the mastery of such methods does nothing for Moscow's feelings of insecurity vis-à-vis more powerful opponents or for its belief that a strong military is a prerequisite for great power status recognition. As demonstrated by the air campaign in Syria in 2015 and also by the numerous large-scale military exercises the country has conducted in recent years, conventional war fighting remains a central concern of Russian strategic thought and military planning.

Since the annexation of Crimea, the understanding of the hybrid warfare concept in the West has broadened. It is now often used not only to describe Russian military tactics, but the Kremlin's approach to foreign policy on a general level. For example, the use of disinformation aimed at Western audiences via state-sponsored media outlets like RT or Sputnik, or through social media and so-called troll factories, is often described as an expression of a hybrid war launched against the West.[41] From an analytical point of view, this conceptual stretching is problematic. As Michael Kofman notes, the notion has become almost meaningless as a result: "The term now covers every type of discernible Russian activity, from propaganda to conventional warfare, and most that exists in between. What exactly does Russian hybrid warfare do, and how does it work? The short answer in the Russia-watcher community is everything."[42] The idea that almost every move can be explained as hybrid warfare does not reflect the complexity of Russian defense and foreign policy. It therefore hinders, rather than aids, a nuanced understanding of current events.[43]

THE MILITARY AS AN INSTRUMENT OF RUSSIAN FOREIGN POLICY

The reason the world's attention was sharply drawn to developments in the Russian military in 2014 was probably not so much the fact that the Crimea operation demonstrated stunning new military prowess or a new, war-winning hybrid warfare approach. More likely, it was because for the first time in the history of the Russian Federation, the country's leadership used armed force for territorial expansion. As has been pointed out many times since, such infringements of another state's sovereignty had not occurred in Europe since the end of World War II, and Moscow's actions were a blatant violation of international law. The fact that Russia had used its military in this way aroused suspicions that military reforms had been pursued by Putin, above all, to enable the goal of further territorial expansion. It created fears that Moscow's actions in Ukraine denoted a dramatic turnaround in foreign policy, a "paradigm shift," that when supported by modernized armed forces would lead to a "seismic change in Russia's role in the world."[44] There were expectations that the annexation of Crimea was part of a bigger plan and that further territorial conquest was highly likely. As the former US secretary of defense Leon Panetta noted, "Putin's main interest is to try and restore the old Soviet Union. I mean, that's what drives him."[45] Such concerns are certainly understandable, especially when it comes to Russia's closest neighbors. However, the role of the military in Moscow's foreign policy, and the Kremlin's views on the utility of force, are more complex than this. As Roy Allison wrote about Crimea, "this resort to military coercion was not simply a reversion to an earlier era of power politics on the European continent. To characterize it thus would obscure the distinct and multifaceted nature of the Russian interventions."[46] While the possibility of further territorial expansion cannot be ruled out, a historically contextualized understanding of the armed forces as an instrument of Russian foreign policy at least suggests that this was not the foremost reason why military modernization was pursued.

As mentioned above, Russian soldiers have been involved in sizable operations across the territory of the former Soviet Union since the end of the Cold War.[47] As such, Moscow's preparedness to use military force as an instrument of foreign policy is not a new development. Already during the early post-Soviet years, these interventions led to concerns that Russia's foreign policy in this region was driven by an imperialist agenda. As Zbigniew Brzezinski wrote in 1994, "regrettably, the imperial impulse remains strong and even appears to be strengthening. . . . Particularly troubling is the growing assertiveness of the Russian military in the effort to regain control over the old Soviet empire."[48] Russia's imperial legacy has informed its decision to use military force in its neighborhood since the end of the Cold War. However, this is not the same as pursuing the goal of recreating the former Soviet Union through territorial conquest.

When the Russian Federation was established, its future role in the region and the world was uncertain. However, the idea that, owing to its history, the country had a special role to play in its neighborhood quickly established itself as a consensus view.[49] The 1993 Russian foreign policy concept unambiguously laid out what Moscow saw as its interests, rights, and responsibilities as the dominant security provider in what it often refers to as its "near abroad." At the same time, the Kremlin made clear its expectation that what it saw as Russia's privileged position should be acknowledged by the international community. As Yeltsin asserted in 1993, "Russia continues to have a vital interest in the cessation of all armed conflict on the territory of the former USSR. Moreover, the world community is increasingly coming to realize our country's special responsibility in this difficult matter. I believe the time has come . . . to grant Russia special powers as a guarantor of peace and stability in this region."[50] The Kremlin's desire to protect what it sees as its "privileged sphere of influence," by military force if necessary, has been a constant feature in Russian foreign policy ever since.

Military interventions in its "near abroad" since the early 1990s have been variously justified with reference to what the Kremlin described as its responsibility to provide security in the region. However, Russia's feeling of responsibility as a guarantor of security was not the only reason for the use of force. Military power was also applied to strengthen the grip over its "sphere of influence," an important element in the country's great power identity and status. During the 1990s Moscow not only used force to bring to an end the "hot" phase of civil wars; in all cases, it also established a lasting military presence in the countries affected, gaining both strategically important outposts as well as a powerful lever of political influence. This has contributed to Russia's lasting control over the region. Unexpectedly for Russia, Yeltsin's appeal to the international community to accept the country's "privileged position" in the former Soviet sphere was never heeded. As neighboring states established their own foreign and security policies, they cooperated with Moscow when it suited them but also explored other options. The West justifiably believed that, as sovereign states, all newly independent states should be allowed to pursue their own interests. Moscow's view that its dominant position in the region was under threat has resulted in increasingly aggressive military action there.

The perception of outside, and specifically Western, encroachment into its "near abroad" has become a dominant theme in the Kremlin's foreign policy discourse. Criticism of NATO's eastward enlargement since the mid-1990s, and since the early 2000s the phenomenon of "color revolutions" in former Soviet states, which Moscow has routinely interpreted as Western instruments used to weaken its position, has been a central theme in this discourse. The war in Georgia in 2008 was justified by the Kremlin in part by the need to provide regional security and to defend Russian troops and citizens against what it described as "Georgian bellicosity toward South Ossetia."[51] However, it is clear that status concerns and the growing feeling that its control over the "near abroad" was weakening were important motivations for the use of force. Unlike the military interventions of the 1990s, this war occurred against the backdrop of an increasingly confrontational tone in Russian foreign policy rhetoric toward the West.[52] Since the so-called Rose Revolution in 2003, Moscow had perceived Georgia as a potential locale for Western intrusion into its "sphere of influence." Georgian president Mikhail Saakashvili, who was elected in 2004, pursued an openly pro-Western foreign policy with the long-term goal of joining NATO, an aspiration that was officially welcomed by the alliance in 2008.[53]

From 2004 onward, Russia's relationship with Georgia had steadily deteriorated, and evidence suggests that Moscow both expected and had planned for the escalation of these tensions.[54] A shelling by Georgian artillery of the South Ossetian capital in 2008 gave the Kremlin an excuse to intervene and force the country firmly back into its orbit. The war left Georgia weakened and made the solution of the territorial disputes over South Ossetia and Abkhazia ever more unlikely. As such, the outcome of the war diminished the prospect of Georgia's NATO membership. As Roy Allison concluded, weakening Georgia in this way "was not just a goal but an *instrument* for

Russia"[55] in the pursuit of higher-order foreign policy objectives: the preservation of its perceived "sphere of influence" and, ultimately, the assertion of its great power aspirations.

When it comes to the use of force in Ukraine in 2014, a similar confluence of factors determined Moscow's decision making. As was the case in Georgia in 2008, Moscow acted on the belief that political developments in Ukraine since the Orange Revolution in 2004 had been engineered by the West in its efforts to encroach into its "sphere of influence." When in February 2014 the United States and other Western governments officially welcomed the new Ukrainian government shortly after the change in power had occurred as a result of the Maidan revolution, the Kremlin interpreted this as evidence of the West's efforts to bring to power a government in Kiev that "would move Ukraine toward the EU and even NATO."[56] That this was a motivation for the use of force in this case was confirmed later by Putin's heavy emphasis on what he claimed was the West's responsibility for Russian actions in his "Crimea speech."[57] Counting on the fact that the new Ukrainian leadership was not in a position to stage an effective military response, Moscow exploited the situation and intervened.

Unlike in Georgia, where the Kremlin chose to weaken the country permanently by recognizing the "independence" of South Ossetia and Abkhazia, in Ukraine it opted for the outright annexation of Crimea in blatant disregard of international law. A strong explanation for this is that Crimea is of extreme strategic importance to Russia, because the Sevastopol naval base is central for power projection in the Black Sea region and beyond. Disputes over Russian basing rights in Crimea had led to tensions in the past, and fears that this could lead to a war with Ukraine were already being expressed during the 1990s.[58] Even the prospect of losing access to Crimea was unacceptable for Russia, and annexation closed the option of any future Ukrainian government of revoking it. Moreover, the annexation of Crimea served to reassert Russia's great power aspirations by sending a signal to its neighbors and to the world that its dominant position in the region is nonnegotiable and will be defended, if required, by any means.

The intervention in the Syrian civil war in 2015 differed from previous uses of force inasmuch as, for the first time since the end of the Cold War, the Kremlin unilaterally intervened beyond the borders of its immediate neighborhood. The reasons for resorting to military power in this case, however, were in line with Moscow's broader views on the utility of force. As was the case in previous interventions, strategic interests and security considerations played a role in Syria. Russia's relations with the latter date back to the Cold War, and the continuation of President Bashar al-Assad's government was seen as conducive to the preservation of its material interests in the country. However, these interests alone were unlikely to have been significant enough to merit an expensive military operation.[59] Russia also had long been concerned with the international reach of religiously motivated extremist and terrorist groups, not least because of the security situation in the North Caucasus. Assisting Assad in defeating groups like the Islamic State, in the Kremlin's eyes, would not only help to return stability and security to Syria but also restrict the potential spread of their activities beyond the Middle East, for example, to Central Asia and, ultimately, to Russia itself.[60]

It is likely that a major motivation for the use of force in Syria was connected to the Kremlin's determination to assert the country's international status. As Angela Stent put it, "Putin's decision to intervene in Syria is rooted in . . . Russian concerns over power and influence."[61] Throughout the post-Soviet years, Moscow had increasingly voiced its indignation not only about what it saw as the West's encroachment into its "sphere of influence," but about what it saw as a unipolar world order and a monopoly on the use of force dominated by the United States. It came to believe that the loss of great power recognition, not least owing to its military weakness, had excluded Russia from having a say in global developments beyond its immediate neighborhood. Its inability to prevent NATO's Operation Allied Force against the Serbian regime in 1999 was of particular importance in this respect.[62] Subsequently, military modernization was prioritized, because this was seen as a necessity for the reassertion of Russia's great power status. As Putin noted in 2012, developing military potential was indispensable "for our partners to heed our country's arguments in various international formats."[63] Having been unable to prevent Western-led regime change in Serbia in 1999, as Russia saw it, a stronger military enabled it to prevent a similar scenario in Syria. As Fyodor Lukyanov concluded, by taking action not only in Ukraine but also in Syria, "Russia made clear its intention to restore its status as a major international player."[64]

Military modernization has made the Russian armed forces more capable, and it has given the Kremlin more opportunity and confidence to use them. However, this does not mean that Moscow's views on the utility of military force have fundamentally changed. Russia has used military force as a flexible tool of foreign policy in the past, and there is little evidence to suggest that today territorial expansion or global domination have become major objectives. There is every reason to assume that Russia will again resort to the use of force in future situations when it perceives this to be in its interest. In its so-called near abroad, these situations most likely will be connected to perceived threats to security and its dominant position in its "sphere of influence," for example, an outbreak of religiously motivated extremism or popular uprisings with the potential of bringing to power a regime unfriendly to Moscow. Globally, future Russian involvement in armed conflicts in regions of strategic importance is also probable, within the limitations of its scope for power projection further afield. Russia's newly found confidence and assertiveness to use its modernized military as a tool of foreign policy undoubtedly poses serious challenges to its neighbors and to the West. The Kremlin's apparent preparedness to use force for protecting its perceived "sphere of influence" by any means is of concern especially for countries it considers to be within this sphere, as it restricts their ability to pursue an independent foreign policy. For the West, the potential escalation of tensions with Russia in situations like Syria is a serious concern. Russian uses of force in certain situations cannot be stopped outright. However, decisions on how to react to an increasingly militarily assertive Russia need to be based on a nuanced understanding of Moscow's views on the utility of force.

CONCLUSION

Successful reforms pursued over the past decade have made the Russian armed forces considerably more capable than they were for much of the post–Cold War years. This has made the country's political leadership more confident in using them. Coupled with an increasingly assertive foreign policy, this has resulted in more aggressive military action and posturing, including the violation of Ukraine's territorial integrity in blatant disregard of international law. All of this has serious implications for international security and for Russia's relationship with its neighbors and with the West. In spite of the significance of these developments, it is important to keep a sense of perspective when it comes to assessing Moscow's military capabilities as well as its intentions for using them.

This chapter showed that although the successes of military modernization have been impressive, Russia is still a long way off from achieving its ambition of maintaining armed forces rivaling those of the world's strongest states. Although it has further enhanced its superiority as the strongest military actor in the immediate neighborhood, significant limitations in its potential for global power projection remain. Russian aspirations for parity in conventional capabilities with the world's most advanced militaries are unlikely to be realized in the near future. Financial limitations in particular will be an obstacle to overcoming shortcomings in manpower and technology. Moscow is already paying a high price for defense, and substantially increasing this would inevitably come at the expense of public spending in other, vital areas. In his inaugural address following the presidential elections in March 2018, Putin noted that, in his view, "the country's security and defense capability are reliably assured" and that his future focus would be on addressing "the most vital domestic development objectives" and ensuring "a new quality of life, wellbeing, security and health" for Russia's citizens.[65] Whether the Kremlin will yet again be prepared to prioritize defense over everything else—the only option that allowed the Soviet Union to achieve superpower status—is thus unclear.

The annexation of Crimea violated a core principle of international law and was an act of aggression with serious consequences that are almost irreversible. The Kremlin's actions will taint Russia's international image and its relations with Ukraine, its other neighbors, and the West for decades to come. Its actions have also heightened fears about the security of Europe and beyond, with potentially grave implications for international peace and stability. The annexation of Crimea does not mean, however, that territorial expansion or global domination by military force has suddenly become the major objective of Russian foreign policy, which continues to revolve around gaining international great power recognition. While this distinction might appear to be slight, it is significant when it comes to decision making by NATO and the West on how to respond to a militarily more assertive Russia. As the experience of the Cold War shows, a policy of containment and the ensuing security dilemma can inadvertently enhance the danger of crisis escalation and instability. What Kimberly Marten describes as an "enhanced and creatively constructed set of deterrent measures,"[66] which demonstrates resolve but also avoids aggravating the Kremlin's beliefs about Western intentions, might therefore be a better option for addressing the array of challenges Russia poses to international security and for preventing the potential escalation of tensions into military conflict.

DISCUSSION QUESTIONS

1. Why did Russia embark on a program of military modernization in 2008?
2. Is contemporary Russia a military great power?
3. Is "hybrid warfare" a threat to Russia's neighbors and to the West?
4. How should the West respond to a more militarily assertive Russia?

SUGGESTED READINGS

Allison, Roy. *Russia, the West, and Military Intervention.* Oxford: Oxford University Press, 2013.

Bukkvoll, Tor. "Russian Special Operations Forces in Crimea and Donbas." *Parameters* 46, no. 2 (2016): 13–21.

Connolly, Richard, and Mathieu Boulège. "Russia's New State Armament Program: Implications for the Russian Armed Forces and Military Capabilities." Chatham House Research Paper, 2018. https://www.chathamhouse.org/publication/russia-s-new-state-armament-program-implications-russian-armed-forces-and-military.

Connolly, Richard, and Cecilie Sendstad. "Russian Rearmament: An Assessment of Defense-Industrial Performance." *Problems of Post-Communism* 64, no. 3 (2017): 112–31.

Marten, Kimberley. "Reducing Tensions between NATO and Russia." Council on Foreign Relations Special Report No. 79 (2017). https://www.cfr.org/report/reducing-tensions-between-russia-and-nato.

McDermott, Roger, Bertil Nygren, and Carolina Vendil Pallin, eds. *The Russian Armed Forces in Transition: Economic, Geopolitical and Institutional Uncertainties.* London: Routledge, 2012.

Persson, Gudrun, ed. *Russian Military Capability in a Ten-Year Perspective—2016.* Swedish Defense Research Agency FOI Report, Stockholm, 2016. https://www.foi.se/en/our-services/fois-reports--publications/summary.html?reportNo=FOI-R--4326--SE.

Renz, Bettina. "Russia and Hybrid Warfare." *Contemporary Politics* 22, no. 3 (2016): 283–300.

———. *Russia's Military Revival.* Cambridge: Polity, 2018.

Thomas, Timothy. "The Evolution in Russian Military Thought: Integrating Hybrid, New-Generation and New-Type Thinking." *Journal of Slavic Military Studies* 26, no. 2 (2016): 554–75.

NOTES

1. Tor Bukkvoll, "Inefficiencies and Imbalances in Russian Defense Spending," in *After "Hybrid Warfare"—What Next? Understanding and Responding to Contemporary Russia*, ed. Bettina Renz and Hanna Smith, Assessment and Research Activities Publication No. 44 (Helsinki: Government's Analysis, 2016), 24, http://tietokayttoon.fi/julkaisu?pubid=14703 (accessed May 1, 2018).

2. Carolina Vendil Pallin, *Russian Military Reform: A Failed Exercise in Defense Decision Making* (London: Routledge, 2009).

3. Anne Aldis and Roger McDermott, eds., *Russian Military Reform, 1992–2002* (London: Frank Cass, 2003).

4. Zoltan Barany, "Defense Reform, Russian Style: Obstacles, Options, Opposition," *Contemporary Politics* 11, no. 1 (2005): 35.

5. Dmitri Trenin, *Post-Imperium: A Eurasian Story* (Washington, DC: Carnegie Endowment for International Peace, 2011), 76.

6. Brian Taylor, *Politics and the Russian Army: Civil-Military Relations, 1689–2000* (Cambridge: Cambridge University Press, 2003), 274.

7. SIPRI Military Expenditure Database, "Data for All Countries 1949–2017," https://www.sipri.org/sites/default/files/SIPRI-Milex-data-1949-2017.xlsx (accessed May 14, 2018).

8. Pavel Baev, "Peacekeeping and Conflict Management in Eurasia," in *Security Dilemmas in Russia and Eurasia*, ed. Roy Allison and Christoph Bluth (London: Royal Institute of International Affairs, 1998), 218.

9. Bettina Renz, "Russian Military Capabilities after 20 Years of Reform," *Survival* 56, no. 3 (2014): 69.

10. Iver Neumann, "Russia as a Great Power 1815–2007," *Journal of International Relations and Development* 11, no. 2 (2008): 128–51.

11. Margot Light, "Russian Foreign Policy," in *Developments in Russian Politics*, eds. Stephen White, Richard Sakwa, and Henry Hale (Basingstoke: Palgrave, 2010), 229.

12. Bettina Renz, "Why Russia is Reviving Its Conventional Military Power," *Parameters* 46, no. 2 (2016): 24–26.

13. Richard Pipes, "Is Russia Still an Enemy?," *Foreign Affairs* 76, no. 5 (1997): 75–76.

14. Bettina Renz, *Russia's Military Revival* (Cambridge: Polity, 2018), 61–83.

15. Vladimir Putin, "TV Address to the Citizens of Russia," March 24, 2000, http://en.special.kremlin.ru/events/president/transcripts/24201 (accessed May 12, 2018).

16. Carolina Vendil Pallin and Frederick Westerlund, "Russia's War with Georgia: Lessons and Consequences," *Small Wars and Insurgencies* 20, no. 2 (2009): 400–424.

17. Margarete Klein, "Towards a 'New Look' of the Russian Armed Forces? Organizational and Personnel Changes," in *The Russian Armed Forces in Transition: Economic, Geopolitical and Institutional Uncertainties*, ed. Roger McDermott, Bertil Nygren, and Carolina Vendil Pallin (London: Routledge, 2012).

18. Johan Norberg, "Training to Fight: Russia's Major Military Exercises, 2011–2014," Swedish Defense Research Agency FOI Report, 2015, https://www.foi.se/reportsummary?reportNo=FOI-R--4128--SE (accessed February 21, 2018).

19. Pavel Aptekar' and Ivan Prosvetov, "Otnoshenie k armii v Rossii perevernulos'," *Vedomosti*, February 22, 2018.

20. Julian Cooper, "Russia's State Armament Program to 2020: A Quantitative Assessment of Implementation, 2011–2015," Swedish Defense Research Agency FOI Report, 2016, 51–52, https://www.foi.se/rapportsammanfattning?reportNo=FOI-R--4239--SE (accessed November 1, 2017).

21. PAK FA stands for "Perspectivney aviatsionnyi kompleks frontovoi aviatsii."

22. Richard Connolly and Cecilie Sendstad, "Russian Rearmament: An Assessment of Defense-Industrial Performance," *Problems of Post-Communism* 64, no. 3 (2017): 112–31; Richard Connolly and Philip Hanson, "Import Substitution and Economic Sovereignty in Russia," Chatham House Research Paper, 2016, https://www.chathamhouse.org/publication/import-substitution-and-economic-sovereignty-russia (accessed November 1, 2017).

23. Richard Connolly and Mathieu Boulège, "Russia's New State Armament Program: Implications for the Russian Armed Forces and Military Capabilities," Chatham House Research Paper, 2018, https://www.chathamhouse.org/publication/russia-s-new-state-armament-programme-implications-russian-armed-forces-and-military (accessed May 10, 2018).

24. Douglas Barrie, "Russia's State Armament Program 2027: A More Measured Course on Procurement," International Institute for Strategic Studies, February 13, 2018, https://www.iiss.org/en/militarybalanceblog/blogsections/2018-f256/february-1c17/russia-state-armament-programme-d453 (accessed May 1, 2018).

25. Aleksandr Golts, "How Many Soldiers Does Russia Have?," *Jamestown Eurasia Daily Monitor* 14, no. 144 (2017), https://jamestown.org/program/many-soldiers-russia (accessed May 1, 2018).

26. Aptekar' and Prosvetov, "Otnoshenie k armii v Rossii." For a detailed account of the problem of *dedovshchina* before the recent reforms, see Dale Herspring, "Dedovshchina in the Russian Army: The Problem That Won't Go Away," *Journal of Slavic Military Studies* 18, no. 4 (2005): 607–29.

27. Sviatoslav Ivanov, "Khotiat li russkie sluzhit?," Gazeta.ru, February 22, 2016, https://www.gazeta.ru/army/2016/02/22/8081159.shtml (accessed May 1, 2018).

28. Golts, "How Many Soldiers Does Russia Have?"

29. Renz, *Russia's Military Revival*, 160–88.

30. Barany, "Defense Reform, Russian Style," 35.

31. House of Commons Defense Committee, "Towards the Next Defense and Security Review: Part Two—NATO," Third Report of Session 2014–15, HC358, July 31, 2014, http://www.publications.parliament.uk/pa/cm201415/cmselect/cmdfence/358/358.pdf (accessed August 12, 2017).

32. Paul Goble, "Russian Military Expert: Moscow Must Focus on Defending Itself against Hybrid Wars," *Jamestown Eurasia Daily Monitor* 15, no. 40 (2018), https://jamestown.org/program/russian-military-expert-moscow-must-focus-defending-hybrid (accessed March 20, 2018).

33. Frank Hoffman, *Conflict in the 21st Century: The Rise of Hybrid Wars* (Arlington, VA: Potomac Institute, 2007).

34. Russian special forces, whose presence in Crimea was initially denied by Putin, who claimed that these unmarked soldiers were "armed civilians," were referred to in the media at the time as "little green men."

35. Johan Norberg, "The Use of Russia's Military in the Crimean Crisis," Carnegie Endowment for International Peace, March 13, 2014, https://carnegieendowment.org/2014/03/13/use-of-russia-s-military-in-crimean-crisis-pub-54949 (accessed August 4, 2017); Maxim Bugriy, "The Crimean Operation: Russian Force and Tactics," *Jamestown Eurasia Daily Monitor* 11, no. 61 (2014), https://jamestown.org/program/the-crimean-operation-russian-force-and-tactics (accessed August 4, 2017).

36. Charles Bartles, "Getting Gerasimov Right," *Military Review* 96, no. 1 (2016): 36.

37. Dima Adamsky, *The Culture of Military Innovation: The Impact of Cultural Factors on the Revolution in Military Affairs in Russia, the US, and Israel* (Stanford, CA: Stanford University Press, 2010), 42–43.

38. Dima Adamsky, "Cross-Domain Coercion—the Current Russian Art of Strategy," *Proliferation Papers* 54 (2015): 25; Raymond Garthoff, "Unconventional Warfare in Communist Strategy," *Foreign Affairs* 40, no. 4 (1961): 566–75.

39. Dima Adamsky, "Through the Looking Glass: The Soviet Military-Technical Revolution and the American Revolution in Military Affairs," *Journal of Strategic Studies* 31, no. 2 (2008): 257–94.

40. Timothy Thomas, "The Evolution in Russian Military Thought: Integrating Hybrid, New-Generation and New-Type Thinking," *Journal of Slavic Military Studies* 26, no. 2 (2016): 555.

41. See, for example, Peter Apps, "Putin's Nuclear-Tipped Hybrid War on the West," May 1, 2018, https://www.reuters.com/article/us-apps-russia-commentary/commentary-putins-nuclear-tipped-hybrid-war-on-the-west-idUSKCN1GD6H2 (accessed May 10, 2018).

42. Michael Kofman, "Russian Hybrid Warfare and Other Dark Arts," March 11, 2016, https://warontherocks.com/2016/03/russian-hybrid-warfare-and-other-dark-arts (accessed November 10, 2017).

43. Bettina Renz, "Russia and Hybrid Warfare," *Contemporary Politics* 22, no. 3 (2016): 293–96.

44. Peter Rutland, "A Paradigm Shift in Russia's Foreign Policy," *Moscow Times*, May 18, 2014.

45. Cited in Centre for Strategic and International Studies (CSIS), "Global Security Forum 2016: Welcoming Remarks and Plenary I—Navigating 21st Century Security Challenges," December 1, 2016, https://www.csis.org/events/global-security-forum-2016-welcoming-remarks-and-plenary-i-navigating-21st-century-security (accessed May 10, 2018).

46. Roy Allison, "Russian 'Deniable' Intervention in Ukraine: How and Why Russia Broke the Rules," *International Affairs* 89, no. 4 (2014): 1258.

47. Renz, *Russia's Military Revival*, 121–59.

48. Zbigniew Brzezinski, "The Premature Partnership," *Foreign Affairs* 73, no. 2 (1994): 72.

49. Roy Allison, *Russia, the West, and Military Intervention* (Oxford: Oxford University Press, 2013), 122–23.

50. Cited in Stephen Page, "The Creation of a Sphere of Influence: Russia and Central Asia," *International Journal* 49, no. 4 (1994): 804.

51. Andrei Tsygankov and Matthew Tarver-Wahlquist, "Duelling Honors: Power, Identity and the Russia-Georgia Divide," *Foreign Policy Analysis* 5, no. 4 (2009): 307.

52. Angela Stent, "Restoration and Revolution in Putin's Foreign Policy," *Europe-Asia Studies* 60, no. 9 (2009): 1090.

53. NATO, "Bucharest Summit Declaration" (press release 49, 2008), https://www.nato.int/cps/ua/natohq/official_texts_8443.htm (accessed August 10, 2017).

54. Mark Kramer, "Russian Policy toward the Commonwealth of Independent States: Recent Trends and Future Prospects," *Problems of Post-Communism* 55, no. 6 (2008): 7.

55. Roy Allison, "Russia Resurgent? Moscow's Campaign to 'Coerce Georgia to Peace,'" *International Affairs* 84, no. 6 (2008): 1065.

56. Samuel Charap and Timothy Colton, *Everyone Loses: The Ukraine Crisis and the Ruinous Contest for Post-Soviet Eurasia* (London: International Institute for Strategic Studies, 2017), 126.

57. Vladimir Putin, "Address by the President of the Russian Federation," March 18, 2014, http://en.kremlin.ru/events/president/news/20603 (accessed May 10, 2018).

58. Dmitri Trenin, *Post-Imperium: A Eurasian Story* (Washington DC: Carnegie Endowment for International Peace, 2011), 44–46.

59. Roy Allison, "Russia and Syria: Explaining Alignment with a Regime in Crisis," *International Affairs* 89, no. 6 (2013): 800–807.

60. Vladimir Putin, "A Plea of Caution from Russia," *New York Times*, September 11, 2013; Derek Averre and Lance Davies, "Russian Humanitarian Intervention and the Responsibility to Protect: The Case of Syria," *International Affairs* 91, no. 4 (2015): 820–21.

61. Angela Stent, "Putin's Power Play in Syria: How to Respond to Russia's Intervention," *Foreign Affairs* 95, no. 1 (2016): 108.

62. Derek Averre, "From Pristina to Tskhinvali: The Legacy of Operation Allied Force in Russia's Relations with the West," *International Affairs* 85, no. 3 (2009): 571–91.

63. Vladimir Putin, "Being Strong: Why Russia Needs to Rebuild Its Military," *Foreign Policy*, February 21, 2012, http://foreignpolicy.com/2012/02/21/being-strong (accessed August 10, 2017).

64. Fyodor Lukyanov, "Putin's Foreign Policy—the Quest to Restore Russia's Rightful Place," *Russia in Global Affairs*, May 4, 2016, http://eng.globalaffairs.ru/redcol/Putins-Foreign-Policy-18133 (accessed August 12, 2017).

65. Vladimir Putin, inaugural speech, May 7, 2018, http://en.kremlin.ru/events/president/news/57416 (accessed May 10, 2018).

66. Kimberly Marten, "Reducing Tensions between NATO and Russia," Council on Foreign Relations Special Report, no. 79 (2017), 3–6.

Index

About the Contributors

Alfred B. Evans Jr., professor emeritus of political science at California State University, Fresno. He is the author of *Soviet Marxism-Leninism: The Decline of an Ideology* (1993). He is also editor or coeditor of three books, including *Change and Continuity in Russian Civil Society: A Critical Assessment* (2006). He has published many book chapters and articles in scholarly journals. His current research focuses on civil society in Russia, with particular emphasis on organizations that engage in public protests.

Stefan Hedlund, professor of Russian studies at Uppsala University, Sweden. His research has mainly focused on institutional dimensions of Russian economic development and attempted reforms through a lens of historical and cultural legacies. He has published a large number of articles and some two dozen books, most recently *Invisible Hands, Russian Experience, and Social Science: Approaches to Understanding Systemic Failure* (2011) and *Putin's Energy Agenda: The Contradictions of Russia's Resource Wealth* (2014).

Kathryn Hendley, William Voss-Bascom Professor of Law and Political Science at the University of Wisconsin, Madison. Her research focuses on legal and economic reform in the former Soviet Union and on how law is actually experienced and used in Russia. Her research has been supported by grants from the National Science Foundation, the Social Science Research Council, the National Council for Eurasian and East European Research, and the International Research and Exchanges Board. She has been a visiting fellow at the Woodrow Wilson Center, the Kellogg Institute for International Affairs at Notre Dame University, the Russian Economic School (Moscow), and the Program in Law and Public Affairs at Princeton University. She has published widely in journals such as *Post-Soviet Affairs*, *Law and Social Inquiry*, and the *American Journal of Comparative Law*.

Janet Elise Johnson, professor of political science at Brooklyn College, City University of New York. She is the author of *Gender Violence in Russia: The Politics of Feminist Intervention* (2009) and *The Gender of Informal Politics: Russia, Iceland and Twenty-First Century Male Dominance* (2018). She has published articles in *Perspectives on Politics*, the *Journal of Social Policy*, *Politics & Gender*, *Communist and Post-Communist Studies*, and *Signs: Journals of Women in Culture and Society*, as well as online in the *Washington Post*'s Monkey Cage, the *Boston Review*, and the *New Yorker*. Over her career, she has been affiliated with various Russian studies institutes, including at Indiana, Miami, and Columbia Universities as well as the University of Helsinki. She writes extensively on gender and politics in Russia.

Maria Lipman, Distinguished Visiting Fellow of Russian Studies at the School of Global and International Studies, Indiana University, Bloomington, in 2017–2018. She was the editor in chief of *Counterpoint*, an online journal published by the Institute for European, Russian, and Eurasian Studies, George Washington University, from 2015 until 2018, and *Pro et Contra*, a policy journal published by the Carnegie Moscow Center from 2003 until 2014. Before joining the Carnegie Moscow Center, Lipman was cofounder and deputy editor of two Russian weekly magazines: *Itogi* (Results), the first weekly newsmagazine in Russia, published in association with *Newsweek*, and *Ezhenedel'ny Zhurnal* (Weekly Journal). From 2001 until 2011 Lipman wrote an op-ed column on Russian politics, media, and society for the *Washington Post*. She has contributed to a variety of Russian and US publications, including the *New Yorker*, and has written an online blog for that magazine since 2012. She has contributed to and coedited several volumes on Russian politics and society. Lipman is a frequent speaker on the international conference circuit and is regularly featured as a Russia expert on a range of international broadcast media. She holds an MA from Moscow State University.

Jeffrey Mankoff, senior fellow and deputy director of the Russia and Eurasia Program at the Center for Strategic and International Studies. He previously was an adviser on Russian affairs at the Department of State, adjunct fellow at the Council on Foreign Relations, and associate director of International Security Studies at Yale University. He has also held fellowships at Harvard, Yale, and Moscow State universities. The author of *Russian Foreign Policy: The Return of Great Power Politics* (2011), his forthcoming book is *Empires of Eurasia: How Imperial Legacies Shape International Security*. He holds a PhD in diplomatic history from Yale.

Alexander M. Nikulin, doctor of economics, director of the Center for Agrarian Studies, Russian Presidential Academy of National Economy and Public Administration (RANEPA). He is the author or coauthor of several books on the rural sociology and agrarian history of Russia. He has published numerous articles and chapters in a wide range of journals and books. His research has been supported by the Open Society Institute, the MacArthur Foundation, the Russian State Scientific Foundation, the Rosa Luxemburg Foundation, INTAS, Oxfam, and the World Bank. His recent books include *Peasant Life Practices: Russia, 1991–2012* (2013) and *Agrarians, Power and Countryside: From Past to Present* (2014). His newest book is *Food Policy and Food Security: Putting Food on the Russian Table* with Stephen Wegren (2018).

Alexandra Novitskaya, PhD candidate in women's, gender, and sexuality studies at Stony Brook University, SUNY. Her research interests are in the intersections of sexuality, national identity, migration studies, and queer theory. Her doctoral dissertation explores the experiences of nonheterosexual Russian-speaking migrants in the United States.

Nikolai Petrov, professor at the National Research University Higher School of Economics (HSE), Moscow. He is a member of the Program on New Approaches to Research and Security in Eurasia (PONARS Eurasia). He is the author or editor of numerous publications dealing with analysis of Russia's political regime, post-Soviet transformation, the socioeconomic and political development of Russia's regions, democratization, federalism, and elections, among other topics. His works include the three-volume *1997 Political Almanac of Russia* and the annual supplements to it. He is the coauthor of *Between Dictatorship and Democracy: Russian Post-communist Political Reform* (2004); *The Dynamics of Russian Politics: Putin's Reform of Federal-Regional Relations*, in two volumes (2004, 2005); *Russia 2025: Scenarios for the Russian Future* (2013); *The State of Russia: What Comes Next?* (2015); and *The New Autocracy: Information, Politics, and Policy in Putin's Russia* (2018).

Thomas F. Remington, visiting scholar, Harvard University, and Goodrich C. White Professor of Political Science (emeritus) at Emory University. He is the author of numerous books and articles on postcommunist politics. His books include *Presidential Decrees in Russia: A Comparative Perspective* (2014); *The Politics of Inequality in Russia* (2011); *The Russian Parliament: Institutional Evolution in a Transitional Regime, 1989–1999* (2001); and, with Steven S. Smith, *The Politics of Institutional Choice: Formation of the Russian State Duma* (2001).

Bettina Renz, associate professor in the School of Politics and International Relations at the University of Nottingham, United Kingdom. She has written and published widely on Russian defense and security policy. Her most recent book is *Russia's Military Revival* (2018).

Richard Sakwa, professor of Russian and European politics at the University of Kent and an associate fellow of Chatham House, United Kingdom. He has published widely on Soviet, Russian, and postcommunist affairs. His recent books include *Postcommunism* (1999); *Contextualising Secession: Normative Aspects of Secession Struggles* (2003), coedited with Bruno Coppieters; an edited volume, *Chechnya: From Past to Future* (2005); *Russian Politics and Society* (2008); and *Putin: Russia's Choice* (2008); *The Quality of Freedom: Khodorkovsky, Putin and the Yukos Affair* (2009); and his study *The Crisis of Russian Democracy: The Dual State, Factionalism, and the Medvedev Succession* was published in 2011. His most recent book is *Russia against the Rest: The Post–Cold War Crisis of World Order* (2017).

Louise Shelley, Omer L. and Nancy Hirst Endowed Chair and University Professor at the School of Policy and Government, George Mason University. She founded and directs the Terrorism, Transnational Crime and Corruption Center (TraCCC). Her most recent books are *Dirty Entanglements: Corruption, Crime, and Terrorism* (2014); *Human Trafficking: A Global Perspective* (2010); and *Dark Commerce: How a New Illicit Economy Is Threatening Our Future* (2018), which was written while she was an inaugural Andrew Carnegie fellow. She is the author of many articles and book chapters on transnational crime, Soviet and Russian crime and justice, and money laundering. Professor Shelley served for six years on the Global Agenda Councils of the World Economic Forum, first on the illicit trade council and then as the inaugural cochair of organized crime. Dr. Shelley appears frequently in the media, lectures widely at universities and multinational bodies, and has testified on numerous occasions before Congress. She is a life member of the Council on Foreign Relations.

Darrell Slider, professor emeritus of government and international affairs at the University of South Florida. He has received numerous awards and authored numerous articles, primarily concerning regional and local politics in Russia and other countries of the former Soviet Union. During the 2017–2018 academic year, he was a Fulbright Research Scholar in Moscow at the Higher School of Economics.

Laura Solanko, senior adviser at the Bank of Finland Institute for Economies in Transition (BOFIT) and adjunct professor at Lappeenranta University of Technology (Finland).

Pekka Sutela, professor at Lappeenranta University of Technology (Finland), adjunct professor at Aalto University of Business (Finland), and visiting distinguished professor at the Paris School of International Affairs (Sciences Po, France). His recent publications include *The Political Economy of Putin's Russia* (2012) and *Trading with the Soviet Union* (2014).

Andrei P. Tsygankov, professor in the Department of Political Science and International Relations at San Francisco State University. A native Russian, he is the author of many books and articles on Russia's international relations. Most recently, he edited *The Routledge Handbook of Russian Foreign Policy* (2018) and authored *The Dark Double: American Media, Russia, and the Politics of Values* (2018).

Stephen K. Wegren, professor of political science at Southern Methodist University. He is the author or editor of seventeen books on the political economy of postcommunist nations. He has published numerous articles and chapters in a wide range of journals and books. His research has been supported by the Social Science Research Council, the National Council for Eurasian and East European Research, the Ford Foundation, the International Research and Exchanges Board, Oxfam, and the Norwegian Research Council. His recent books include *Land Reform in Russia: Institutional Design and Behavioral Responses* (2009) and *Rural Inequality in Divided Russia* (2014). His newest book is *Food Policy and Food Security: Putting Food on the Russian Table* with Alexander Nikulin (2018).

Jeanne L. Wilson, Shelby Cullom Davis Professor of Russian Studies and professor of political science at Wheaton College in Norton, Massachusetts. She is also a research fellow at the Davis Center for Russian and Eurasian Studies at Harvard University. She is the author of *Strategic Partners: Russian-Chinese Relations in the Post-Soviet Era* (2004). She is also the author of a number of articles and book chapters, including recent articles in *European Politics and Society*, *Problems of Post-Communism*, *Politics*, *Europe-Asia Studies*, and *East European Politics*. Her current research focuses on issues of identity and status in Russia and China.